Communications in Computer and Information Science 1648

More information about this series at https://link.springer.com/bookseries/7899

Jorge Herrera-Tapia ·
Germania Rodriguez-Morales ·
Efraín R. Fonseca C. ·
Santiago Berrezueta-Guzman (Eds.)

Information and Communication Technologies

10th Ecuadorian Conference, TICEC 2022
Manta, Ecuador, October 12–14, 2022
Proceedings

 Springer

Editors
Jorge Herrera-Tapia ⓘD
Universidad Laica Eloy Alfaro de Manabí
Manta, Ecuador

Germania Rodriguez-Morales ⓘD
Universidad Técnica Particular de Loja
Loja, Ecuador

Efraín R. Fonseca C. ⓘD
Universidad de las Fuerzas Armadas ESPE
Quito, Ecuador

Santiago Berrezueta-Guzman ⓘD
CEDIA
Cuenca, Ecuador

ISSN 1865-0929   ISSN 1865-0937 (electronic)
Communications in Computer and Information Science
ISBN 978-3-031-18271-6   ISBN 978-3-031-18272-3 (eBook)
https://doi.org/10.1007/978-3-031-18272-3

This Springer imprint is published by the registered company Springer Nature Switzerland AG
The registered company address is: Gewerbestrasse 11, 6330 Cham, Switzerland

Preface

The tenth edition of the Ecuadorian Congress of Information and Communication Technologies (TICEC 2022) was held in the city of Manta from October 12 to 14, 2022, in hybrid mode, on the campus of the Universidad Laica Eloy Alfaro de Manabí (ULEAM).

TICEC is one of the most important conferences in Ecuador on information and communication technologies (ICTs). This event brings together researchers, educators, professionals, and students from different parts of the world to disseminate research results and develop academic activities related to developing and implementing new ICT applications in multiple fields.

This year, this important academic and scientific event was organized by ULEAM and the Corporación Ecuatoriana para el Desarrollo de la Investigación y la Academia (CEDIA). The conference included the oral presentation of scientific full papers that were distributed across three principal topics:

- Data Science
- ICTs Applications
- Software Development

This tenth edition of TICEC received manuscripts written by 223 authors from 11 countries. All articles were analyzed for similarity with previous works and were peer reviewed (double-blind) by members of the TICEC 2022 Program Committee, consisting of 150 highly experienced researchers from 40 countries. We assigned at least three reviewers to each manuscript to ensure a high-quality and careful review process. Based on the peer review results, 20 full papers were accepted, representing an acceptance rate of under 30%.

October 2022

Jorge Herrera-Tapia
Germania Rodriguez-Morales
Efraín R. Fonseca C.
Santiago Berrezueta-Guzman

Organization

Honorary Committee

Cecilia Paredes	CEDIA, Ecuador
Marco Zambrano	Universidad Laica Eloy Alfaro de Manabí, Ecuador
Juan Pablo Carvallo Vega	CEDIA, Ecuador

General Chair

Jorge Herrera-Tapia	Universidad Laica Eloy Alfaro de Manabí, Ecuador

Program Committee Chairs

Germania Rodriguez-Morales	Universidad Técnica Particular de Loja, Ecuador
Efraín R. Fonseca C.	Universidad de las Fuerzas Armadas, Ecuador
Marcos Orellana	Universidad del Azuay, Ecuador
Juan Pablo Salgado	Universidad Politécnica Salesiana, Ecuador
Pablo Pérez-Gosende	Universidad Politécnica Salesiana, Ecuador

Organizing Committee

Klever Delgado Reyes	Universidad Laica Eloy Alfaro de Manabí, Ecuador
César Cedeño Cedeño	Universidad Laica Eloy Alfaro de Manabí, Ecuador
Dolores Muñoz Verduga	Universidad Laica Eloy Alfaro de Manabí, Ecuador
Renato Intriago Plaza	Universidad Laica Eloy Alfaro de Manabí, Ecuador
Victor Chávez Moreira	Universidad Laica Eloy Alfaro de Manabí, Ecuador
Gabriela Sión Saltos	Universidad Laica Eloy Alfaro de Manabí, Ecuador
Galia Rivas Toral	CEDIA, Ecuador
Ana Isabel Ordoñez	CEDIA, Ecuador
Santiago Ruilova	CEDIA, Ecuador
Francisco Toral	CEDIA, Ecuador

Santiago Morales	CEDIA, Ecuador
Erick Brito	CEDIA, Ecuador
Santiago Berrezueta-Guzman	CEDIA, Ecuador

Program Committee

Adam Wojciechowski	Lodz University of Technology, Poland
Agustin L. Herrera-May	Universidad Veracruzana, Mexico
Agustín Yagüe	Universidad Politécnica de Madrid, Spain
Alex Fernando Buitrago Hurtado	Universidad Externado de Colombia, Colombia
Alexandros Liapis	ESDA Lab, Greece
Alexandros Spournias	ESDA Lab, Greece
Alvaro Llaria	University of Bordeaux, France
Alvaro Suarez	Universidad de Las Palmas de Gran Canaria, Spain
Ángel Alberto Magreñán	Universidad de La Rioja, Spain
Angel Hernandez-Martinez	Universidad Nacional Autónoma de México, Mexico
Ankit Maurya	Indian Institute of Technology Roorkee, India
Antonio Mogro	Tecnológico de Monterrey, Mexico
Arash Arami	University of Waterloo, Canada
Arcangelo Castiglione	University of Salerno, Italy
Artur Rydosz	AGH University of Science and Technology, Poland
Belen Bermejo	University of the Balearic Islands, Spain
Belen Curto	Universidad de Salamanca, Spain
Benoît Parrein	Ecole polytechnique de Nantes, France
Bugra Alkan	London South Bank University, UK
Carlos Abreu	Instituto Politécnico de Viana do Castelo, Portugal
Carme Quer	Universitat Politècnica de Catalunya, Spain
Cecilio Angulo	Universitat Politècnica de Catalunya, Spain
Chao Min	Nanjing University, China
Che-Wei Lin	National Cheng Kung University, Taiwan
Christos Antonopoulos	University of Peloponnese, Greece
Christos Mourtzios	Aristotle University of Thessaloniki, Greece
Christos Panagiotou	ESDA Lab, Greece
Claudia Ayala	Universitat Politècnica de Catalunya, Spain
Claudia Marzi	Italian National Research Council, Italy
Coral Calero	Universidad de Castilla-La Mancha, Spain
Corina Namaj	University of Istanbul, Turkey
Cristian Vasar	Politehnica University of Timisoara, Romania
Dan Pescaru	Universitatea Politehnica din Timisoara, Romania
Darius Andriukaitis	Kaunas University of Technology, Lithuania

David Valiente	Miguel Hernandez University, Spain
Dhruba Panthi	Kent State University at Tuscarawas, USA
Diego Brandao	CEFET/RJ, Brazil
Dionisis Kandris	University of West Attica, Greece
Eduardo Almentero	Universidade Federal Rural do Rio de Janeiro, Brazil
Eduardo Juarez	Universidad Politécnica de Madrid, Spain
Eike Petersen	Universität zu Lübeck, Germany
Engin Zeydan	Centre Tecnològic de Telecomunicacions de Catalunya, Spain
Emil Pricop	Petroleum-Gas University of Ploiesti, Romania
Fabio Arena	Kore University of Enna, Italy
Firas Raheem	University of Technology, Iraq
Francisco Prieto-Castrillo	Universidad Politécnica de Madrid, Spain
Gabor Sziebig	The Arctic University of Norway, Norway
George Adam	University of Thessaly, Greece
Gerasimos Vonitsanos	University of Patras, Greece
Giuseppe Ciaburro	Università degli Studi della Campania Luigi Vanvitelli, Italy
Gyanendra Prasad Joshi	Sejong University, South Korea
Ho-Lung Hung	Chienkuo Technology University, Taiwan
Hugo Almeida-Ferreira	Polytechnic Institute of Oporto, Portugal
Ibraheem Kasim Ibraheem	Baghdad University, Iraq
Ioan Viorel Banu	Gheorghe Asachi Technical University of Iasi, Romania
Iosif Szeidert	Politehnica University of Timisoara, Romania
Irina Georgiana Mocanu	Politehnica University of Bucharest, Romania
Isabel Sofia Sousa Brito	Instituto Politécnico de Beja, Portugal
Iván Pau	Universidad Politécnica de Madrid, Spain
Ivan Virgala	Technical University of Košice, Slovakia
Jai Singh	Charles Darwin University, Australia
Janusz Dudczyk	WB Electronics S.A. Poland
Jari Hannu	University of Oulu, Finland
Jason Wu	Texas A&M Transportation Institute, USA
Javier Gomez	Universidad Autónoma de México, Mexico
Jean-Fu Kiang	National Taiwan University, Taiwan
Jerwin Prabu A.	Bharati Robotic Systems India Pvt Ltd, India
Jessica Maradey	Universidad Autonoma de Bucaramanga, Colombia
Jianbin Qiu	Harbin Institute of Technology, China
John Castro	Universidad de Atacama, Chile
José Martinez-Carranza	Instituto Nacional de Astrofísica, Óptica y Electrónica, Mexico

Mohiuddin Ahmed	Edith Cowan University, Australia
Natasa Zivic	University of Siegen, Germany
Noman Naseer	Pusan University, South Korea
Noor Zaman	Taylor's University, Malaysia
Omar Abdul Wahab	Université du Québec en Outaouais, Canada
Panagiota (Yota) Katsikouli	University of Copenhagen, Denmark
Patricio Galdames	Universidad del Bio-Bio, Chile
Paul Nicolae Borza	Transilvania University of Brasov, Romania
Piotr Borkowski	Maritime University of Szczecin, Poland
Prasanta Ghosh	ICEEM, India
Przemysław Mazurek	West Pomeranian University of Technology, Poland
Raúl Antonio Aguilar Vera	Universidad Autónoma de Yucatán, Mexico
Robert Alexandru Dobre	Politehnica University of Bucharest, Romania
Roberto Murphy	INAOE, Mexico
Roemi Fernandez	Universidad Politecnica de Madrid, Spain
Rosaria Rucco	University of Naples Parthenope, Italy
Rostom Mabrouk	Bishop's University, Canada
Rui Zhao	University of Nebraska Omaha, USA
Ruoyu Su	Memorial University of Newfoundland, Canada
Saleh Mobayen	University of Zanjan, Iran
Samanta Kolsch	Steinbeis-Hochschule Berlin, Germany
Samuel Ortega-Sarmiento	University of Las Palmas de Gran Canaria, Spain
Sara Paiva	Oviedo University, Spain
Shaibal Barua	Mälardalen University, Sweden
Shernon Osepa	Internet Society, The Netherlands
Silvia Grassi	Università degli Studi di Milano, Italy
Stavros Souravlas	University of Macedonia, Macedonia
Stefano Mariani	Università degli Studi Modena e Reggio Emilia, Itlay
Sule Yildirim-Yayilgan	Norwegian University Science and Technology, Norway
Sunday-Cookeyn Ekpo	Manchester Metropolitan University, UK
Thomas Usländer	Fraunhofer IOSB, Germany
Tomasz Bieniek	Institute of Electron Technology, Poland
Tuan Nguyen-Gia	University of Turku, Finland
Utkarsh Singh	depsys SA, Switzerland
Valerio Baiocchi	Sapienza University of Rome, Italy
Vera Ferreira	Federal University of the Pampa, Brazil
Vinayak Elangovan	Penn State Abington, USA
Vladimir Sobeslav	University of Hradec Kralove, Czech Republic
Wojciech Zabierowski	Lodz University of Technology, Poland

Xavier Franch   Universitat Politècnica de Catalunya, Spain
Yanhua Luo   University of New South Wales, Australia
Yu Huang   Chinese Academy of Sciences, China
Zoltán Ádám Tamus   Budapest University of Technology, Hungary

Contents

ICT's Applications

An Online BCI System Based in SSVEPs to Control IoT Devices 3
Johanna Carolina Cerezo Ramirez, José Luis Murillo López,
and Sang Guun Yoo

Collision Avoidance Simulation Using Voronoi Diagrams in a Centralized
System of Holonomic Multi-agents 18
Leduin José Cuenca Macas and Israel Pineda

Intelligent Electromyograph for Early Detection of Myopathy
and Neuropathy Using EMG Signals and Neural Network Model 32
Evelyn Aguiar-Salazar, Bryan Cerón-Andrade,
Andrea Valenzuela-Guerra, Daniela Negrete-Bolagay,
Xiomira Fiallos-Ayala, Diego Suntaxi-Dominguez,
Fernando Villalba-Meneses, Andrés Tirado-Espín,
and Diego Almeida-Galárraga

Underwater Wireless Sensor Networks and Cryptographic Applications 46
Fabián Cuzme-Rodríguez, Pablo Otero, Miguel-Ángel Luque-Nieto,
Mauricio Domínguez-Limaico, and Henry Farinango-Endara

Design of a Sensor Network for Drinking Water Control in the Maria
of Merced Educational Unit 59
Manuel Eduardo Vinces Mendieta, Marely del Rosario Cruz Felipe,
and Darwin Patricio Loor Zamora

Drinking Water and Sewerage at the Universidad de las Fuerzas Armadas
ESPE and Implementation of an Internet of Things Flowmeter 73
David Vinicio Carrera Villacrés, Rodney Alberto Garcés,
Alfonso Rodrigo Tierra Criollo, Ricardo Duran, and Geovanny Raura

Indicators to Evaluate Elements of Industry 5.0 in the Textile Production
of MSMEs 85
Pablo Flores-Siguenza, Bernarda Vásquez-Salinas,
Lorena Siguenza-Guzman, Rodrigo Arcentales-Carrion,
and Dolores Sucozhañay

Technological Accessibility and Digital Health Education Associated
with the Use of Smart Healthcare by Obstetricians in Peru 101
    Yuliana Mercedes De La Cruz-Ramirez,
    Santiago Angel Cortez-Orellana, Augusto Felix Olaza-Maguiña,
    and Nadezhda Tarcila De La Cruz-Ramirez

Data Science

Adaptation of a Process Mining Methodology to Analyse Learning
Strategies in a Synchronous Massive Open Online Course 117
    Jorge Maldonado-Mahauad, Carlos Alario-Hoyos,
    Carlos Delgado Kloos, and Mar Perez-Sanagustin

Ecuador Agricultural Product Price Forecast: A Comparative Study
of Deep Learning Models 137
    Sherald Noboa, Erik Solís, and Erick Cuenca

Assessing the COVID-19 Vaccination Process via Functional Data Analysis ... 152
    Guido Tapia-Riera, Lenin Riera-Segura, Christian Calle-Cárdenas,
    Isidro R. Amaro, and Saba Infante

A Methodology to Develop an Outdoor Activities Recommender Based
on Air Pollution Variables 171
    Pablo Arévalo, Marcos Orellana, Priscila Cedillo,
    Juan-Fernando Lima, and Jorge Luis Zambrano-Martinez

Improving with Metaheuristics the Item Selection in Parallel Coordinates
Plot 186
    David Cordero-Machuca, Juan-Fernando Lima, and Marcos Orellana

Implementation of Clustering Techniques to Data Obtained from a Memory
Match Game Oriented to the Cognitive Function of Attention 201
    Marcos Orellana, María-Inés Acosta-Urigüen,
    and Reinerio Rodríguez García

Q-Learning in a Multidimensional Maze Environment 217
    Oscar Chang, Stadyn Román Niemes, Washington Pijal,
    Arianna Armijos, and Luis Zhinin-Vera

Cyberbullying Through the Lens of Data Science 231
    Alexandra Bermeo, María-Inés Acosta-Urigüen, Marcos Orellana,
    and Sebastián I. Valdivieso Albán

Software Development

Comparative Study of Image Degradation and Restoration Techniques 253
   Washington Pijal, Israel Pineda,
   and Manuel Eugenio Morocho-Cayamcela

IOWA Rough-Fuzzy Support Vector Data Description 266
   Ramiro Saltos and Richard Weber

Preparation of a Social Engineering Attack, from Scratch to Compromise:
A USB Dropper and Impersonation Approach 281
   Jorge Sánchez Freire and Benjamín Garcés

Information Security at Higher Education Institutions: A Systematic
Literature Review 294
   Daisy Imbaquingo-Esparza, Javier Díaz, Mario Ron Egas,
   Walter Fuertes, and David Molina

Author Index 311

ICT's Applications

An Online BCI System Based in SSVEPs to Control IoT Devices

Johanna Carolina Cerezo Ramirez[1,2], José Luis Murillo López[1,2], and Sang Guun Yoo[1,2(✉)] (iD)

[1] Departamento de Informática y Ciencias de la Computación, Escuela Politécnica Nacional, Quito, Ecuador
{johanna.cerezo,jose.murillo01,sang.yoo}@epn.edu.ec
[2] Smart Lab, Escuela Politécnica Nacional, Quito, Ecuador

Abstract. Internet of Things allows devices to communicate each other and with users. This way, people can control and monitor these devices using mobile applications, voice commands, gestures, among others. It is a technology that makes people's life easier. However, people with severe physical disabilities cannot take advantage of this technology since the way of controlling smart devices were designed for people without disabilities. In this situation, it is necessary to find other means of communication such as Brain-Computer Interface, which is a technology that seeks to connect the user's brain activity with any external applications. Steady State Visually Evoked Potentials have been one of the most widely used brain patterns due to its simplicity and precision. In this work, a Brain-Computer Interface system based on SSVEP was built to control IoT devices. The brainwaves generated by the SSVEP stimuli were acquired using a portable electroencephalography device and then classified using Canonical Correlation Analysis algorithm and translated into operational commands to navigate through an application to control different IoT devices using the MQTT protocol. The final prototype was tested on fifteen volunteers, achieving an average accuracy of 97.61%, requiring an average time of 9.7 s to turn on a smart light bulb and 16.68 s to turn it off.

Keywords: SSVEP · Brain-computer interface · BCI · Internet of Things · IoT · CCA · MQTT

1 Introduction

Internet of Things (IoT) is the interconnection of different types of devices to create a smart environment, allowing people to control or access electronic devices in their environment using voice commands, gestures, or movements [1]. The popularity of this technology has greatly increased in recent years because of cost reduction and ease of use of smart devices [2]. Although one might think that IoT is an all-inclusive technology, this is a hasty conclusion. Even though this technology makes life easier to most of the people, it does not consider people with severe movement disabilities who are unable to perform any kind of movement or even speak e.g., people suffering from Motor Neuron Disease (MND), which is a set of neurodegenerative disorders related to upper

J. Herrera-Tapia et al. (Eds.): TICEC 2022, CCIS 1648, pp. 3–17, 2022.
https://doi.org/10.1007/978-3-031-18272-3_1

or lower motor neuron degeneration leading to progressive loss of body movement [3]. By 2016, patients with MND reached 330918 people worldwide. In addition, the number of people who have been permanently or temporally disabled due to traffic accidents ascends between 10 to 50 million [4]. In this situation, the creation of Brain Computer Interfaces (BCI) solutions could help to the mentioned excluded population.

BCI is a communication system that translates brain activity signals into understandable commands for computers or other smart devices [5]. When implementing a BCI system, there are a variety of brain patterns that can be used. Some of them are: P300, Motor Imagery, Error Potentials, Intentional Blinking, and Steady-State Visually Evoked Potentials (SSVEPs). SSVEPs are signals that are natural responses generated by the brain when the user is exposed to a visual stimulus flickering at frequencies between 3.5 and 75 Hz [6]. The advantages of SSVEP are that they have a high transfer rate, can be easily generated at a low cost [7], can be detected noninvasively through electroencephalography (EEG), and require little training to get used to the system [8].

There are different algorithms that can be used to classify signals generated by SSVEPs, the most popular being Canonical Correlation Analysis (CCA) [9]. Other methods such as Fast Fourier Transform (FFT) and Linear Discriminant Analysis (LDA) have also been used traditionally. On the other hand, the use of Artificial Intelligence algorithms has increased. Some of them are Support Vector Machine (SVM), Convolutional Neural Network (CNN) and Adaptative Feedforward Neural Network (AFNN). They offer more accuracy but require more time and data to be trained.

CCA is a classical method for determining the relationship between at least two sets of multidimensional variables [10]. It has been identified as the most widely used algorithm in the development of SSVEP-based BCIs because of its high stability and performance [11]. Its popularity has increased because it is less user-dependent than other algorithms and allows the use of harmonic frequencies [9].

The objective of this work is to build a solution that allows people with severe movement disabilities to control IoT devices through their brainwaves. This objective will be achieved by developing an SSVEP-based BCI that will collect brain signals using a noninvasive acquisition technique. The visual stimuli for the SSVEP signals will be generated by using light-emitting diodes (LEDs) flickering at different frequencies.

2   State of Art

Several studies have proposed SSVEPs based BCI systems to improve the quality of life of people with temporary or permanent mobility disabilities. These systems enabled the control of a medical bed [12], a feeding system for hospital patients [13], and robotic arms [14–16]. There are studies that implement SSVEPs based BCI systems to control smart devices. In [17], blinds and a light are controlled using four stimuli (8, 9, 11 and 12 Hz) with a success rate of 87% and an average time of 4 s. The main limitation of the system is that it needs two stimuli to control on and off actions of each device. Therefore, the number of stimuli will increase when more devices need to be controlled.

In [18], an offline system was built to control a light, a fan, a television, and an alarm clock using four stimuli (10, 11, 12 and 13 Hz). This work achieved a success rate of 84,8% but was tested with only two users. The system needs only one stimulus to control each device. However, for each device added to the system, the number of stimuli must increase as well and only two actions (on/off) can be performed per device.

In [19], SSVEP stimuli are generated using the Augmented Reality (AR) technology and they are used to control home appliances. This work achieved a success rate of 92.8%. However, this work does not give enough information to replicate the prototype i.e., number and frequency of stimuli. Additionally, the work does not mention which devices they were able to control nor the action they were able to execute.

In [20], AR is combined with SSVEPS to develop a system capable of controlling a light bulb, an elevator, and a coffee machine. This solution achieved a success rate of 87.5% on 7 users. This work used 4 stimuli (6, 7, 8 and 9 Hz), and a QR code to identify the devices that the user wants to control. Depending on the device to be controlled, glasses show the stimuli with the actions that can be executed. Although this is an interesting approach, it was not intended for people with physical disabilities, as users had to move from one place to another to access the QR codes assigned to the devices.

In [21], an online system was built to control a light bulb, a television and blinds using a combination of SSVEPs, with 4 stimuli (4, 6, 19 and 15 Hz), and an eye-tracking system implemented through HoloLens. The system was tested with 7 users and achieved a success rate of 76.1% for SSVEPs and 89.3% for the combination with the eye-tracking system. An action was assigned for each stimulus and to use this prototype the user has to walk around the room to switch between devices, which means that this solution could not be used by people with movement disabilities.

Several SSVEP based BCI systems have been developed in recent years but most of them use a non-scalable approach, such as using one stimulus per device with limited on and off actions. The present work aims to develop an SSVEP-based BCI to navigate through a Graphic User Interface (GUI) that will list the available devices to control and the actions to perform. Thus, the number of devices and actions available will not depend on the number of stimuli of the system.

3 Methodology

Incremental methodology is a software engineering method based on a step-by-step implementation as an expanding model [22]. In this methodology, the product is created in several stages. In each stage or increment, features are added until the final version is reached. Each increment has four stages [23]. The first is analysis, where requirements and specifications are gathered. This is followed by the design; once the requirements are understood a plan is made to fulfill them. Next is the coding phase, where the code is created. And finally, there is the testing phase, where the prototype is tested.

In this work, an adaptation of the incremental methodology will be used. Since the prototype to be developed goes beyond software development, the coding phase has been replaced by a development phase that will cover the implementation of the prototype's different features. The other stages will remain the same.

Once the prototype is built, the Action Research methodology will be used. This methodology is based on the relationship between experimentation and knowledge generation [24]. Although this methodology was built to study social phenomena, it has recently gained popularity among other fields, especially in computer science [25]. This is because it prioritizes knowledge generation, so it is considered a generic empirical research method. The phases depend on the research approach, but it should include the following five steps: (1) Diagnosing, (2) Action Planning, (3) Action Taking, (4) Evaluating and (5) Specify Learning. This methodology fits the last phase of this work's needs since it allows defining the best course of action to test the complete prototype.

4 Development of the Solution

The proposed solution will contain four increments that will contribute to building the final prototype. In the first increment, the user interface that will show the actions and available IoT devices will be built. The second increment will focus on implementing the communication with IoT devices through a Message Queuing Telemetry Transport (MQTT) broker. In the third increment, the SSVEPs stimuli generated by LED lights will be deployed. In the fourth increment, the classification algorithm and the signals' acquisition strategy will be developed. And, in the last phase, the final prototype will be tested. The architecture of the final prototype is shown in Fig. 1.

4.1 First Increment

In this increment, the application with the user interface that shows the list of available actions and devices was built.

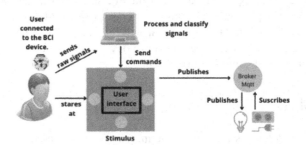

Fig. 1. System architecture

Analysis. In order to provide easy navigation to the user, the interface will be composed of a main menu listing a shortcut to all the actions. It will also contain an option to access a different listing where the devices will be grouped by rooms, and when a device is selected, the available actions for such device will be displayed.

Design. Mockups of the GUI were created to show the available actions in the center of the screen surrounded by four buttons. At the top is the accept button, used to perform the action. To navigate between actions, two buttons are used: one arrow to go left and one to go right. At the bottom of the screen is a button to go back or close the application.

As shown in Figs. 2 and 3, two mockups were made with different styles. The dark style was chosen because it is more comfortable for users' eyes.

The user interface will be built using the Electron framework that allows building native desktop applications using HTML, CSS, and JavaScript. Applications developed with Electron are multiplatform and can be executed over different operating systems [26]. To guarantee information persistence, the SQLite database will be used, since it is a serverless and lightweight database engine that does not need a server.

Fig. 2. Mockup of the user interfaces in light style.

Fig. 3. Mockup of the user interface in dark style.

Fig. 4. Screenshot of the developed user interface.

Development. The coding of the application was done based on the parameters, technologies and frameworks listed in the previous subsections. Figure 4 shows the developed user interface.

Test. The tests consisted of verifying the navigation of the interface with four people and the results were all correct.

4.2 Second Increment

In this increment, an infrastructure for the IoT devices was built and it was integrated to the user interface application.

Analysis. In this phase, it was necessary to implement an infrastructure that allows connecting the user interface with IoT devices (a smart bulb and a smart power strip with four plugs). This connection must be secure and fast.

Design. A Message Queuing Telemetry Transport (MQTT) broker will be used to send the user-selected action in the GUI to the device using the publish/subscribe messaging queue model. The chosen MQTT broker is Beebotte MQTT which is based on a channel and resource model, where each channel can be related to several resources. It runs on version 3.1.1 of the MQTT protocol and provides SSL and non- SSL connections through the 1883 and 8883 ports, respectively [27]. In addition, it provides a reliable communication bridge using WebSockets, REST and MQTT.

Development. A project was created on Beebotte platform with one channel and five resources, for one smart bulb and four sockets of a smart power strip. A Python program was developed to subscribe to the MQTT broker; and execute the device selected actions. Finally, the ability to publish actions to the MQTT broker was added to the GUI.

Test. The correct communication between the user interface and the IoT devices was verified. These tests were conducted with four people who were asked to turn on/off the light and the first plug of the smart strip. The results were all satisfactory. Delay tests were also performed to verify the time it took for the prototype to execute an action. For this purpose, the smart devices were turned on and off 35 times and the average time was measured. The results of these tests are shown in Table 1.

Additionally, an extra analysis was performed to determine the delay corresponding to the communication through MQTT. For this experiment, two timestamps were recorded. The first one when the message to activate the IoT device is sent from the GUI and the second one when it arrives to the subscribed device. This test was also performed 35 times and the result is shown in Table 2.

Table 1. Average time on turning on/off smart devices.

Device	Action	Time (s)
Smart bulb	On	1.57
	Off	1.40
Smart Power Strip	On	0.42
	Off	0.38

Table 2. Average time of MQTT communication

Device	Action	Time (s)
Smart bulb	On	0,082
	Off	0,087
Smart Power Strip	On	0,094
	Off	0,084

From the results shown in Tables 1 and 2, it is evident that communication through MQTT takes a trivial time of 0.08 s in the case of the smart bulb. Which means that it does not have a great impact on the performance of the device activation. The rest of the time corresponds to the time that the device takes for its activation.

4.3 Third Increment

In this phase, the SSVEPs stimulus were implemented using LEDs.

Analysis. Since the goal of this work is to implement a system based on SSVEPs, it is necessary to implement a device capable of generating the visual stimuli. Four stimuli are needed to navigate the user interface: accept, left, right and back. In addition, the user interface must be placed around the stimuli, so that the user can observe it while looking at the stimuli.

Design. To generate the stimuli, two options were considered: LEDs and an LCD display. An LCD display may present problems in correctly representing several stimuli flashing at different frequencies at the same time, making the SSVEP response weak [28, 29]. In addition, only frequencies obtained by dividing the refresh rate of the display by an integer can be used [30]. Due to these limitations, it was decided to use LEDs, since the number of frequencies that can be represented is large, because there is no constraint such as the refresh rate that restricts the frequencies that can be used [31].

SSVEP stimuli usually originate from frequencies represented by integers in the mid-low frequency band. However, the decision of which frequencies to use is usually made arbitrarily by the researcher. Other works have used frequencies between 8 and 12 Hz [17], 10 and 13 Hz [18], 6 and 9 Hz [20], 7 and 10 Hz [32, 33] with good results. In this work, frequencies located in the middle band were chosen i.e., 7, 8, 9 and 10 Hz.

In some studies, only the O2 and O1 channels of the international 10/20 system are used to acquire SSVEPs' signals [34–36]. In some cases, Oz channel is also used because it has the closest location to the visual cortex and therefore a good detection of the SSVEP response [37]. Additionally, it is possible to place electrodes in additional channels like POz, P3 and P4 as done in [38] and [18]. However, OZ, O1 and O2 channels have been defined as the main locations to acquire user's brain activity elicited by SSVEPs as such activity is more clearly and consistently detected [37]. For these reasons, in this work OZ, O1 and O2 channels were used.

In addition, the stimuli will be placed in a diamond position, with a 600x1024 px LCD screen placed in the middle, displaying the GUI while the stimuli match the position of the GUI buttons. It was also decided to use white LEDs since several studies have shown that this color has good results with SSVEPs stimuli [39–41].

Development. The LEDs visual stimuli were generated by using a Raspberry Pi with an application developed in Python which controls the frequency of LEDs. The frequencies were distributed as 7 Hz on top, 8 Hz on the right, 9 Hz on the bottom and 10 Hz on the left. The LEDs were placed in a 49 cm square panel, each one covered by a diffuser filter to reduce the eye fatigue of users from looking directly at the LEDs [41].

Test. In this stage, tests were performed to verify that the frequency generated for each stimulus was correct. For this purpose, a 20-s signal was recorded from the occipital lobe (O1, O2 and Oz). The recorded data was then plotted to verify that the peaks reached in the amplitude vs. frequency plot matched the frequency generated by the stimulus. This test was carried out with 4 people, and the stimuli were correctly generated for each frequency. The results are shown in the following figures (see Figs. 5, 6, 7, 8).

4.4   Fourth Increment

In this increment, signal acquisition and filtering processes, and a CCA-based classification algorithm were implemented. These tasks were integrated with the user interface application.

Analysis. To identify the stimulus that the user is looking at among the four frequencies, it is necessary to implement a classification algorithm of brain signals gathered from an EEG device.

Design. For the collection of the brain signals, the Electroencephalography (EEG) device called OpenBCI was used. OpenBCI is an opensource and low-cost platform that allows monitoring the electrical activity of the brain, muscles, and heart. On the other hand, for the processing and classification of the brain signals, a special software called OpenVibe was used, since it allows real time acquisition, filtering, classification, and visualization of brain signals [42]. Additionally, OpenVibe was selected since it supports OpenBCI. The classification of the signals will be carried out using Canonical Correlation Analysis (CCA), a multiclass classification algorithm that does not require training and has an average precision of 81.5% [9]. Communication between the classification algorithm and the user interface will be implemented through sockets.

Development. In the OpenVibe tool, a brainwave classification scenario that makes use of the CCA was modified. In this scenario, multiple steps are configured for acquisition, filtering, and processing of brain signals. The acquisition client was configured to receive data from the O1, O2 and Oz channels. A band pass filter was configured for the frequencies between 1 and 40 Hz. Additionally, the length of the signal to be collected for classification and the time window were configured i.e., a 3-s signal taken every 0.5 s.

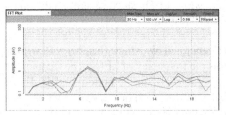

Fig. 5. The graph of the 7 Hz recording

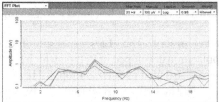

Fig. 6. The graph of the 8 Hz recording

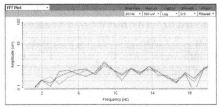

Fig. 7. The graph of the 9 Hz recording

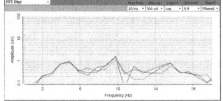

Fig. 8. The graph of the 10 Hz recording

The classification algorithm (CCA) that this scenario uses was developed in Python, and it was configured to work with four frequencies that will be received as parameters. In this algorithm, the input signal is compared with 4 reference signals, which correspond to the frequencies of 7, 8, 9 and 10 Hz, to find their correlation and emit a classification.

The algorithm output corresponds to the class number assigned to the frequencies following the order in which the frequencies were inserted in the scenario's parameters. In this case, for 7 Hz, the corresponding class is 1; for 8 Hz, the corresponding class is 2, and so on, in such a way that we will obtain the equivalence between action in the interface, frequency and classification shown in Table 3.

Based on this equivalency table, the navigation in the user interface consists of stare at the stimulus on the right or left to move in the correspondent direction, stare at the top stimulus to execute the action, and stare at the bottom stimulus to exit the program.

Table 3. Correspondence between interface actions, frequencies, and their classification

Frequency (Hz)	Classification	Interface Action
7	1	Accept
8	2	Right
9	3	Return
10	4	Left

The algorithm emits a classification every 0.5 s, but this is not suitable for the system because the interface's control becomes unstable, since too many commands are executed per second. For this reason, a second stage was implemented, in which the last 8 classifications are stored in an array, of which 75% must belong to the same class to emit a valid classification.

Since the system can generate noise signal when the user switches his/her sight from one stimulus to another, or from one stimulus to the user interface, an inactivity time of 2.5 s was added when a valid classification has been sent. During this time the classifications made by the algorithm will not be considered to avoid unwanted selections in the interface.

The classifications recognized by the algorithm are transmitted to the user interface where the action that corresponds to them are performed. The GUI was also modified to change the color of the button (to green) for 2 s when it is activated, to give extra feedback to the user on which actions they are executing when observing the stimuli.

Test. During this testing stage, the functionality of the prototype was verified (see Fig. 9). It was possible to use the SSVEP stimuli to move between the list of actions of the interface. Two users were logged into OpenBCI and asked to navigate in the user interfaces and perform actions. The prototype worked perfectly, and users were able to navigate and execute actions through the interface without errors.

Fig. 9. Prototype in use

4.5 Test of the Integrated Prototype

At this stage, the Action Research methodology was used to define the best course of action to evaluate the functionality of the prototype.

Diagnosing. The tests performed in the fourth increment were limited, which means that they could not be considered reliable since the sample of users was too small.

Action Planning and Taking. At this stage, the test to be performed with the volunteers were defined. The test will consist in turning on and off the smart light bulb and one socket of the smart power strip. This process was performed to cover from the simplest to the most complex navigation steps in the user interface.

First, the user will have to turn the bulb on and off. Turning on is the first command of the interface, so it only requires accepting the action i.e., stare at the upper stimulus. To turn off the bulb, it is necessary to scroll to the right once and select the option. Secondly, the user will have to turn one socket of the smart power strip on and off. To turn it on, it requires scrolling to the right twice and selection the option; while turning it off, it requires a further scroll to the right and then the select the command.

The process for placing the electrodes on the user's scalp consisted of (1) finding the Inion, i.e., the most prominent part of the occipital bone; the Oz channel is located in the central part of this area. (2) Separate the hair with hairpins by drawing an imaginary horizontal straight line on the scalp over Oz. (3) Sanitize the scalp surface. (4) Apply conductive paste on Oz and then place the electrode over the paste. (5) Find the location of the O1 (left) and O2 (right) channels by measuring about half-inch from Oz. (6) Repeat step 4 for the channels O1 and O2. (7) Pass the electrodes leads over the user's head to the front. (8) Sanitize the earlobes, apply conductive paste, and then place the electrodes over the paste. (9) Cover the earlobe electrodes with tape to prevent them from falling off. (10) Connect the electrodes to the OpenBCI Cyton.

Evaluating. Tests were carried out on fifteen volunteers, five women and ten men with an age range between 20 to 25 years, who declared not suffering from epilepsy. This verification was necessary since observing the SSVEPs could cause seizures in people with this disorder. Before starting the tests, the user was familiarized with the stimuli. Each user had to see each stimulus for 20 s and it was explained that they can blink while performing the tests, since this activity does not affect the results. Then, the subject was placed in front of the LCD screen with the GUI, and he/she was explained how to navigate through it, that is, the equivalence between the stimuli and the interface shown in Table 3. In addition, they were told that when a button is activated, it will change to green color immediately and then the device will be activated. Next, a familiarization test with navigation was carried out through the interface, using only the stimuli. Finally, the users were asked to carry out the four actions defined above, these are: turn the bulb on and off, and turn a socket of the smart power strip on and off. And the time required to perform each action and the data issued by the classification were recorded. The results and the learnings of this methodology are specified in the section below.

5   Results and Discussion

5.1   Results

The average time obtained to turn on the smart bulb was 9.70 s and the average time to turn it off was 16.04 s. And the average time to turn on the smart power strip was 26.80 s and to turn it off was 21.89 s. These results are shown in Tables 4 and 5.

Table 4. Tests results for the smart bulb   **Table 5.** Tests results for the smart strip

	On (s)	Off (s)
AVG	9,70	16,68
MIN	7,02	14,07
MAX	13,16	40,54

	On (s)	Off (s)
AVG	26,80	21,89
MIN	21,76	13,6
MAX	42,88	68,52

From the 126 classifications performed in all of 15 subjects, only 3 were incorrect. This means that the model delivered a success rate of 97.61% when identifying the stimuli that were observed by the user.

5.2   Discussion

IoT device's control through a BCI system offers a whole new range of possibilities to manipulate electronic devices with unusual but effective methods, which could help people with physical disabilities. For this purpose, different brain patterns can be used, but the SSVEPs have several advantages. They can be acquired non-invasively (by placing electrodes with conductive cream directly on the scalp); stimuli can be easily generated, and the pattern accurately detected; it can be implemented at low-cost; and an SSVEP-based BCI requires little or no training to use (in this work a simple five-minute explanation was enough).

In the present work, five gold cup electrodes were used to acquire EEG brain signals using the Cyton biosensing board (OpenBCI V3) connected to a PC via a Bluetooth dongle. This system uses four SSVEP stimuli which were generated using a Raspberry

Pi 3B + and displayed using LED diodes covered by a diffusing filter. A 600 x 1024px LCD screen was used to show the GUI application. Finally, the four stimuli were mounted on a 49 x 49 cm wooden board, each on half of each side of the board, as well as the LCD screen that was mounted in the middle of the board.

It is also important to indicate that the final prototype can be considered efficient since it can control five devices, four sockets of the smart power strip and one smart bulb, in real time; and it can perform 14 actions (two actions for each socket of smart power strip and six for the smart bulb) using only four stimuli. In similar studies such as [17] and [18], the number of available devices/actions is limited by the number of stimuli configured in the system, since each stimulus corresponds to one action. Those approaches are not scalable in the long term because to control more devices more stimuli must be added. Therefore, in this perspective, the proposed solution outperforms previously implemented ones (see Table 6).

Table 6. Result comparison with other SSVEP-based IoT device control studies

Reference	Precision (%)	Number of Stimuli	Number of devices controlled	Stimulus type
[17]	87%	4	2	LCD
[18]	84,8%	4	4	LED
[19]	92.8%	Unknown	Unknown	Augmented Reality
[20]	85.7%	2–4	3	Augmented Reality
Proposed system	97.61%	4	5	LED

However, the proposed solution also presents some minor limitations. Firstly, the size of the board where the screen and stimuli are placed is considerable (49x49 cm). Secondly, since the SSVEP requires the user to focus completely on the stimulus they wish to activate, the environmental noises can affect the activation speed of different devices of the system.

Other considerations to be aware of are: (1) after long periods of use, users register visual fatigue due to the discomfort caused by observing the LEDs for a long time and (2) the use of this system is contraindicated for people suffering from epilepsy as it could cause convulsions.

6 Conclusions

In the present work, SSVEP responses generated from stimuli delivered by LEDs flashing at four different frequencies (7, 8, 9 and 10 Hz) were transformed into operational commands to control different IoT devices using a CCA-based classification algorithm.

As the final product of this work, a functional prototype consisting of several components was obtained. These components are (1) the user brain signals acquisition using the OpenBCI EEG, (2) the visual stimuli generated by LEDs flashing at different frequencies to trigger the SSVEP brain response in the user, (3) the brain signal processing and classification system using OpenViBE, (4) the user interface, which has the list of available IoT devices to control and its actions, and uses the output from the classification algorithm for navigation, and (5) the IoT devices (i.e., a light bulb and a power strip with four individual sockets) which receive the action selected by the user on the GUI through a MQTT broker.

Given the freedom to connect any electrical device to each of the sockets on the power strip, the variety of electrical appliances that could be controlled is wide, and therefore, the system could be adapted to the user's needs. Additionally, the prototype is scalable, since more smart devices can be added to the system if can be controlled through developer´s API.

Finally, the tests conducted on 15 users provided promising results. An average precision of 97.61% was obtained through all the tests. The average time to turn on and off the smart bulb was 9.70 and 16.04 s, respectively. As well as turning on and off one of the sockets of the power strip required an average time of 26.80 and 21.89 s, respectively. We believe that these results confirm the real possibilities of implementing the developed prototype in real life solutions for helping people with severe movement disabilities.

References

1. Gubbi, J., Buyya, R., Marusic, S., Palaniswami, M.: Internet of Things (IoT): a vision, architectural elements, and future directions. Futur. Gener. Comput. Syst. **29**(7), 1645–1660 (2013). https://doi.org/10.1016/j.future.2013.01.010
2. Bhayani, M., Patel, M., Bhatt, C.: Internet of Things (IoT): In a Way of Smart World. **438**, 343–350 (2016)
3. Logroscino, G., et al.: Global, regional, and national burden of motor neuron diseases 1990–2016: a systematic analysis for the Global Burden of Disease Study 2016. Lancet Neurol. **17**(12), 1083–1097 (2018). https://doi.org/10.1016/S1474-4422(18)30404-6
4. Global status report on road safety. Geneva: World Health Organization; 2018. Licence: CC BYNC-SA 3.0 IGO (2018)
5. Hoffmann, U., Vesin, J.-M., Ebrahimi, T.: Recent Advances in Brain-Computer Interfaces. (2007). https://doi.org/10.1109/MMSP.2007.4412807
6. Beverina, F., Palmas, G., Silvoni, S., Piccione, F., Giove, S.: User adaptive BCIs: SSVEP and P300 based interfaces. PsychNology J. **1**, 331–354 (2003)
7. Chen, J., Zhang, D., Engel, A.K., Gong, Q., Maye, A.: Application of a single-flicker online SSVEP BCI for spatial navigation. PLoS ONE **12**(5), 1–13 (2017). https://doi.org/10.1371/journal.pone.0178385
8. Zhang, L., Liu, J., Wu, X., Guo, X., Zhou, B., Ye, Z.: Implement an asynchronous online SSVEP-based brain computer interface. In: Proceeding - 2017 10th International Congress Image Signal Processing Biomedical Engineering Informatics, CISP-BMEI 2017, vol. 2018-January, pp. 1–5 (2018). https://doi.org/10.1109/CISP-BMEI.2017.8302169
9. Witten, D.M., Tibshirani, R.J.: Extensions of sparse canonical correlation analysis with applications to genomic data. Stat. Appl. Genet. Mol. Biol. **8**(1), (2009). https://doi.org/10.2202/1544-6115.1470

10. Zheng, P., Gao, X.: Fixed-point CCA algorithm applied to SSVEP based BCI system. In: Proceeding 2013 IEEE Symposium Computational Intelligence Cognitive Algorithms, Mind, Brain, CCMB 2013 - 2013 IEEE Symposium Series Computational Intelligence SSCI 2013, no. 1, pp. 107–114 (2013). https://doi.org/10.1109/CCMB.2013.6609173

11. Poveda Zavala, S., Luis Murillo López, J., Ortíz Chicaiza, K., Guun Yoo, S.: Review of steady state visually evoked potential brain-computer interface applications: technological analysis and classification. J. Eng. Appl. Sci. **15**(2), 659–678 (2019). https://doi.org/10.36478/jeasci.2020.659.678

12. Peng, N., et al.: Control of a nursing bed based on a hybrid brain-computer interface. In: 2016 38th Annual International Conference of the IEEE Engineering in Medicine and Biology Society (EMBC), pp. 1556–1559 (2016). https://doi.org/10.1109/EMBC.2016.7591008

13. Perera, C.J., Naotunna, I., Sadaruwan, C., Gopura, R.A.R.C., Lalitharatne, T.D.: SSVEP based BMI for a meal assistance robot. In: 2016 IEEE International Conference on Systems, Man, and Cybernetics (SMC), pp. 2295–2300 (2016). https://doi.org/10.1109/SMC.2016.7844580

14. Yang, C., Wu, H., Li, Z., He, W., Wang, N., Su, C.: Mind control of a robotic arm with visual fusion technology. IEEE Trans. Ind. Informatics **14**(9), 3822–3830 (2018). https://doi.org/10.1109/TII.2017.2785415

15. Zhang, C., Kimura, Y., Higashi, H., Tanaka, T.: A simple platform of brain-controlled mobile robot and its implementation by SSVEP. In: The 2012 International Joint Conference on Neural Networks (IJCNN), pp. 1–7 (2012). https://doi.org/10.1109/IJCNN.2012.6252579

16. Pelayo, P., Murthy, H., George, K.: Brain-computer interface controlled robotic arm to improve quality of life. In: 2018 IEEE International Conference on Healthcare Informatics (ICHI), pp. 398–399 (2018). https://doi.org/10.1109/ICHI.2018.00072

17. Zhao, R., Qiao, Y., Zhu, Y., Wang, Y.: A SSVEP intelligent home service system based on CCA. In: 2017 3rd IEEE International Conference on Control Science and Systems Engineering (ICCSSE), pp. 495–499 (2017). https://doi.org/10.1109/CCSSE.2017.8087982

18. Virdi, P., Syal, P., Kumari, P.: Home automation control system implementation using SSVEP based brain computer interface. In: 2017 International Conference on Inventive Computing and Informatics (ICICI), pp. 1068–1073 (2017). https://doi.org/10.1109/ICICI.2017.8365304

19. Park, S., Cha, H.S., Kwon, J., Kim, H., Im, C.H.: Development of an Online home appliance control system using augmented reality and an SSVEP-based brain-computer interface. 8th International Winter Conference Brain-Computer Interface, BCI 2020, (2020). https://doi.org/10.1109/BCI48061.2020.9061633

20. Saboor, A., et al.: SSVEP-based BCI in a smart home scenario. In: Rojas, I., Joya, G., Catala, A. (eds.) IWANN 2017. LNCS, vol. 10306, pp. 474–485. Springer, Cham (2017). https://doi.org/10.1007/978-3-319-59147-6_41

21. Putze, F., Weib, D., Vortmann, L.M., Schultz, T.: Augmented reality interface for smart home control using SSVEP-BCI and eye gaze. Conference Proceeding - IEEE International Conference System Man Cybern., vol. 2019-October, pp. 2812–2817 (2019). https://doi.org/10.1109/SMC.2019.8914390

22. Saeed, S., Jhanjhi, N.Z., Naqvi, M., Humayun, M.: Analysis of software development methodologies. Int. J. Comput. Digit. Syst. **8**(5), 445–460 (2019). https://doi.org/10.12785/ijcds/080502

23. Ganney, P.S., Pisharody, S., Claridge, E.: Software engineering. In: Clinical Engineering, Elsevier, pp. 131–168 (2020)

24. Susman, G.I., Evered, R.D.: An assessment of the scientific merits of action research. Adm. Sci. Q. **23**, 582–603 (1978)

25. Staron, M.: Action Research in Software Engineering (2020)

26. Electronjs.org. Electron | Build cross-platform desktop apps with JavaScript, HTML, and CSS (2021). https://www.electronjs.org Accessed 1 May 2021

27. Beebotte.com. Beebotte MQTT Support (2021). https://beebotte.com/docs/mqtt Accessed 2 May 2021
28. Zhu, D., Bieger, J., Garcia Molina, G., Aarts, R.M.: A survey of stimulation methods used in SSVEP-based BCIs. Comput. Intell. Neurosci., vol. 2010, (2010). https://doi.org/10.1155/2010/702357
29. Wu, Z., Lai, Y., Xia, Y., Wu, D., Yao, D.: Stimulator selection in SSVEP-based BCI. Med. Eng. Phys. **30**(8), 1079–1088 (2008). https://doi.org/10.1016/j.medengphy.2008.01.004
30. Sugiarto, I., Allison, B., Gräser, A.: Optimization strategy for SSVEP-based BCI in spelling program application. In: Proceedings - 2009 International Conference Computational Engineering Technology ICCET 2009, vol. 1, pp. 223–226 (2009). https://doi.org/10.1109/ICCET.2009.189
31. Zander, T., Roussel, N.: Optimizing the use of SSVEP-based brain-computer interfaces for human-computer interaction To cite this version: Andéol Évain Optimizing the Use of SSVEP-based Beaudouin-Lafon for Human-Computer Interaction Gernot Müller-Putz (2017)
32. Volosyak, I., Gembler, F., Stawicki, P.: Age-related differences in SSVEP-based BCI performance. Neurocomputing **250**, 57–64 (2017). https://doi.org/10.1016/j.neucom.2016.08.121
33. Mouli, S., Palaniappan, R.: Eliciting higher SSVEP response from LED visual stimulus with varying luminosity levels. 2016 International Conference Students Applied Engineering ICSAE 2016, pp. 201–206 (2017). https://doi.org/10.1109/ICSAE.2016.7810188
34. Gao, X., Xu, D., Cheng, M., Gao, S.: A BCI-based environmental controller for the motion-disabled. IEEE Trans. Neural Syst. Rehabil. Eng. **11**(2), 137–140 (2003). https://doi.org/10.1109/TNSRE.2003.814449
35. Lee, P.L., et al.: An SSVEP-actuated brain computer interface using phase-tagged flickering sequences: a cursor system. Ann. Biomed. Eng. **38**(7), 2383–2397 (2010). https://doi.org/10.1007/s10439-010-9964-y
36. Brunner, C., Allison, B., Altstätter, C., Neuper, C.: A comparison of three brain-computer interfaces based on event-related desynchronization, steady state visual evoked potentials, or a hybrid approach using both signals. J. Neural Eng. **8**, 25010 (2011). https://doi.org/10.1088/1741-2560/8/2/025010
37. Ng, B., Bradley, A.P., Cunnington, R.: Stimulus specificity of a steady-state visual-evoked potential-based brain-computer interface. J. Neural Eng. **9**(3) (2012). https://doi.org/10.1088/1741-2560/9/3/036008
38. Chen, X., Wang, Y., Nakanishi, M., Jung, T.P., Gao, X.: Hybrid frequency and phase coding for a high-speed SSVEP-based BCI speller. In: 2014 36th Annual International Conference IEEE Engineering Medicine Biology Society EMBC 2014, pp. 3993–3996 (2014). https://doi.org/10.1109/EMBC.2014.6944499
39. Cao, T., Wan, F., Mak, P., Mak, P.-I., Vai, M., Hu, Y.: Flashing color on the performance of SSVEP-based brain-computer interfaces. In: Conference Proceedings IEEE Engineering Medicine Biology Society, vol. 2012, pp. 1819–1822 (2012). https://doi.org/10.1109/EMBC.2012.6346304
40. Aljshamee, M., Mohammed, M., Choudhury, R.-U.-A., Malekpour, A., Luksch, P.: Beyond Pure Frequency and Phases Exploiting: Color Influence in SSVEP Based on BCI. Comput. Technol. Appl., vol. 5 (2014). https://doi.org/10.17265/1934-7332/2014.02.008
41. Murillo, et al.: Study of the Influences of Stimuli Characteristics in the Implementation of Steady State Visual Evoked Potentials based Brain Computer Interface Systems. In Press
42. OpenViBE. Discover OpenViBE (2021). http://openvibe.inria.fr/discover/ Accessed 2 May 2021

Collision Avoidance Simulation Using Voronoi Diagrams in a Centralized System of Holonomic Multi-agents

Leduin José Cuenca Macas[(✉)][ID] and Israel Pineda[ID]

Yachay Tech University, Hacienda San José s/n Proyecto Yachay,
Urcuquí, Imbabura 100115, Ecuador
{leduin.cuenca,ipineda}@yachaytech.edu.ec

Abstract. This work solves the Collision Avoidance problem in a simulation of a centralized system of holonomic multi-agents in a two dimensional space free of static obstacles. For this, we propose an implementation of three modules in an architecture: Threat Assessment Strategy (TAS), Path Planning Strategy (PPS), and Path Tracking Strategy (PTS). The Buffered Voronoi Cells represent the TAS. The PPS modules use two algorithms: the Analytical Geometric Algorithm (AGA) and the Receding Horizons Control (RHC) based on Quadratic Programming (QP) Algorithm. Finally, PTS controls the tracking according to fixed distance magnitudes in each iteration. The analysis of the results considers the computational execution time, the number of steps until convergence, and the calculation of optimal values. Also, these results are compared with the Optimal Reciprocal Collision Avoidance (ORCA) algorithm. In this way, our proposal successfully addresses and solves the collision avoidance problem but takes more execution time and number of steps compared with the ORCA algorithm. Besides, the number of steps of AGA is closer to ORCA, producing promising results with an accuracy of 95%.

Keywords: Collision avoidance · Voronoi diagrams · Convex optimization · Quadratic programming · Path planning · Simulation

1 Introduction

Collision Avoidance (CA) is the process of preventing two or more physical objects from having intersecting boundaries in space-time, taking variables like time and distances into account. In this way, CA is studied due to its practical applications, mainly in path planning for ships [1], autonomous robots [2], aircraft and unmanned aerial vehicles [3], using different mathematical and computational techniques such as geometric analysis, control modeling with optimization, game theory, dynamical systems, and artificial intelligence [4]. Therefore, this problem challenges researchers to simulate the natural ability of complex living beings or processes to avoid physical collisions and react accurately.

J. Herrera-Tapia et al. (Eds.): TICEC 2022, CCIS 1648, pp. 18–31, 2022.
https://doi.org/10.1007/978-3-031-18272-3_2

In the present work, we deal with CA algorithms for centralized autonomous holonomic multi-agent. We use the safe distance-based method as a Threat Assessment Strategy (TAS). A combination of Optimization and Geometrical-based strategies with heuristics to break deadlocks serve as Path Planning Strategy (PPS). Moreover, the Path Tracking Strategy (PTS) uses Euclidean geometry. The project proposal involves using Buffered Voronoi Cells (BVC), Analytical Geometric Algorithm (AGA), and Quadratic Programming (QP) based Receding Horizons Control (RHC) algorithm. The generated algorithms only require detecting the relative positions with a centralizing character. Therefore, it is very suitable for online deployment, as it does not require a concurrent communication network. We demonstrate the capabilities of our algorithm by comparing it to the Optimal Reciprocal Collision Avoidance (ORCA) in a benchmark simulation scenario, and we present the results of over 2160 experimental trials in total. Our work follows the ideas of Zhou et al. [5].

2   Related Work

2.1   Collision Avoidance

There are at least two CA Design Control Architectures for autonomous agents [2]: the Multi-Layer CA System divides responsibility for different objectives into layers, and the Unified-Design CA System combines two blocks for integrated objectives and identical control inputs. Both architectures usually comprise several sub-modules or strategies: TAS, PPS and PTS.

TAS provides an assessment and subsequent warnings of the potential threat to CA. The result of the TAS calculation is the key to triggering the subsequent actions of the CA architecture. In this way, TAS feeds the decision-making strategy on the appropriate action of the moving object. In addition, TAS takes care of the threshold or tolerance limits around obstacles or any physical object in the environment. Once this object violates certain conditions, the CA system activates the path planning module to re-plan the current trajectory. The risk can be measured by any means, including distance, speed, and acceleration of the moving object relative to the elements of the environment [4].

The PPS re-plans a collision-free route while the vehicle moves once the TAS identifies the potential collision threat. This new route may differ from the previous route planned by the PPS. In addition, an ideal PPS considers the risk of collisions involved in changing the current kinematics of the vehicle. First, the strategy guarantees enough space for the mobile to maneuver without frontal or side collisions. Then it needs to make sure that there is no potential risk with another obstacle after the maneuver. Finally, the new trajectory must consider the mechanical limitations and internal implications of the moving object [2].

PTS algorithms act as a path following controller to ensure the vehicle or mobile robot successfully avoids collisions. An enfficient PTS timely tracks the reference re-planned path by producing the required low-level control actions and output suitable interventions. For this reason, different scenarios demand particular CA actions [2].

2.2 Voronoi Diagrams

Given a set of two or more but a finite number of distinct points in the Euclidean plane, we associate all the locations in that space with the closest members of the set of points concerning the Euclidean distance. The result is a tessellation is called *Voronoi Diagram* generated by the point set, and the regions consti-tuting the Voronoi diagram are called *Voronoi cells*. New compressed cells can be generated within each cell according to the safety radius distance. These new cells are the *Buffered Voronoi Cells*. Figure 1 shows this description graphically.

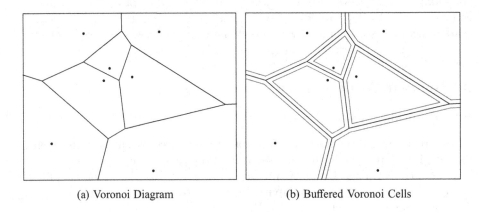

(a) Voronoi Diagram   (b) Buffered Voronoi Cells

Fig. 1. Example of Voronoi diagrams

2.3 Multi-agent Navigation

We can categorize the multi-agent systems based on the different views of plan-ning approaches into two classes: centralized and decentralized [6]. We call Cen-tralized Policy for multi-agents to a plan to generate collective actions starting from the states of the global system, solving the problems of the agents in a unified way. On the other hand, in a decentralized system, the agents partially observe the global system state and make local decisions. Thus, the planned mapping from local knowledge to local actions is called a Decentralized Policy for multi-agent.

3 Methodology

3.1 Model Proposal

We propose a simulation architecture for a holonomic multi-agent system in a two-dimensional environment free of obstacles. Our proposed architecture uses three main components: TAS, PPS, and PTS. The simulation uses Voronoi Dia-gram as the core of its TAS. The PPS component can use either AGA or the

QP-based RHC algorithm; both algorithms have the same input parameters, but with the difference that the QP-based RHC algorithm has a solver for the optimization problem. Additionally, the PPS has heuristics to break deadlocks during navigation. We use Euclidean distance for PTS. The two architecture variations (AGA and QP-based RHC) are compared with the ORCA algorithm to contrast result metrics.

3.2 Two-Dimensional Environment

The environment is represented by a two-dimensional Cartesian plane. Both main axes contain the real set of numbers for the coordinates generation. Thus, the position of the robots and the Voronoi vertices are any real coordinates. The initial and final positions of the simulated agents are antipodal and form a circular figure centered at the point $(0, 0)$. Let N be the number of robots; the distance from each position to $(0,0)$ equals $4 \times \sqrt{N}$ plus an offset belonging to the set $[-\frac{1}{0.4 \times N}, 0)$. The distance formula is selected to generate configurations similar to Zhou et al. [5]. There is an approximation for Voronoi infinity vertices for practical purposes. The magnitude generated for their respective infinity edges is equal to 20 times the number of simulated robots; for example, if there exist five robots, then the magnitude is equal to 100. There are no static obstacles or passages, just moving robots defined as common obstacles. The precision of the numeric values depends on the programming language of the implementation; in this case, Python.

3.3 Heuristics to Deal with Deadlock

Deadlock is an imminent problem in CA. It happens when some robots block the paths of each other so that they cannot reach their goal. For those robots whose goal positions are not inside their own BVC, in a deadlock situation, each robot must be at the closest point to the goal position on its BVC. The closest point in the BVC of robot i, g_i^*, to the goal $p_{i,f}$, must be either at a vertex or on edge such that a line from $p_{i,f}$ to g_i^* is perpendicular to this edge.

No existing algorithm can provably avoid deadlock without central computation to our best knowledge. Instead, most distributed algorithms attempt to alleviate the problem through sensible heuristics. Similarly, we propose two heuristic methods that perform well in solving deadlock. At the same time, we establish a deadlock threshold value due to the limited range of numerical data types of programming languages.

The first heuristic is the Right-Hand Rule, which detours each robot from its right side when encountering other robots in deadlock situations. If the application of this heuristic causes the robot to leave its BVC, then we prefer not to move the robot in that step. This preference is made until the movement of other robots can break the deadlock or allow the movement of the blocked robot.

The second one considers the previous positions, ensuring a high level of breaking deadlock situations, abrupt and zigzag movements. In this case, we analyzed the distance between previous positions with the closest point in the BVC.

3.4 QP-Based Receding Horizons Control Algorithm

The Quadratic Programming Based Algorithm has its foundations on the Receding Horizon Control, also known as Model Predictive Control. Its applications include scenarios such as industrial and chemical process control, supply chain management, stochastic control in economics and finance, revenue management, hybrid vehicles, automotive and aerospace applications [7].

With RHC, an optimization problem is solved at each time step to determine a plan of action over a fixed time horizon. Then, the first input from the plan is applied to the system. Next time we repeat the planning process, solving a new optimization problem with the time horizon shifted one step forward. The optimization problem estimates future quantities based on available information at each time step. The control policy involves feedback since real-time measurements determine the control input [8]. In this way, we model the following optimization problem,

Problem 1 (Receding Horizon Path Planning).

$$
\min_{\overline{p}_1,\ldots,\overline{p}_T} J_i = \sum_{t=0}^{T-1} \left(\left(\overline{p}_{i,t} - p_{i,f}\right)^{\mathsf{T}} Q \left(\overline{p}_{i,t} - p_{i,f}\right) + u_{i,t}^{\mathsf{T}} R u_{i,t} \right) \tag{1}
$$
$$
+ \left(\overline{p}_{i,T} - p_{i,f}\right)^{\mathsf{T}} Qf \left(\overline{p}_{i,T} - p_{i,f}\right)
$$

subject to:

$$
\overline{p}_{i,t+1} = A\overline{p}_{i,t} + Bu_{i,t}, \; t = 0, \cdots, T-1, \tag{2}
$$
$$
\overline{p}_{i,t} \in \overline{V}_i, \; t = 1, \cdots, T, \tag{3}
$$
$$
\overline{p}_{i,0} = p_i, \tag{4}
$$
$$
\|u_{i,t,x}\| \leq u_{x,max}, \; t = 0, \cdots, T-1, \tag{5}
$$
$$
\|u_{i,t,y}\| \leq u_{y,max}, \; t = 0, \cdots, T-1. \tag{6}
$$

In Problem 1, the cost function J_i is a summation of the intermediate state and terminal costs. In Eq. 1, $p_{i,f}$ is the final position, $\overline{p}_{i,0}$ to $\overline{p}_{i,T}$ and $u_{i,0}$ to $u_{i,T-1}$ are the path and inputs to be planned, respectively. The positive definite or semi-definite matrices Q, R, and Q_f are weight factors to balance the three costs. The decision variables for this standard QP problem are $\overline{p}_{i,1}$ to $\overline{p}_{i,T}$. Constraint 2 ensures that the path is feasible with the dynamics of the robots. In the present work, the holonomic robots do not need to fix the matrix values because they can move in any direction, and their velocity is the same. Constraint 3 restrains the planned path inside the corresponding BVC $\overline{\mathcal{V}}_i$ of robot i. This constraint can be written explicitly in the form of a set of linear inequalities:

$$\overline{p}_{i,t}^\mathsf{T} \epsilon_j \leq 0, \qquad t = 1, \cdots, T, j \in \{1, \cdots, N\}, j \neq i, \tag{7}$$

where ϵ_j is a vector representing an edge of $\overline{\mathcal{V}}_i$ that separates robot i from robot j. Constraint 4 makes sure the planned positions start from the current position of the robot, and, finally, the lower and upper bounds for the input $u_{i,t}$ are written component-wisely in constraints 5 and 6.

We use the Python-embedded modeling language CVXPY to solve the QP problem [9]. It allows expressing a convex problem naturally that follows the mathematical conventions rather than in the restrictive standard form of solvers. However, the usage of CVXPY is similar to a usual Python library. Algorithm 1 contains the most fundamental parts of the pseudocode to solve the QP problem and get the closer coordinate in the robot cell to its final position.

Algorithm 1: QP Solver

Data: agent, r, T
Result: $\overline{p}_T$
1 initialize m, A, B, R, Q, Q_f, $\overline{p}$, u, $u_{max,x}$, $u_{max,y}$;
2 cost $= 0$;
3 constraints $= [\ ]$;
4 $p_i =$ agent initial position;
5 $p_f =$ agent final position;
6 Add $\overline{p}_{i,0} = p_i$ to constraints;
7 **for** t *in range(T)* **do**
8 $\quad$ Sum $(\overline{p}_t - p_f)^\mathsf{T} Q (\overline{p}_t - p_f) + u_t^\mathsf{T} R u_t$ to cost;
9 $\quad$ Add $\overline{p}_{t+1} = A\overline{p}_t + Bu_t$ to constraints;
10 $\quad$ Add $\|u_{0,t}\| \leq u_{max,x}$ to constraints;
11 $\quad$ Add $\|u_{1,t}\| \leq u_{max,y}$ to constraints;
12 $\quad$ **for** *each position of agent neighbors* **do**
13 $\quad\quad$ $p_j =$ neighbor position;
14 $\quad\quad$ Add $p_t - \frac{p_i+p_j}{2}^\mathsf{T}(p_j - p_i) + (r * \|p_j - p_i\|) \leq 0$ to constraints;
15 $\quad$ **end**
16 **end**
17 Sum $(\overline{p}_T - p_f)^\mathsf{T} Q_f (\overline{p}_T - p_f)$ to cost;
18 **for** *each position of agent neighbors* **do**
19 $\quad$ $p_j =$ neighbor position;
20 $\quad$ Add $p_T - \frac{p_i+p_j}{2}^\mathsf{T}(p_j - p_i) + (r * \|p_j - p_i\|) \leq 0$ to constraints;
21 **end**
22 Solve the CVXPY problem();

3.5 Analytical Geometrical Algorithm

The QP-based RHC Algorithm generates a control policy optimal over the planning horizon at the expense of solving a QP problem online at each time step. Furthermore, we can solve the QP with an Analytical Geometric Algorithm for the particular case of no intermediate cost terms, which executes much faster than the QP, while CA is still guaranteed.

Consider the case where the intermediate state and the control input costs are equal to zero, and the terminal cost exists. However, all the constraints of the optimization problem are the same. This simplification can be considered as a one-step greedy strategy that drives the robot to move to its goal position as soon as possible. With this simplification, the moving object should direct towards a point in the convex polygon borders closest to its goal position [5].

Algorithm 2 outlines the basic AGA procedure. The input parameters are the number of robots N, the magnitude of the safety radius r, the magnitude of movement m in each step, the magnitude of deadlock tolerance δ, the magnitude of movement ϵ to break deadlock, and the number of previous positions ω to evaluate if a deadlock situation exists.

Algorithm 2: Analytical Geometric

Data: N, r, m, δ, ϵ, ω, robots

1 **if** *not Collision Free Configuration* **then**
2   Change the initial or final configuration;
3   break;
4 **end**
5 **while** *not current positions = final positions* **do**
6   Generate Voronoi Diagram;
7   Generate BVC;
8   **for** *agent in robots list* **do**
9   **if** *not Final position inside BVC* **then**
10   Get the closest point inside BVC;
11   Check deadlock;
12   cycle $= 1$;
13   **while** *cycle* $< \omega$ **and** *not deadlock* **do**
14   **if** *deadlock* **then**
15   Apply right-hand heuristic;
16   **end**
17   Increment cycle in 1;
18   **end**
19   **else**
20   The closest point is the final position;
21   **end**
22   Move the robot to its closest point;
23   **end**
24 **end**

The explanation of Collision Free Configuration and generation of the closest point to final in a cell mentioned in the procedure is below.

- **Collision Free Configuration.** For the group of N robots with the same safety radius r, *A collision free configuration* is one where the distance between positions of robot p_i and robot p_j satisfies:

$$\|p_i - p_j\| \geq 2r, \forall i,j \in 1,2,\cdots,N, i \neq j. \tag{8}$$

- **BVC Closest Point.** Let $\mathcal{V} = (\epsilon, e)$ represents a convex polygon in ^{2}, where ϵ is the set of edges and e is the set of vertices. For any point $g \in^2$, the closest point $g^* \in \mathcal{V}$ to g is either g itself, or on an edge ϵ^* of $\mathcal{V}$, or is a vertex e^* of $\mathcal{V}$.

3.6   Optimal Reciprocal Collision Avoidance Algorithm

The task is for each robot A to independently (and new simultaneously) select a new velocity v_A^{new} for itself such that all robots are guaranteed to be collision-free for at least a preset amount of time r when they would continue to move at their new velocity. As a secondary objective, the robots should select their new velocity as close as possible to their preferred velocity. The robots cannot communicate with each other and can only use observations of the current position and velocity of the other robot. However, each robot may assume that the other robots use the same strategy to select a new velocity. Note that this problem cannot be solved using central coordination, as the robot itself only knows the preferred velocity of each robot [10].

In this work, we use the RVO2 library as the ORCA algorithm implementation [11]. It is an open-source implementation and has a simple API for third-party applications. In this way, the user specifies static obstacles, agents, and the preferred velocities of the agents. The simulation is performed step-by-step via a simple call to the library. Thus, the simulation is fully accessible and manipulable during runtime. Furthermore, the algorithm ensures that each agent exhibits no oscillatory behaviors.

3.7   Analysis Method

We defined the ways to study the model proposed in this subsection. First, a series of experiments evaluate and compare the performance of the model proposed in Sect. 4.2. These experiments were designed with specific research intentions:

1. We are executing pseudo-random spatial configurations of the agents to check the consistency in the construction of the Voronoi Diagram.
2. Next, suitable values for parameters in AGA and QP-Based RHC Algorithm appear.
3. Finally, the proposed algorithms and ORCA are compared using the best performing AGA and QP-Based RHC Algorithm.

We defined a set of measures for testing the algorithms. These measures helped us understand the performance of algorithm in terms of duration and calculation of optimum values. The performance measures are the following.

- **Execution Time (ET)** is a measure of execution duration in units of time. It is the time from starting movement until all robots reach the final positions. The execution time is represented as follows:

$$ET = t_f - t_i. \tag{9}$$

Thus, ET is the total execution time, t_f is the final time, and t_i is the initial time.
- **Steps Number (ST)** is a measure of duration in terms of iterations. It is the number of iterations until all robots reach the final position. This measure depends on the algorithm design, mainly of the movement magnitude.
- **Effectiveness in Distance Traveled (ED)** measures how close the path traveled is to the shortest distance, understood as a straight line from the starting point to the end. This effectiveness is represented as:

$$ED = \frac{\sum_{i=1}^{N} a_i}{\sum_{i=1}^{N} b_i}. \tag{10}$$

In this equation, N is the total number of robots, a_i represents the shortest distance for robot i from its started position to the final position, and b_i is the total distance traveled by robot i. This measure is only used for AGA parameters analysis.
- **Sum Cost (SC)** represents the sum of the means of all the previous measures for the selection of the best AGA parameter value. The SC follows the next model:

$$\min \left\{ \frac{ET_i}{\sum_{j=1}^{k} ET_j} + \frac{ST_i}{\sum_{j=1}^{k} ST_j} + \frac{1 - ED_i}{\sum_{j=1}^{k}(1 - ED_j)} \right\}, \tag{11}$$

where k represents the number of values that one of the parameters can take and $i \in \{1, \cdots, k\}$.

4   Results and Discussion

4.1   Construction of Voronoi Diagram

Figure 2 shows one experiment with all the corresponding geometric structures. The Voronoi Diagram is drawn with thick gray lines. The dashed gray lines are the straight lines from the current positions of agents to their goal positions. Also, the executed trajectories, BVC, and goal positions have the same color as the robot, and the thick dark lines are the planned paths from our algorithm for each robot in its cell. We can see in Fig. 2a an initial configuration with five robots and a safety radius equal to 0.3. In Fig. 2b, we can see the robots in the middle of the execution. In Fig. 2c, we can see all robots direct to their goal position. Finally, Fig. 2d shows the final state of the system.

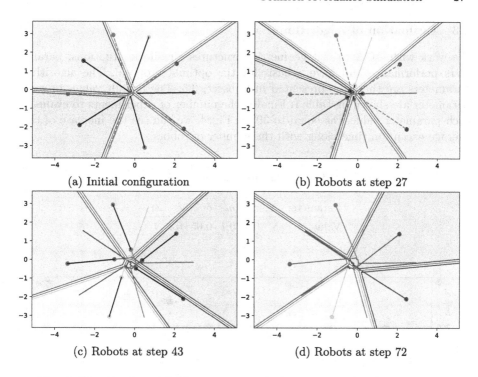

(a) Initial configuration

(b) Robots at step 27

(c) Robots at step 43

(d) Robots at step 72

Fig. 2. Visualization of AGA execution with the respective BVC generation

4.2   Deadlock

The blocking situation was addressed satisfactorily in all the experiments. In Fig. 3a, we can see blue, cyan, and magenta robots in deadlock situation. Next, we can see in Fig. 3b the next state after dealing with deadlock using the right-hand rule heuristic.

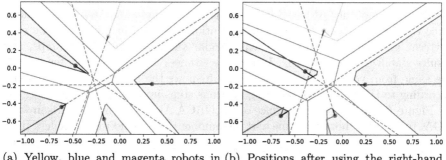

(a) Yellow, blue and magenta robots in deadlock.

(b) Positions after using the right-hand rule heuristic.

Fig. 3. Deadlock situation. (Color figure online)

4.3 Evaluation of Algorithms

We work with AGA to test geometric structures, deadlock situations, parameters performance and have a basis for the optimal proposal. The algorithm parameters are the same presented in Subsect. 3.5. The default values of each parameter are shown in Table 1. Finally, the number of experiments to evaluate each parameter value was equal to 30. In Fig. 4, we can see the increase of the average execution time along with the number of robots.

Table 1. Default parameters values in AGA evaluation

Parameter	N	r	m	δ	ϵ	ω
Value	5	0.1	0.1	0.05	0.1	1

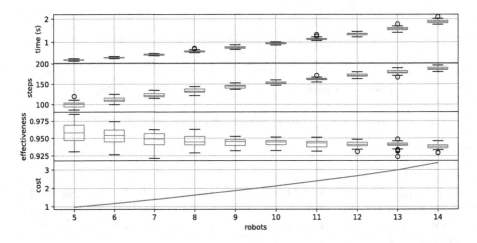

Fig. 4. Time in seconds, number of steps and effectiveness vs number of robots in AGA

The results of the QP-based RHC algorithm are similar to AGA performance since there is a growing trend of the execution time and instability in the step patterns and effectiveness up to a particular value. In the case of steps, the results stabilize from value six. In the effectiveness case, the results tend to be the same from value five onwards. Figure 5 shows the number of system steps according to the number of receding horizons steps in solver.

Figure 6 shows the performance of the ORCA Algorithm in comparison with AGA. In this way, both the time and the number of steps of ORCA are less than AGA for a range of values from five to fourteen robots. However, for the number of steps, AGA comes close to ORCA.

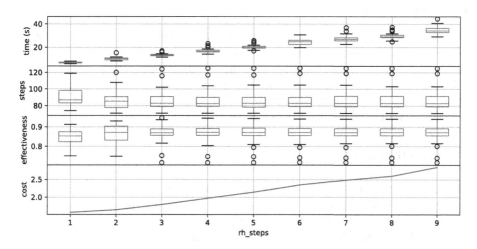

Fig. 5. Time in seconds, number of steps and effectiveness vs number of in QP-based RHC algorithm.

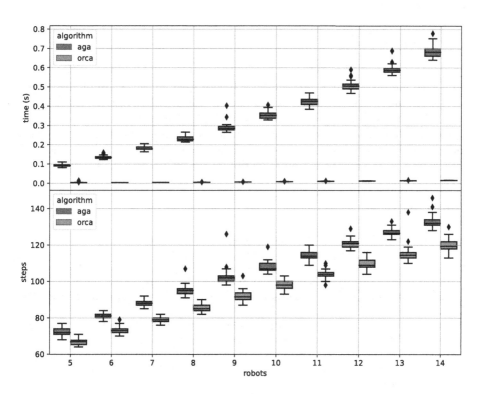

Fig. 6. ORCA and AGA performance in time and number of steps vs number of robots.

4.4 Implementation

The experiments were executed in a computer with a Intel ® Core ™ i7-10750H CPU @ 2.60 GHz processor with 6 CPU Cores, 12 Logical processors, 15.5 GB RAM, 64-bit system type running on Ubuntu 20.04.4 Operating System. The following repository has our algorithm implementation, performance, and experimental setup for reproducibility purposes: https://github.com/pepeleduin/Collision-Avoidance-Algorithms-in-2D-using-Voronoi-Diagrams.

5 Conclusions

We conclude that the Analytical Geometric Algorithm successfully addressed and solved the execution time limitations and the number of steps to converge towards the solution. On the other hand, the Receding Horizon Control algorithm based on Quadratic Programming requires more execution time. We did not always get optimal results working with heuristics, but we obtained good-enough solutions that are close to the performance of the Optimal Reciprocal Collision Avoidance algorithm. However, the algorithm produces promising results with an accuracy of around 95%.

5.1 Future Work

We consider using techniques such as High-Performance Computing to experiment with more significant problems for future work. The nature of the agent system and the environment can be modified to analyze the behavior of the algorithms. In this way, concurrency could be applied to decentralize the system and expand the dimension of the environment. In addition, the simulation visualization can be improved to better appreciate the behavior of the agents. Finally, other solvers could find better optimization of the solution of the problem.

References

1. Zaccone, R., Martelli, A.: A collision avoidance algorithm for ship guidance applications. J. Marine Eng. Technol. **19**(sup1), 62–75 (2020)
2. Hamid, U., Saito, Y., Zamzuri, H., Rahman, M., Raksincharoensak, P.: A review on threat assessment, path planning and path tracking strategies for collision avoidance systems of autonomous vehicles. Int. J. Veh. Autonomous Syst. **14**(2), 134–169 (2018)
3. Huang, S., Teo, R., Tan, K.: Collision avoidance of multi unmanned aerial vehicles: A review. Ann. Rev. Control **48**, 147–164 (2019)
4. Dahl, J., de Campos, G., Olsson, C., Fredriksson, J.: Collision avoidance: A literature review on threat-assessment techniques. IEEE Trans. Intell. Veh. **4**(1), 101–113 (2018)
5. Zhou, D., Wang, Z., Bandyopadhyay, S., Schwager, M.: Fast, on- line collision avoidance for dynamic vehicles using buffered voronoi cells. IEEE Robotics Autom. Lett. **2**(2), 1047–1054 (2017)

6. Xuan P., Lesser, V.: Multi-agent policies: from centralized ones to decentralized ones. In: Proceedings of the First International Joint Conference on Autonomous Agents and Multiagent Systems, pp. 1098–1105 (2002)
7. Camacho, E., Alba, C.: Model predictive control. Springer Science & Business Media (2013)
8. Mattingley, J., Wang, Y., Boyd, S.: Receding horizon control. IEEE Control Syst. Mag. **31**(3), 52–65 (2011)
9. Diamond, S., Boyd, S.: CVXPY: a Python-embedded modeling language for convex optimization. J. Mach. Learn. Res. **17**(83), 1–5 (2016)
10. Carbone, C., Ciniglio, U., Corraro, F., Luongo, S.: A novel 3d geometric algorithm for aircraft autonomous collision avoidance. In: Proceedings of the 45th IEEE Conference on Decision and Control, pp. 1580–1585. IEEE (2006)
11. Van den Berg, J., Lin, M., Manocha, D.: Reciprocal velocity obstacles for real-time multi-agent navigation. In: 2008 IEEE International Conference on Robotics and Automation, pp. 1928–1935. IEEE (2008)

Intelligent Electromyograph for Early Detection of Myopathy and Neuropathy Using EMG Signals and Neural Network Model

Evelyn Aguiar-Salazar[1,2], Bryan Cerón-Andrade[1,3], Andrea Valenzuela-Guerra[1],
Daniela Negrete-Bolagay[1], Xiomira Fiallos-Ayala[1], Diego Suntaxi-Dominguez[1],
Fernando Villalba-Meneses[1,4], Andrés Tirado-Espín[5],
and Diego Almeida-Galárraga[1(✉)]

[1] School of Biological Sciences and Engineering, Universidad Yachay Tech, Urcuquí 100650,
Ecuador
dalmeida@yachaytech.edu.ec
[2] Faculty of Medical Sciences, Universidad UNIANDES, Ambato 180166, Ecuador
[3] Faculty of Medical Sciences, Universidad UNIANDES Sede Santo Domingo, Santo
Domingo 230104, Ecuador
[4] Aragón Institute of Engineering Research (I3A), Universidad de Zaragoza, 50018 Zaragoza,
Spain
[5] School of Mathematical and Computational Sciences, Universidad Yachay Tech,
Urcuquí 100650, Ecuador

Abstract. The present work proposes developing an electromyograph to give a
reliable diagnosis for detecting neuromuscular diseases. Neuropathy is a condition
that affects neurons, and in myopathy, the muscle fiber does not work correctly.
Developing a highly accurate diagnostic system based on EMG readings would
provide a promising way to improve the evaluation of neuromuscular disorders.
If the features are efficiently extracted, it is possible to obtain outstanding sorting
performance. This research is carried out in two phases (hardware and software).
First, the electromyogram was developed with sensors that allow the acquisition of
bioelectric signals generated by the skeletal muscles with non-invasive electrodes.
For recording the EMG signal, a differential pre-amplification was made, and three
filters were used to obtain the minimum noise in the signal. Second, a Convolutional Neural Network (CNN) of type ResNet-34 was developed in Python. A
database obtained from various articles with similar studies was built; data was
a set of images of EMG signals divided into three classes: healthy, neuropathy,
and myopathy. The images of these three classes are similar in time domain and
frequency, so this network classifies healthy images of EMG signals from showing
patterns of pathology. An EMG-based feature extraction method is proposed and
implemented that uses a neural network to detect healthy conditions, myopathy,
and neuropathy. Finally, according to the performance evaluation of this method,
it has a precision of 98.57%.

Keywords: Electromyography · Neural networks · Medical conditions ·
Pathology · Smart device

J. Herrera-Tapia et al. (Eds.): TICEC 2022, CCIS 1648, pp. 32–45, 2022.
https://doi.org/10.1007/978-3-031-18272-3_3

1   Introduction

Neuropathy is a condition in which neurons are affected, the individual experiences numbness in their limbs [1]. This condition can cause gait impairment, such as difficulty walking, climbing stairs, or maintaining balance [2]. In the USA, the number of people with this condition is approaching 20,000 [3]. The estimated prevalence of neuropathies in the general population is about 2%; in adults from 55 years old, it can reach 8% [4]. Myopathy is a muscular condition where the physiological function of the muscle fiber is altered and can be produced for some reasons as muscle cramps, stiffness, and spasms [2, 5]. In 2005 the USA's statistics data determined that approximately 2.97 million patients have been diagnosed with myopathy [3].

To give an accurate diagnosis to patients suffering from these pathologies, electromyography (EMG) is used. The EMG allows the extraction of muscle signals, and subsequently, the interpretation of those patterns to the patients by the medical staff is necessary [6]. However, the number of neurological experts is limited, so an automatic system that helps diagnosis, periodic detection, and monitoring is required [3]. Therefore, it is possible to reduce the medical costs that clinical examinations could represent per patient, thanks to the early detection of these muscular diseases. The electromyogram helps to detect diseases through the analyses of pattern recognition applications by using analytical methods [7]. For instance, fast and short-term Fourier transforms (FFT and SFT) are used to study stationary signals and then for the non-stationary signals [8, 9]. Pattichis and Pattichis processed the signal at different resolution levels (multiresolution analysis) by using the continuous Wavelet transform (WT) [10].

As a consequence of WT function having continuous derivatives, i.e., allowing decompose a continuous function efficiently, signal processing is reduced and avoid unwanted signals [8, 11]. Many others, such as autoregressive (AR), Root mean square (RMS), Quadratic phase coupling (QPC), have emerged [12, 14]. These techniques provide an extensive spectral to study the signals. However, it is necessary to extract the coefficients from each stage of the construct functional approximation to the original signal. It implies the analysis by classifiers such as Artificial Neural Network (ANN), Support Vector Machines (SVM) [15], Logistic Regression (LR), Linear Discriminant Analysis (LDA) [8, 16]. For the determination of muscle fatigue for an automated system, estimation of knee joint angle for control of leg prostheses determination of muscle contraction during human walking, among others [17].

Neural networks are computer systems inspired by the learning characteristics and structure of biological neuron networks, and they also have applications for the detection of muscle diseases [18]. A study identified three spectral analysis methods (AR, FFT, Cepstral analysis) to characterize myoelectric signals and classify neuropathy and myopathy using neural network classifiers [14]. The combination of SVM with FTT provides the area under the ROC curve (receiver operating characteristic) of 0.953, which is within the acceptable range [14]. Likewise, other researchers used the Probabilistic Neural Network (PNN), a classifier that can map any input pattern to a series of classifications. A diagnosis of neuromuscular diseases has the advantage of a training process and is an inherent parallel structure [19].

It is necessary to perform an image classification or normalization of contrast and brightness and noise elimination [20]. Therefore, research-based on image recognition using artificial neural networks explicitly performs feature extraction using grayscale and binarization, transforming the image into two colours, black and white. Also, in this work, the Python programming language was chosen [10]. This project's objective includes the investigation and interpretation of EMG signals using an electromyogram. Then, signals are further analyzed using a CNN that provides better analysis tools that allow diagnosing these musculoskeletal conditions (healthy, neuropathy, and myopathy) by analyzing the images of EMG signals.

2   Materials and Methods

The research implies the following modules: first, obtaining and processing the signal, so here, choose the components and the amplifiers to avoid distortions of the signal's information as the noise. Second, extract and store the information from the signals provided by the prototype to transform the signal. Third, extract signals with pathologies of a database, in this case, signals of myopathy and neuropathy. Finally, apply neural networks as classificatory according to the different parameters considered (see Fig. 1).

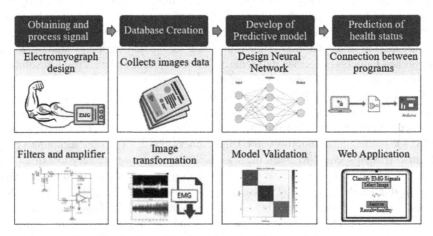

Fig. 1. Flow diagram of the working methodology.

2.1   Obtaining and Process Signal

The myoelectric signal represents the electrical activity resulting from the excitability of muscle fibers due to muscle concentration. The amplitude of this signal varies from μV to values of the order of 10 mV [21]. In this research, three non-invasive 3M 2560 Red Dot™ foam electrodes whose dimensions are 4x4 cm were used to detect the EMG signal. They are comfortable for patients, occlusive for fluids, and easy to handle. The solid gel of the electrodes allows uninterrupted and high-quality marks and minimizes the degree of skin irritation. Thus, two electrodes detect variation of signal (millivolts), placed on the biceps at a distance between them of 3 cm, and the third is used as a reference on the elbow. The electrodes make an ion exchange of tissue from the living body to an electronic device that triggers the appearance of a potential difference (voltage). For the treatment and processing of the read signal, an electronic board was developed with various components such as resistors, operational amplifiers, and capacitors. The board consists of three stages (see Fig. 2).

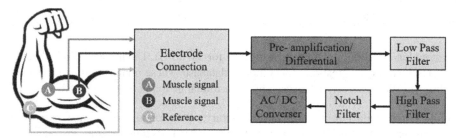

Fig. 2. Block diagram of the EMG circuit (hardware).

First Stage. The signal received from electrodes passes through an instrumental amplifier made up of three operational amplifiers and some resistors. It has two parts: a preamplification and a differential part. The primary signal is to amplify (gain) the difference between two input signals. The input signal amplitude oscillates in a range from 1 to 10 mV. For the treatment of the signal, an output that ranges from 1 V to 10 V is required. Approximately 1000 times profit is required.

Second Stage. At this stage, the required cutoff frequencies for the three filters must be defined [22]. The literature recommends using a cutoff frequency of 10 Hz to 300 Hz since the signal outside this range has much noise [2]. Besides, the 60 Hz frequency must be eliminated due to the interference generated with the country's electricity grid. Three filters are used: low pass, high pass, and notch, whose cutoff frequencies are 300 Hz, 10 Hz, and 60 Hz.

Third Stage. Corresponding to the conversion ADC, analogue to a digital signal, is accomplished with microprocessors such as Arduino. The values sent from the Arduino board to the computer's serial port are taken through the Python pyserial module. Moreover, these data are plotted as a function of time and amplitude.

The system's transfer function is obtained to predict the shape of the EMG signal without the need to solve complex differential equations [23]. Thus, for each phase, a transfer function is calculated for the amplification and the three filters. Then, multiplication of these series functions is performed to result in the entire system's transfer function. (See Fig. 3).

2.2 Database Creation

Simulated signals were extracted from various works carried out to evaluate the proposed method, classified into three categories: healthy, myopathy, and neuropathy, these signals

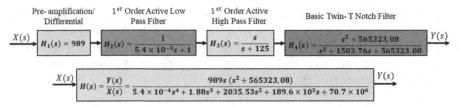

Fig. 3. The transfer function of each stage of the EMG circuit.

are stored in image form with their respective format (JPG). The images were collected and classified for the creation of a complete database. These images will be processed to discover some characteristics used by the artificial neural network to classify EMGs.

Image Transformation. Use OpenCV library, then choose the transformation: grayscale (in signals the colour does not matter), binarization (separate the signal of interest from the rest of the image), and segmentation (in three parts each signal) (see Fig. 4).

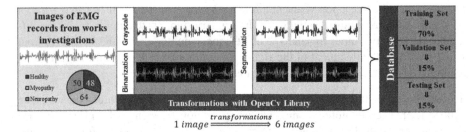

Fig. 4. Process of database creation.

Datasets of the Database. Supervised learning uses a database to teach a model of performing a task or predicting a value (or values). For this, three subsets must be created: Training set: to train the model; validation set: to make sure the models are not overfitting; Test set: to determine the model's accuracy. In general, the training, validation, and test dataset are divided by a ratio of 70%, 15%, 15%, respectively. It is shown in Table 1.

Table 1. Database of EMG signal images, with different conditions

Conditions	Healthy	Myopathy	Neuropathy	Total
Database	144	192	150	486

2.3 Develop the Predictive Model

It collaborated with a pre-trained model of a neuronal network containing the weights and biases representing the features of the dataset it was trained on. The neural network used is a CNN of type ResNet-34 that contains 34 layers used for image classification tasks. The Neural Network was developed in TensorFlow, and to use the Fastai library in Python was employed. It is a pre-trained model on the ImageNet dataset. However, it is different from traditional NN because it takes the residuals from each layer and uses them in subsequent connection layers (similar to residual NN for text prediction).

The residual building block of the ResNet34 layer consists of multiple convolutional layers (Conv), batch normalization (BN), rectified linear unit (ReLU) activation functions, and shortcuts. The output of the residual building block can be expressed as y = F(x) + x. Where F is the residual function, x is the input, and y is the output of the residual function. The entire residual network consists of the first convolutional layer and several basic blocks. ResNet-34 contains 33 convolutional layers, a top pooling layer with a size of 3 × 3, an intermediate pooling layer, and a fully connected layer. A classic ResNet-34 model has rectified nonlinearity (ReLU) activation, and batch normalization (BN) is applied to the back of all convolutional layers in the "basic block". In contrast, the SoftMax function is applied to the last layer (see Fig. 5).

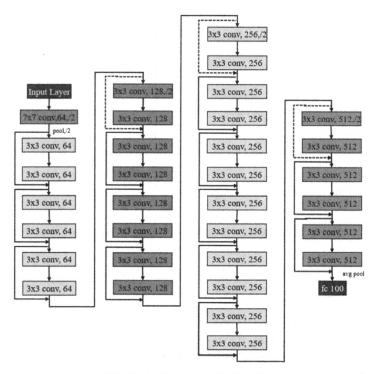

Fig. 5. Architecture of ResNet-34.

2.4 Prediction of Health Status

The connection between the electromyograph and the neural network was by a web application. This tool allows patients to use it from a web server via the Internet, reducing installation problems. This application works with a single screen where the electromyograph's image is uploaded and predicts the signal status (healthy, myopathy, or neuropathy). The web application was developed in Python and worked with the Heroku platform, where the database is stored in the cloud.

3 Results

3.1 Obtaining and Process Signal

The electromyograph was created to extract the filtered EMG signal from the individual. Besides, a neural network for signal analysis was implemented to discriminate whether a person has myopathy or neuropathy; this is a healthy individual. In the first instance, the EMG signal that was extracted from the created device is presented clean. It can be seen in Fig. 6. This signal results from signal amplification and filtering used the low pass, high pass, and notch filters, with cutoff frequencies of 300 Hz, 20 Hz, and 60 Hz, respectively.

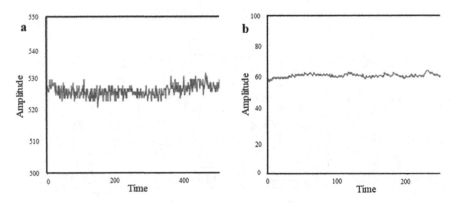

Fig. 6. EMG signal in ms (a) with noise and (b) without noise.

3.2 Neural Network

The neural network was trained 41 epochs, and this process took less than 5 min. The error on the training set of data, training loss is 0.193424, the error after running the validation set of data through the trained network, validation loss is 0.060876, and the error rate was 0.014286. These values are obtained from the learning rate ranging from 1×10^{-6} to 1×10^{-4}.

Subsequently, the efficiency of the neural network was evaluated using the confusion matrix (see Fig. 7). The primary diagonal data are represented (painted blue), which indicates the number of hits in the model. In this case, 22 have been correctly classified as EMG healthy, 24 as EMG myopathy, and 23 as EMG neuropathy, which generates a total of 70 data, of which 69 are correctly classified with an accuracy rate 98.57%. The lower diagonal shows the false negatives or type II error (the disease is not detected when, in fact, it does present); there is no such error. In contrast, the upper diagonal reflects the classifier errors: false positives or error type I (the disease is detected but does not present). In effect, just one actual value of the neural network regarding neuropathy is confused with myopathy in the predicted one.

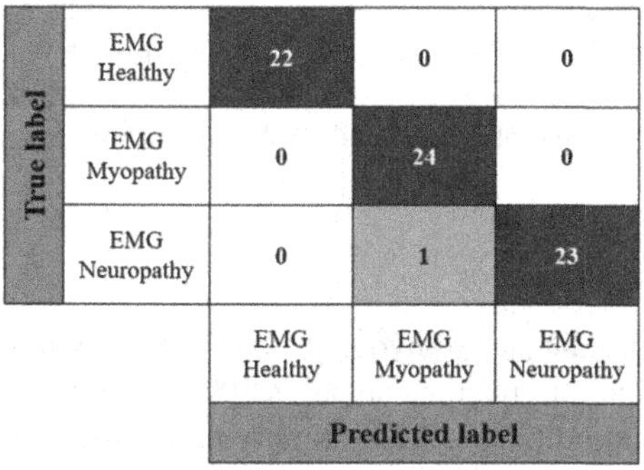

		EMG Healthy	EMG Myopathy	EMG Neuropathy
True label	EMG Healthy	22	0	0
	EMG Myopathy	0	24	0
	EMG Neuropathy	0	1	23
		EMG Healthy	EMG Myopathy	EMG Neuropathy
		Predicted label		

Fig. 7. Confusion matrix.

3.3 Web Application

The web application requires access to internet and to have any device capable of being a Web server. The device must have an operating system that can run as a Web server, capable of delivering HTML5 content. It must also have an Intel® 847 Processor, 1.10 GHz, and a minimum Ram of 512 MB. These features are the basics in any computer, cell phone or tablet. Finally, this tool does not require the device to have a certain amount of storage or hard disk space as it works online. The web application makes the prediction approximately two seconds after pressing the "Analyze" button. It provides the advantage of executing an immediate and easy diagnosis using the electromyograph developed in this study. The result from the web application (see Fig. 8).

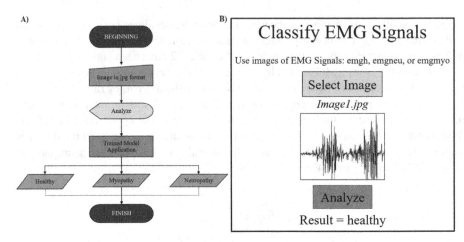

Fig. 8. A) Flowchart of the trial process and B) Web application screen and components

4 Discussion

To develop the hardware, the electromyograph was necessary to have some considerations. The appropriate gain to read the signal is 1000 times due to the range in which it is found from micro to millivolts. After amplifying the positive and negative signals from the two electrodes, a differentiation was made to find the muscle's potential. Then, the removal of electronic noise and interference of the circuit was carried out through filters.

The EMG signal's optimal frequency range is from 10 Hz to 300 Hz, whose maximum potential is 100 Hz [21]. The supplied electrical network has a frequency of 60 Hz, which creates interference with the circuit. For this reason, this frequency is eliminated with the notch filter. Furthermore, the conversion of the signal from analogue to digital was through Arduino. Finally, it was observed that the received signal is wildly oscillating due to environmental interferences, power sources, and lack of circuit isolation, among others. Hence, an offset circuit must be implemented, allowing handling the signal in the y axis and a ground controller circuit to maintain a constant signal.

A transfer function was necessary to establish a frequency function that exceeds these tolerance limits with an approximation process [24]. The transfer function of the analogue circuit allows us to set up the mathematical model of the system and its components and relevant information such as poles and zeros [23, 25]. Small electrodes ($r < 5$ mm) are preferable over larger ones to avoid loss of information. In EMG amplifiers, analogue notch filters help reduce power line-induced interference at 50 Hz or 60 Hz. These filters removed both the interference and spectral components of the EMG signal. Additionally, notch filters introduce a non-linear phase response below and above the center frequency.

To develop the software, a problem was the lack of a database of EMG images. To this was created a standardized database which corresponds to the initial images found in publicly available papers, and then it was applied image transformation: grayscale, binarization, and segmentation. It is so; the database contained 486 images of 3 classes. To increase the reliability of the system, the current designed dataset should be further expanded. To evaluate the results' relevance was to calculate three metrics: specificity, sensitivity, and accuracy calculus from the confusion matrix. It is shown in Table 2.

Table 2. Different detection methods presented in the literature

Method	Learning technique	Disease	Metrics (%)			Ref
			Sen	Spcf	Acc	
CNN model ResNet-34	DP. CNN and classifier	Healthy, neuropathy and myopathy	100	97,91	98,57	-
EEMD-FastICA-LDA	DP. Noise-assisted data analysis method, by using Fast ICA algorithm and LDA classifier	NMD	-	-	98.00	[26]
SVM classifier	DP. Feature extraction by CWT and using the RBF kernel	NMD	74.73	96.94	91.01	[27]
KNN classifier	DP. Feature extraction by CWT and using 9 nearest neighbors	NMD	75.12	96.83	91.11	[27]
WNN	DP. Classification of EMG signals using WNN	NMD	92.00	94.00	90.70	[28]
CNN classifier	DP. Obtain probability score characterizing whether the muscle image belongs to a diagnosis class	Normal and myositis	81.20	89.90	86.60	[29]
RF classifier	ML. Image features vector as input and each tree provides a vote to classify the disease	Normal and myositis	71.80	91.90	83.00	[29]

(continued)

Table 2. (*continued*)

Method	Learning technique	Disease	Metrics (%)			Ref
			Sen	Spcf	Acc	
SVMs classifier	ML. Algorithms to analyze, and eliminate to find the optimal number of parameters to classification	Types of SMA	-	89.00	92.80	[30]
ANN	DP. Evaluation of Muscle Diseases Using ANN Analysis of 31P MR Spectroscopy Data	Amyopathic Dermatomyositis	-	-	97.70	[31]
CNN model ResNet50 plus SVM classifier	DP. CNN and classifier	COVID-19	97.47	93.47	95.38	[32]

** Sen: Sensitivity, Spcf: Specificity, Acc: Accuracy, ML: Machine Learning, DP: Deep Learning, CNN: Convolutional Neural Network, EEMD: Ensemble Empirical Mode Decomposition, ICA: Independent Component Analysis, LDA: Linear Discriminant Analysis, NMD: Neuromuscular disorders, SVM: Support vector machine, CWT: Continuous Wavelet Transform, RBF: Radial Basis Function: K Nearest Neighbor (supervised ML algorithm), RF: Random Forest, SVMs: Support vector machines, SMA: spinal muscular atrophy ANN: Artificial Neural Networks, WNN: Wavelet Neural Networks

The method of Deep Learning (DP) selected was CNN because it worked with images. This neural network represents an innovation in the study of these two diseases. The present method obtains better results than others that are in the literature. It was compared with other classifiers for the EMG signal, the same CNN model ResNet50, and other DP models and Machine Learning (ML) techniques. Consequently, our model has high sensitivity (97.91%) and high accuracy (98.57%), which means values are comparable to current DP techniques.

5 Conclusion

The project met the proposed objectives. It first created an electromyograph that extracts the clean EMG signal from the individual, using three filters: low pass, high pass, and notch. The development of hardware was a process that incorporated clinical knowledge, understanding of neuromuscular physiology, and pathology to obtain an EMG signal as accurately as possible. The detection of neuromuscular pathologies depends on a correct EMG analysis in all phases of muscle movement.

Second, implementing a neural network for signal analysis allows predicting whether a person has myopathy, neuropathy, or is a healthy individual. The database of the

Neural Network was made up of images and represented an innovation in how diagnoses of diseases are carried out. The results obtained in the classification of myoelectric signals exposed the high growth and implementation of neural networks as classification mechanisms. This computational model allows us to identify the myoelectric signal patterns present in each pathology with a precision rate of 98.57%%. These positive results may be applicable to a larger database but using the same methodology. In other words, the fundamentals used can be generalized in different cases with the certainty that the results will be equally effective.

Third, based on the experimental results, the electromyogram's functionality, and the neural network, when working together, allows the detection of pathologies in real-time. In natural settings, this device could help clinicians make a correct diagnosis of neuromuscular disorders. Therefore, the prediction model used in this study is significant in the clinical field since it helps to improve the precision of the diagnosis and increases the speed at which the treatment can be applied to a patient, allows periodic monitoring, and reduces medical expenses.

For future perspectives, the implementation and improvement of signal taking must be sought using a plate and other components to allow noise isolation and decrease the margin of error that the developed apparatus presents to date. Also, images of EMG records of people could be obtained with myopathy and neuropathy to obtain data from more muscles and more subjects, expanding and creating a consistent database. Another aspect of the diagnosis that should be investigated is the severity of the disease (mild, moderate, severe, and chronic states). This will create an intelligent system capable of processing images, measurements, and signs to diagnose neuromuscular disorders considering all the characteristics mentioned above.

References

1. Gupta, A., Sayed, T., Garg, R., Shreyam, R.: Emg signal analysis of healthy and neuropathic individuals. IOP Conf. Ser. Mater. Sci. Eng. **225**, 012128 (2017). https://doi.org/10.1088/1757-899x/225/1/012128
2. Kanwade, A., Bairagi, V.: Feature Extraction of EMG Signals in Time and Frequency Domain for Myopathy, Neuropathy and Healthy Muscle. In: International Conference Electrical Electronics Engineering Trends, Communication Optimisation Sciences, pp. 917–921 (2016)
3. Artameeyanant, P., Sultornsanee, S., Chamnongthai, K.: An EMG-based feature extraction method using a normalized weight vertical visibility algorithm for myopathy and neuropathy detection. Springerplus **5**(1), 1–26 (2016). https://doi.org/10.1186/s40064-016-3772-2
4. Kraychete, D.C., Sakata, R.K.: Painful peripheral neuropathies. Rev Bras Anestesiol. **61**, 641–648 (2011)
5. Bevilacqua, J., Earle, N.: Miopatías inflamatorias. Rev. Médica Clínica Las Condes. **29**, 611–621 (2018) https://doi.org/10.1016/j.rmclc.2018.09.002
6. Paganoni, S., Amato, A.: Electrodiagnostic evaluation of myopathies. Phys. Med. Rehabil. Clin. N. Am. **24**, 193–207 (2013). https://doi.org/10.1016/J.PMR.2012.08.017
7. Wu, Y., Martínez, M., OrizaolaBalaguer, P.: Overview of the application of EMG recording in the diagnosis and approach of neurological disorders. Electrodiagnosis New Front. Clin. Res. (2013). https://doi.org/10.5772/56030
8. Bue, B.D., Merényi, E., Killian, J.M.: Classification and diagnosis of myopathy from emg signals*. work. data min. Med. Heal. Conjunction with 13th SIAM International Conference Data Min. (SDM-DMMH), Austin, TX. (2013)

9. Suquilanda-Pesántez, J.D., et al.: Prediction of Parkinson's disease severity based on Gait signals using a neural network and the fast fourier transform. In: XV Multidisciplinary International Congress on Science and Technology, pp. 3–18, Springer, Cham (2020). https://doi.org/10.1007/978-3-030-68080-0_1

10. García, P.P.: Reconocimiento de imágenes utilizando redes neuronales artificiales (2013)

11. Thukral, R., Singh, M.: Analysis of EMG signals based on wavelet transform-a review. J. Emerg. Technol. Innov. Res. **2**, 3132 (2015)

12. Belkhou, A., Jbari, A., Belarbi, L.: A continuous wavelet based technique for the analysis of electromyography signals. In: Proceedings 2017 International Conference Electrical Information Technologies ICEIT 2017. pp. 1–5 (2018). https://doi.org/10.1109/EITech.2017.8255232

13. Koçer, S.: Classifying myopathy and neuropathy neuromuscular diseases using artificial neural networks. Int. J. Pattern Recognit. Artif. Intell. **24**, 791–807 (2010). https://doi.org/10.1142/S0218001410008184

14. Liu, Y., Gligorijevic, I., Matic, V., De Vos, M., Van Huffel, S.: Multi-sparse signal recovery for compressive sensing. In: Proceedings Annual. International Conference IEEE Engineering Medicine Biology Society EMBS. pp. 1053–1056 (2012). https://doi.org/10.1109/EMBC.2012.6346115

15. Yanchatuñaa, O.P., Pereiraa, J.P., Pilaa, K.O., Vásqueza, P.A., Veintimillaa, K.S., Villalba-Menesesa, G.F., Almeida-Galárragaa, D.: Skin Lesion Detection and Classification Using Convolutional Neural Network for Deep Feature Extraction and Support Vector Machine

16. Swaroop, R., Kaur, M., Suresh, P., Sadhu, P.K.: Classification of myopathy and neuropathy EMG signals using neural network. Proceedings IEEE International Conference Circuit, Power Computational Technologies ICCPCT 2017 (2017). https://doi.org/10.1109/ICCPCT.2017.8074406

17. Phinyomark, A., Limsakul, C., Phukpattaranont, P.: Application of wavelet analysis in EMG feature extraction for pattern classification. Meas. Sci. Rev. **11**, 45–52 (2011). https://doi.org/10.2478/v10048-011-0009-y

18. Alim, O.A., Moselhy, M., Mroueh, F.: EMG signal processing and diagnostic of muscle diseases. 2012 2nd Int. Conf. Adv. Computational Tools Engineering Applications ACTEA 2012. pp. 1–6 (2012). https://doi.org/10.1109/ICTEA.2012.6462866

19. Shaw, L., Bagha, S.: Online Emg Signal Analysis for diagnosis of Neuromuscular diseases by using PCA and PNN. Int. J. Eng. Sci. **4**, 4453–4459 (2012)

20. Oliva Rodríguez, A.: Desarrollo de una aplicación de reconocimiento en imágenes utilizando Deep Learning con OpenCV (2018)

21. Weir, R.: Design of Artificial Arms and Hands for Prosthetic Applications. In: Standard Handbook of Biomedical Engineering & Design. **32**, 1–60 (2004)

22. Pérez, A., Avilés, O., Mauledoux, M.: Diseño y Construcción de un Sistema de Emulación de Movimiento de Miembro Superior a Través de Electromiografía (EMG) (2017)

23. Ishii, T., Narita, N., Endo, H.: Evaluation of jaw and neck muscle activities while chewing using EMG-EMG transfer function and EMG-EMG coherence function analyses in healthy subjects. Physiol. Behav. **160**, 35–42 (2016). https://doi.org/10.1016/J.PHYSBEH.2016.03.023

24. Merletti, R., Botter, A., Troiano, A., Merlo, E., Alessandro, M.: Technology and instrumentation for detection and conditioning of the surface electromyographic signal : state of the art. Clin. Biomech. **24**, 122–134 (2009). https://doi.org/10.1016/j.clinbiomech.2008.08.006

25. Johnson, D.H.: Transfer Functions. In: Fundamentals of Electrical Engineering I. pp. 56–59 (2014)

26. Naik, G.R., Selvan, S.E., Nguyen, H.T.: Single-channel EMG classification with ensemble-empirical-mode-decomposition-based ICA for diagnosing neuromuscular disorders. IEEE Trans. Neural Syst. Rehabil. Eng. **24**, 734–743 (2016). https://doi.org/10.1109/TNSRE.2015.2454503

27. Belkhou, A., Achmamad, A., Jbari, A.: Classification and diagnosis of myopathy EMG signals using the continuous wavelet transform. 2019 Sci. Meet. Electr. Biomed. Eng. Comput. Sci. EBBT 2019. pp. 1–4 (2019). https://doi.org/10.1109/EBBT.2019.8742051

28. Subasi, A., Yilmaz, M., Ozcalik, H.R.: Classification of EMG signals using wavelet neural network. J. Neurosci. Methods. **156**, 360–367 (2006). https://doi.org/10.1016/j.jneumeth.2006.03.004

29. Burlina, P., Billings, S., Joshi, N., Albayda, J.: Automated diagnosis of myositis from muscle ultrasound: exploring the use of machine learning and deep learning methods. PLoS ONE **12**, 1–15 (2017). https://doi.org/10.1371/journal.pone.0184059

30. Srivastava, T., Darras, B.T., Wu, J.S., Rutkove, S.B.: Machine learning algorithms to classify spinal muscular atrophy subtypes. Neurology **79**, 358–364 (2012). https://doi.org/10.1212/WNL.0b013e3182604395

31. Kari, S., Olsen, N.J., Park, J.H.: Evaluation of muscle diseases using artificial neural network analysis of 31P MR spectroscopy data. Magn. Reson. Med. **34**, 664–672 (1995). https://doi.org/10.1002/mrm.1910340504

32. Zschorlich, V.R.: Digital filtering of EMG-signals. Electromyogr. Clin. Neurophysiol. **29**, 81–86 (1989)

Underwater Wireless Sensor Networks and Cryptographic Applications

Fabián Cuzme-Rodríguez[1,2]([✉]) [iD], Pablo Otero[2] [iD], Miguel-Ángel Luque-Nieto[2] [iD], Mauricio Domínguez-Limaico[1] [iD], and Henry Farinango-Endara[1] [iD]

[1] Universidad Técnica del Norte, Avenido 17 de Julio, Ibarra 100105, Ecuador
{fgcuzme,hmdominguez,hpfarinangoe}@utn.edu.ec
[2] Instituto de Ingeniería Oceánica, Universidad de Málaga, Málaga, Spain
pablo.otero@uma.es, maluque@ic.uma.es

Abstract. Underwater wireless sensor networks (UWSNs) are a technology that is gaining ground in the field of research, oriented to generate applications that allow the monitoring of the underwater environment, oil bases, pollution control, and natural disasters. This type of networks, as well as terrestrial wireless sensor networks (TWSN), must apply security to protect the communication and transmission of information between nodes. Therefore, an analysis of the challenges related to cryptographic security that UWSNs must consider for the development of robust, secure, lightweight, and efficient cryptographic algorithms is addressed. A review of primitive cryptographic algorithms adapted to secure communication protocols in underwater environments is conducted, as well as some general and specific considerations for the development of cryptographic algorithms for underwater environments. This review seeks to establish an analysis to improve or propose cryptographic algorithms that meet the established security considerations.

Keywords: Underwater sensor networks (UWSNs) · Terrestrial wireless sensor networks (TWSNs) · Cryptography

1 Introduction

71% of water in the oceans covers most of the earth's surface [1], where much of the underwater environment is still unexplored. Underwater networks have become a broad field of research applied to different areas of the underwater environment such as monitoring and discovery of the marine environment, control, and supervision of oil extraction, coastal protection, and disaster warning, among others. [2]. Submarine communications have been used in the military field since its beginnings. In 1945, the United States of America developed the submarine telephone for submarine communications during the Second World War [3].

Underwater wireless sensor networks (UWSN) have focused their research on network construction or protocol management, leaving security unattended [4]. This type of network uses acoustic waves because they operate underwater, rather than radio

J. Herrera-Tapia et al. (Eds.): TICEC 2022, CCIS 1648, pp. 46–58, 2022.
https://doi.org/10.1007/978-3-031-18272-3_4

frequency (RF) waves, which suffer from excessive attenuation in the underwater environment. [5, 6].

UWSNs have particular characteristics such as a low propagation velocity of about 1500m/s, its speed is slower compared to a signal propagated through the air 3×10^8 m/s [7]. Another feature is the bandwidth limited to a few kHz and fast varying channel with a high bit error rate (BER) [8], the latter is due to signal attenuation, noise, multipath effect, Doppler spread and water temperature [9, 10].

Typical security threats can present themselves at any layer of the TCP/IP architecture [11], from the physical layer to the application layer. At this point it should be noted that not all solutions developed and applied in terrestrial wireless sensor networks may be an adoption option for UWSNs, so the field of application of a security solution must be adequately understood, from this point of view it is important to differentiate between underwater wireless sensor networks (UWSN) and terrestrial wireless sensor networks (TWSN), see Table 1 [4, 9].

Table 1. Differences between UWSN and TWSN

Features	UWSN	TWSN
Architecture	Mostly 3D	Mostly 2D
Topology	Highly dynamic, due to water	Static or slightly dynamic
Node movement	Movement with the water current	Static
Deployment	Dispersed	Dense
Communication medium	Acoustic or optical signals	Radiofrequency signals
Medium speed	Acoustic Speed 1500 m/s	RF speed at the speed of light 3×108 m/s
Propagation delay	High	Low
Frequency	Low frequency, between Hz to kHz	High frequency, between MHz to GHz
Bandwidth	Increased bandwidth at short distances	Bandwidth does not change over different distances
Link quality	The high bit error rate	Relatively better
Energy requirements	Limited	Less Limited
Node robustness	Minor	Major
Computational complexity	Complex	Less complexity
Memory requirements	Limited	Less Limited
Environmental conditions	Bad	Good
Implementation cost	More expensive	Lower cost

As shown in Table 1, some characteristics are considered that make UWSNs to be treated in a different way, where security plays an important role in the establishment of secure underwater networks.

This paper attempts to address a discussion of the cryptographic security challenges faced by wireless sensor networks in underwater environments. Giving an overview of the progress of related research in this field and to be able to define guidelines to further delve into the security issues faced by UWSNs.

The rest of the article is organized as follows. Section 2 discusses two architectures defined by other studies and topics related to UWSNs. Section 3 briefly explains the motivations for the research conducted. Section 4 defines the security attacks on UWSNs, the problems of cryptographic primitives, cryptographic algorithms developed, and the proposal for approaching the design of algorithms for these environments, and finally Sect. 5 concludes by summarizing the guidelines for future research in this field.

2   Underwater Wireless Sensor Networks

UWSNs were defined as network comprising broad categories of underwater nodes. The categories of underwater nodes range from underwater sensors, buoys, autonomous surface vehicles (ASVs), autonomous underwater vehicles (AUVs), etc. UWSN's three-dimensional network architecture comprises all of the above-mentioned subsea nodes [12].

In general, underwater events are initially identified locally by the sensor nodes and then the information from these events is communicated to the surface sink through automatic mobile nodes or multiple hops using acoustic communication to reach the satellites or ground stations and the information reaches the monitoring centers, see Fig. 1 [13].

Among all the node types listed above, sensor nodes play a vital role if UWSNs are involved; depending on the specific application requirement, a wide range of sensor nodes will be deployed, such as surface sinks, and sensor nodes with floating buoys, low-power grids, and autonomous underwater vehicles.

In [4] two types of malicious attacks against UWSNs are classified; the first type is based on attacks on sensor nodes, which although effective is not very practical for real environments because the sensor nodes are sparsely deployed and it is difficult to destroy several nodes, it can cause serious damage if a receiver node is destroyed. The second type of attack is oriented to network protocols, which occur more frequently because if the network protocol stops working it would affect all node communication and the network would be rendered useless. In this case, we can consider the network architecture proposed to achieve integral management in each of the layers, see Fig. 2.

In Fig. 2, the TCP/IP architecture is shown with certain differences in the physical layer due to the use of the acoustic channel. On the right side, cross-cutting characteristics are established that relate to power management, topology, quality of service, mobility, and security. These features support the communication protocol stack in UWSNs.

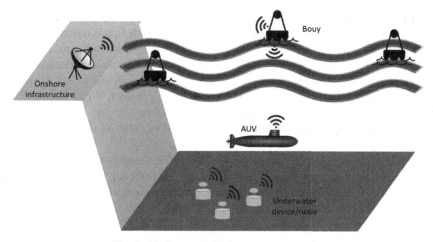

Fig. 1. Underwater wireless sensor networks

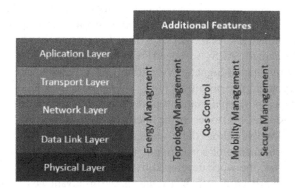

Fig. 2. UWAN network architecture

2.1 Problems Related to UWSNs

According to [10] there are some problems that UWSNs must face in general, including environmental effects, cognitive communication, MAC problems, channel utilization, localization, routing, optimal packet size selection, and energy efficiency.

The environmental effect directly affects the speed of sound, where temperature, water pressure, depth, and salinity affect the speed of sound. Cognitive communication is related to the communication frequencies available in the underwater channel, these are limited because most artificial and natural acoustic systems use frequencies from 1 kHz to 100 kHz, so the acoustic channel may be saturated.

Another problem is related to media access control (MAC) mechanisms, where frequency division multiple access (FDMA) is not appropriate due to the restricted bandwidth of the acoustic channel, and time division multiple access (TDMA) is not efficient due to the propagation delays of the acoustic channel. But there are methods applicable to this environment such as space division multiple access (SDMA). Another variant of TDMA for acoustic channel access is UA-MAC. Channel utilization is also related to the bandwidth that can be used for communications in this environment.

Localization is another problem to be faced in these environments because of having mobile nodes that must give exact locations and are prone to change location due to sea currents that exist in the environment. Also, routing problems affect the energy consumption of the nodes, mobility is another factor to consider, where the change of the topology is an analysis that has been addressed, where the communication of the nodes and the corresponding hops must be maintained to reach all the nodes available in the topology.

The size of the packet to be transmitted is another important factor to consider, since it is related to the characteristics of the protocol, the load offered, and the bit error rate. Thus, an inadequate packet size reduces network performance, while in another context an adequate packet size increases efficiency.

3 Motivations

The development of secure networks has occurred since the beginning of traditional communications in computer systems, where the development of cryptographic systems of symmetric and asymmetric keys such as DES (Data Encryption Standard), 3DES (Triple Data Encryption Standard), AES (Advanced Encryption Standard), RSA (Rivest, Shamir, and Adleman), DSA (Digital Signature Algorithm), ECC (Elliptic curve cryptography) are considered cryptographic primitives [14].

In this context, cryptographic variants have been developed for devices with limited resources (RAM, ROM, CPU) to secure the Internet of Things (IoT) or terrestrial wireless sensor networks (TWSNs). From these studies, we can indicate the one developed by [15], where the performance of some cryptographic variants on a Raspberry Pi board is analyzed. Likewise, the work developed by [16] where some techniques of several authors are analyzed to determine their advantages and disadvantages. From the latter, the techniques used in the BLOWFISH algorithm can be pointed out on a programmable gate array (FPGA) allowing good encryption and decryption times, but the implementation costs are a disadvantage.

The cryptographic systems developed so far for IoT or TWSNs environments are not suitable for UWANs, this remains a challenge for this type of environment. The research developed so far has started from cryptographic primitives based on ultralight encryption schemes [17], these address some communication problems oriented to confidentiality, integrity, and authentication in UWSNs [11]. Despite the research efforts carried out so far in the UWSNs, there are still open gaps that must be solved, such as the computational load required for the operation of cryptographic algorithms, energy consumption, the proper use of the available channel capacity, key sizes, vulnerability to known and new attacks.

4 Challenges Related to Cryptographic Security

Section 1 and 2 have been addressing general topics of the UWSNs, concerning the problems presented by these communication environments, in this section focuses on the analysis of the specific cryptographic problems and challenges that must be considered for the development or improvement of cryptographic algorithms.

4.1 Security Attacks on UWSNs

Considering the features and applications of UWSNs, many algorithms have been developed to ensure their secure functionality; in [18] it is commented that a large part of these works is related to access control, authentication, peer key establishment, and defense against an attack.

Previously, major research was motivated and researched on traditional cryptographic information and data authentication to develop the relationships between sensor nodes. However, cryptographic methods are sometimes not very efficient and effective [19]. Unreliable communications over wireless channels can make communication between nodes susceptible by allowing sensor nodes to compromise and publish security information to malicious nodes. The compromised entity of the network appears as a legitimate node, so it is easy for the adversary to execute the attacks. When an attack occurs on a node, this node behaves abnormally, such as altering the message of other members, discarding data, or spreading excessive data.

To understand some attacks on UWSNs, [1] compiles studies on specific security attacks that exploit the underwater acoustic channel; highlights attacks on location, packet delivery, and synchronization. Of which we can indicate the following: Jamming, Wormhole, Sybil, Sinkhole, Blackhole, Spoofing, and Flooding.

4.2 Problems of Cryptographic Primitives

Cryptography is a fundamental mechanism for securing networks regardless of the environment where it is applied. Some of the characteristics of UWSNs must be considered to affect the applicability of cryptographic primitives to offer authentication, confidentiality, integrity, and non-repudiation. Thus, some problems studied in [11] are addressed.

Ciphertext Expansion. In the encryption process, they include some mechanisms to modify the original text, such as message filling, modification identification codes, and authentication, which make the length of the message increase. This affects the increase in transmission time and greater consumption of bandwidth and energy. While ciphertext is negligible in a traditional network, it is an important parameter to consider in UWSNs [20]. This study as an example it establishes a message expansion of 18% considering 128-bit AES encryption with an average message of 720 bits; likewise, applying integrity with an SHA-256 resume function that generates a 256-bit output, causes an additional overhead of 35% considering the same message size.

Asymmetric Key Cryptography. It is widely adopted in systems with extensive computational resources, allowing the exchange and distribution of symmetric keys and digital signatures in a secure way. This type of cryptography is not applicable for wireless devices with limited resources, so the search for asymmetric key cryptographic variants is indispensable. A public key cryptographic primitive is elliptic curve cryptography (ECC) [14], delivering the same levels of security with smaller keys compared to RSA.

Symmetric Key Cryptography. One of the advantages of symmetric key encryption over asymmetric key encryption is that less time is required in the encryption and decryption process. The problem in this type of cryptography is that the key must be shared previously before starting a communication, which can be a risk in case the secret key is compromised, considering that you have an insecure communication environment and channel [21].

4.3 Cryptographic Algorithms Applied to Secure Protocols

In [20], a secure routing protocol and a set of cryptographic primitives (SeFLOOD) that protect confidentiality and integrity in the underwater communication channel are proposed. The cryptographic suite it proposes, covers confidentiality with the 128-bit AES encryption algorithm combined with the Cipher Text Stealing (CTS) technique that alters the processing of the last two blocks of plaintext, giving a reordered transmission of the last two blocks of ciphertext and no expansion. In terms of integrity, it uses 4-byte digests resulting from truncating the actual value of the hash function, converting the overhead of about 4.4% of the average message to UWSNs. For key management, because symmetric cryptography is used, it applies a secure and scalable key change protocol for resource-constrained devices (S2RP) [23], key management with this method is suitable for UWSNs as it provides an efficient proof of key authenticity, and also requires some key change messages according to the number of nodes, which is a scalable mechanism. The key authentication mechanism relies on key rings, based on Lamport's one-time password technique, this key ring will be a set of symmetric keys so that each key is the hash pre-image of the previous one (see Fig. 3), therefore, given a key $K^{(i)}$ in the keychain, anyone can compute the following previous keys $K^{(j)}, j \leq i$, but only the creator of the keychain can compute the following keys $K^{(j)}, j > i$; the keys are revealed in the reverse order of creation, so an authenticated key in the keychain can authenticate the following revealed keys by simply applying the hash function $K^{(i)} = h(K^{(i+1)})$.

$$K^{(i-1)} = \pi h(k^{(i)}), i = n, \dots, 1$$

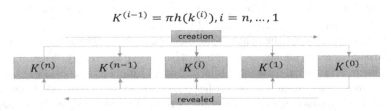

Fig. 3. Keychain.

This cryptographic suite applied to the FLOOD routing protocol adds a negligible additional overhead of less than 6%, the discovery overhead is only consumed at network startup and is then amortized over the lifetime of the system. The design of this secure routing protocol complies with Lampson's well-known recommendations for computer system design [24].

In [25], a security framework (SecFUN) for UWSNs, providing confidentiality, integrity, authentication, and non-repudiation, based on AES building blocks in Galois counter mode (GCM) and algorhythms digital signature is presented. For symmetric key-based encryption and authentication, the GCM version of SecFUN uses 128-bit AES for encryption, authentication, and integrity are provided by calculating the message authentication code (MAC) in the Galois field. The inputs for GCM operation are a symmetric key (K), an initialization vector (IV), a plaintext (P) and any additional data A to be authenticated. The output is a cipher text (C) and an authentication tag (T), the latter tag allows the authenticity of the message to be verified without the need for decryption operations. For asymmetric key-based authentication within ECC, they consider schemes that require bilinear maps (pairing-based cryptography) specifically the Boneh-Lynn-Shacham (BLS) and Zhang-Safavi-Naini-Susilo (ZSS) schemes, both schemes belong to the family of short signatures of around 160 bits, with a security level of 280 and are computationally efficient. Signatures of less than 160 bits are also proposed based on multivariate cryptographic schemes (HFE, HFEv- and Quartz) [26], these are based on the difficulty of solving systems of quadratic polynomial equations for enough quadratic unknowns, this makes them much more flexible than ECC based schemes because they allow to handle shorter signatures and to establish the desired security level. Among the digital signature schemes considered, the study relies on Quartz because it provides 128-bit signatures and a security level of 280.

As the SecFUN security framework uses the channel-aware routing protocol (CARP) to evaluate cryptographic primitives considering energy consumption and end-to-end latency its results demonstrate a flexible security solution in terms of energy and latency.

In [22], key generation based on received signal strength (RSS), three approaches of Aono, Mathur, and Patwari, which are key extraction algorithms based on the signal with which the nodes communicate, are analyzed. For the evaluation of the key generation approaches performance metrics such as: Key generation rate which specifies the average number of secret bits extracted from each RSS measurement; Bit mismatch rate which specifies the ratio of mismatched bits between the keys produced by two participants to the key length; and Randomness which considers a number series to be random if the smallest algorithm capable of specifying it on a computer has approximately the same number of information bits as the series itself. Applying this mechanism in UWSNs sets some challenges such as the long transmission time of a sounding signal because the transmission time of a sounding could be thousands of times longer than in terrestrial environments; the other challenge is the asymmetric RSS measurements that can occur in acoustic channels due to the half-duplex characteristics of the acoustic nodes and the fast variation of the underwater channel, these measurements are not symmetric.

To solve the challenges of the underwater channel, soft filters such as the symmetric moving average filter are applied to reduce the discrepancies between the shared keys. Considering reductions of 100% for Aono, 63% for Mathur, and 20% for Patwari.

In [27], it presents an 8-round lightweight iteration block cipher algorithm for communicating UWSNs based on chaotic theory (see Eq. 1) and increases the keyspace by changing the iteration number.

$$x_{n+1} = \mu x_n (1 - x_n) \tag{1}$$

where μ is a parameter, $\mu \in [0, 4]$; when $x_0 \in (0, 1)$, no matter how many iteration rounds exist we will always obtain $x_n \in (0, 1)$.

The logical operation applied to reduce the computational and storage overhead of the nodes, is a simple bit-by-bit exclusive-or (XOR) logical operation, see Eq. 2. The encryption process is a combination of the left and right sides each of 32 bits, the interaction of the 8 rounds follows a process similar to the Feistel structure, without exchanging the last round to facilitate the decryption process.

$$b_i \oplus (a_i \oplus b_i) = a_i \rightarrow (i = 0, 1, \ldots, n-1),$$

$$a_i \oplus (a_i \oplus b_i) = b_i \rightarrow (i = 0, 1, \ldots, n-1). \tag{2}$$

where a_i or b_i is a binary bit and the sum of the bits of the binary code is n. The symbol "$\oplus$" indicates the XOR operation.

The performance analysis was based on three important points such as the security analysis such as the change of the key in each round, besides being resistant to plaintext attacks; storage cost which is another limitation in UWSNs is also considered in the analysis where the proposed algorithm has a low storage capacity; and finally, the performance efficiency is considered optimal because its execution is faster. The comparisons were carried out with other cryptographic algorithms such as AES-128, Blowfish, and PRESENT.

In [28], one of the most recent studies analyzed published in 2020, a secure energy-efficient cooperative routing (SEECR) protocol for UWSNs is proposed, adding a strong defense mechanism to combat attacks in underwater environments. The proposed SEECR protocol uses multi-hop networks using the cooperative technique, whereby data that is generated from the source node is forwarded to the destination on a hop-by-hop basis. An initialization setup is established where each sensor calculates its weight based on the residual energy and depth which is transmitted to the neighboring nodes via handshake messages. For the messaging node movement scheme, node depth thresholds are set to maintain the network lifetime and operability. In the process of eliminating attacker nodes, each sensor node stores packets sent and received from neighboring sensor nodes, and then performs a comparison, in case the comparisons are not equal, it can be identified as an attacker node.

Additionally, [28] evaluates SEECR with the AMCTD (Adaptive Mobility of Courier Nodes in Threshold-optimized DBR) protocol, known within UWSNs routing. Some evaluation criteria were established such as the number of active nodes, transmission loss, throughput, energy consumption, and end-to-end delay. This evaluation was defined in scenarios with and without attacks. This proposed solution presents significant security improvements in the routing of UWSNs along with efficient energy consumption that allows sensor nodes to have a longer lifetime in the network.

.

4.4 Discussion

When referring to security, the CIA triangle is always considered [23], regardless of the environment where you want to implement security, each one establishes a scope of application that allows systems to deliver acceptable security within their scope of operation, framed in confidentiality that means keeping something secret, the integrity that defines the non-alteration of information in transit or in storage and the availability that defines that the information, service or node is always available when required. UWSNs should also consider this definition to design secure systems; but other concepts must be linked to security systems such as authentication (Who wants to communicate), authorization (Who can access a resource or network), and auditing (What is happening in the network or node), this allows you to have confidence in the network or service that is offered or you want to offer, in our analysis would be in a UWSN.

Considering and starting from this analysis as shown in Fig. 4, the CIA triangle is presented with the security concepts defined in the previous paragraph that must be linked in the search for comprehensive security. The architecture defined by [4], adapted in Fig. 2, is considered to be an important contribution to the development and secure deployment of UWSNs, where transversal characteristics are established that must be developed for the protocol stack in a general way and support the security process. This is considered because you cannot have good security if you do not manage it properly.

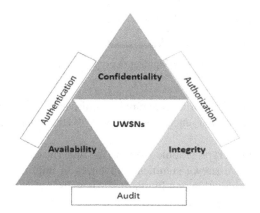

Fig. 4. General security considerations.

In this context, the cryptographic systems that are to be implemented in the UWSNs also require some considerations, some of them start from the general security shown in Fig. 4, consequently, it is defined in Fig. 5 some considerations that the cryptographic algorithms oriented to the UWSNs must conceive in the design.

In Fig. 5, some considerations are established such as robustness which encompasses the hardness and simplicity of the algorithm that is not easily vulnerable to different existing attacks. Low memory and CPU consumption are an important considerations due to the limitations that sensor nodes have. Low power consumption is another factor that should be considered because it should consume as little energy as possible to extend the life of the node connected to the network. Lightweight is related to block sizes, key, encryption/decryption time, and performance. Finally, the optimization of bandwidth that allows optimizing its use available in this environment, which is also a limited component.

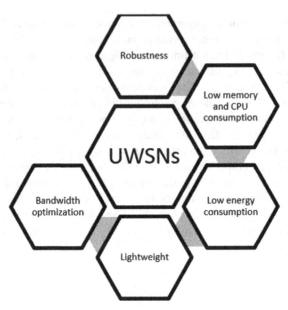

Fig. 5. Considerations for the development of cryptographic algorithms for UWSNs.

In this sense, the analysis of cryptographic primitives is paramount for the development of an algorithm that encompasses most of the considerations shown in Fig. 5.

The development of cryptographic systems for underwater environments such as [17, 20, 21, 24, 26] have shown significant advances in improving security in these hostile environments and with many limitations. They also serve as a basis for further improvement of the proposed security schemes since they do not cover all the layers or modalities of attacks that can be generated in these environments. The purpose of this study is to generate a lightweight cryptographic proposal that is under current security needs.

5 Conclusions

Although the last 5 years there have been investigations related to the security of UWSNs, there are still many gaps to investigate such as creating lighter algorithms that allow optimizing the use of limited bandwidth in this type of network.

Cryptographic primitives have been a good basis for the development of algorithms for devices with limited resources, but they must be further improved for their applicability in the harsh environments where UWSNs work.

For the development of future cryptographic algorithms, they must be aware of the computational load, energy consumption, key sizes, and number of rounds of algorithms, which allow secure communication without sacrificing computational resources that could affect the efficiency of underwater communications.

References

1. Yisa, A.G., Dargahi, T., Belguith, S., Hammoudeh, M.: Security challenges of Internet of Underwater Things: a systematic literature review. Trans. Emerg. Telecommun. Technol. (2020). https://doi.org/10.1002/ett.4203
2. Lal, C., Petroccia, R., Pelekanakis, K., Conti, M., Alves, J.: Toward the development of secure underwater acoustic networks. IEEE J. Ocean. Eng. **42**(4), 1075–1087 (2017). https://doi.org/10.1109/JOE.2017.2716599
3. Zheng, J., Zhou, S., Liu, Z., Ye, S., Liu, L., Yin, L.: A new underwater sensor networks architecture. In: Proceedings 2010 IEEE International Conference on Information Theory and Information Security, ICITIS 2010, pp. 845–848 (2010). https://doi.org/10.1109/ICITIS.2010.5689713
4. Han, G., Jiang, J., Sun, N., Shu, L.: Secure communication for underwater acoustic sensor networks. IEEE Commun. Mag. **53**(8), 54–60 (2015). https://doi.org/10.1109/MCOM.2015.7180508
5. Li, N., Martínez, J.-F., Meneses Chaus, J., Eckert, M.: A Survey on Underwater Acoustic Sensor Network Routing Protocols. Sensors **16**(3), 414 (2016). https://doi.org/10.3390/s16030414
6. Shanthi, M.B., Anvekar, D.K.: Secure Localization for Underwater Wireless Sensor Networks Based on Probabilistic Approach. In: 2018 Second International Conference on Advances in Electronics, Computers and Communications (ICAECC), pp. 1–6 (2018). https://doi.org/10.1109/ICAECC.2018.8479451
7. Liu, Z., Deng, X., Li, J.: A secure localization algorithm based on reputation against wormhole attack in UWSNS. In: 2017 International Symposium on Intelligent Signal Processing and Communication Systems (ISPACS), pp. 695–700 (2017). https://doi.org/10.1109/ISPACS.2017.8266566
8. Zhang, Y., Li, B.: Underwater acoustic channels characterization for underwater cognitive acoustic networks. In: Proceedings - 3rd International Conference Intelligent Transportation Big Data Smart City, ICITBS 2018, vol. 2018-Janua, pp. 223–226 (2018). https://doi.org/10.1109/ICITBS.2018.00065
9. Das, A.P., Thampi, S.M.: Secure communication in mobile underwater wireless sensor networks. In: 2015 International Conference Advances Computational Communication Informatics, ICACCI 2015, pp. 2164–2173 (2015). https://doi.org/10.1109/ICACCI.2015.7275937
10. Awan, K.M., Shah, P.A., Iqbal, K., Gillani, S., Ahmad, W., Nam, Y.: Underwater wireless sensor networks: a review of recent issues and challenges. *Wireless* Communications and Mobile Computing, vol. 2019 (2019). https://doi.org/10.1155/2019/6470359
11. Jiang, S.: On securing underwater acoustic networks: a survey. IEEE Commun. Surv. Tutorials, p. 1,(2018). https://doi.org/10.1109/COMST.2018.2864127
12. Manikandan, T.T., Sukumaran, R., Christhu Raj, M.R., Saravanan, M.: Network model for improved localization performance in uwsn:a node deployment perceptive. In: Proceedings of the 4th International Conference on Electronics, Communication and Aerospace Technology, ICECA 2020, pp. 695–701 (2020). https://doi.org/10.1109/ICECA49313.2020.9297406
13. Nayyar, A., Ba, C.H., Cong Duc, N.P., Binh, H.D.: Smart-IoUT 1.0: a smart aquatic monitoring network based on internet of underwater things (IoUT). In: Duong, T.Q., Vo, N.-S. (eds.) INISCOM 2018. LNICSSITE, vol. 257, pp. 191–207. Springer, Cham (2019). https://doi.org/10.1007/978-3-030-05873-9_16
14. Dhanda, S.S., Singh, B., Jindal, P.: Lightweight cryptography: a solution to secure IoT. Wireless Pers. Commun. **112**(3), 1947–1980 (2020). https://doi.org/10.1007/s11277-020-07134-3

15. Khan, N., Sakib, N., Jerin, I., Quader, S., Chakrabarty, A.: Performance analysis of security algorithms for IoT devices. 5th IEEE Reg. 10 Humanit. Technol. Conf. 2017, R10-HTC 2017, vol. 2018-Janua, pp. 130–133 (2018). https://doi.org/10.1109/R10-HTC.2017.8288923

16. Naru, E.R., Saini, H., Sharma, M.: A recent review on lightweight cryptography in IoT. Proc. Int. Conf. IoT Soc. Mobile, Anal. Cloud, I-SMAC 2017, pp. 887–890 (2017). https://doi.org/10.1109/I-SMAC.2017.8058307

17. Peng, C., Du, X., Li, K., Li, M.: An ultra-lightweight encryption scheme in underwater acoustic networks. J. Sensors 2016 (2016). https://doi.org/10.1155/2016/8763528

18. Souza, E., Wong, H.C., Cunha, I., Loureiro, A.A.F., Vieira, L.F.M., Oliveira, L.B.: End-to-end authentication in under-water sensor networks. In: Proceedings - International Symposium on Computers and Communications, pp. 299–304 (2013). https://doi.org/10.1109/ISCC.2013.6754963

19. Ahmed, M.R., Aseeri, M., Kaiser, M.S., Zenia, N.Z., Chowdhury, Z.I.: A novel algorithm for malicious attack detection in UWSN (2015). https://doi.org/10.1109/ICEEICT.2015.7307516

20. Dini, G., Lo Duca, A.: A Secure communication for underwater acoustic sensor networks. Sensors **12**(11), 15133–15158 (2012). https://doi.org/10.1109/MCOM.2015.7180508

21. Luo, Y., Pu, L., Peng, Z., Shi, Z.: RSS-based secret key generation in underwater acoustic networks: advantages, challenges, and performance improvements. IEEE Commun. Mag. **54**(2), 32–38 (2016). https://doi.org/10.1109/MCOM.2016.7402258

22. Dini, G., Savino, I.M.: S2RP: A secure and scalable rekeying protocol for wireless sensor networks. In: 2006 IEEE International Conference on Mobile Ad Hoc and Sensor Systems, MASS, vol. 1, pp. 457–466 (2006). https://doi.org/10.1109/MOBHOC.2006.278586

23. Lampson, B.: Hints and Principles for Computer System Design. **74**(1934), 535–546 (2019)

24. Ateniese, G., Capossele, A., Gjanci, P., Petrioli, C., Spaccini, D.: SecFUN: Security framework for underwater acoustic sensor networks. MTS/IEEE Ocean. 2015 - Genova Discov. Sustain. Ocean Energy a New World, pp. 1–9 (2015). https://doi.org/10.1109/OCEANS-Genova.2015.7271735

25. Courtois, N.T., Daum, M., Felke, P.: On the security of HFE, HFEv- and quartz. In: Desmedt, Y.G. (ed.) PKC 2003. LNCS, vol. 2567, pp. 337–350. Springer, Heidelberg (2003). https://doi.org/10.1007/3-540-36288-6_25

26. Saeed, K., Khalil, W., Ahmed, S., Ahmad, I., Khattak, M.N.K.: SEECR: secure energy efficient and cooperative routing protocol for underwater wireless sensor networks. IEEE Access **8**, 107419–107433 (2020). https://doi.org/10.1109/ACCESS.2020.3000863

Design of a Sensor Network for Drinking Water Control in the Maria of Merced Educational Unit

Manuel Eduardo Vinces Mendieta[1]([☒]) [ID], Marely del Rosario Cruz Felipe[2] [ID], and Darwin Patricio Loor Zamora[1,2] [ID]

[1] Instituto de Posgrado, Universidad Técnica de Manabí, Portoviejo, Manabí, Ecuador
{mvinces7026,patricio.loor}@utm.edu.ec
[2] Facultad de Ciencias Informáticas, Universidad Técnica de Manabí, Portoviejo, Manabí, Ecuador
marely.cruz@utm.edu.ec

Abstract. The excessive consumption of drinking water in the María of the Merced Educational Unit brings with it the need to establish control over it, being a private entity that is located in the Portoviejo canton of the province of Manabí in Ecuador; it is here where it is proposed for this research to design a wireless sensor network over the educational institution. For this purpose, the ZigBee communications protocol was used since this technology allows creating the scope of the network, delimited by approximately 140 square meters, in addition to providing adequate management of battery performance and bandwidth. Several tree, star, and mesh topology scenarios were defined and evaluated by simulation using effective transfer rate, latency, and packet loss parameters. As a result, the tree topology is the most suitable for use in this context. To validate the results, a quasi-experiment was defined in which significant differences between the three topologies were analyzed using the Kruskal Wallis test, allowing the results to be corroborated by statistical tests.

Keywords: Latency · Packet loss · Throughput · WSN · ZigBee

1 Introduction

Two aspects are required to achieve autonomous data collection and processing: the technology to equip elements such as sensors or actuators in a wireless environment and the communication protocols.

Wireless Sensor Networks (WSN) are a particular type of network used within a wireless personal area network (WPAN); among their characteristics is that they are low speed, mainly because of their low power capacity; typically, each of these sensors is used in areas with difficult network access. The tremendous acceptance of this type of network is given with the advanced implementation of electronic devices managed with microcontrollers of tiny size, with high performance and low power consumption, conducive to using these devices in multiple applications [1].

J. Herrera-Tapia et al. (Eds.): TICEC 2022, CCIS 1648, pp. 59–72, 2022.
https://doi.org/10.1007/978-3-031-18272-3_5

Currently, there are several types of networks that can be framed within WSNs; these are types defined for specific applications, such as wireless sensor multimedia networks (WSMNs), underwater sensor networks (USNs), body area networks (BANs), vehicular area sensor networks (VANs), among others [2].

The agile and efficient transfer of data is a priority in WSNs, even more so when there is a limited battery life, which degrades network performance and decreases network lifetime; advances have shown that the method of avoiding collisions between packets can have a minimum latency, likewise, greater energy efficiency so that in the end the network lifetime is extended [3].

A dynamic system for monitoring and control of WSNs operating with the ZigBee communication protocol allows interactive communication with sensors, manipulation of the number of nodes in the network, as well as management of the communication system data controller with a user-friendly interface to manage and visualize the information provided by the nodes, thus achieving better performance in control applications and sensor networks, as they work with small data packets, low power consumption, and low sending rate, providing secure communication.

WSNs can be deployed by many nodes used within a delimited area to collect data on physical or environmental conditions, such as temperature, humidity, pressure, etc. Performance evaluation within the wireless network is essential because it checks the feasibility of the network architecture and protocol algorithms and provides performance optimization guidelines. Among the different candidates, simulation offers a cost-effective way forward. Recently, researchers have developed many simulation models for other platforms, including OPNET, NS-2, TOSSIM, EmStar, OMNeT++, J-Sim, ATEMU, and Avrora [5].

In the case of WSNs, the usefulness of these networks is found in many areas. This scenario is coupled with the fact that ZigBee technology is based primarily on low power consumption, low cost, durability, and reliability. To determine the excellent performance in terms of basic topologies using OPNET simulation, we can show two types of scenarios for both fixed and mobile nodes on the topologies supported by ZigBee (tree, star, and mesh) where they were compared concerning the network parameters in terms of throughput (bits/s), Mac load (bits/s) and end-to-end delay (in seconds); differences were obtained in the results generated by fixed and mobile nodes in the ZigBee network depending on these parameters [6].

To improve some performance metrics in the ZigBee network, the proper placement of the nodes is considered very important, and through the OPNET Modeler simulator, the effect of the mobility of the ZigBee network coordinator could be extensively analyzed and evaluated; on tins research, the conclusion was that, with the proper placement of the routers in different positions and with an appropriate variation of the routing of them, substantial differences in performance were observed with the routing algorithm of the ZigBee mesh network [7].

Sim Several researchers have done similar working OPNET's Riverbed simulator to consider and analyze different scenarios in WSNs. Most of these research works were based on various quality parameters from which appreciable results were obtained and documented. Compared with other simulators, OPNET is the most suitable for simulating the behavior of real-world networks; since it provides a complete simulation environment, many simulation studies have been carried out on sensor networks using the ZigBee wireless communications protocol [8].

The Maria de la Merced Educational Unit in the city of Portoviejo is a confessional and boarding school for children and adolescents who opt for a liberating integral education style of the Mercedarian charism; Over time, it has been growing in infrastructure, and within it, there are essential services that are not controlled for their proper use including drinking water, where high costs are paid monthly on the consumption of these items, for not having a regulated control over this service, which is often reflected in the discomfort of those who manage the expenses within the educational institution.

With all of the above, this article proposes the design of a WSN using the ZigBee wireless communications protocol, which is ideal for use in essential services, including the control of drinking water; planning is developed using OPNET simulation software, where the tree, star and mesh topologies will be compared according to the metrics of effective transfer rate (throughput), latency and packet loss; whose objective is to identify which scenario would be the most appropriate for the control of the drinking water service within the WSN for the UEMM.

The article is structured as follows: Sect. 2 shows the applied mathematics and methods, Sect. 3 presents the results, and Sect. 4 draws the conclusions.

2 Materials and Methods

The development of this article was based on determining the most appropriate topology for a WSN using the ZigBee wireless communications protocol as a control method for the UEMM facilities on the drinking water service, in which the network design was performed by simulation with the use of OPNET software, defining as main elements within the simulation fixed nodes that were located according to the geographical plane taken as reference the educational institution; on that simulated space scenarios were created where metrics were applied to measure the performance of the WSN.

For this research, a normality test was performed on the approach proposed as an alternative hypothesis where, if different sensor network topologies are analyzed by simulation with the OPNET tool, the proposed network for the control of drinking water service in the UEMM will be obtained, from the analysis of the results got it was possible to identify whether a parametric or non-parametric data test was applied, thus validating the distribution of the data obtained in the simulations, i.e. when the populations from which the sample was taken are strongly asymmetric. Figure 1 shows the process of getting the design within the WSN to control the drinking water service within the educational institution facilities.

2.1 Analysis of the Current Situation at the UEMM

In this section, an analysis of the facilities belonging to the UEMM was made, taking as a first point the area designed for the WSN, which is located in the province of Manabí, in the canton of Portoviejo; it has an approximate size of 140 square meters, as can be seen in Fig. 2, where the scope of the investigation was delimited.

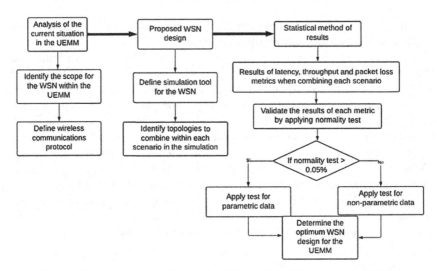

Fig. 1. The process to be followed to obtain the WSN design for the UEMM

Fig. 2. Location of UEMM facilities for WSN design

Today we find many standards that can be used in short-range networks, each developed for a specific type of application, which today can be used in sensor and actuator networks. Figure 3 shows a set of wireless network standards classified by data rate axes and network types.

Based on the representative data in Fig. 3, three wireless communication technologies within the range of a wireless personal area network (WPAN) were considered as detailed in Table 1, highlighting some of their main characteristics to compare each of these technologies.

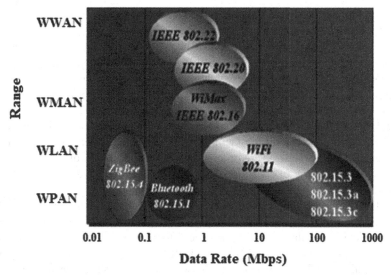

Fig. 3. Network types and data rates to be defined in the WSN

Table 1. Comparison chart between ZigBee Bluetooth and WiFi.

Details	ZigBee 802.15.4	Bluetooth 802.15.1	WiFi 802.11
Current consumption (mA)	30	65–170	350
Network capacity (nodes)	65000	30	7
Battery life (days)	>365	7	1
Transmission speed (Kbps)	250	1000–3000	54000
Transmission power (mW)	1–2	1–100	40– 200
Radio frequency (GHz)	0,868; 0,915; 2,4	2,4	2,4
Working range (meters)	70–300	<300	100

Among the three technologies compared, we can say that the ZigBee wireless communications protocol stood out from the other technologies because of its low power consumption and longer battery life. Its ease of implementation [9] made it worthy of being the technology that forms part of the design for the WSN as a method of controlling the drinking water service within the UEMM facilities.

2.2 Proposed WSN Design

The method used for this research was a simulation, where it can be evidenced that several programs allow designing a complete network model; among these simulation tools are Network Simulator 2 (NS2), NS3, OMNET, OPNET, and MATLAB, which support the development functions of the ZigBee wireless communication protocol; all the named simulators provide discrete event simulation for the evaluation of various parameters in the network that researchers use widely.

OPNET simulation is the platform that becomes the primary tool that provides solutions for the estimation of wireless network designs and applications; it supports the network model based on ZigBee wireless communication protocol, which consists of coordinators, routers, and end devices; these elements can be set within a network scenario as fixed or mobile [10].

The design of the WSN began with the analysis of the current reality in the UEMM, where the lack of control over the facilities of the drinking water service was found; on the design, three scenarios were proposed, each with 17 nodes, of which 13 are end devices that have the task of collecting data; one of the nodes acted as coordinator and the other three remaining as Routers, all located as fixed points.

The dimensions of the simulation were 140 by 160 square meters for the WSN; in each design, the ZigBee coordinator device was configured with its network parameters, defining the corresponding tree, star, and mesh topologies in each scenario. Figure 4 shows the design created with OPNET to identify the location of the drinking water facilities within the UEMM, where each sensor device was placed on strategic points within the institution.

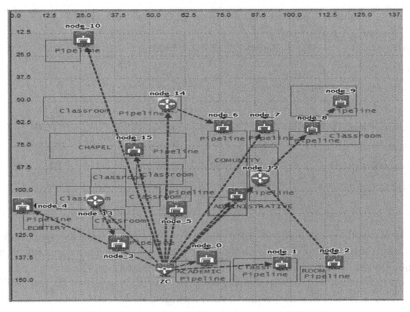

Fig. 4. Design of the WSN as a scenario for UEMM

In each of the scenarios created in the OPNET simulator, combinations were made between tree, star, and mesh topologies, using ZigBee technology; from this, in each combined system, a metric was executed to measure the performance of the network where throughput, latency, and packet loss were calculated; allowing with this process to identify the best control scenario for the WSN over the drinking water service facilities within the UEMM.

The results of the WSN simulation were carried out with a total time of six hours, distributed in three simulations of two hours for each scenario with combined topologies, from which independent samples were obtained for each of the metrics analyzed in each of the network scenarios.

2.3 Statistical Method of Results

To demonstrate the best design, a statistical analysis was performed, for which the normality of the data was initially checked and, based on the result, a corresponding test was applied. Then, using the simulation samples, a normality test was performed using the Kolmogorov-Smirnov test to demonstrate whether the proposed network performance metrics comply with a normal distribution.

Since the distributions of the throughput, latency, and packet loss metrics were not normal and according to [11] for this case, Kruskal Wallis tests [12] were used for the nonparametric analysis of the data. The SPSS statistical program was used for this data analysis using a 95% confidence interval and a significance level of 5%.

Statistics Used. The combined effective throughput, end-to-end delay (latency), and packet loss were evaluated in all scenarios. Packet loss is calculated according to [13] from the metrics provided by the simulator for packets sent and received.

3 Results and Validation

This section presents the results obtained from the network design through simulation. With these data, the validation tests obtained from the normality tests and the test for parametric or non-parametric data are performed to determine the best WSN scenario to be used within the UEMM facilities.

3.1 Simulation Results

The results of the WSN simulation were obtained by creating three scenarios. First, the tree, star, and mesh topologies were combined in each system, allowing the network performance to be measured using throughput, latency, and packet loss metrics. The results obtained from the simulations comparing the three topologies within the WSN are shown below.

Throughput Metrics for the WSN. In Fig. 5, we identify a notable significant difference within the WSN when comparing the performance of the tree topology has a considerable increase in its effective transfer rate. In contrast, when observing the mesh and star topologies, their performance is much lower, and there is a significant difference.

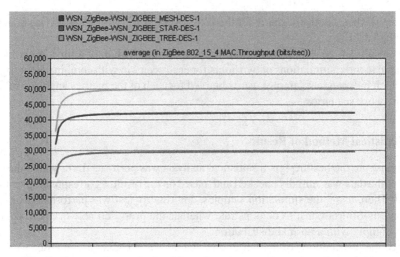

Fig. 5. Comparative analysis of throughput in tree, star, and mesh topologies

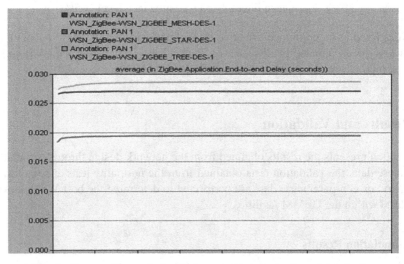

Fig. 6. Comparative analysis of latency in tree, star, and mesh topologies

Latency Metrics for the WSN. Figure 6 shows the behavior of latency in each of the combined topologies, where it can be identified that the star topology is the one that offers a better decrease in delay, being this topology more efficient compared to the mesh and tree topologies; denoting that there is a significant difference within the WSN when comparing the end-to-end delay on this scenario the combined topologies.

Packet Loss Metric for the WSN. Figure 7a shows on the application layer the packets received where it generated more traffic on the tree topology. In contrast, the mesh and star topology maintains a lower margin of packages received, denoting a significant difference within the WSN on the traffic received in the combined scenarios.

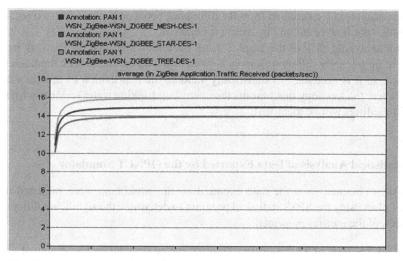

Fig. 7a. Comparative analysis of traffic received on tree, star, and mesh topologies

Figure 7b shows in the application layer the packets sent where more traffic was generated in the tree and mesh topology that remain with the same traffic margin. In contrast, the star topology maintains a lower margin of packets sent, denoting a significant difference within the WSN on the traffic sent in the combined scenarios.

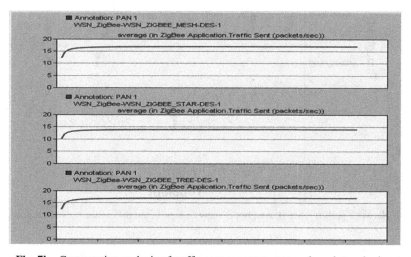

Fig. 7b. Comparative analysis of traffic sent over tree, star, and mesh topologies.

The packet loss is calculated from the difference between packets sent and received, from which the final result on this metric is obtained.

After analyzing each of the graphs, it has been identified that the network performance is significantly different from each other when different network topologies are deployed, so it is necessary to statistically validate the distribution of this data in the WSN, where the topology that best fits the control of drinking water services within the UEMM facilities will be identified.

3.2 Statistical Analysis of Data Exported by the OPNET Simulator

The results obtained from the data exported on the simulation were validated using whisker plots using the SPSS statistical program to determine the significant differences with each of the metrics presented.

Statistical Analysis of Throughput. Figure 8, where the whisker box is plotted, shows that the tree topology performs better within the WSN than the mesh and star topologies, showing a significant difference between them.

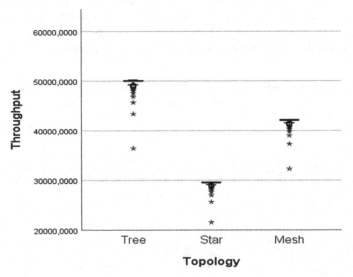

Fig. 8. Network performance (throughput) shows a significant difference between topologies

Statistical Analysis of Latency. It can be observed in Fig. 9 that, in the statistical sample, the latency in the star topology. It has a lower end-to-end delay than the mesh and tree topologies, so it can be noted that there is a slightly significant difference in this parameter.

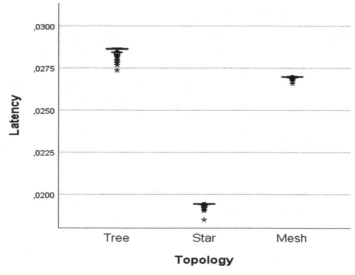

Fig. 9. Network throughput (latency) shows little significant difference between topologies

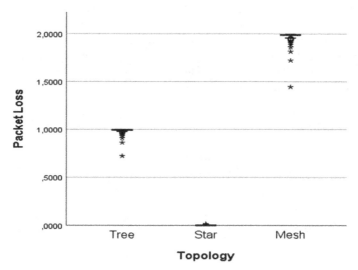

Fig. 10. Network performance (packet loss) shows little significant difference between topologies

Statistical Analysis of Packet Loss. The representation of the samples obtained in Fig. 10 shows that the star topology has less packet loss than the tree and mesh topology, showing a significant difference in this statistical result.

3.3 Validation by Normality Testing

Next, the validation of the data is defined using a normality test on the data obtained from the three topologies where three independent samples of more than 50 data were obtained, where the Kolmogórov-Smirnov test was applied, getting results as shown in Table 2, where the significance of the P-value in each of the metrics is equal to 0%.

Table 2. Results normality test applying Kolmogorov-Smirnov test on 300 data obtained from the metrics in the simulation

Metrics	Statistician	gl	Sig. P-value
Throughput	0,228	300	0,000
Latency	0,339	300	0,000
Packet loss	0,162	300	0,000

With these results, having a P-value equal to 0,000 indicates that the metrics do not follow a normal distribution. Therefore, the data will be validated using nonparametric tests.

Non-parametric Tests. Since there was no normality in the data, a non-parametric test was applied to identify that the topologies had independent samples; since there were more than two groups, it was determined that the test to be performed was the Kruskal Wallis test on the data obtained from the simulation.

Table 3. Contrast statistics in the Kruskal Wallis test on metrics

Metrics	H de Kruskal Wallis	gl	Sig. P-value
Throughput	263,176	2	0,000
Latency	265,781	2	0,000
Packet loss	271,788	2	0,000

Table 3 shows the value of the Kruskal Wallis H statistic on 2 degrees of freedom, where the asymptotic significance of the P-value obtained is less than 0.05; therefore, the null hypothesis is rejected, and it is concluded that the parameters of latency, throughput, and packet loss differ between the three topologies.

The three proposed scenarios are valid. However, it is presented as the best scenario to work within the WSN according to the graphs analyzed on two of the three metrics is defined as the star topology, which has better results in terms of latency and packet loss over the other two topologies in tree and mesh.

4 Conclusions

In this research, it was determined that the tree topology is the most appropriate to be used as a method of control over the facilities of the Educational Unit Maria de la Merced, which was defined based on the Kruskal Wallis test having a very significant difference in the effective transfer rate compared to the other metrics of latency and packet loss where no significant difference was denoted between the topologies.

The design of the WSN is a proposal for the educational institution that will innovate the control of drinking water systems, creating a process that will serve as an extension to other essential services, thus ensuring the excellent use of resources within the institution.

References

1. Arellano Aucancela, A., Avila-Pesántez, D., Jennyfer, E.P., Hervas Parra, C.: Evaluación de una red de Sensores Inalámbrica para detección de Incendios Forestales. Rev. Tecnológica ESPOL **28**, 115–130 (2015). https://www.researchgate.net/publication/297208802
2. Romero García, N.V.: Análisis y evaluación del parámetro de calidad de servicio (QoS) en red ZigBee con un nodo coordinador. Univ. Catol. Santiago Guayaquil **4**(2), 9–15 (2017)
3. Jayachitra, V.P., Geetha, G., Vijay, K.S., Jayachitra, V.P., Geetha, G., Vijay, K.S.: Energy-delay efficient unified routing protocol for wireless sensor networks. Circuits Syst. **7**(6), 995–1007 (2016). https://doi.org/10.4236/CS.2016.76084
4. Alvarado Medellin, P., Aguilar Escarcia, S.P., Ramírez Aguilrera, A.M., Ortiz Gómez, R.: Dynamic system for monitoring and control wireless sensor networks operating under ZigBee comunication protocol. Ing. Investig. y Tecnol. **20**(1), 1–9 (2019). https://doi.org/10.22201/fi.25940732e.2019.20n1.003
5. Shi, L., Ren, H., Peng, M.: Enhanced simulation model of ZigBee wireless sensor network. DEStech Trans. Comput. Sci. Eng. (Cece), 26–31 (2017). https://doi.org/10.12783/dtcse/cece2017/14369
6. Adaramola, O.J., Olasina, J.R.: Network investigation and performance analysis of ZigBee technology using OPNET. J. Adv. Comput. Eng. Technol. **4**(4), 209–218 (2018)
7. Alvarado-Medellin, P., Aguilar-Escarcia, S.P., Ramírez-Aguilera, A.M., Ortiz-Gómez, R.: Sistema dinámico para el monitoreo y control de redes inalámbricas de sensores que operan bajo el protocolo de comunicación ZigBee. Ing. Investig. y Tecnol. **20**(1), 0 (2019). https://doi.org/10.22201/fi.25940732e.2019.20n1.003
8. Marghescu, C., Pantazica, M., Brodeala, A., Svasta, P.: Simulation of a wireless sensor network using OPNET. In: 2011 IEEE 17th International Symposium for Design and Technology in Electronic Packaging, SIITME 2011 - Conference Proceedings, pp. 249–252 (2011). https://doi.org/10.1109/SIITME.2011.6102728
9. Tobón, D., et al.: Recuperación de Datos en Dispositivos de Almacenamiento SSD Utilizando File Carving. RISTI Rev. Iber. Sist. e Tecnol. Inf. **13**(1), 490–499 (2014). https://doi.org/10.17013/risti.n.pi-pf
10. Zhao, W., Xie, J.: OPNET-based modeling and simulation study on handoffs in Internet-based infrastructure wireless mesh networks. Comput. Netw. **55**(12), 2675–2688 (2011). https://doi.org/10.1016/J.COMNET.2011.04.013
11. Alhayani, B., Abdallah, A.A.: Manufacturing intelligent Corvus corone module for a secured two way image transmission under WSN. Eng. Comput. (Swans. W.) **38**(4), 1751–1788 (2020). https://doi.org/10.1108/EC-02-2020-0107/FULL/XM

12. Alhayani, B., Abbas, S.T., Mohammed, H.J., Mahajan, H.B.: Intelligent secured two-way image transmission using corvus corone module over WSN. Wirel. Pers. Commun. **120**(1), 665–700 (2021). https://doi.org/10.1007/s11277-021-08484-2

13. Vallejo, J.: Implementación de escenarios de simulación de redes de acceso utilizando la plataforma Opnet, pp. 1–125 (2018). http://201.159.223.180/bitstream/3317/11985/1/T-UCSG-POS-MTEL-125.pdf. Accessed 30 June 2022

Drinking Water and Sewerage at the Universidad de las Fuerzas Armadas ESPE and Implementation of an Internet of Things Flowmeter

David Vinicio Carrera Villacrés[1,2,3]($\boxtimes$) (iD), Rodney Alberto Garcés[1],
Alfonso Rodrigo Tierra Criollo[1], Ricardo Duran[1], and Geovanny Raura[1]

[1] Departamento de Ciencias de la Tierra y la Construcción, Carrera de Ingeniería Civil,
Universidad de las Fuerzas Armadas ESPE, Sangolquí 171103, Ecuador
dvcarrera@espe.edu.ec

[2] Facultad de Ingeniería en Geología, Minas, Petróleos y Ambiental, FIGEMPA, Carrera de
Ingeniería Ambiental, Universidad Central del Ecuador, Quito 170129, Ecuador

[3] Grupo de Investigación en Contaminación Ambiental GICA, Grupo de Investigación en
Geoespacial, Quito, Ecuador

Abstract. The Universidad de las Fuerzas Armadas ESPE is an institution that in 2022 celebrates 100 years of creation. The current main campus was built in 1989 and approximately provides its facilities to 14,187 people every day, including students, professors, and workers located in Sangolquí, Ecuador, Southamerica. The drinking water and sewerage pipes of the university are more than 33 years old, which makes an assessment of their operation urgent. The objectives of the article were to collect the information on the drinking and sanitary water drainage to know the state of the pipes, through measurements of the supplies of drinking water and pressures, therefore, to propose a solution installing a first IoT flowmeter that provides real-time information on water consumption in a building of the university and study the dynamics of the series generated with recurrence maps. The average pressure on the campus was approximately 20 m of water column (mwc), which was acceptable, however, in the south of the main campus, low pressures of less than 10 mwc were obtained with the drinking water and sewage pipes in poor condition. The supply of drinking water was 213.16 L per capita per day. The implementation of the IoT flowmeter was complicated by the deterioration of the material of most of the pipes, however, it was possible to install the first flowmeter in the administrative building, which demonstrated the technical feasibility of controlling water consumption. In real-time on a university test place. The recurrence maps provided recurring series with a period of 20 h.

Keywords: Flowmeter · IoT · Recurrence maps

© The Author(s), under exclusive license to Springer Nature Switzerland AG 2022
J. Herrera-Tapia et al. (Eds.): TICEC 2022, CCIS 1648, pp. 73–84, 2022.
https://doi.org/10.1007/978-3-031-18272-3_6

1 Introduction

1.1 University of the Armed Forces

In 1989, the construction of infrastructure and sanitary and hydraulic networks of the main campus of the University of the Armed Forces ESPE, located in what was then a farm in the Valle de los Chillos with approximately 40 ha [1]. Currently, the institution has 33 years of operation.

The main campus is made up of 26 buildings, among which the following stand out: Administrative Building, residence, library, student blocks A, B, C, and D, laboratories, and coliseum, among others.

With a work team from the construction department, a tour of all the university buildings was carried out, checking connections and locks that are suitable for the work of installing an IoT flowmeter. Thus, the administration building was reached, which is one of the most used buildings of the university every working day.

1.2 Drinking-Water and Sewerage

Those responsible for drinking water systems have to adopt emergency actions focused on satisfying the demand and the continuity of services that can be interrupted by the age of the infrastructure, the variation in pressures, the interruption of electrical energy, breaks in distribution systems, landslides, earthquakes, floods, among other activities [2].

In countries of Latin America, the Caribbean, and the world in the last 20 years there has been a downward trend in the consumption of drinking water per inhabitant. The design bases did not contemplate this decrease, which is why an inefficient economic investment is being made from the investment, operation, and maintenance costs of the resulting infrastructure, for example, in the city of Brussels between 2005 and 2012 there was a reduction in domestic consumption about 30% [3].

The time interval in which drinking water and sewerage will provide the service at its full potential is known as the optimal design period, it is based on economic aspects, and the useful life of the infrastructure. It is recommended that drinking water and sewerage this time be between 10 and 20 years [4]. ESPE their drinking water and sewerage are more than 30 years old.

1.3 Flowmeter IoT

Thinger.io allows communication with IoT devices, through a series of REST API services, providing subscription mechanisms for updating information in real-time. The developed system is similar to the one proposed by [5] and it is based on an IoT flowmeter that allows obtaining water consumption data that is sent to the cloud [6], as shown in Fig. 1.

An ESP8266 microcontroller was used as an IoT node, to which a two-inch diameter water flow sensor (DFC15) was connected, which allows sensing the average flow rate in liters per minute and the volume of consumption in liters. The data is presented through

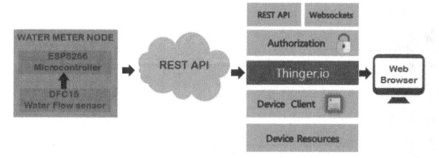

Fig. 1. Infrastructure technology of Thinger.io

a dashboard that can be accessed from a personal computer or mobile device through a web browser.

The device was installed in one of the university campus buildings in the drinking water distribution column. From there, three sensor cables (positive, data, and negative) extend, which are directed to a pass box where the microcontroller that transmits the data through a Wi-Fi network is located (Fig. 2).

Fig. 2. Flowmeter IoT installed in the administrative building of the university

The dashboard configured on the Thinger.io platform presents the record of consumption data through time series as shown in Fig. 3.

1.4 Flowmeter IoT Data Analysis with Recurrence Maps

There are several nonlinear techniques or measures to determine the complexity of a time series, for example, the correlation dimension, Lyapunov exponents, Poincaré maps, Hurst coefficient, and visual recurrence analysis, among others [7–9] and [10].

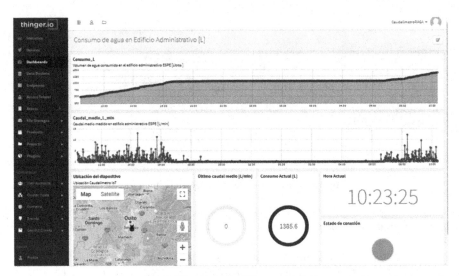

Fig. 3. Dashboard of Flowmeter IoT

These techniques allow for the identification of non-linear presences and possibly chaotic behaviors in these series.

To determine the behavior of a time series to detect existing patterns or structural changes, recurring map analysis (Visual Analysis of Recurrence-VAR) is used. The recurrence maps are a set of points, equally spaced in a square matrix of N × N (N is the total data of the time series), where the axes represent the chronological sequence of the vectors in the constructed space.

When the recurrence map shows an identifiable structure or pattern, the series indicate a sign of determinism; otherwise, the series indicate a sign of randomness [11]. This technique allows us to investigate the trajectory (system dynamics) in m-dimensional phase space through a two-dimensional representation of its recurrences. This recurrence in the state of time i at a different time j is visualized within a two-dimensional square matrix (recurrence matrix). The recurrence graph is a qualitative process that allows us to observe signs of the system's behavior to locate hidden recurring patterns.

The objectives of the work were to collect the information on the drinking water and sewerage pipes to know their conditions of materials and breakdowns of the systems from the supply wells, and outlets to the public sewer, through campaigns of measurement of flows and pressures, monitoring and visits to on-site networks, thus, determining the best place to implement a flowmeter with the Internet of Things (IoT), which provides real-time information on water consumption in a building of the University and analyze that data with recurrence maps.

2   Methodology

2.1   Study Zone

Figure 4 shows the location map of the University of the Armed Forces ESPE with images of the most problematic points in the drinking water and sewerage.

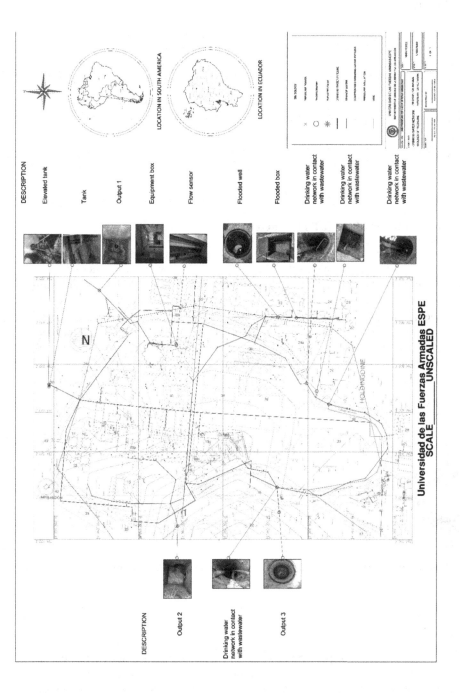

Fig. 4. Location map of the University with images of the most problematic points of the drinking water and sewage network

Table 1 presents the methodology for collecting hydro-sanitary information from the university's ESPE main campus.

Table 1. Description of the work methodology

No.	Activity	Methodology	Reference
1	Drinking water	Field work with maintenance staff of the university	[12]
2	Sewerage		
3	Pressures in the provision of drinking water		

2.2 Implementation of the IoT Flowmeter

An IoT device capable of measuring the volume of water that passes through the point of a drinking water network was created; based on a water flow control meter with the LCD screen or quantitative liquid controller, the programming of an Arduino board with internet access and a platform that receives the data sent by the IoT equipment (Fig. 5). The Thinger.io platform was used to receive the data sent by the IoT equipment, since it offers users a reception of data a minute after it has been generated, showing the data generated in a graphic and dynamic display panel, being able to access him in any part of the day and the world.

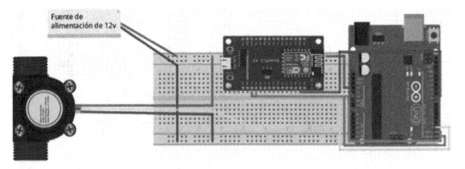

Fig. 5. The connection between the flow sensor, Arduino UNO and NODEMCU

2.3 Data Processing

The time series analysis was performed using flow data (liters per minute). These data were recorded with an interval of one minute in the months of February, March, July, August, September, October, and November 2021, obtaining their respective monthly time series. From these monthly series, the accumulated flow was taken for each hour, thus generating the series that will be used for the analysis of the respective recurrent maps [10]. To topologically reconstruct an original multidimensional system from a scalar time series in an equivalent way, the Takens theorem [13] was used, for which a time delay of seven was used, and with a dimension.

3   Results and Discussions

3.1   Drinking Water, Pressures, and Sewerage with Problems Encountered

For the evaluation of the drinking water pipes and sewerage, on-site visits were made with the technical maintenance staff of the University and the students on the subject of drinking water and sewerage, and a manometer was built to measure the water pressure at strategic points of the campus (Fig. 6).

Fig. 6. Gathering of information on the drinking water and sewerage

Table 2 shows the results of the pressures taken in the drinking water pipes.

Table 2. The pressure obtained in the drinking water pipes of the University

Node	Pressure (meter water column)	Node	Pressure (meter water column)	Node	Pressure (meter water column)
J-1	19,55	J-9	15,96	J-17	9,51
J-2	20,37	J-10	12,13	J-18	9,64
J-3	14,27	J-11	4,44	J-19	12,68
J-4	30,14	J-12	7,07	J-20	23,07
J-5	36,43	J-13	11,95		
J-6	28,79	J-14	24,24		
J-7	28,19	J-15	21,88		
J-8	21,63	J-16	27,56		

The average pressure in the University was approximately 20 m water column, which explains a good pressure at most points of the drinking water network [14]. In nodes 11 and 12 there is pressures less than 10 m water column, that is, low pressures [15], these are located at the farthest point of the network south of the university in the transportation department.

The University is supplied with water resources through aquifers (underground water) from two wells; its location is in the North. The first well has an exit flow of 10 l/s, supplying the facilities during business days, Monday through Friday, due to its better water quality; the second well has a flow of 25 l/s, which supplies on the weekends [16].

The pipes are in poor condition of the drinking water of the university campus at various points shows wear with small leaks that over time become large volumes of wasted water, likewise, it was appreciated that the stopcocks have problems due to age [12].

The sewerage has been in operation for more than 30 years, therefore, the pipes are in bad condition, since it was found that in several wells the stairs were corroded and several bottoms were eroded, making it difficult for the correct evacuation of solids and liquids, especially in the pipes that discharge residual water from the coliseum, transport, and CICTE in the south of the University [12].

3.2 Measurement of the Population of the Universidad de las Fuerzas Armadas ESPE

The Construction and Development Department of the University provided a full-scale plan of the university, from which the useful area of all the buildings where tutorials are given was extracted and this was divided into 1.6 m^2, which is the minimum area recommended by the technical standards from Ecuador. And educational infrastructure standards according to agreement 483-12 [17], except in places such as the library, coliseum, bar, dining room, and auditoriums where the maximum capacity allowed was taken.

Information on the administrative and teaching staff was requested from the university's human talent department with memorandum No. ESPE-DCTC-2021-1929-M [18]. With this information, the saturation population of the campus was obtained, which included 12,428 students, 1,759 teachers, administrators, and university workers.

3.3 Implementation of IoT Flowmeter

The drinking water pipes of the university were evaluated, and it was difficult in most sections to install the flowmeter due to the poor condition of the material. The pipe was in better condition and the best place to get power and internet was the Administration building located in the northeast of the university.

In the year 2021, the month of February, there were data records for 6 days, for March 13 days, for July 6 days, for August 31 days, for September 30 days, for October 31 days, for November 22 days. From these data and with the values of the delay time and the immersed dimension, the respective recurrence maps were constructed for the respective months and can be seen in Fig. 7.

From a visual analysis of the recurrence maps, it is possible to observe how the areas change in most of the series, which indicates the presence of discontinuities. In addition, the series has different structures grouped in the form of a grid; indicating that they have different behaviors and would help in the detection of structural changes [10].

It can also be seen that in all the months the recurrence points form lines parallel to the main diagonal, giving indications of a possible deterministic structure, and with a period of approximately 20 h. It can be seen that the points form parallel and perpendicular lines to the main diagonal, indicating the presence of a symmetrical and periodic structure over time [9].

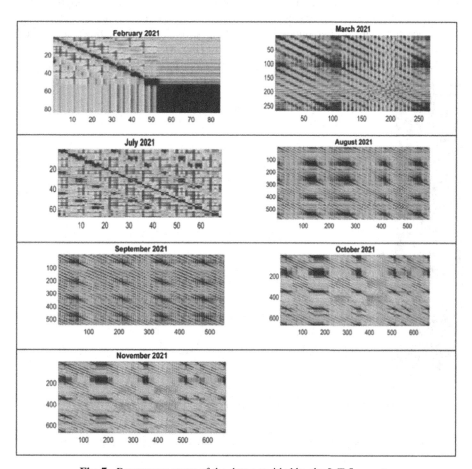

Fig. 7. Recurrence maps of the data provided by the IoT flowmeter

From the visual analysis, the different structures presented by the recurrence maps of the time series give clues about their dynamic behavior. However, to determine its behavior in a more objective and precise way, it is necessary to have data for a whole year and to use new analysis techniques. For this reason, future work will be carried out with the quantitative analysis of these recurrence maps using different Recurrence Quantification Analysis - RQA metrics.

3.4 Determination of the Drinking Water Supply at the University

From the information collected by the human talent department [18] and the flows obtained from the published work [16], it turned out that the provision of drinking water at the university was 213.16 L per capita per day, an endowment five times greater than the recommendation in the Ecuadorian regulations for universities, which is 40 to 60 l per capita per day [19]. As a first approximation, the university would be well supplied with drinking water, however, the IoT flowmeter marks a consumption in the early morning hours when there are no personnel 3,040 L, that is, it will be the subject of another investigation to account for the waters that are lost (Fig. 8).

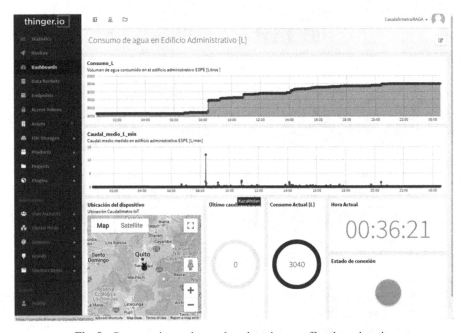

Fig. 8. Consumption at dawn when there is no staff at the university

The implementation of IoT sensors to measure meteorological variables have shown that the sustainable management of resources is possible to avoid waste, as well as improve production processes [20]. It is possible to relate the measured variables and their environment as demonstrated by [21].

4 Conclusions

The drinking water and sewerage pipes at the University of the armed forces are in poor condition with critical points in the south in the part of the coliseum and the logistics and transport department. The water that supplies the university comes from two wells with a flow of 35 L per second and the total population surveyed was 14,187 people, therefore, the provision of drinking water was 213.16 L per capita per day. The average pressure in the drinking water pipes was approximately 20 mwc with points of low pressure in the southern area of the university. The recurrence maps of the data generated by the IoT flowmeter resulted in a recurrence of 20 h. The installation of the IoT flowmeter was complicated because the pipes are in poor condition, however, it was possible to install the first flowmeter in the administrative building, demonstrating the technical feasibility and providing preliminary information during off-hours occupation of the university facilities of 3040 L.

References

1. Bravo, K.: Historia de la Universidad de las Fuerzas Armadas, Primera ed. Sangolqui (2014)
2. Arteaga, D.: Plan de respuesta para sistemas de agua potable: Enfoque en la pandemia COVID-19. Banco Int. del Desarro, pp. 1–66 (2020). https://publications.iadb.org/publicati ons/spanish/document/Plan-de-respuesta-para-sistemas-de-agua-potable-Enfoque-en-la-pan demia-COVID-19.pdf
3. Paez Rubio, T., Alberti, J., Rezzano Tizze, N.: Tendencia del consumo de agua potable y eficiencia en la inversión en infraestructura de agua y saneamiento: Estudio de caso en América Latina (2020). https://publications.iadb.org/es/node/29620
4. CONAGUA: Datos Básicos Para Proyectos De Agua Potable Y Alcantarillado (Basic Data for Potable Water and Sewage Projects) (2015)
5. Abioye, E.A., et al.: IoT-based monitoring and data-driven modelling of drip irrigation system for mustard leaf cultivation experiment. Inf. Process. Agric. 8(2), 270–283 (2021). https://doi.org/10.1016/j.inpa.2020.05.004
6. Thinger.io: Console.thinger.io (2022). https://console.thinger.io/login
7. Wolf, A., Swift, J.B., Swinney, H.L., Vastano, J.A.: Determining Lyapunov exponents from a time series, pp. 285–317 (1985)
8. Tierra, A., Luna, M., Staller, A., Pilapanta, C., Romero, R., Porras, L.: Hurst coefficient estimation by rescaled range and wavelet of the ENU coordinates time series in GNSS network. IEEE Lat. Am. Trans. 16(4), 1064–1069 (2018). https://doi.org/10.1109/TLA.2018.8362138
9. Tierra, A., León, R., Alexis Tinoco, S., Cañizares, C., Amores, M., Porras, L.: Visual analysis of recurrence of time series of the coordinates ENU in the GPS stations. Bol. Ciencias Geod. 24(4), 470–484 (2018). https://doi.org/10.1590/S1982-21702018000400029
10. Ayala, M.F., Tierra, A., Carrera-Villacrés, D.V.: Variables meteorológicas en la estación anal-ysis of the dynamics of time series from meteorological variables in the climatological station chone, Ecuador. GEOACTA 43(1), 51–67 (2019). https://revistas.unlp.edu.ar/geoacta/article/view/13319
11. Eckmann, J.-P., Kamphorst, S.O., Ruelle, D.: Recurrence plots of dynamical systems. Europhys. Lett. 4(9), 973–977 (1987). https://doi.org/10.1209/0295-5075/4/9/004
12. Garcés Alarcón, R.A.: Diagnóstico y propuesta de mejora de agua potable y alcantarillado en la Universidad de las Fuerzas Armadas ESPE Matriz implementando caudalímetros inteligentes IoT (2022)
13. Sugihara, G., et al.: Detecting strange attractors in turbulence. J. Anim. Ecol. 84(6), 388–400 (2012)
14. SEMARNAT and CONAGUA, Manual de Agua Potable, Alcantarillado y Saneamiento Man-ual de Agua Potable, Alcantarillado y Saneamiento Desinfección Para Sistemas de Agua Potable y Saneamiento Comisión Nacional del Agua (2010)

15. Comisión Nacional del Agua, Manual de Agua Potable, Alcantarillado y Saneamiento Diseño de Redes de Distribución de Agua Potable (2007)
16. Carrera-Villacrés, D., Bahamonde-coyago, C., Mancheno-criollo, C., Mena-Castro, R., Moreira-Pin, J., Ordóñez-Ríos, M.: Dynamic model of SARS-CoV-2 spread and drinking water consumption impact at Universidad de las Fuerzas Armadas ESPE. Int. J. Adv. Sci. Eng. Inf. Technol. **12**(3), 994–1000 (2022). https://doi.org/10.18517/ijaseit.12.3.14682
17. Vidal, G.: Normas técnicas y estándares para el diseño de espacios educativos (2012). https://educacion.gob.ec/wp-content/uploads/downloads/2013/01/ACUERDO-483-12.pdf
18. ESPE: Memorando Nro. ESPE-DCTC-2021–1929-M, Sangolqui (2021)
19. N. Norma Ecuatoriana de la Construcción: Norma hidrosanitaria NHE agua. In: Norma Ecuatoriana de la Construcción Capítulo 16, p. 16, 17 (2011)
20. Carrera-Villacrés, D., Villacrés, J.L.C., Braun, T., Zhao, Z., Gómez, J., Quinteros-Carabalí, J.: Fog harvesting and iot based environment monitoring system at the ilalo volcano in ecuador. Int. J. Adv. Sci. Eng. Inf. Technol. **1**, 407–412 (2020). https://doi.org/10.18517/ijaseit.10.1.10775
21. Vinicio Carrera-Villacrés, D., et al.: Relationship between the morphometric and physicochemical parameters of the Urkuhuayku microbasin where the Urku Yaku 2.0 fog collector sytem tower is located. In: LACCEI International Multi-conference for Engineering, Education and Technology, p. 11 (2020). https://doi.org/10.18687/LACCEI2020.1.1.161

Indicators to Evaluate Elements of Industry 5.0 in the Textile Production of MSMEs

Pablo Flores-Siguenza[1] , Bernarda Vásquez-Salinas[2] ,
Lorena Siguenza-Guzman[3,4] , Rodrigo Arcentales-Carrion[5] ,
and Dolores Sucozhañay[2(✉)]

[1] Department of Applied Chemistry and Systems of Production, Faculty of Chemical Sciences, Universidad de Cuenca, Cuenca, Ecuador
`pablo.floress@ucuenca.edu.ec`
[2] Interdisciplinary Department of Space and Population (DIEP), University of Cuenca, Cuenca, Ecuador
`{bernarda.vasquez,dolores.sucozhanay}@ucuenca.edu.ec`
[3] Department of Computer Sciences, Faculty of Engineering, Universidad de Cuenca, Cuenca, Ecuador
`lorena.siguenza@ucuenca.edu.ec`
[4] Research Centre Accountancy, Faculty of Economics and Business, KU Leuven, Leuven, Belgium
[5] Faculty of Economic and Administrative Sciences, Universidad de Cuenca, Cuenca, Ecuador
`rodrigo.arcentales@ucuenca.edu.ec`

Abstract. Textile MSMEs are going through a period of instability and greater difficulty in executing their operations due to factors derived from the pandemic, globalization, policies, and environmental and social needs. This is driving companies to abandon classic methods and turn to the use of innovative concepts as manners to promote sustainability and resilience. One of these concepts is Industry 5.0, which, according to the European Commission, focuses on sustainable manufacturing and operator well-being and complements Industry 4.0 as it seeks to improve factory efficiency through technology by placing the human being at the center of development. At the same time, it minimizes environmental and social impacts and enhances resilience. Aware that implementing these new trends is a challenge for MSMEs, this study contributes to the generation of indicators to evaluate elements of Industry 5.0 in the textile production of MSMEs, supporting the development and implementation of strategies focused on this area. The construction of the set of indicators is based on a 3-phase framework that consists of doing a systematic literature review, selecting the indicators by a process of analysis and comparison, and expanding their characteristics through elaborating data sheets. As part of the results, 172 indicators completed a rigorous selection and validation process. These will serve as the basis for developing sustainable, resilient, and human-centered production models that can be carried out in future research.

Keywords: Industry 5.0 · Indicators · Sustainability · MSMEs · Textile industry

J. Herrera-Tapia et al. (Eds.): TICEC 2022, CCIS 1648, pp. 85–100, 2022.
https://doi.org/10.1007/978-3-031-18272-3_7

1 Introduction

Current events, such as globalization, technological development, global warming, and the recent COVID19 pandemic have caused important changes in the production and marketing of all kinds of goods in different industries [1]. An example of this can be seen in textile MSMEs, where the instability and complexity of their operations have increased. These events have motivated their production models to become resilient, withstand periods of crisis and high variability, and be sustainable [2].

Nevertheless, achieving sustainability is one of the most critical challenges for companies due to among others their economic difficulties [3]. Yet, it is worthen due to its multiple benefits. For example, balanced integration of economic performance, environmental impact, and social inclusion, increased productivity, new market niches, improved image, reduced environmental and labor risks, among others [4].

Initially, the concept of Industry 4.0 sought, in addition to applying new technologies in the industry, to address ecological needs related to green production. However, this concept lost its focus over time on sustainability issues to focus on the application of technologies to increase the efficiency and flexibility of production [5]. A new approach is then generated, that of Industry 5.0, which seeks the transformation of the manufacturing sector, no longer focusing only on the application of technologies to improve productivity but also seeking to achieve social objectives, allowing it to be a provider of prosperity, respecting environmental limits and putting the welfare of workers at the center of the production process [6].

The three key elements of the Industry 5.0 approach are sustainability, which in turn is divided into three dimensions, economic, environmental and social. Together they generate strategies that seek to ensure the needs of the present without compromising the needs of future generations. The next element is human empowerment, which places the human being at the center of all development and seeks a better relationship between man and machine/technology. The last element, resilience, allows companies to adapt to a changing environment and plan strategies that guarantee the continuity of their operations.

Therefore, researching, developing, and implementing models, tools and indicators with an Industry 5.0 approach will contribute significantly to the economic reactivation of MSMEs since three fundamental elements are comprehensively addressed: sustainability, human empowerment, and resilience. This study aims to generate a set of indicators to evaluate elements of Industry 5.0 in the textile production of MSMEs starting from a conceptual definition of Industry 5.0 and its elements. This set of indicators will become a tool to guide companies toward Industry 5.0

2 Related Research

A brief bibliographic search on Industry 5.0, its elements and current application was carried out. Unfortunately, little information is observed in the world literature regarding not only MSMEs but in all types of industries. Some studies address the transition from Industry 4.0 to 5.0, especially technological development [7, 8]. Others cover specific strategies for Industry 5.0. For example, they study technological enablers for a transition to a smart circular economy [9], analyze human empowerment techniques in the digital age [6], and investigate the influence of emotional intelligence in the workforce [10].

Regarding the three elements of Industry 5.0, as far as we know no studies are on resilience and human empowerment, and regarding sustainability there is quite a lot of information, not specifically with the industry 5.0 approach but in a general way. According to Malek and Desai [11], the main strategies currently being researched in sustainable development are supply chains, circular economy, business model development and smart factories. However, there is little information on textile MSMEs, and most research focuses on environmental problems and the reduction of their impacts [12, 13].

From this brief literature review, there is still little, or no information on tools to evaluate the Industry 5.0 elements, which we are convinced will be helpful and, above all, a guide for companies and MSMEs that are just starting to venture into sustainability, resilience, and human empowerment as a global vision.

Some research projects have initiated the development of indicators to address sustainability and resilience in a general manner. For example, the project "Incorporation of sustainability concepts in the management models of Micro, Small and Medium Textile Enterprises" (SUMA) [14, 15], and the project "Model of distribution of resilient plans for MSMEs with a focus on productivity and occupational safety" (ResilTex) [16]. Both projects have generated valuable information in this area of interest since they have studied textile MSMEs and have established models and guidelines that fit the context. However, although these projects have already obtained sustainability and resilience indicators, they have not yet considered the industry 5.0 approach in their development.

3   Methodology

A methodological framework was established to generate a set of indicators that evaluate elements of Industry 5.0 in textile production (Fig. 1). This structure guided each step followed to meet the objective of this study.

Knowing that a precise understanding of the Industry 5.0 concept and its elements is vital to subsequently identify and define a set of indicators related to this approach, a **Systematic Literature Review (SLR)** based on Fink's methodology [17] was developed, which it consists of seven steps to guarantee the rigor and quality of the results.

1) Selection of research questions: with the help of the PICO strategy [18], three research questions were formulated, a) How is industry 5.0 and its elements currently being defined? b) What Industry 5.0 strategies are currently applied in the operations of textile companies? and c) What indicators of sustainability, resilience, and human empowerment are applied in the textile industry in the Industry 5.0 field?
2) Definition of database sources: the selected databases were Scopus, Web of Science, Scielo, and Latindex Catalogue.
3) Selection of search terms: structured search strings were defined: "Industry 5.0" & "Textile", "Industry 5.0" & "Sustainability" OR "Resilience" OR "Empowerment human being".

4) Application of practical selection criteria: the selected studies are in Spanish and English, from scientific journals published between 2012 and 2022, and belong to one of these thematic areas, Environmental, Social Sciences, Engineering, Business and Management, Multidisciplinary, and Economics.

5) Application of methodological criteria: in addition to the above criteria, studies had to have valid research designs, reliable data sources, and significant results.

6) Review of documentation: The sample was reviewed in the Atlas.ti software, which supports the organization, analysis, and interpretation of the results.

7) Synthesis of results: Fig. 2 summarizes the number of articles comprising the sample analyzed, consisting of 121 papers detailed in Appendix A.

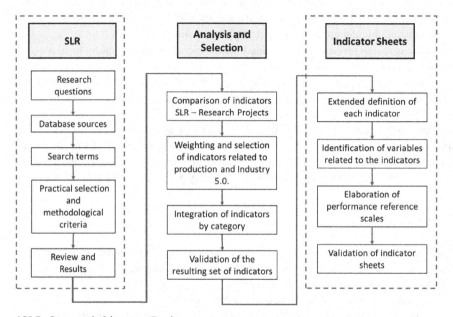

*SLR: Systematic Literature Review

Fig. 1. Guiding framework for the generation of the set of indicators.

A second set of indicators is obtained from the information generated in the SUMA and ResilTex projects. Once both sets of indicators have been obtained, in the next phase (**Analysis and Selection**), a comparison is made between them to verify similarities and differences. Next, a weighting matrix was proposed to select only the indicators related to Industry 5.0 and production in textile companies. Finally, the two bases were integrated by categories and validated by a panel of experts.

To complement the final set of indicators determined in phase two, **Indicator Sheets** were prepared following the methodology used by SUMA, which consisted of establishing an expanded definition of the indicator, identifying variables related to the indicator, and constructing a reference scale considering optimistic and pessimistic scenarios. These sheets were also validated by experts from the academic and the textile sector.

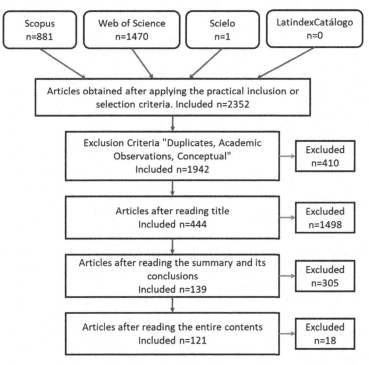

Fig. 2. Flow chart of the methodology applied in SLR

4   Results and Discussion

In view of the importance and thoroughness of the SLR, the results are divided into two sections. The first section presents the main findings of the SLR through a meta-analysis and a descriptive analysis. The second section focuses on the selection of indicators and the preparation of data sheets.

4.1   Results of the Systematic Literature Review

In reference to the meta-analysis of the sample obtained, the increase in the number of publications over the years stands out, especially from 2017, as shown in Fig. 3. This increase is also evidenced when analyzing the time in two periods. For example, between 2012 and 2016, the average number of articles was 6.4 per year, while from 2017 to 2021, the average increased to 17.4 per year. Similarly, the rebound that exists in the years 2020 and 2021 is evident, until 2019 the average number of publications per year was 8.5. Compared to 2020 (22 articles), there is an increase of approximately 251% and, compared to 2021 (29 articles), the increase amounts to 331%. This analysis is consistent with the growing importance and relevance of the concepts of sustainability, Industry 4.0 and Industry 5.0 for academia, business, and policy makers [11].

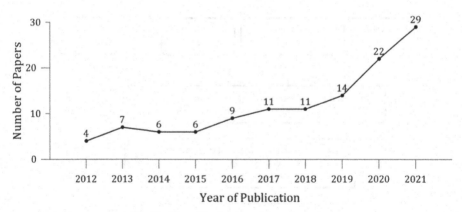

Fig. 3. Time distribution of sample papers

Other statistical data of the sample indicate that there are 24 case studies in textile companies, followed by 10 cases in the automotive sector, the two main ones. Several sectors were considered, not only textiles, due to the topicality of the concepts investigated and the scarcity of information about them. The 121 articles in the sample have been published in 92 different journals. Only 14 journals have more than two publications, containing 36% of the total sample. Finally, the publications correspond to 36 countries, of which 23 have more than two publications. The first ten countries represent 61% of the sample, with India, China, Brazil, and the United Kingdom standing out with more than eight papers each.

For the descriptive analysis of the sample, the study focused on the research questions raised. Thus, Table 1 helps answer the first research question, "How is Industry 5.0 and its elements currently defined?" The table mentions five definitions given by different authors of the analyzed sample. However, these definitions have similarities, which allows generalizing and saying that Industry 5.0 is about complementing and leveraging the advantages and technology of Industry 4.0, putting the human being at the center of development, and integrating elements of sustainability and resilience to generate positive impacts in the operations of the industries.

Regarding the elements of Industry 5.0, sustainability is defined as a set of strategies to find a balanced integration of economic performance, environmental impact, and social inclusion to benefit current and future generations [4]. Human empowerment, the basis of Industry 5.0, places the human being at the center of economic or production processes, establishing a close collaboration between highly trained personnel and technology to create unique or individualized products/services [5]. The last element, resilience, refers to the ability to adapt to adverse situations, unforeseen events, and setbacks, and having the ability to anticipate, respond, and adapt to sudden changes and disruptions to survive and thrive [19].

Table 1. Main definitions of industry 5.0

Definition	Reference
Industry 5.0 can be considered as the answer to the demand of renewed human-centric industrial paradigm, starting from the reorganisation of the production processes to then generate positive implications first within the business perspectives and secondly towards all the components belonging to the innovation ecosystem. Industry 5.0 relies on three core elements: human-centricity, sustainability, and resilience	[20]
Industry 5.0 complements industry 4.0 by specifically putting research and innovation at the service of the transition to a sustainable, human-centric, and resilient industry	[21]
Industry 5.0 envisions the development of human-centered, resilient, and sustainable smart manufacturing systems that are able to make use of real-time pervasive networks to support coordinated and complex processes	[22]
Industry 5.0 or a 'human touch' revolution, is a human-centered society that balances the economic advancement with the resolution of social problems by a system that highly integrates cyberspace and physical space	[10]
Industry 5.0 emphasis on empowering the human being and his co-existence with automation. This era of industrial upheaval attempts to take the Industry 4.0 to a new milestone by integrating humans and machines in the smart factory	[6]

Regarding the second research question, "What Industry 5.0 strategies are currently applied in the operations of textile companies", Table 2 summarizes by area of interest the main strategies, which are mainly focused on sustainability, followed by the development of innovative technologies, human empowerment, and resilience.

In terms of sustainability strategies, models are highlighted to balance economic, environmental, and social variables [23], business networks and efforts to achieve SDGs [24], support frameworks in sustainability planning [25], and aspects social as society 5.0 [9, 20]. Furthermore, strategies focused on developing innovative technologies mainly explain their usefulness in Industry 4.0 and how they can evolve to Industry 5.0 [8]. On the other hand, those that refer to human empowerment investigate physical comfort [26], emotional comfort [10], and the design of work environments [27]. Finally, resilience-related strategies focus on business resilience assessment frameworks [19].

Table 2. Main strategies of industry 5.0 applied in company operations

Area	Strategy	Features
Sustainability	Society 5.0	Involves all actors in a dynamic way, enhances the individual-technology relationship in favor of sustainable development

(continued)

Table 2. (*continued*)

Area	Strategy	Features
	Frameworks for the sustainable development of industries	Support in planning and çonceptual innovation
	Cluster network model	Managing and integrating SDGs into the daily operations of SMEs
	Structural equation analysis of data	Establishes relationships between social and economic performance
Technological development and innovation	Development of digital technologies	Key element for the expansion of the circular economy
	Block chain-enabled, fog computing	Increased transaction security and deepened traceability
	Intelligent autonomy	Robots that interact directly with humans
	Artificial intelligence	Automated decisions through interconnected networks
Human Empowerment	Workstation design	Design and development of occupational environments, to constitute symbiotic and coevolutionary sociotechnical systems
	Exoskeletons	Improving worker positioning and fatigue
	Emotional intelligence	Worker performance, adaptability to Industry 5.0
Resilience	Resilience assessment model	Business resilience assessment framework

In response to the third research question, "What indicators of sustainability, resilience, and human empowerment are applied in the textile industry in Industry 5.0?". Tables 3 and 4 are constructed from information extracted from the sample. Table 3 summarizes the 64 indicators identified in sustainability element, classified by dimension and category. While Table 4 shows the 38 indicators identified for the elements of human empowerment and resilience, also classified by category.

Table 3. Indicators used in the sample corresponding to sustainability element

Dimension	Category	Indicator
Economic	Cost management	Equipment cost. Cost of materials. Cost of services. Acquisition cost
	Corporate management	Amount invested in competitiveness plans. Machine setup time. Quantified money in manufacturing waste. Percentage of plant flexibility. Inventory and stocks. Quality of products and services
	Products	New products per year. Innovation and insertion in international markets. Originality of the product based on its percentage of market share. Uniqueness
	Operating results	Profit. Costs. Revenues. Number of performance indicators used
	Suppliers	Standards for suppliers. Just-in-time delivery
	Customers	Number of complaints per customer/region. Customer satisfaction. Delivery time
	Infrastructure	Proximity to transportation hubs. Availability of alternative transportation. Availability of storage facilities. Manufacturing facilities available
Social	Salary and benefits	Salary paid to employees. Bonuses paid annually to employees
	Job satisfaction	Level of employee satisfaction. Absenteeism. Employee turnover
	Occupational Health and safety	Company health and safety programs. Average distance traveled by employees to the company. Employee life expectancy
	Human resources Management	Labor availability. Percentage of skilled labor. Recruitment and selection. Training plans and activities. Evaluation plans
	Community	Number of community development programs

(continued)

Table 3. (*continued*)

Dimension	Category	Indicator
Environment	Environmental management	Environmental policy. Environmental objectives. Environmental care structure. Disclosure of environmental performance information. Main environmental impacts. Suppliers' relationship with the environment
	Responsibility	Waste treatment/disposal. Consumption of hazardous materials
	Consumption	Quantity of water consumed. Quantity of energy consumed. Quantity of paper used
	Life cycle	Product life cycle analysis
	Recycling	Material reduced annually. Actions to reuse materials. Actions to promote recycling
	Pollution	Effluents. Soil. Air. Auditory
	Green image	Participation in environmental initiatives. Ratio of green clients to total

4.2 Analysis and Selection of Indicators

As mentioned in the methodology, the selection of the set of indicators corresponding to the second phase of the study begins with a comparison between the sustainability indicators obtained in the literature and the indicators of the SUMA project. Although some indicators of both subsets, despite not having the same name, have similarities and their objective is the same. Therefore, they are considered similar for this study. In this manner, the duplication of indicators during integration is avoided. In addition, the same procedure is carried out between the resilience indicators found and those of the ResilTex Project.

The results of this comparison process show that the indicators with the most notable similarities are environmental dimension with 80.95% and that, in general, there is a similarity of 57.81%, i.e., 37 indicators found in the literature do not resemble any of the SUMA indicators.

In the next step, a weighting matrix was made to filter the indicators that focus on the production area aligned with the concepts and elements of Industry 5.0 and can be applied to the context of textile MSMEs. The matrix considers the following criteria: relevance to the elements, applicability, access to information, and impact area. Ten academics, two textile entrepreneurs, and two professionals from the production area of textile companies in Azuay province participated in the process.

Table 4. Indicators used in the sample corresponding to the elements of human empowerment and resilience.

Element	Category	Indicator
Human empowerment	Worker behavior	Emotional responses (affection). Confidence. Attitudes. Acceptance. Personal growth. Situational awareness
	Training	Number of hours of training received. Absorption of knowledge. Implementation of trained strategies
	Performance	Efficiency. Effectiveness. Autonomy. Adaptability to new environments. Teamwork. Adaptability to robot-human environment
	Physical ergonomics	Physical workload. Safety. Physical Fatigue. Physical Comfort. Workplace Design
	Cognitive ergonomics	Mental workload. Concentration/attention. Training in mental strengthening. Awareness
	Management	Empowerment Policies. Implementation of tools to help workers
Resilience	Assets and resources	Material. Social. Financial. Networking. Intangible
	Dynamic competitiveness	Flexibility. Rebounding. Robustness. Networking
	Learning and culture	Leadership, operations management and, decision making. Collectivity and sense-making. Employee well-being

Lastly, the indicators obtained were validated by a panel of experts, resulting in a final set of 172 indicators detailed in Appendix B. These indicators will be used to evaluate elements of Industry 5.0 in textile production. Furthermore, this final set of indicators was grouped by categories, shown in Table 5, along with the respective element, dimension, and number of indicators.

As a complement, this study's third and last phase consisted of preparing technical sheets for each of these incorporated indicators. The technical sheet contains complete information on the indicator in terms of its concept, variables involved, and reference scale, all of which will allow a better practical application and, above all, a quantification of the indicators as they are implemented.

The structure of the sheets can be seen in Fig. 4, which refers to the "Absenteeism rate" indicator.

Table 5. Number of indicators in the final set by element, dimension and category.

Element	Dimension	Category	# Indicators
Sustainability	Economic	Economic profitability. Business diversity. Long-term investments. Liquidity. Solvency. Management. Profitability	14
	Social	Employment relationship. Freedom of association and collective bargaining. Occupational health and safety. Fair wages. Social benefits/social security. working hours. Forced labor. Child labor. Equal opportunities. Worker development. Behavior in the event of dismissal. Sexual harassment. Community	65
	Environment	Environmental management. Energy. Water. Materials. Waste. Emissions. Effluents. Ambient noise	73
Human empowerment	NA	Specific training. Physical ergonomics. Cognitive ergonomics. Management	12
Resilience	NA	Assets and resources. Dynamic competitiveness. Learning and culture. Infrastructure	8

5 Conclusions

The study has generated a set of 172 indicators that evaluate elements of Industry 5.0 in the textile production of MSMEs. For this, the study has used a third-phase framework that began with a systematic literature review, an analysis of the characteristics of the indicators, and finally, elaborating conceptual sheets for each indicator with comprehensive information about them.

Regarding the study's first phase, the SLR analyzed a sample of 121 articles in a critical, transparent, and reproducible manner. The findings evidence the growing interest in issues of sustainability and Industry 5.0, going from four articles published in 2012 to 29 in 2021. The strategies that consider an Industry 5.0 approach and are currently most researched are those related to sustainability, followed by the development of innovative technologies, human empowerment, and resilience. In addition, the SLR allowed the result of a conceptual definition of Industry 5.0 and its elements, a fundamental step in identifying and constructing indicators related to this approach.

From the literature, 102 indicators have been obtained, presenting relatively scarce information regarding their definition, applicability, and evaluation. For this reason, its analysis, comparison with other projects, weighting, validation, integration, formation of categories, and elaboration of conceptual sheets is necessary and fundamental to obtain a robust set of indicators with detailed information and, above all, 100% applicable to our context.

Code:	Name:			
S-11-063	Absenteeism rate			
Definition:	This indicator seeks to determine if the company has a mechanism to evaluate the absenteeism of its personnel and compare it with the average rates of its sector to improve the presence of employees in the organization.			
Dimension/ Subdimension:	Behavior in the event of dismissal		**Stakeholder**	Worker
Related variables				
The indicator is based on two criteria that companies must meet to define their performance. a. The company evaluates the rate of employee absenteeism. b. The company generates measures to improve its absence rate.				
All criteria are defined according to an affirmative or negative answer from the person in charge.				
Performance reference scale				
Performance	**Score**	**Range/Interval**	**Description**	
Unacceptable	-2	N/A	The performance benchmark on the scale is not defined.	
Inadequate	-1	N/A	The performance benchmark on the scale is not defined.	
Standard	0	The company does not evaluate its absenteeism rate.	If the company does not perform an analysis of its absenteeism rate and the causes of the results, it is considered to have a standard performance. Since it is not a legal obligation to evaluate this issue.	
Well	1	The company evaluates its absenteeism rate.	If the company performs an analysis of absenteeism and its causes, it is considered a good performer. It reflects the efforts in analyzing personal behavior	
Excellent	2	The company evaluates and generates measures for improvement.	If the company analyzes absenteeism rates and periodically reviews or updates them, it is considered to have outstanding performance.	

Fig. 4. "Absenteeism rate" indicator sheet

The rigorousness followed in obtaining this set of indicators, the integration of information from various projects, and the participation of academia, entrepreneurs, and professionals in the construction and validation process make the results of this research a valuable tool for both researchers and entrepreneurs who are taking their first steps in the field of Industry 5.0.

Acknowledgments. The authors would like to thank to "Corporación Ecuatoriana para el Desarrollo de la Investigación y Academia – CEDIA" for the financial support given to the present research, development, and innovation work through its CEPRA program, especially for the CEPRA XVI-2022 Pros-5.0. In addition, this research was partially funded by the University of Cuenca, Technical University of Ambato and University of Azuay.

Appendix A - List of References Considered in the SLR

The list of references used in the SLR can be found online at https://imagineresearch.org/industry5_appendixa/.

Appendix B – Set of Indicators and Sheets

Set of resulting indicators can be found online at https://imagineresearch.org/industry5_appendixb/.

References

1. Acioli, C., Scavarda, A., Reis, A.: Applying Industry 4.0 technologies in the COVID–19 sustainable chains. Int. J. Prod. Perform. Manag. (2021, ahead-of-print). https://doi.org/10.1108/IJPPM-03-2020-0137
2. Luna-Altamirano, K.A., Sarmiento-Espinoza, W.H., Calle-Masache, O.R., Ramón-Poma, G.M.: Modelo de sustentabilidad para la reactivación de las Mipymes textiles de la ciudad de Cuenca-Ecuador. Dominio de las Ciencias **7**, 325–337 (2021). https://doi.org/10.23857/dc.v7i1.1645
3. Abreu, M., Ferreira, F., Proença, J., Ceglia, D.: Collaboration in achieving sustainable solutions in the textile industry. J. Bus. Ind. Mark. (2020, ahead-of-print). https://doi.org/10.1108/JBIM-01-2020-0041
4. Lopes de Sousa Jabbour, A.B., Ndubisi, N.O., Roman Pais Seles, B.M.: Sustainable development in Asian manufacturing SMEs: progress and directions. Int. J. Prod. Econ. **225**, 107567 (2020). https://doi.org/10.1016/j.ijpe.2019.107567
5. Breque, M., De Nul, L., Petridis, A.: Industry 5.0: towards a sustainable, human-centric and resilient European industry. https://aeneas-office.org/2022/01/04/industry-5-0-towards-a-sustainable-human-centric-and-resilient-european-industry/
6. Kumar, R., Gupta, P., Singh, S., Jain, D.: Human empowerment by Industry 5.0 in digital era: analysis of enablers. In: Phanden, R.K., Mathiyazhagan, K., Kumar, R., Paulo-Davim, J. (eds.) Advances in Industrial and Production Engineering, pp. 401–410. Springer, Singapore (2021). https://doi.org/10.1007/978-981-33-4320-7_36
7. Margherita, E., Braccini, A.M.: Socio-technical perspectives in the Fourth Industrial Revolution - Analysing the three main visions: Industry 4.0, the socially sustainable factory of Operator 4.0 and Industry 5.0. Presented at the 23 November 2021 (2021)
8. Alvarez-Aros, E., BERNAL-TORRES, C.: Technological competitiveness and emerging technologies in industry 4.0 and industry 5.0. Anais da Academia Brasileira de Ciências **93** (2021). https://doi.org/10.1590/0001-3765202120191290
9. Fraga-Lamas, P., Lopes, S., Fernández-Caramés, T.: Green IoT and edge AI as key technological enablers for a sustainable digital transition towards a smart circular economy: an Industry 5.0 use case. Sensors **21**, 5745 (2021). https://doi.org/10.3390/s21175745
10. Chin, S.: Influence of emotional intelligence on the workforce for Industry 5.0. J. Hum. Resour. Manag. Res. **2021** (2021). https://doi.org/10.5171/2021.882278
11. Malek, J., Desai, T.N.: A systematic literature review to map literature focus of sustainable manufacturing. J. Clean. Prod. **256**, 120345 (2020). https://doi.org/10.1016/j.jclepro.2020.120345

12. Sahinkaya, E., Yurtsever, A., Çınar, Ö.: Treatment of textile industry wastewater using dynamic membrane bioreactor: impact of intermittent aeration on process performance. Sep. Purif. Technol. **174**, 445–454 (2017). https://doi.org/10.1016/j.seppur.2016.10.049

13. Nouren, S., et al.: Sweet lime-mediated decolorization of textile industry effluents. Pol. J. Environ. Stud. **28** (2018). https://doi.org/10.15244/pjoes/81090

14. Sucozhañay, G., Cabrera, F., Sucozhañay, D., Guaman, R., Siguenza-Guzman, L., Vanegas, P.: Toward a sustainability balanced scorecard for managing corporate social responsibility: a conceptual model. In: García, M.V., Fernández-Peña, F., Gordón-Gallegos, C. (eds.) Advances and Applications in Computer Science, Electronics and Industrial Engineering. AISC, vol. 1307, pp. 279–298. Springer, Singapore (2021). https://doi.org/10.1007/978-981-33-4565-2_18

15. Sigcha, E., Martinez-Moscoso, A., Siguenza-Guzman, L., Jadan, D.: PESTEL analysis as a baseline to support decision-making in the local textile industry. In: Botto-Tobar, M., Zamora, W., Larrea Plúa, J., Bazurto Roldan, J., Santamaría Philco, A. (eds.) ICCIS 2020. AISC, vol. 1273, pp. 144–156. Springer, Cham (2021). https://doi.org/10.1007/978-3-030-59194-6_13

16. Flores-Siguenza, P., Siguenza-Guzman, L., Lema, F., Tigre, F., Vanegas, P., Aviles-González, J.: A systematic literature review of facility layout problems and resilience factors in the industry. In: Botto-Tobar, M., Montes León, S., Torres-Carrión, P., Zambrano Vizuete, M., Durakovic, B. (eds.) ICAT 2021. CCIS, vol. 1535, pp. 252–264. Springer, Cham (2022). https://doi.org/10.1007/978-3-031-03884-6_19

17. Fink, A.: Conducting Research Literature Reviews: From the Internet to Paper. SAGE Publications, Thousand Oaks (2019)

18. Santos, C.M. da C., Pimenta, C.A. de M., Nobre, M.R.C.: The PICO strategy for the research question construction and evidence search. Revista Latino-Americana de Enfermagem **15**, 508–511 (2007). https://doi.org/10.1590/S0104-11692007000300023

19. Mezzour, G., Boudanga, Z., Benhadou, S.: Smart pandemic management through a smart, resilient and flexible decision-making system. ISPRS Int. Arch. Photogramm. Remote Sens. Spat. Inf. Sci. **4443**, 285–294 (2020). https://doi.org/10.5194/isprs-archives-XLIV-4-W3-2020-285-2020

20. Carayannis, E.G., Morawska-Jancelewicz, J.: The futures of Europe: Society 5.0 and Industry 5.0 as driving forces of future universities. J. Knowl. Econ. (2022). https://doi.org/10.1007/s13132-021-00854-2

21. Gürdür Broo, D., Kaynak, O., Sait, S.M.: Rethinking engineering education at the age of industry 5.0. J. Ind. Inf. Integr. **25**, 100311 (2022). https://doi.org/10.1016/j.jii.2021.100311

22. Fraga-Lamas, P., Varela-Barbeito, J., Fernández-Caramés, T.M.: Next generation auto-identification and traceability technologies for Industry 5.0: a methodology and practical use case for the shipbuilding industry. IEEE Acces **9**, 140700–140730 (2021). https://doi.org/10.1109/ACCESS.2021.3119775

23. Gupta, S., Racherla, U.: Interdependence among dimensions of sustainability: evidence from Indian leather industry. Manag. Environ. Qual. Int. J. **29** (2017). https://doi.org/10.1108/MEQ-06-2017-0051

24. Jiménez, E., de la Cuesta-González, M., Boronat-Navarro, M.: How small and medium-sized enterprises can uptake the sustainable development goals through a cluster management organization: a case study. Sustainability **13**, 5939 (2021). https://doi.org/10.3390/su1311 5939

25. Lee, Z.-Y., Chu, M.-T., Chen, S.-S., Tsai, C.-H.: Identifying comprehensive key criteria of sustainable development for traditional manufacturing in Taiwan. Sustainability **10**, 3275 (2018). https://doi.org/10.3390/su10093275

26. Gašová, M., Gašo, M., Štefánik, A.: Advanced industrial tools of ergonomics based on Industry 4.0 concept. Procedia Eng. **192**, 219–224 (2017). https://doi.org/10.1016/j.proeng.2017. 06.038

27. Bednar, P.M., Welch, C.: Socio-technical perspectives on smart working: creating meaningful and sustainable systems. Inf. Syst. Front. **22**(2), 281–298 (2019). https://doi.org/10.1007/s10 796-019-09921-1

Technological Accessibility and Digital Health Education Associated with the Use of Smart Healthcare by Obstetricians in Peru

Yuliana Mercedes De La Cruz-Ramirez[1]([⊠]) [ID], Santiago Angel Cortez-Orellana[2] [ID], Augusto Felix Olaza-Maguiña[1] [ID], and Nadezhda Tarcila De La Cruz-Ramirez[3] [ID]

[1] Universidad Nacional Santiago Antúnez de Mayolo, Centenario 200, Huaraz 02002, Peru
{ydelacruzr,aolazam}@unasam.edu.pe
[2] Universidad Peruana Los Andes, Giráldez 231, Huancayo 12000, Peru
d.scortez@upla.edu.pe
[3] Hospital Víctor Ramos Guardia, Luzuriaga 1248, Huaraz 02001, Peru

Abstract. This research was conducted to determine the association of the technological accessibility and digital health education with the use of smart healthcare by obstetricians in a high Andean city of Peru. A cross-sectional research was carried out with 276 obstetricians who worked during 2021 in the Huaylas Sur Health Network of Huaraz (3052 masl), Peru. An online questionnaire was applied between January and February 2022, whose results were processed using the SPSS V23.0 program, as well as the Chi square statistical test. It was evidenced that the majority of obstetricians made an occasional use of the services based on smart healthcare during the development of their professional activities (45.7%). There was limited access to computer devices (50.3%), medical applications (56.9%) and Internet connection (50.4%). Most of the obstetricians did not have digital health education training regarding the use of digital health tools (76.1%), information management (79.0%), digital content creation (77.5%) and collaborative network work (73.2%). All the aforementioned aspects had a statistically significant relationship with the use of smart healthcare ($p < 0.05$). It was concluded that the level of technological accessibility and the digital health education that obstetricians have are associated with the use of the services of smart healthcare during the development of their professional activities in 2021. The digital literacy of health workers is an important and urgent need to improve the quality of patient care, together with overcoming the existing digital divide in the Peruvian population.

Keywords: Digital divide · Digital health education · Obstetrics · Smart healthcare

1 Introduction

The application of smart healthcare in the different health activities has meant many benefits for patients and health professionals, who have not only been able to increase

J. Herrera-Tapia et al. (Eds.): TICEC 2022, CCIS 1648, pp. 101–113, 2022.
https://doi.org/10.1007/978-3-031-18272-3_8

their communication possibilities, but have also improved the certainty of their diagnoses and the effectiveness of their treatments [1–4]. These benefits have been demonstrated in various studies worldwide [5–7], with emphasis on the countries of North America and Europe, in which, in addition to the advances presented, new risk reduction strategies are emphasized to prevent adverse events that could occur during the application of smart healthcare systems.

However, the reality described in the preceding paragraph is not related to what is observed in most South American countries, in which the implementation of smart healthcare has been limited, among other reasons, due to lack of resources and lack of commitment from the government authorities. Thus, for example, in a study carried out in Brazil, it is highlighted that the constant growth of applications has not corresponded with the limitations of Internet connection, especially in the regions farthest from large urban centers and with less economic development [8].

Another extremely important aspect that is directly related to health professionals is their level of digital literacy [9, 10], which, according to some studies, is much higher in workers who work in private health institutions and in the area of medicine [11, 12], the same not happening with professionals from other health specialties. In this way, it is highlighted that according to the specialty of the service providers and the type of work they perform, the knowledge and skills they have acquired over the years in the field of telehealth can help them improve the efficiency of their work, maximize their potential and reduce the risk of transmitting infections [11].

The reality of the application of smart healthcare in Peru has many interesting aspects to highlight, due to the disparity in the quality of care provided in the different health institutions. Thus, advances have been observed in the use and dissemination of the benefits of smart healthcare in private institutions located in the largest and most important cities in Peru, whose staff generally have basic knowledge of digital health education and have access to various technological tools [13, 14]. The opposite happens with the workers of public institutions, whose work is focused on the care of the most remote and poor population groups in Peru, where there is a lack of training, resources, equipment and infrastructure [15, 16].

This research addresses the reality and problems previously described in health professionals in the specialty of obstetrics, whose level of digital literacy has not been previously addressed in sufficient detail. Likewise, the level of use carried out by these professionals with respect to services based on smart healthcare is unknown in the scientific literature, especially in places far from the interior of Peru, such as the high Andean city of Huaraz, whose population is served mainly by professionals who work in the Huaylas Sur Health Network, which is completely publicly managed.

Thus, this research has sought to answer the following questions:

What is the level of technological accessibility of the obstetricians who work in the Huaylas Sur Health Network?

What digital health education training do the obstetricians who work in the Huaylas Sur Health Network have?

What is the level of use of smart healthcare carried out by the obstetricians who work in the Huaylas Sur Health Network?

Is there an association between the level of technological accessibility and the use of smart healthcare carried out by the obstetricians who work in the Huaylas Sur Health Network?

Is there an association between digital health education training and the use of smart healthcare carried out by obstetricians working in the Huaylas Sur Health Network?

According to the questions formulated in the research, the general objective was to determine the association of the technological accessibility and digital health education with the use of smart healthcare by obstetricians in the Huaylas Sur Health Network of Huaraz, Peru.

2 Methodology

2.1 Research Design and Population Under Study

A cross-sectional research design was applied, for which the population consisted of 328 obstetricians who worked during 2021 in the Huaylas Sur Health Network of Huaraz.

Within the inclusion criteria, it was considered to obstetricians who worked as permanent and/or temporary employees, regardless of their age and gender. The only exclusion criteria were the condition of work license and therefore the non-performance of care activities during the year 2021, as well as the refusal to participate in the study.

It is important to clarify that of the total population mentioned above, 40 obstetricians participated in the execution of the pilot test in order to validate the relevance of the data collection instrument; while 12 obstetricians refused and/or did not respond to the virtual request to answer the online questionnaire. In this way, the final participation of 276 obstetricians was achieved, the results of which are disclosed in the corresponding section of this article.

2.2 Variables

Demographic Variables. Age (25–49 years, ≥ 50 years), gender (male, female), employment status (permanent employee, temporary employee) and years of work experience (1–14 years, ≥ 15 years).

Research Variables. The following variables were taken into account:

Technological Accessibility of Obstetricians. The accessibility to computing devices (never, sometimes, always), medical applications (never, sometimes, always) and Internet connection (never, sometimes, always) was evaluated.

Digital Health Education. The training of obstetricians regarding the use of digital health tools (yes, no), information management (yes, no), digital content creation (yes, no) and collaborative networking (yes, no) was evaluated.

Use of Services Based on Smart Healthcare. The frequency of use in general during the development of their professional activities in 2021 (never, monthly, weekly, daily) was evaluated.

2.3 Data Collection Procedure

In order to comply with the data collection, a questionnaire was developed in which all the information corresponding to the demographic and research variables described in the preceding section was considered, with a total of 12 questions (Appendix section).

The validity and reliability of the questionnaire was evaluated, for which in the first case the expert judgment method was applied, achieving the participation of 8 experts in telemedicine, to whose answers the Kendall's concordance test was applied, demonstrating the validity of content ($p = 0.001$). In the case of reliability, it was evaluated with a pilot test with 40 obstetricians through the application of the test-retest technique with an interval of 5 weeks, at the end of which the intraclass correlation coefficient and the kappa index were applied, showing that the questionnaire was a reliable evaluation instrument, obtaining 0.819 and 0.871, respectively; as well as a Cronbach's alpha index of 0.836.

The opinion of the experts was taken into account to improve the wording of the questions in the final version of the questionnaire, whose content was recorded in an online form using Google Forms. The invitation for voluntary participation, together with the link to the online questionnaire and the informed consent statement, were sent to the obstetricians' personal emails. The respective follow-up was carried out through the WhatsApp application, for which we had the support of the authorities of the Huaylas Sur Health Network, who, after evaluating the study protocol and the respective authorization, provided the necessary information. The entire application process of the final version of the online questionnaire was carried out during the months of January and February 2022.

2.4 Statistical Analysis

The information collected was processed using the SPSS V23.0 program. A descriptive analysis of the variables under study was applied, for which absolute frequencies and percentages were recorded in the results tables. The Chi-square statistical test was used in order to evaluate a possible association between the variables under study, with a significance level of $p < 0.05$.

2.5 Ethical Considerations

The recommendations made known by the World Medical Association and the Declaration of Helsinki [17] were strictly respected, especially with regard to voluntary participation, the virtual completion of an informed consent declaration and the protection of the confidentiality of the data of the study participants. Likewise, the research protocol was reviewed and approved prior to its execution by the Ethics Committee of the Santiago Antúnez de Mayolo National University, an institution located in the same geographic area in which the study population lived, that is, in the city of Huaraz-Peru.

3 Results

Table 1 shows that of the 276 obstetricians who answered the final version of the questionnaire, most of them were female (95.3%), with 50 years old or older (65.2%), whose employment status was temporary, that is, hired by the Peruvian government to provide their professional services for a certain period (59.4%), with at least 15 years of professional experience (61.6%).

Table 1. Demographic characteristics of obstetricians.

Characteristic	n	%
Age:		
- 25–49 years	96	34.8
- ≥ 50 years	180	65.2
Gender:		
- Male	13	4.7
- Female	263	95.3
Employment status:		
- Permanent employee	112	40.6
- Temporary employee	164	59.4
Years of work experience:		
- 1–14 years	106	38.4
- ≥ 15 years	170	61.6

It is evidenced that the highest percentage of obstetricians occasionally used services based on smart healthcare during the development of their professional work in 2021, with a monthly frequency of use (45.7%); while 18.5% of obstetricians said they had never used such services (Table 2). Likewise, the majority of obstetricians who made occasional use had limited access to computing devices (50.3%), medical applications (56.9%) and Internet connection problems (50.4%). As a result of the statistical analysis, it was shown that the level of technological accessibility of obstetricians has a statistically significant relationship with the use of the services of smart healthcare (p < 0.05).

Table 2. Technological accessibility according to use of services based on smart healthcare.

Technological accessibility	Use of services based on smart healthcare								Total		Chi-Square results
	Never		Monthly		Weekly		Daily				
	n	%	n	%	n	%	n	%	n	%	
Computing devices:											
- Never	0	0	48	17.4	9	3.3	34	12.3	91	33.0	$X^2 =$
- Sometimes	27	9.8	78	28.3	31	11.2	3	1.0	139	50.3	148.305
- Always	24	8.7	0	0	22	8.0	0	0	46	16.7	p < 0.001
Total	51	18.5	126	45.7	62	22.5	37	13.3	276	100	

(*continued*)

Table 2. (*continued*)

Technological accessibility	Use of services based on smart healthcare								Total		Chi-Square results
	Never		Monthly		Weekly		Daily				
	n	%	n	%	n	%	n	%	n	%	
Medical applications:											
- Never	0	0	34	12.3	3	1.1	30	10.8	67	24.2	$X^2 =$ 166.884 $p < 0.001$
- Sometimes	23	8.3	92	33.4	35	12.7	7	2.5	157	56.9	
- Always	28	10.2	0	0	24	8.7	0	0	52	18.9	
Total	51	18.5	126	45.7	62	22.5	37	13.3	276	100	
Internet connection:											
- Never	0	0	17	6.2	3	1.1	27	9.7	47	17.0	$X^2 =$ 172.690 $p < 0.001$
- Sometimes	11	4.0	91	33.0	27	9.8	10	3.6	139	50.4	
- Always	40	14.5	18	6.5	32	11.6	0	0	90	32.6	
Total	51	18.5	126	45.7	62	22.5	37	13.3	276	100	

On the other hand, regarding training in digital health education (Table 3), it was observed that the majority of obstetricians who made occasional use of services based on smart healthcare during the year 2021, did not have training related to use of digital health tools (76.1%), information management (79.0%), digital content creation (77.5%) and collaborative networking (73.2%). After analyzing these results, it was found that the digital health education of obstetricians has a statistically significant relationship with the use of the services of smart healthcare ($p < 0.05$).

Table 3. Digital health education according to use of services based on smart healthcare.

Digital health education	Use of services based on smart healthcare								Total		Chi-Square results
	Never		Monthly		Weekly		Daily				
	n	%	n	%	n	%	n	%	N	%	
Use of digital health tools:											
- Yes	3	1.1	30	10.9	17	6.2	16	5.7	66	23.9	$X^2 =$ 17.131 $p = 0.001$
- No	48	17.4	96	34.8	45	16.3	21	7.6	210	76.1	
Total	51	18.5	126	45.7	62	22.5	37	13.3	276	100	
Information management:											
- Yes	2	0.7	36	13.1	18	6.5	2	0.7	58	21.0	$X^2 =$ 21.145 $p < 0.001$
- No	49	17.8	90	32.6	44	16.0	35	12.6	218	79.0	
Total	51	18.5	126	45.7	62	22.5	37	13.3	276	100	

(*continued*)

Table 3. (*continued*)

Digital health education	Use of services based on smart healthcare								Total		Chi-Square results
	Never		Monthly		Weekly		Daily				
	n	%	n	%	n	%	n	%	N	%	
Digital content creation:											
- Yes	7	2.6	39	14.2	15	5.4	1	0.3	62	22.5	$X^2 =$ 15.850 $p = 0.001$
- No	44	15.9	87	31.5	47	17.1	36	13.0	214	77.5	
Total	51	18.5	126	45.7	62	22.5	37	13.3	276	100	
Collaborative networking:											
- Yes	16	5.8	24	8.7	27	9.8	7	2.5	74	26.8	$X^2 =$ 14.436 $p = 0.002$
- No	35	12.7	102	37.0	35	12.7	30	10.8	202	73.2	
Total	51	18.5	126	45.7	62	22.5	37	13.3	276	100	

4 Discussion

The findings of this research in relation to the general objective raised, have allowed us to find that technological accessibility and the digital health education of obstetricians are associated with the use of the services of smart healthcare during the development of their professional activities in the Huaylas Sur Health Network of Huaraz in 2021. This finding is related to the conclusions reported by other researchers [18, 19], although in different contexts, in which the problem of lack of resources and low digital literacy also constituted an important barrier to the implementation of new information technologies during population health care.

In this regard, recent review articles [20–22] have released an interesting compilation of the wide variety of computing devices and medical applications that exist on the market, with multiple benefits, among which the health care of pregnant women and their newborns occupies a transcendental place. However, the lack of access to these technological resources, especially in the poorest countries, has meant not taking advantage of these benefits, with serious consequences for people's health. This level of technological accessibility that health professionals have has also been addressed in this research, finding that in the case of obstetricians, such accessibility has been limited in relation not only to computing devices, but also to medical applications.

Another issue that is transcendental in the analysis of technological accessibility problems presented by health professionals is the digital gap that exists with respect to the Internet access, a problem that is still important, especially in more distant places, such as the communities where the obstetricians of the Huaylas Sur Health Network work. Thus, it is evidenced that the economic cost of connecting to the Internet is not recognized by the health authorities as part of work activities, which limits the access of professionals. Various studies have highlighted that even in the best implemented places, difficulties in connecting to the Internet have been observed [12], a situation that has been worse in countries with limited resources, where health professionals who work in primary care health institutions, receive low economic remuneration and therefore cannot access to better work resources [23].

Digital health education, for its part, presents very serious deficiencies in the obstetric staff that works in the institutions of the Huaylas Sur Health Network, having found in the present study that the majority of obstetricians do not have training related to transcendental aspects such as the use of digital health tools, information management, digital content creation and collaborative networking. This finding apparently is not only observed in Peru, but also in more developed countries, such as Canada [24], where it was reported that only 21.9% of health professionals wanted to maintain the use of virtual digital tools, among other things because they considered that despite the change in practices during the COVID-19 pandemic, there were still many deficiencies in the use of applications and computer resources, affecting timely access to health care.

With regard to information management in health institutions, little training on this subject was observed in obstetrics professionals, which would not allow putting into practice the benefits evidenced in previous studies, such as the secure management of medical data, as well as the protection of privacy through intelligent health systems [25], especially in health emergency situations [26].

Another important aspect is related to the creation of digital content on which a study carried out in Turkey found a positive feedback feeling regarding the virtual creative content strategies that professionals had to implement to meet the health needs of their patients [27]. This last finding is contrary to what was observed in the present study, where the majority of obstetricians stated that they did not have training related to the creation of digital content.

On the other hand, collaborative networking has also been evidenced as an aspect on which there is very little training in the obstetricians participating in this study, a situation that is also related to the need for personal interaction that many professionals still consider important in their professional performance [12].

It is also worth mentioning that the occasional use of smart healthcare services by obstetricians, is probably due to the limited dissemination that still exists on this subject in Peru [16, 23], as a result of access limitations, for example, to the Internet. Thus, the planning of health personnel development policies is a pending task for the current Peruvian government [28].

A separate point deserves the circumstances in which the provision of health services has been developed during the year 2021, due not only to the still significant presence of infections due to COVID-19, but also to the exhaustion and difficulties that have evidenced among professionals after long months of work overload, a reality that has also affected professionals in Obstetrics. In this regard, although it is highlighted that the COVID-19 pandemic has developed a wide range of digital literacy skills among health professionals [9], has also become noticeable the weaknesses and lack of training in some countries such as Peru, where little importance had been given to digital health education [15, 16].

In addition to the previously mentioned aspects, it is important to make known the limitations presented in this study, such as the difficulty of evaluating a greater number of training topics regarding digital health education, having only considered the best known, according to the literature reviewed in the area of health. Likewise, the low number of peer-reviewed publications of researchers in Peru, as well as the cross-sectional research design developed and the online application modality of the data collection instrument, as a result of the limitations that still exist during 2021 due to the state of health emergency decreed by the Peruvian authorities, meant the impossibility of addressing other aspects of the variables under study; aspects that could be taken into account in future studies.

What is mentioned in the preceding paragraph does not affect the importance of the findings found regarding the use of smart healthcare among obstetric professionals, as well as its level of technological accessibility and digital health education, contributions that not only stand out for being a medical specialty dedicated to the health care of women and newborns, but also because it describes a little-known reality in a high Andean city in the Sierra del Peru, with different characteristics from the large cities of the Peruvian coast such as Lima, which motivates new areas of research.

5   Conclusions and Future Steps

5.1   Conclusions

The level of technological accessibility and the digital health education that obstetricians have are associated with the use of the services of smart healthcare during the development of their professional activities in the Huaylas Sur Health Network in 2021. In this way, it was also concluded the limited access to computing devices, medical applications and Internet connection, together with little training regarding the use of digital health tools, information management, digital content creation and collaborative networking, limitations that were also observed in the occasional use of smart healthcare services by obstetricians during the development of their professional activities.

5.2   Future Steps

The aforementioned conclusions serve as a basis to raise the need to promote digital literacy of health workers, in order to improve the quality of patient care, as well as streamline and enhance the professional performance of workers. In this way, it is the responsibility of the authorities, the implementation of concrete actions aimed at overcoming the existing digital gap in the Peruvian population, especially in the most remote and poorest places. Likewise, university authorities should consider the inclusion of subjects related to bioinformatics within the curricula of health careers, in order to promote early training in topics of digital health education such as smart healthcare, being also the responsibility of obstetricians and health professionals in general, to procure their constant updating and training.

Acknowledgements. To the obstetricians who work in the Huaylas Sur Health Network of the city of Huaraz, for their participation and permanent commitment in carrying out their duties in favor of the poorest population of Peru. To the authorities of the Huaylas Sur Health Network, for all the facilities provided during the execution of the research.

Appendix

Table 4.

Table 4. Questionnaire applied to obstetricians.

Section 1: *Demographic variables*
Q1. Age:
(a) 25–49 years
(b) ≥ 50 years
Q2. Gender:
(a) Male
(b) Female
Q3. Employment status:
(a) Permanent employee
(b) Temporary employee
Q4. Years of work experience:
(a) 1–14 years
(b) ≥ 15 years
Section 2: *Perception about technological accessibility of obstetricians*
Q1. Access to computing devices:
(a) Never
(b) Sometimes
(c) Always
Q2. Access to medical applications:
(a) Never
(b) Sometimes
(c) Always
Q3. Access to Internet connection:
(a) Never
(b) Sometimes
(c) Always
Section 3: *Yes/no questions about digital health education of obstetricians*
Q1. Use of digital health tools (Yes or No)
Q2. Information management
Q3. Digital content creation
Q4. Collaborative networking

(*continued*)

Table 4. (*continued*)

Section 4: *Perception about use of services based on smart healthcare by obstetricians*
Q1. Frequency of use of smart healthcare:
(a) Never
(b) Monthly
(c) Weekly
(d) Daily

References

1. Diwakar, M., et al.: Directive clustering contrast-based multi-modality medical image fusion for smart healthcare system. Netw. Model. Anal. Health Inform. Bioinform. **11**(1), 1–12 (2022). https://doi.org/10.1007/s13721-021-00342-2
2. Zhang, S., Chhetry, A., Zahed, M.A., Sharma, S., Park, C., Yoon, S., Park, J.Y.: On-skin ultrathin and stretchable multifunctional sensor for smart healthcare wearables. npj Flex. Electron. **6**(11), 1–12 (2022). https://doi.org/10.1038/s41528-022-00140-4
3. Wang, L., Xi, S., Qian, Y., Huang, C.: A context-aware sensing strategy with deep reinforcement learning for smart healthcare. Pervasive Mob. Comput. **83**, 101588 (2022). https://doi.org/10.1016/j.pmcj.2022.101588
4. Shreya, S., Chatterjee, K., Singh, A.: A smart secure healthcare monitoring system with internet of medical things. Comput. Electr. Eng. **101**, 107969 (2022). https://doi.org/10.1016/j.compeleceng.2022.107969
5. Liu, Y.: Risk management of smart healthcare systems: delimitation, state-of-arts, process, and perspectives. J. Patient Saf. Risk Manag. **27**(3), 129–148 (2022). https://doi.org/10.1177/25160435221102242
6. Shahzad, S.K., Ahmed, D., Naqvi, M.R., Mushtaq, M.T., Iqbal, M.W., Munir, F.: Ontology driven smart health service integration. Comput. Methods Programs Biomed. **207**, 106146 (2021). https://doi.org/10.1016/j.cmpb.2021.106146
7. Kurapati, K.: Proactive and intelligent healthcare management using IoT. In: Proceedings of the 2022 International Conference on Advances in Computing, Communication and Applied Informatics (ACCAI), pp. 1–7. Institute of Electrical and Electronics Engineers Inc., Chennai (2022). https://doi.org/10.1109/ACCAI53970.2022.9752579
8. De Freitas, D., de Medeiros, V., Gonçalves, G.E.: Towards a control-as-a-service architecture for smart environments. Simul. Model. Pract. Theory **107**, 102194 (2021). https://doi.org/10.1016/j.simpat.2020.102194
9. McBeath, K.C.C., Angermann, C.E., Cowie, M.R.: Digital technologies to support better outcome and experience of care in patients with heart failure. Curr. Heart Fail. Rep. **19**(3), 75–108 (2022). https://doi.org/10.1007/s11897-022-00548-z
10. Muppavarapu, K., Saeed, S.A., Jones, K., Hurd, O., Haley, V.: Study of impact of telehealth use on clinic "no show" rates at an academic practice. Psychiatr. Q. **93**, 689–699 (2022). https://doi.org/10.1007/s11126-022-09983-6
11. Breton, M., et al.: Telehealth in primary healthcare: a portrait of its rapid implementation during the covid-19 pandemic. Healthcare Policy **17**(1), 73–90 (2021). https://doi.org/10.12927/HCPOL.2021.26576

12. Breton, M., et al.: Telehealth challenges during COVID-19 as reported by primary healthcare physicians in Quebec and Massachusetts. BMC Fam. Pract. **22**(1), 192 (2021). https://doi.org/10.1186/s12875-021-01543-4

13. Garcia, S., et al.: Implementation of telemedicine in the Americas: barriers and facilitators. Pan Am. J. Public Health **45**, 1498313 (2021). https://doi.org/10.26633/RPSP.2021.131

14. Condori, L., Berrú, R.: Telehealth systems in the monitoring of patients of medical clinics: a systematic review across a 10-year period. In: Larrondo, M.M., Zapata, L.F., Aranzazu-Suescun, C. (eds.) 19th LACCEI International Multi-Conference for Engineering, Education Caribbean Conference for Engineering and Technology: "Prospective and Trends in Technology and Skills for Sustainable Social Development" and "Leveraging Emerging Technologies to Construct the Future", LACCEI 2021, pp. 1–6. Latin American and Caribbean Consortium of Engineering Institutions, Virtual Online (2021). https://doi.org/10.18687/LACCEI2021.1.1.69

15. Monetegro, P., Pinillos, L., Young, F., Aguilar, A., Tirado-Hurtado, I., Pinto, J.A., Vallejos, C.: Telemedicine and the current opportunities for the management of oncological patients in Peru in the context of COVID-19 pandemic. Crit. Rev. Oncol. Hematol. **157**, 103129 (2021). https://doi.org/10.1016/j.critrevonc.2020.103129

16. Novoa, R.H., et al.: Maternal perinatal telemonitoring in the context of the coronavirus disease 2019 pandemic in a tertiary health center in Peru. Am. J. Perinatol.2022https://doi.org/10.1055/a-1787-6517

17. World Medical Association. Declaration of Helsinki – Ethical principles for medical research involving human subjects. https://www.wma.net/policies-post/wma-declaration-of-helsinki-ethical-principles-for-medical-research-involving-human-subjects/. Accessed 01 Jul 2022

18. Budhwani, S., et al.: Challenges and strategies for promoting health equity in virtual care: findings and policy directions from a scoping review of reviews. J. Am. Med. Inform. Assoc. **29**(5), 990–999 (2022). https://doi.org/10.1093/jamia/ocac022

19. Truong, M., Yeganeh, L., Cook, O., Crawford, K., Wong, P., Allen, J.: Using telehealth consultations for healthcare provision to patients from non-Indigenous racial/ethnic minorities: a systematic review. J. Am. Med. Inform. Assoc. **29**(5), 970–982 (2022). https://doi.org/10.1093/jamia/ocac015

20. Fujioka, J.K., et al.: Challenges and strategies for promoting health equity in virtual care: protocol for a scoping review of reviews. JMIR Res. Protoc. **9**(12), e22847 (2020). https://doi.org/10.2196/22847

21. Shaw, J., Brewer, L.C., Veinot, T.: Recommendations for health equity and virtual care arising from the COVID-19 pandemic: narrative review. JMIR Formative Res. **5**(4), e23233 (2021). https://doi.org/10.2196/23233

22. Monaghesh, E., Hajizadeh, A.: The role of telehealth during COVID-19 outbreak: a systematic review based on current evidence. BMC Public Health **20**(1), 1193 (2020). https://doi.org/10.1186/s12889-020-09301-4

23. Alvarez-Risco, A., Del-Aguila-Arcentales, S., Yáñez, J.A.: Telemedicine in Peru as a result of the COVID-19 pandemic: perspective from a country with limited internet access. Am. J. Trop. Med. Hyg. **105**(1), 6–11 (2021). https://doi.org/10.4269/ajtmh.21-0255

24. Johnson, C., Dupuis, J.B., Goguen, P., Grenier, G.: Changes to telehealth practices in primary care in New Brunswick (Canada): a comparative study pre and during the COVID- 19 pandemic. PLoS ONE **16**(11), e0258839 (2021). https://doi.org/10.1371/journal.pone.0258839

25. Chang, J., Ren, Q., Ji, Y., Xu, M., Xue, R.: Secure medical data management with privacy-preservation and authentication properties in smart healthcare system. Comput. Netw. **212**, 109013 (2022). https://doi.org/10.1016/j.comnet.2022.109013

26. Eslami, P., Kalhori, S.R.N., Taheriyan, M.: eHealth solutions to fight against COVID-19: a scoping review of applications. Med. J. Islam Repub. Iran **35**(1), 1–14 (2021). https://doi.org/10.47176/mjiri.35.43

27. Karadag, A., Sengul, T.: Challenges faced by doctors and nurses in wound care management during the COVID-19 pandemic in Turkey and their views on telehealth. J. Tissue Viability **30**(4), 484–488 (2021). https://doi.org/10.1016/j.jtv.2021.09.001

28. Rees, G., Peralta, F., Scotter, C.: The implications of COVID-19 for health workforce planning and policy: the case of Peru. Int. J. Health Plann. Manag. **36**, 190–197 (2021). https://doi.org/10.1002/hpm.3127

Data Science

Adaptation of a Process Mining Methodology to Analyse Learning Strategies in a Synchronous Massive Open Online Course

Jorge Maldonado-Mahauad[1]([⊠]), Carlos Alario-Hoyos[2], Carlos Delgado Kloos[2], and Mar Perez-Sanagustin[3]

[1] Department of Computer Science, Universidad de Cuenca, Cuenca, Ecuador
jorge.maldonado@ucuenca.edu.ec
[2] Department of Telematics Engineering, Universidad Carlos III de Madrid, Getafe, Spain
{calario,cdk}@it.uc3m.es
[3] Institute de Recherce Informatique de Toulouse, Université de Toulouse, Toulouse, France
mar.perez-sanagustin@irit.fr

Abstract. The study of learners' behaviour in Massive Open Online Courses (MOOCs) is a topic of great interest for the Learning Analytics (LA) research community. In the past years, there has been a special focus on the analysis of students' learning strategies, as these have been associated with successful academic achievement. Different methods and techniques, such as temporal analysis and process mining (PM), have been applied for analysing learners' trace data and categorising them according to their actual behaviour in a particular learning context. However, prior research in Learning Sciences and Psychology has observed that results from studies conducted in one context do not necessarily transfer or generalise to others. In this sense, there is an increasing interest in the LA community in replicating and adapting studies across contexts. This paper serves to continue this trend of reproducibility and builds upon a previous study which proposed and evaluated a PM methodology for classifying learners according to seven different behavioural patterns in three asynchronous MOOCs of Coursera. In the present study, the same methodology was applied to a synchronous MOOC on edX with $N = 50{,}776$ learners. As a result, twelve different behavioural patterns were detected. Then, we discuss what decision other researchers should made to adapt this methodology and how these decisions can have an effect on the analysis of trace data. Finally, the results obtained from applying the methodology contribute to gain insights on the study of learning strategies, providing evidence about the importance of the learning context in MOOCs.

Keywords: Learning analytics · Learning behaviour · Learning strategies · Process mining · Massive open online courses

1 Introduction

One of the greatest challenges of Massive Open Online Courses (MOOC) learners is to be able to self-direct and self-regulate their learning process and adjust their strategies according to the particular context in order to achieve their learning objectives

J. Herrera-Tapia et al. (Eds.): TICEC 2022, CCIS 1648, pp. 117–136, 2022.
https://doi.org/10.1007/978-3-031-18272-3_9

[29]. In the past years, and due to the massive amount of data collected from MOOC platforms, several researchers in the Learning Analytics (LA) community have focused on the analysis of learners' trace data to unveil their learning strategies and propose new classifications accordingly [19, 22]. Several methods and techniques have been applied to analyse these trace data, such as unsupervised machine learning techniques, sequence mining algorithms, transition graphs or hidden Markov models [13, 19]. All these methods are event-based approaches; where an event is defined as an action of the learner with the course content, tools or learning platform functionalities. However, recently researchers from the Process Mining (PM) field, who are experts in the analysis of data processes, proposed novel methods to unveil learning strategies from big data looking for other representations to understand how self-regulated learning processes occurs [2, 3, 15]. Process Mining techniques can be used to discover models that describe and represent sequences of interactions between learners and course materials [3]. In these recent studies, PM techniques have shown to be very robust to understand users' interactive workflows within a particular system in both structured and unstructured processes. Moreover, compared with other techniques such as sequence mining, transition graphs or hidden Markov models, whose outputs are difficult to relate with natural learning processes and to draw meaningful insights about them. In this sense, PM provides encouraging results for understanding learning processes [6]. Moreover, is a suitable approach for studying learning strategies, as a dynamic regulatory activity carried out during a learning task [25], facilitating the discovery of end-to-end learning process models using the recorded events. But, despite the encouraging results obtained using PM techniques, results from one study do not necessarily apply to other contexts. So, there has been an increasing interest in LA research in replicating studies across contexts [9, 10, 16], although studies of this nature are still scarce in part due to the variation of the instructional conditions [11]. Therefore, new analyses with different data should be done to understand the validity of PM methods in other learning environments and contribute providing more evidence about the impact of the learning context on learners' behaviour and study strategies. To continue this trend of reproducible science, this work builds upon the analytical methodology proposed in a previous study by [18] for unveiling students' learning strategies in self-paced MOOCs in Coursera. In that research, seven different learning strategies were identified, and learners were classified into three groups: samplers, comprehensive, and targeting learners. In the present study, we adapt this particular PM methodology and analyse its application in a MOOC deployed over the edX platform, delivered in a synchronous mode, where the digital resources were developed in English language and consisted in video-lectures, graded and non-graded assessments and other resources. The aim of this adaptation effort is two-fold: (1) to understand whether we could replicate (partially or totally) the analysis conducted in [18] and what methodological decisions we had to change for this purpose and; (2), to extend the current knowledge about students' learning strategies in MOOCs and the influence of the learning context.

2 Related Work

2.1 Analysis of Learning Strategies in MOOCs: Methods and Techniques

To study SRL strategies in online environments, researchers have followed two different approaches: Aptitude-based and Event-based approaches [7]. Aptitude-based approaches offer insights about how learners believe they are using their learning strategies while studying (e.g., self-reports). Event-based approaches conceive learning strategies as a set of events (i.e., actions) that learners perform while they are studying. Event-based approaches overcome some of the weaknesses of aptitude-based approaches, since the former use detailed records of each learner's behaviour, engagement, and other types of interactions with course contents to extract conclusions about their behaviour. However, observing learning strategies in MOOCs, even when these manifest as a set of events or actions, involves several challenges, such as: (a) how to transform traces of fine/coarse-grained data into interpretable behaviour (learning strategies); (b) how to identify and observe behavioural changes; and (c) how to understand whether an observable behaviour relates to a particular learning strategy or to more than one [23].

Recent advances in the evolving disciplines of LA and PM have contributed to overcome these challenges. LA focuses on the human interpretation of data and could provide insights into learning strategies [4], while PM focuses on the application of computational techniques on event-based learning activities to discover sequence of learning behaviour [3]. Examples of these advances are the work done by [21], who applied PM techniques in a MOOC of Coursera with 43,218 learners to understand their learning processes analysing how they performed watching video-lectures and taking assessments. In [18] they used the fuzzy miner algorithm to extract seven types of learning strategies from learners enrolled in four MOOCs of Coursera. Other authors such as [14] used PM to explore learners' quiz-taking behaviour and interaction patterns in a learning management system. Finally, authors in [3] also used PM and clustering techniques to describe the learning behaviour of four groups of learners.

These prior works set the basis to start considering PM as a suitable technique for analysing sequences of learning behaviour. However, more examples and replication studies are needed since both the methodological decisions involved in the use of PM and the context in which the data is gathered may strongly condition the final results.

2.2 Learning Strategies Across Contexts

One of the most important concerns in today's scientific community is that of reproducibility. A key domain in which reproducibility has been identified as a particularly important problem is that of Psychology [23]. Psychology researchers have observed a systematic trend wherein results from studies carried out in one (original) context do not reliably transfer or generalise to other contexts [23, 26]. Examples of contextual factors and changes include everything from demographic variables of participants to the physical or virtual environment in which the study is carried out. This trend has highlighted that fact that results from scientific experiments should always be: (1) sufficiently contextualised and reported on accordingly and (2) replicated across different contexts.

Research in education has found that, just as is the case in Psychology research, the outcomes regarding the impact on learning are also highly dependent on context. Several studies have found that learning outcomes and learner engagement are highly dependent on the context in which the learning occurs [20, 27]. This issue has recently begun to be explored in the LA literature by examining the effect of a course structure/design on passing rates [5]. By leveraging the literature on learning design (the science of structuring and sequencing instructional activities) [17] found that certain course designs (context) lead to significantly different passing rates than others [5]. [8] also demonstrated in a replication study that classifications of learners according to their behaviour varies from a MOOC deployed in Coursera or in FutureLearn, a platform created for promoting a socio-constructivist learning approach [4].

2.3 Research Questions

Two research questions drive this study with the aim of understanding how the methodology for detecting learning strategies proposed in [18] adapts to other learning contexts:

RQ1: To what extend can we replicate (partially or totally) the methodology applied in the previous study by [18] to extract students' learning strategies in a MOOC?

RQ2: How do students' learning strategies in this new context differ from those from the previous study?

The objective of the *RQ1* is to analyse and discuss what the methodological decisions are needed for applying the same methodology in a different context and see the implications on the final analysis. Regarding *RQ2*, as shown in prior research, learning is highly dependent on context, and the structure and characteristics of a course can have a direct effect on learners' behaviour. In order to understand whether the learning strategies found in [18] vary in this new context, we will analyse two aspects: (1) the learners' behavioural patterns in a synchronous MOOC in edX; and (2) how learners can be classified according to their behaviour and learning outcomes.

3 Method

Some decisions were taken during the process to adapt the methodology developed by [18] to the new learning context. We specified in the text indicating *[Decision-X]*, where "X" corresponds to the number of the methodological decision taken.

3.1 Context: MOOC and Sample

This study used data from one MOOC on "Introducción a la programación en Java" offered by Universidad Carlos III de Madrid in edX. The course was taught in English and the materials were organised into five modules. This MOOC included video-lectures and numerous interactive activities as formative and summative assessments. Figure 1 presents the course structure. This MOOC followed a synchronous approach, and the contents were released weekly. The course was open from April 28th, 2015 until June 30th of the same year. The estimated learners' workload was between five to seven hours per week. To pass the course the learners needed to obtain 60% of the final grade. Summative assessments (exams) had a weight of 75% of the final grade. The rest, 25% of the grade, was assigned to programming activities that consisted of two peer assessments. The final study sample comprised $N = 50{,}776$ online learners that at least completed one video-lecture in the MOOC. The sample selection differs from the study by [18], study in which the subjects were selected based on if they had answered or not a self-reported SRL survey *[Decision-1]*.

Week 0	
General Topic	VL VL VL VL VL
Week 1	
Topic 1	VL AF AF AF VL AF AF AF VL AF AF
Topic 2	VL AF AF AF AF VL VL AF AF AF AF AF AF
Topic 3	VL AF AF VL AF AF AF AF
Topic 4	VL VL AF VL AF AF
LAB 1	VL AF AF AF AF AF AF AF AF AF AF
RECAP	VL VL VL VL
EXAM 1	AS
SELF-EVALUATION	AF AF AF AF AF AF AF
SELF-EVALUATION	VL
Week 2	
Topic 1	VL AF AF VL AF AF AF AF AF
Topic 2	VL AF AF VL AF
Topic 3	VL VL AF AF AF
Topic 4	VL AF VL AF VL AF VL AF
LAB 2	VL AF AF AF AF AF AF AF AF
RECAP	VL VL VL
EXAM 2	AS
SELF-EVALUATION	AF AF AF AF AF AF AF AF
SELF-EVALUATION	VL

Week 3	
Topic 1	VL AF VL AF VL AF AF AF
Topic 2	VL VL AF AF AF AF
Topic 3	VL AF VL AF VL AF AF VL AF AF
Topic 4	VL VL AF VL AF VL AF AF
LAB 3	VL AF AF AF
RECAP	VL VL VL VL VL VL VL
EXAM 3	AS
PEER ASSESSMENT 1	AS
SELF-ASSESSMENT 1	AF
SELF-EVALUATION	AF AF AF AF AF AF AF
SELF-EVALUATION	VL
Week 4	
Topic 1	VL AF VL AF AF VL AF
Topic 2	VL AF VL AF AF AF VL VL
Topic 3	VL AF AF VL AF VL AF
Topic 4	VL AF AF AF VL AF AF VL AF AF VL VL
LAB 4	VL AF AF AF AF AF AF AF AF
RECAP	VL VL
EXAM 4	AS
SELF-EVALUATION	AF AF AF AF AF AF AF AF AF
SELF-EVALUATION	VL
Week 5	
Topic 1	VL AF AF VL AF VL AF AF
Topic 2	VL AF VL VL AF VL
Topic 3	VL AF VL AF VL AF AF VL AF VL AF
Topic 4	VL VL VL
LAB 5	VL AF AF AF AF AF
RECAP	VL VL
EXAM 5	AS
PEER ASSESSMENT 2	AS
SELF-EVALUATION	VL

Fig. 1. Structure of the course presenting the contents of each week. VL = video-lecture, AF = formative-assessment, AS = summative-assessment.

3.2 Procedure

To extract students' learning strategies, we followed the stages proposed in [18]. Specifically, they adapted the PM2 methodology [6], and defined four phases to obtain the process model from learners' behaviour in interaction with the course content: (1) extraction stage, (2) event log generation, (3) model discovery and (4) model analysis.

Extraction Stage. The data used in this study were related to learners' commitment with the MOOC contents. These contents were presented in the course as a sequence of different digital resources such as video-lectures, and formative/summative activities. In [18] they only considered interactions with video-lectures and summative activities. In the present study, we extended the data employed to characterise the learners' interaction with the course content by considering the following resources: *LTI* activities (integrating an external development environment called *Codeboard*), graded activities, navigation between modules, tabs and clicks on the home page in edX *[Decision-2]*. Each time a learner interacted with a digital resource in edX, a log with a learning event was generated and stored. This raw data was organised in different files classified in general data, forums, and personal data containing information about learners' behaviour.

Event Log Generation Stage. For creating the event log in this stage, we built upon the two conceptual assumptions defined in [18]: (1) to adopt the same definition of study session as a period of time in which the MOOC platform registered continuous activity of a learner within the course, with intervals of inactivity no greater than 45 m and; (2) to adopt the same definition of an interaction as an event triggered by a learner when this interact with resources from the MOOC. In comparison with the authors in [18], where they defined only six possible interactions, we defined ten types of possible interactions (Table 1) depending on the MOOC structure and the digital resource the learner interacted with *[Decision-3]*. This extension on the number of interactions was a necessary step in order to consider the content provided in the course. Table 1 presents the ten types of interactions defined, which are related to video-lectures, assessments, home view page, and navigation between modules and tabs.

As a result, we defined an event log that contained: (a) the user identification, (b) a time stamp, (c) the interaction performed, and (d) the number of the session in which the event was triggered when learners engaged with MOOC contents. Table 2 presents part of the event log used as an example. We also defined success in a synchronous MOOC based on the grades that learners achieved during the course (at least 60% of the grade in the course), as authors in [18] also did. On the contrary, we did not include the SRL profile as part of the event log *[Decision-4]*.

Model Discovery Stage. Given the exploratory context of this study in which it was necessary to handle complex processes, we selected the same Disco algorithm and their implementation in the Disco commercial tool [12] as authors in [18] also did. The resulting process model was confirmed using the implementation of the Celonis algorithm. Both implementations use a variation in the fuzzy miner algorithm that produced interesting synopses of the learning process in comparison with other techniques [24].

Model Analysis Stage. As a result of the previous stages, we generated a process model that contained learners' behaviour (see Fig. 2). Then, we analysed the observed behaviour in order to unveil learning strategies. For this stage, we identified the most frequent interaction sequences performed by learners that characterised each session, that is the learner's path followed in the MOOC within a session (see Fig. 3). As authors in [18] did, we ordered the different variants of the sessions from the most common to the least common. The most common ones were assigned to a category that described a session pattern. For example, we analysed the first variants of these sessions and observed that comprised interactions consisting in beginning a video-lecture, then completing or reviewing a video lecture and then ending the session. Therefore, a pattern of *"Only video-lecture"* was defined (i.e., learners working in sessions only with video-lectures).

Table 1. Types of interactions defined based on course resources

Course resource	Interaction	Description
Video-lecture	Begin	Begin but not complete watching a video-lecture that was not previously completed
	Complete	Complete watching more than the 75% of the video-lecture for the first time
	Review	Watch (part of) a video-lecture that was completely watched in the past
LTI activity	Assessment Formative	Attempt to solve a non-graded activity at the first time
	Assessment Formative Review	Go back to a non- graded assessment that was previously visited
Graded activity	Assessment Summative Try	Attempt to solve a graded activity without achieve it
	Assessment Summative Complete	Successful attempt to solve a graded assessment for the first time
	Assessment Summative Review	Go back to a graded assessment that was previously completed successfully
Home Page	Home View	Go to the home page of the course
Modules, Tabs	Navigation	Go through modules (vertically) or tabs (horizontally) looking for specific content

Table 2. Example of the minimal columns of the event log generated

UserId	Time stamp	Interaction	# Session
28	1434522567	Assessment-Formative	1
28	1434522567	Video-Lecture-Complete	1
161	1430520885	Assessment-Formative	1
161	1430520885	Navigation	1
161	1430520885	Navigation	1

Authors in [18] recommend repeating this procedure several times for analysing the rest of the variants in the sessions. This was done using the same Python script developed ad hoc to do this classification task. As a result, we obtained twelve types of sessions (interaction patterns) that learners made.

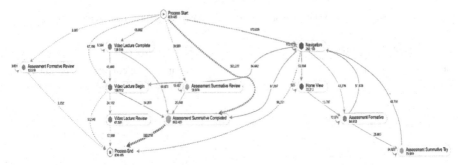

Fig. 2. Full process model obtained using Celonis software, containing all the interactions by sessions. The process model shows ten possible interactions that learner can perform with the course content. Thick dotted line represents the most common path followed by learners.

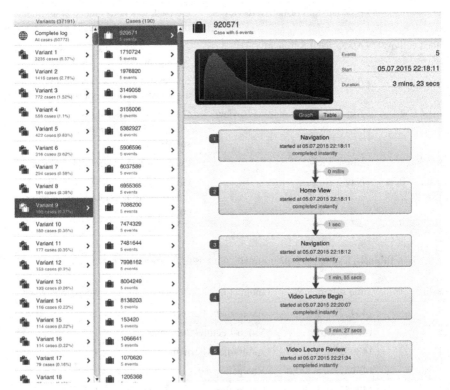

Fig. 3. List of the 37,191 variants of sessions obtained using Disco software performed by 50,776 learners in the MOOC. The "variant 9" shows five interactions (events) with four interaction sequences and time associated with the duration of the session.

4 Results

4.1 RQ1: To What Extend Can We Replicate (Partially or Totally) the Methodology Applied in the Previous Study by [18] to Extract Learners' Learning Strategies in a MOOC?

Most of the process in [18] could be applied to the new MOOC. However, some methodological decisions were made to adapt to the structure and data collected in the edX platform, especially in the data-set extraction and log-data construction. In this section we present what were these decisions.

Study Sample [Decision 1]. The study sample of the synchronous MOOC deployed in edX was composed of online learners that at least completed one video-lecture, unlike in the case of the previous study in which the sample was composed of learners who completed an SRL survey. This decision was made because two other previous studies [18, 19] observed that learners' behaviour in the platform was not related with the self-regulatory profile reported in that questionnaire, which is also related to the discussion about the validity of self-reported data in psychological studies [28].

Mapping the Nature of Interactions with Course Resources [Decision 1 and 3]. The MOOC structure of the edX course contained more digital resources compared with the ones in Coursera due to the course design characteristics (video-lectures, formative activities, graded activities, navigation between modules, tabs and clicks on the home page). Accordingly, we mapped the course resources with the possible interactions of the learners and defined ten types of interactions instead of the six defined in the previous study (asynchronous MOOC in Coursera).

Self-reported Information [Decision 4]. This study did not include a self-reported SRL profile of the students (as it was done in [18]) as part of the event log. This variable was found to not have an influence in the process of exploring the patterns of the behaviour found. However, knowing the self-reported profile of the learners helps to have a better understanding of the characteristics of the students and relate their profile to their actions. To sum up, these four decisions lead us to adapt the methodology used in [18] in the context of this study.

4.2 RQ2: How do Learners' Learning Strategies in This New Context Differ from Those from the Previous Study?

To answer this research question, two analyses were conducted. Next, we present the results of these analyses.

a) Analysis of Learners' Behavioural Patterns in a Synchronous MOOC in edX. We obtained twelve types of interaction sequence patterns that learners made when they engaged with the MOOC (see Table 3). The description of each interaction sequence pattern was grounded upon whether a session only contained a certain type of interaction (e.g., sessions consisting of *only-video-lectures* without any assessment activity) or whether the session contained certain type of interaction sequences between interactions that are considered important for the learning process (e.g., sessions where learners went from *trying a summative-assessment* to a *video-lecture* activity). Once the most common sessions patterns were extracted from the main process model (see Fig. 2), we obtained a specific process model for each pattern (see example in Fig. 4). Twelve distinct types (patterns) of sessions were extracted: *(1) Only assessment-summative-complete*: Session pattern in which learners worked only passing graded assessments. This is the most common type of session: 44.11% of the total number of sessions corresponded to this type. *(2) Only video-lecture to assessment-summative-complete*: Session pattern in which learners began working with video-lectures (either beginning, completing) and then successfully solved a graded assessment (summative) for the first time (see Fig. 4): 13.44% of the sessions corresponded to this type.

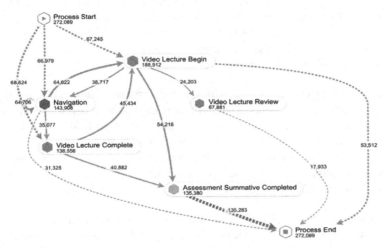

Fig. 4. Only video-lecture to assessment summative complete session pattern performed by learners in a MOOC

(3) Only video-lecture: Session pattern in which learners worked only with video-lectures. Learners performed sessions that consisted of watching at least one video-lecture and did not contain assessment activities. Learners could begin, complete, review video-lectures or perform combinations of them (i.e., begin and then complete, begin and then review, complete and then review): 10.78% of the sessions corresponded to this type. *(4) Only assessment-summative*: Session pattern in which learners worked only with summative assessments. Learners performed sessions that consisted in trying at least one summative assessment and did not watch any video-lecture. Learners could try, complete, review summative assessments or performed combinations of them (i.e., try and then complete, try and then review, complete and then review) while they were interacting with the course: 10.03% of the sessions corresponded to this type. *(5) Only assessment-formative*: Session pattern in which learners worked only with formative assessments. Learners performed sessions that consisted of attempting at least one formative assessment and did not watch any video-lecture. Learners could attempt or review

formative assessments or perform combinations of them (i.e., attempt an assessment and then end the session, attempt and then review, review and then end the session): 9.59% of the sessions corresponded to this type. *(6)Combined:* Session pattern in which learners combined from two up to four sessions patterns mentioned in this section: when the combination is up to two, all types of sessions were considered as part of this combined session pattern; when the combination is up to three, sessions consisting in work only with video-lectures and only with assessments were not considered as part of this combined session pattern; when the combination is up to four, sessions consisting in working only with video-lectures, only with assessments and explore were not considered as part of this combined session pattern: 4.15% of the sessions corresponded to this type. *(7) Only-assessment:* Session pattern in which learners worked between formative and summative assessments in the same session. Learners could attempt to solve or review a non-graded assessment activity (formative) and try to complete (pass) a graded assessment activity (summative) while they were interacting with the course: 2.27% of the sessions corresponded to this type. *(8) Only video-lecture to assessment-formative:* Session pattern in which learners began working with video-lectures (either beginning, completing or reviewing) and then attempted to solve a non-graded activity at the first time: 2.24% of the sessions corresponded to this type. *(9) Explore:* Session pattern in which learners worked only beginning video-lectures (without completing) or attempting some non-graded formative assessments. *(10) Assessment-summative-try to Only-video-lecture:* Session pattern in which learners attempted to solve a graded activity incorrectly and then worked with video-lectures (begin, complete, review video-lectures or combinations of them). *(11) Video-lecture-complete to assessment-summative-try:* Session pattern in which learners completed a video-lecture and then attempted to solve a graded activity without managing to do it. *(12) Others:* We have classified as other to those sessions that were long and disperse, as they do not fit into any of the above-mentioned session patterns.

Table 3. Percentage of session patterns performed by learners (N = 800,485 sessions)

Session patterns	# Sessions (%)
(1) Only assessment-summative-complete	353,090(44.11%)
(2) Only video-lecture → assessment-summative-complete	107,623(13.44%)
(3) Only video-lecture	86,306(10.78%)
(4) Only assessment-summative	80,310(10.03%)
(5) Only assessment-formative	76,791(9.59%)
(6) Combined	33,253(4.15%)
(7) Only assessment	18,205(2.27%)
(8) Only-video-lecture → assessment-formative	18,000(2.24%)
(9) Explore	10,095(1.26%)
(10) Assessment-summative-try → only-video-lecture	9,463(1.18%)
(11) Others	6,644(0.83%)
(12) Video-lecture-complete → assessment-summative-try	705(0.08%)

b) Learners' Classification According to Their Behaviour and Learning Outcomes.
To answer this question learners ($N = 50,776$) were grouped based on the identified sessions patterns. We use the agglomerative hierarchical clustering as in [18]. The resulting dendrogram was used to identify the optimal number of clusters (qualitative). Then, using the *Gaussian mixture* and *K-means* clustering techniques, we confirmed the number of clusters based on the silhouette score (quantitative). This led to selecting the solution with four clusters (see Fig. 5). Table 4 describes the resulting clusters in terms of: (a) the ten session patterns used for grouping the learners (we discarded video-lecture-complete to assessment-summative-try and others given that both types are less than 1% of all sessions), (b) the mean in terms of session performed, (c) the number of learners, (d) the number of learners that passed/failed the course.

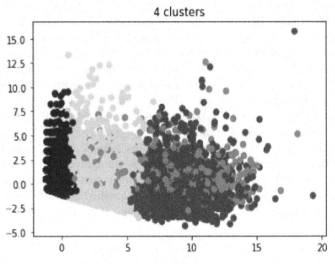

Fig. 5. Scatter Plot with silhouette score 0.571

The resulting clusters indicate different types of learning strategies deployed by learners while they were facing the MOOC. If we look for specific differences between the different clusters, we can describe them as follows (see Table 4; Table 5; Table 6 and Fig. 5):

Cluster 0 – Sampling Learners: This cluster was composed of learners that on average visited only once or twice the course exploring the course content. Specifically, they visited the video-lectures and follow through the proposed path by the course to visit formative assessments but without attempting or ending any activity proposed, just exploring the content to see the big headlines. This cluster is composed of the largest number of learners ($n = 30,415$), but they fail passing the course.

Cluster 1 – Targeting Learners: This cluster was composed of learners that on average performed a low number of sessions. Although they were active learners, they had low activity in the course in comparison with the next groups (clusters 2 and 3, see Table

Table 4. Means of session patterns per cluster performed by learners (N = 800,485)

Session patterns	Cluster 0	Cluster 1	Cluster 2	Cluster 3
	M (SD)	M (SD)	M (SD)	M (SD)
Assessment-summative-try → only-video-lecture	.00(.07)	.29(.62)	1.49(1.63)	1.62(1.68)
Combined	.01(.11)	1.26(1.33)	3.91(3.40)	4.08(3.36)
Explore	.14(.38)	.23(.56)	.39(.66)	.62(.85)
Only-assessment-summative-complete	.00(.00)	**10.79**(13.66)	**47.03**(32.67)	**69.15** (27.79)
Only-assessment	.00(.08)	.74(1.10)	1.43(1.31)	2.04(1.35)
Only-assessment-formative	**.76**(.095)	1.78(2.31)	5.70(4.90)	**9.54**(5.42)
Only-assessment-summative	.00(.07)	**2.65**(3.88)	**9.96**(6.93)	**14.03**(6.19)
Only-video-lecture	.33(.68)	**2.22**(3.18)	**9.94**(8.63)	**15.90**(9.63)
Only-video-lecture → assessment-formative	**.37**(.617)	.32(.73)	.40(.72)	.37(.64)
Only-video-lecture → assessment-summative-complete	.00(.00)	**2.86**(4.30)	**15.92**(11.81)	**24.59**(10.64)
N_sessions_on_average_per_cluster	1.69(1.37)	23.37(25.59)	97.77(61.68)	142.761(45.77)
N_learners	**30,415**	**17,829**	**651**	**1,881**
Fail_course	30,415	17,786	492	1,005
Pass_course	**0**	**43**	**159**	**876**

4, Table 5 and Table 6). They worked superficially with the course materials. These learners after watching video-lectures attempted to pass summative assessments leaving formative assessment aside (sessions were mainly oriented to passing the summative assessments). This behaviour shows that learners in this cluster focused on passing the course more than on achieving a deep understanding of the contents and self-evaluating their progress. This cluster is composed of a great number of learners ($n = 17,829$), but only a few of them passed the course ($n = 43$, compared with clusters 2, 3).

Cluster 2 – Low Comprehensive Learners: This cluster was composed of learners that on average performed a large number of sessions in comparison with the previous two groups (clusters 0, 1). They worked intensively with the course materials. These learners watched the video-lectures, attempted formative and then summative assessments (which is the path designed by the instructors in the course). They focused on summative more than formative assessments (see Table 4, Table 5 and Fig. 6). Also, after watching video-lectures they intended to pass summative assessments and worked less with formative assessments (in comparison with cluster 3). However, learners in this cluster performed more sessions working with summative assessments than with formative ones. In this cluster, a large number of learners passed the course ($n = 159$, in comparison with cluster 1).

Cluster 3 – Highly Comprehensive Learners. This cluster was composed of learners that on average performed a large number of sessions and worked with more intensity with the course contents than learners in the rest of the clusters (see Table 4; Table 5 and Fig. 6). Learners in cluster 3 performed more sessions that consisted in working with video-lectures before they passed a summative assessment. Also, they performed more sessions either with formative or summative assessments in comparison with learners in cluster 2. This behaviour showed the intention of learners to achieve a deep understanding of the contents and self-evaluate their progress. Learners in this cluster also performed sessions in which they worked intensively only with video-lectures in comparison with the rest of the learners in the different clusters.

Finally, Table 6 presents comparisons between the four clusters based on the distributions of the session patterns. Between clusters 2 and 3 there are no statistically significant differences, while pair comparisons between clusters 0–1, 1–2, 1–3 showed statistically significant differences.

To analyse the relationship between students' learning behavioural patterns and their performance in the course we followed the same methodology applied in [18] and compared how learners performed the different sessions patterns depending on their achievements (passing or not passing the course). However, learners in clusters 2 and 3, classified as low and highly comprehensive learners respectively, behaved differently in terms of passing the course. Although learners in these clusters worked on average the same number of sessions in the course (no statistical differences observed), their study strategies differ (Table 7).

Table 5. Differences in session patterns between cluster 2–3

Session patterns	Cluster 2	Cluster 3	t	p	r
	M	M			
Assessment-summative-try → only-video-lecture	1.49	1.62	−.95	.342	.06
Combined	3.91	4.08	−1.44	−.49	.07
Explore	.39	.62	−6.94	< .001***	.39
Only-assessment-summative-complete	**47.03**	**69.15**	−8.02	< .001***	.49
Only-assessment	1.43	2.04	−5.38	< .001***	.33
Only assessment-formative	5.70	**9.54**	−8.91	< .001***	.50
Only assessment-summative	9.96	**14.03**	−6.91	< .001***	.43
Only video-lecture	9.94	**15.90**	−7.86	< .001***	.45
Only-video-lecture → assessment-formative	.40	.37	.50	.61	.03
Only video-lecture → assessment-summative complete	**15.92**	**24.59**	−8.63	< .001***	.51
N_sessions_on_average_per_cluster	97.77	142.76	−17.05	< .001***	.49
N_learners	**651**	**1,881**			

Note: *** p < .001; marks statistically significant differences.

Table 6. Comparison between clusters of learners based on the session patterns

Cluster #	Cluster #	χ2	p
0	1	281.35	< .001***
1	2	194.99	< .001***
1	3	529.99	< .001***
2	3	15.18	.231

Note: *** p < .001 marks statistically significant differences.

Highly comprehensive learners (cluster 3): (a) worked more in sessions that consisted in watching video-lectures and then passing summative assessments, (b) worked more with formative assessments and worked in combination with summative and formative assessments, and (c) on average explored more the course contents.

In contrast, *low comprehensive learners* (cluster 2): (a) worked more in sessions in which they tried to pass a summative assessment (but failed) and then went back to work with video-lectures (begin, complete or review), and (b) worked more with combinations of the different session patterns in comparison with highly comprehensive learners. In addition, *low comprehensive learners* tried to pass summative assessments but when failing, they work in video-lectures, probably trying to find information in the video-lectures that helped them to pass the summative assessments. In contrast, *highly comprehensive learners* worked first with video-lectures and then passed summative assessments. This behaviour suggests that this type of learner is trying to achieve a deep understanding of the contents and self-evaluate their progress working more with formative assessments.

Table 7. Differences in session patterns performed on average by learners in clusters 2–3 that passed the course

Session patterns	Cluster 2 (pass)	Cluster 3 (pass)	t	p	r
	M	M			
Assessment-summative-try → only-video-lecture	2.25	1.49	4.89	< .001***	.32
Combined	5.89	3.82	6.24	< .001***	.40
Explore	.34	.50	−3.07	< .002**	.17
Only-assessment	1.90	2.12	−2.04	< .045**	.13
Only-assessment-formative	10.94	11.85	−2.08	< .038**	.14
Only-video-lecture → assessment-summative complete	30.62	31.85	−2.20	< .028**	.13
N_sessions_on_average_per_cluster	88.81	88.814	−.0029	.998	.000
N_learners	**159**	**876**			

Note. ** p < .05, *** p < .001 marks statistically significant differences.

5   Conclusion and Discussion

5.1   Summary of Results

Even if conducting the same study across different context is complicated by variations in instructional conditions [11], in this study we made an effort of replicability and applied the PM methodology in [18] to a data set of a synchronous MOOC in the edX platform. Two main results were obtained. Firstly, the PM methodological approach can be replicated, but it requires taking three key decisions that are dependent to the context of application: (1) the sample size, which will vary from experiment to experiment; (2) mapping the nature of the interactions based on the structure of the MOOC under analysis, but keeping the metric of session and interaction; and (3) eliminating students' SRL profile obtained from a SRL-questionnaire as a control measure. Secondly, the adaptation of this methodological approach extends the findings in [18] by identifying new learning strategies that are highly dependent on the course structure. In contrast to the six self-regulatory patterns and three groups of learners identified in the prior work, we identified twelve patterns and four groups: 1) Sampling learners, 2) Targeting learners, 3) Low Comprehensive learners, and 4) Highly Comprehensive learners.

5.2   Implications

The present findings have implications both for (a) the methods used in the LA community for analysing trace data, and (b) for theory and practice of SRL. **Regarding the implications in LA methods**: This paper sheds some light on the aspects to be considered when doing replication studies using students' trace data. Replicating an analytical method requires taking decision about how raw data is processed. In order to evaluate the reproducibility of the results, these decisions should be carefully reported, especially when they require some level of pre-processing or abstraction. When applying PM approaches, the data pre-processing and data abstraction is key. For example, how students' work session is defined or how student's interactions with the course content are mapped into a logfile may have an impact on how learners' strategic patterns are observed. This study shows that, when replicating methodological approaches based on PM, the granularity of the data when defining students' interaction should maintained from one study to another. That is, if student's interaction with the course content is defined by interaction with a particular resource, this should be the level of granularity for the analysis, and no combinations of interactions should be considered for the analysis. In current literature, most of studies take as a reference the interactions with the course content as a basis [13, 24], however, this could vary when changing platform, since the nature of the data collected may vary. The results of this study emphasize the importance of including the decision-making process on data preprocessing as part of any analysis in order to be able to compare the results from one study to another. Moreover, this pre-processing should consider simplifying the raw data by keeping only those types of interaction that could be translated from one platform to another, even if this means losing some data in the process. Of course, simplifying the data may mean also simplifying the results, but more studies of this type should be reported so that the community arrives to agreements such as a standard of a minimum logfile to facilitate replication studies. **Regarding the implications for SRL theory and practice:** The adaptation of this methodology extends the findings in [18] by identifying new learning strategies that are highly dependent on the course structure. Twelve sessions patterns and four groups of learners were found. Learners classified as sampling and targeting in this study are similar to those found in [18]. However, in contrast to the prior work, *Comprehensive learners* can be classified into *highly* and *low* comprehensive. *Highly comprehensive learners* seemed to be deeper learners following the designed path of the course, trying to achieve a deep understanding of the contents and self-evaluating their progress through the intensive work with formative activities. In contrast, *low comprehensive learners* seemed to be more strategic, following a pattern that consisted in passing summative activities and working less with formative ones. While in the prior work, [18] analysed a MOOC with only summative assessment activities, the MOOC in the present study included more than 160 formative activities. These results suggest that the strategies adopted by the learners are highly dependent on the context, and in particular, on the course content and structure. Moreover, these results align with prior work that show how course structure and design conditions students' behaviour [1, 17]. However, more studies, and particular A/B experimental experiments, should be conducted in order to provide robust evidences on how context affects learners' behaviour. Moreover, and beyond replication efforts, we believe that the identified behavioural patterns can inform the design of learning environments by either supporting the implementation of precise learner modelling or by providing enough scaffolding to at-risk learners who remain working actively in the MOOC.

5.3 Limitations

The findings of this study are subject to some limitations given the nature of the data and methodological choices. First, this study is based on learners' behavioural data that were automatically collected by the MOOC platform, so the analyses are limited to the data provided. Second, and for the effort of replication, the set of interactions obtained for analysing the learners' behaviour through study sessions were simplified to consider video-lectures, assessments (either summative or formative) and navigation interactions. Considering data such as the students' forum activity may alter the strategic patterns encountered. Future work will expand this study considering data from collected by other researchers from other courses and platforms in order to conduct a meta-analysis following the same methodology.

Acknowledgments. This paper was supported by the ANR LASER (156322) and Vicerrectorado de Investigación de la Universidad de Cuenca. The authors acknowledge PROF-XXI, which is an Erasmus+ Capacity Building in the Field of Higher Education project funded by the European Commission (609767-EPP-1-2019-1-ES-EPPKA2-CBHE-JP).

References

1. Alario-Hoyos, C., et al.: Understanding learners' motivation and learning strategies in MOOCs. Int. Rev. Res. Open Distrib. Learn. **18**(3), 119–137 (2017)
2. Alonso-Mencía, M.E., et al.: Self-regulated learning in MOOCs: lessons learned from a literature review. Educ. Rev., 1–27 (2019)
3. van den Beemt, A., et al.: Analysing structured learning behaviour in massive open online courses (MOOCs): an approach based on process mining and clustering. Int. Rev. Res. Open Distrib. Learn. **19**(5) (2018)
4. Boekaerts, M.: Self-regulated learning: a new concept embraced by researchers, policy makers, educators, teachers, and students. Learn. Instr. **7**(2), 161–186 (1997)
5. Davis, D., et al.: Toward large-scale learning design: categorizing course designs in service of supporting learning outcomes. In: Proceedings of the Fifth Annual ACM Conference on Learning at Scale, p. 4 (2018)
6. van Eck, M.L., Lu, X., Leemans, S.J.J., van der Aalst, W.M.P.: PM^2: A process mining project methodology. In: Zdravkovic, J., Kirikova, M., Johannesson, P. (eds.) CAiSE 2015. LNCS, vol. 9097, pp. 297–313. Springer, Cham (2015). https://doi.org/10.1007/978-3-319-19069-3_19
7. Endedijk, M.D., Brekelmans, M., Sleegers, P., Vermunt, J.D.: Measuring students' self-regulated learning in professional education: bridging the gap between event and aptitude measurements. Qual. Quant. **50**(5), 2141–2164 (2015). https://doi.org/10.1007/s11135-015-0255-4
8. Ferguson, R., Clow, D., Beale, R., Cooper, A.J., Morris, N., Bayne, S., Woodgate, A.: Moving through MOOCS: pedagogy, learning design and patterns of engagement. In: Conole, G., Klobučar, T., Rensing, C., Konert, J., Lavoué, É. (eds.) EC-TEL 2015. LNCS, vol. 9307, pp. 70–84. Springer, Cham (2015). https://doi.org/10.1007/978-3-319-24258-3_6
9. Ferguson, R., Clow, D.: Consistent commitment: patterns of engagement across time in massive open online courses (MOOCs). **2**, 55–80 (2015). https://doi.org/10.18608/jla.2015.23.5
10. Gardner, J., et al.: Replicating MOOC predictive models at scale. In: L@S, p. 1 (2018)
11. Gašević, D., et al.: Learning analytics should not promote one size fits all: the effects of instructional conditions in predicting academic success. Internet High. Educ. **28**, 68–84 (2016)
12. Günther, C.W., Rozinat, A.: Disco: discover your processes. BPM (Demos). **940**, 40–44 (2012)
13. Jovanović, J., et al.: Learning analytics to unveil learning strategies in a flipped classroom. Internet High. Educ. **33**, 74–85 (2017)

14. Juhanák, L., et al.: Using process mining to analyze students' quiz-taking behavior patterns in a learning management system. Comput. Hum. Behav. **92**, 496–506 (2017)
15. Kizilcec, R., Pérez-Sanagustín, M., Maldonado, J.J.: Self-regulated learning strategies predict learner behavior and goal attainment in massive open online courses. Comput. Educ. **104**, 18–33 (2017). https://doi.org/10.1016/j.compedu.2016.10.001
16. Kizilcec, R.F., Brooks, C.: Diverse big data and randomized field experiments in MOOCs. Handb. Learn. Analytics, 211–222 (2016)
17. Laurillard, D.: Teaching as a design science: Building pedagogical patterns for learning and technology. Routledge (2013)
18. Maldonado-Mahauad, J., et al.: Mining theory-based patterns from big data: identifying self-regulated learning strategies in massive open online courses. Comput. Hum. Behav. **80**, 179–196 (2018)
19. Matcha, W., et al.: Detection of learning strategies: A comparison of process, sequence and network analytic approaches. In: Scheffel, M., Broisin, J., Pammer-Schindler, V., Ioannou, A., Schneider, J. (eds.) EC-TEL 2019. LNCS, vol. 11722, pp. 525–540. Springer, Cham (2019). https://doi.org/10.1007/978-3-030-29736-7_39
20. Meyer, J.H.F., Muller, M.W.: Evaluating the quality of student learning. I—an unfolding analysis of the association between perceptions of learning context and approaches to studying at an individual level. Stud. High. Educ. **15**(2), 131–154 (1990)
21. Mukala, P., et al.: Exploring students' learning behaviour in MOOCs using process mining techniques. Eindhoven. BPM Center Report BPM-15-10. BPMCenter.org, Eindhoven Google Scholar (2015)
22. Pardo, A., et al.: Generating actionable predictive models of academic performance. In: Proceedings of the Sixth International Conference on Learning Analytics & Knowledge - LAK 2016, pp. 474–478 (2016). https://doi.org/10.1145/2883851.2883870
23. Pashler, H., Wagenmakers, E.-J.: Editors' introduction to the special section on replicability in psychological science: a crisis of confidence? Perspect. Psychol. Sci. **7**(6), 528–530 (2012)
24. Saint, J., Gašević, D., Pardo, A.: Detecting learning strategies through process mining. In: Pammer-Schindler, V., Pérez-Sanagustín, M., Drachsler, H., Elferink, R., Scheffel, M. (eds.) EC-TEL 2018. LNCS, vol. 11082, pp. 385–398. Springer, Cham (2018). https://doi.org/10.1007/978-3-319-98572-5_29
25. Sonnenberg, C., Bannert, M.: Discovering the effects of metacognitive prompts on the sequential structure of SRL-processes using process mining techniques. J. Learn. Analytics **2**(1), 72–100 (2015)
26. Stanley, D.J., Spence, J.R.: Expectations for replications: are yours realistic? Perspect. Psychol. Sci. **9**(3), 305–318 (2014)
27. Trigwell, K., Prosser, M.: Improving the quality of student learning: the influence of learning context and student approaches to learning on learning outcomes. High Educ. (Dordr) **22**(3), 251–266 (1991)

28. Veletsianos, G., et al.: The life between big data log events: learners' strategies to overcome challenges in MOOCs. AERA Open **2**(3), 2332858416657002 (2016). https://doi.org/10.1177/2332858416657002
29. Winne, P.H., Hadwin, A.F.: Studying as self-regulated learning. Metacognition Educ. Theor. Pract. **93**, 27–30 (1998)

Ecuador Agricultural Product Price Forecast: A Comparative Study of Deep Learning Models

Sherald Noboa$^{(\boxtimes)}$ (ID), Erik Solís (ID), and Erick Cuenca (ID)

Yachay Tech University, Urcuquí, Ecuador
{sherald.noboa,erik.solis,ecuenca}@yachaytech.edu.ec

Abstract. The application of forecasting techniques in the agriculture industry started with a commodity prediction almost a century ago. However, currently, the same application is not explored in the same field. For instance, in Ecuador, farmers have to suffer the volatility of prices of agriculture products during all the growing stages since they do not count on any forecasting method for preventing future events. Therefore, this work aims to reduce the gap of knowledge by presenting the implementation of five deep learning algorithms which forecast weekly and monthly prices of avocado, red onion, and cucumber from the wholesale market of Ibarra city in Ecuador. Results have shown that single models are still suitable for forecasting, although, the best performance comes from compound models such as Conv-LSTM-MLPs. Likewise, with proper hyperparameter tuning, the last model showed an error reduction (MAE) of 23% for weekly avocado prices.

Keywords: Forecasting · Commodity · Deep learning · Hyperparameter tuning

1 Introduction

Humanity developed agriculture some centuries ago, and since then this field has evolved thanks to new technological inventions. Currently, many institutions with different funding sources have been able to create reliable data collection techniques to take advantage of data. For example, in India, Microsoft uses artificial intelligence sensors to detect pest attacks, and notify farmers immediately through voice calls [23]. Likewise, the United Kingdom, through public funds, uses machine learning methods combined with advanced sensor techniques to predict the yield of the wheat harvest [19]. In short, with the growing demand for food, the agricultural supply chain should be guaranteed. Besides, governments, farmers, and intermediaries should be active participants in the decision-making that leads to sustainable agriculture. In the Ecuadorian context, the agricultural sector is one of the fundamental pillars of its economy, accounting for 9% of the gross domestic product. That is, it occupies the fourth most important

© The Author(s), under exclusive license to Springer Nature Switzerland AG 2022
J. Herrera-Tapia et al. (Eds.): TICEC 2022, CCIS 1648, pp. 137–151, 2022.
https://doi.org/10.1007/978-3-031-18272-3_10

economic sector for this country [20]. However, prices of agricultural products in wholesale markets in Ecuador tend to be volatile. For example, in the last ten years of record prices, in the Ibarra wholesale market, the price of a 50 kg bag of red onions tend to vary from $10 to $45 in less than 6 months[1]. Therefore, farmers could take advantage of more convenient prices if they have adequate information. Indeed, this volatility could be mitigated with the help of a forward price prediction approach.

The prediction of future prices using data recorded over a similar interval of time is called time series forecasting, and it is a field of interest in many wealthy industries such as pharmaceuticals, aerospace, and financial [4]. This interest is because we are living in a world where each second many data are created, and it can be collected over time. Thus, taking advantage of those data make any company more valuable and competitive in their respective market [3]. Nonetheless, less industrialized fields such as agriculture in developing countries such as Ecuador have been little explored in the use of forecasting techniques. Under this context, a forecasting process can be a decisive tool used by farmers in order to get better information before growing their products. A common scenario for farmers is that earning of their harvest is conditioned to the market prices and after the final balance of income and expenses, they may present money losses. Even worst, some farmers grow their products with loans, so in the end, farmers end up with more debt [1]. Therefore, a good price prediction can make a difference in considering the next crop and consequently a profitable harvest.

According to the literature, Artificial Neural Networks (ANN) can be applied for time series forecasting [9, 25, 27]. Indeed, in the last ten years, their usage has become mainstream thanks to many data based on applications that use Machine Learning (ML) and Deep Learning (DL) algorithms [32]. DL form part of ML methods, which are based on ANN. For instance, DL models focus on speech recognition and machine translation in the field of natural language processing (NLP). Notice that these applications work with text which is a sequence of words, in other words, a type of sequential data. Likewise, these models also work with another type of sequential data, as time series [10]. For example, multilayer perceptrons (MLPs) is a ML method that works with sequential data. However, there exist other models called Recurrent Neural Networks (RNN) that were created especially for working with sequential data. Besides, this model has evolved into Long-Short Term Memory (LSTM) which solved most RNN first problems [11]. Indeed, since DL models are based on ANN, they can be mixed with other models or features. For instance, a convolution layer from Convolutional Neural Networks (CNN) can be combined with a LSTM for the prediction of short-term wind speed [8]. In short, DL models have shown their potential in real-world applications, so they have become the default choice when working with sequential data.

---

[1] http://sinagap.mag.gob.ec/sina/PaginasCGSIN/VisorReporte.aspx,   last   access: June 2022.

There is an unexplored study gap for predicting time series using DL models applied in agricultural product prices in Ecuador. Besides, the literature suggests several DL methods for forecasting time series; however, we must take into account the features of the series, which can positively or negatively affect [15]. Therefore, for the above reasons, this work aims to test five DL models and compare their forecasting performance. The methods used for this purpose are MLPs, RNN, bidirectional LSTM, Conv-LSTM, and Conv-LSTM-MLPs. The datasets consist of weekly and monthly prices of avocado, red onion, and cucumber from the Ibarra, Ecuador wholesale market.

This paper is organized as follows. Section 2 describes the related works researched. The proposed methodology is presented in Sect. 3. The experiments are performed in Sect. 4, while the results are discussed in Sect. 5. Finally, Sect. 6 concludes this study and presents future work.

2   Related Works

Currently, the trend for forecasting commodities prices is DL models based on ANN [25]. For instance, Yu et al. [30] and Ribeiro et al. [22] forecast prices on wholesale markets in China and Brazil, respectively. They used ANN architectures that currently are no longer used as main models. However, the insights behind their studies are that ANN are fantastic at mapping non-linearities, and mixing models improve results. Nowadays, most of the studies reviewed for time series forecasting show a clear dominance of RNN models [25].

Notice that RNN are the facto models used for sequential data as time series. For example, Weng et al. [28] forecast cucumber prices in China and proved that RNN performed better than BPNN and ARIMA models for daily, weekly, and monthly data. Moreover, the most used RNN model is LSTM due to its concept of long-term dependencies, which makes it even better than traditional RNN for forecasting data. To illustrate, Sabu et al. [23] forecast monthly arecanut prices in India and found that the LSTM model can obtain incredible results in comparison with a traditional forecasting method such as ARIMA, SARIMA or HoltWinter's Seasonal method. Likewise, Nassar et al. [18] and Alameer et al. [2] presented hybrid models based on RNNs to forecast different agricultural products and coal fluctuations prices, respectively. In both studies, the DNN-LSTM and ATT-CNN-LSTM models outperform traditional ML algorithms, classic statistical models, and the LSTM model.

Nevertheless, not all the studies suggest the superiority of DL models. For example, Ly et al. [14] forecast one agricultural product as cotton and one commodity as oil and demonstrated that with the proper tuning of ARIMA, it can get slightly better results than LSTM. Lastly, Ly et al. [14] also suggested that mixing both models improve significantly the results. Therefore, mixing several models can be a good option in order to get the advantages of each model.

Most of the studies do not use the concept of hyperparameter tuning for the training part of their models, which normally tend to minimize the error. Another important aspect to take into consideration is the training and testing ratio. It seems like there is not a consensus for this ratio like in Weng et al. [28] study where 98% of the dataset was used for training, whereas most of the studies use a ratio of 80:20 or 70:30. Furthermore, few authors clearly explain how the datasets were treated before the data were fed into the DL models, except the authors that describe the sliding window technique [2, 14, 26].

Common things about the studies and their data used to forecast commodities or agricultural products were that most of the authors picked monthly data. Moreover, the period of these observations seems to be irrelevant because there is a significant variance between all the authors' studies evaluated here. Finally, the cost functions for the forecasting performance criteria vary among several options, such as Mean Absolute Percentage Error (MAPE), Mean Absolute Error (MAE), Root Mean Square Error (RMSE), and Mean Squared Error (MSE) [18, 28, 32].

3   Methodology

The proposed methodology consists of five main steps, as shown in Fig. 1. Each step is described in detail in the following.

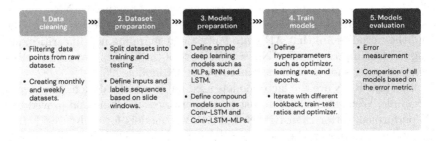

Fig. 1. Flowchart of the proposed methodology.

3.1   Data Cleaning

The original data came in a .xls format, downloaded manually from the Public Agricultural Information System of Ecuador (SIPA) website[2]. This platform has historical prices of any agricultural product that has been produced in Ecuador. For example, our data for avocados consists of historical prices of one box of 55 pounds. Likewise, for cucumber and red onion, the prices represent a bag of 100 pounds. All the datasets have records from 6/6/2011 up to 8/2/2021, and they all are valued in dollars (USD). Besides, each data originally has 949 registers of prices in about ten years; however, there is no consensus on the date of registration. Thus, for a proper data feeding process for our models, we need to clean and put the data in a time series format such as weekly and monthly registers. Normally, time series have a frequency, i.e., all the data must be weekly or monthly. Therefore, after the filtering process, the datasets contain 472 and 118 records weekly and monthly, respectively.

[2] http://sipa.agricultura.gob.ec/index.php, last access: June, 2022.

3.2   Data Preparation

For all the models used in this study, the starting ratio for training and testing was 70:30. Which means 70% of all registers in the datasets will be used for training and the remaining part for testing. Since the ratio portion is important, it will be changed for other experiments. After that, the sliding window method is applied to all the training data points. This procedure is necessary because we want to capture all the possible patterns. This method consists of shifting a window with a fixed width called the look-back parameter. The window is going to slide one step at a time. As a result, the training dataset is divided into several mini-sets. The information inside the look-back hyperparameter is called inputs features, and the next value at the right edge of the window is called a label [17]. For this study, the look-back hyperparameter was 4. The next step after the creation of multiple sequences based on the sliding window approach is to shuffle and batch these sequences. In fact, the batch size was set to a fixed value of 32 since this number is recommended by some authors for smaller datasets [12,25]. Lastly, mixing the data is important because it ensures a better data distribution during training, reducing the variance and the overfitting scenario.

3.3   Models Preparation

Table 1 presents the five model architectures proposed to compare. Each model is described in detail in the following sections.

Table 1. Features of the five proposed models.

Features	Models				
	MultiLayer perceptron	Recurrent neural network	Bidirectional LSTM	Conv-LSTM	Conv-LSTM-MLPs
Input layer (1)	10 neurons	40 neurons	32 neurons	32 neurons	32 neurons
Hidden layers	2 layers: 20 & 10 neurons	2 layers: 2 RNN stack with 40 cells each one	2 layers: 2 LSTM stack with 32 cells each one	3 layers: 1 conv, & 2 LSTM stack with 32 cells each one	5 layers: 1 conv, 2 LSTM stack with 32 cells each one, & 2 layers with 30 and 20 neurons
Output layer (1)	1 neuron	1 neuron	1 neuron	1 neuron	1 neuron
Activation function	RELU	tanh	tanh, Sigmoid	RELU, tanh, Sigmoid	RELU, tanh, Sigmoid

Multilayer Perceptrons (MLPs). This model consists of a feedforward neural network with four layers in total. The input layer contains ten input nodes, and the second and third layers are hidden layers with twenty and ten neurons, respectively. Finally, the output layer has only one node for the predictions. This model is being tested since some authors recommended it as a starting point when working with ANN [21].

Recurrent Neural Network (RNN). Remember that MLPs networks work for general purposed data; meanwhile, RNN models were created for sequential data, i.e., a time series such as our datasets. This model works with two recurrent neural networks stacked one after another [31]. It means that two layers are working together, and both networks are helping each other to capture most of the information that our time series have. Note that the RNN networks are in the model's hidden part, and each layer network has forty RNN cells.

Bidirectional LTSM. LSTM network was the solution for the vanishing gradient problem that RNN used to have when processing longer sequences. Likewise, there exists a variation of the traditional LSTM model. The main change with the traditional LSTM network is that now two LSTM layers are stacked one after another, and each layer has a different flow of information [24]. Thus, the name bidirectional means that one of the layers has a forward direction, and the other layer has a backward direction. Thus, the network is learning information in two ways, which can be an advantage when the dataset shows no patterns.

Conv-LSTM. This model can be called a compound model since we are using the convolution feature of CNN. The advantage of using a convolution layer at the beginning of the model is that this operation maps spatial features normally present in images. However, the same concept can be applied to time series. In detail, the convolution layer has 32 filters, the kernel size is 3×3, and the activation function is *RELU*. In this layer, the input data change a bit since the convolution feature works with 3D input shape data; however, this issue is addressed with an increase in the dataset dimension. The next LSTM layers consist of two LSTM stacks, one after another, which have 32 LSTM cells [8].

Conv-LSTM-MLPs. This model is a little more complex than the above model. Now, at the end of the LSTM layers, the model added a MLPs structure that, in theory, should reduce the error measurement. This happens because the Conv-LSTM layers capture the most important patterns presented in time series, and MLPs are in charge of the generalization of those patterns [16]. In other words, we are combining the advantages of each architecture. Moreover, the Conv and LSTM layers have the same features as the above described. Lastly, the MLPs added have two layers with 30 and 10 neurons.

3.4   Training Models

The training part for all the five models proposed is the same. It consists of fine-tuning hyperparameters such as optimizer, learning rate, and the number of epochs. The aim of tuning these hyperparameters is to find the values that best fit the proposed models.

Optimizer. The optimizer is the algorithm in charge of the learning process, which seeks to minimize the loss function, i.e., it determines the correct weight parameter values. This work has tested two optimizers: Stochastic Gradient Descent with momentum (SGDm) and Adam. SGDm is a traditional optimizer that, on certain occasions, performs better than Adam if the correct momentum value is found [7]. Likewise, Adam is implemented due to its features such as faster convergence, sparse gradients on noisy problems, etc. [13].

Learning Rate. The learning rate (LR) is a hyperparameter of the optimizer that determines how fast or slow the model will learn. In general, a high learning rate accelerates the convergence of the model to a suboptimal solution. In contrast, a low learning rate produces a not conversion of the model [29]. For this work, a scheduler callback function was implemented with SGDm to find the optimal LR for all the proposed models. Therefore, each model will have a different LR value. It consists of starting with a low learning rate, but after some epochs, it will increase. Then, after complete training with different LR values, we plot it against the loss for each model and find at which value the models converged.

Epochs. This hyperparameter indicates the number of passes that the entire training dataset has completed through the model [5]. Thus, the number of epochs is important because the correct number guarantees proper learning; in other cases, the model could not learn. For this purpose, we choose a high number of training epochs and plot it against the loss for all the models. In our work, the loss shows stability at 200 epochs.

3.5   Models Evaluation

The error measurement calculates the distance between the forecast value and the ground truth. Usually, the error measurement can be classified depending on the task being performed. In our case, the most used metrics for a regression task are Mean Absolute Error (MAE) or Mean Square Error (MSE). On the one hand, MSE tends to prior larger errors, i.e., one higher error is enough to get a high number with this metric. However, on the other hand, MAE tends to evaluate each error one by one. Therefore, it does not penalize large errors as much as the MSE. Thus, the MAE metric will be used in this work because we aim to get higher accuracy in the forecast values [6].

4   Experiments

This section presents three experiments developed for this work. It is worth mentioning that for all the experiments, step forecasting is carried out.

4.1   Materials

This work was implemented using Python3 and two Python-based DL frameworks: TensorFlow 2.6.0 and Keras API 2.4.0. The environment that gathers all these technologies is Google Colaboratory (Colab), which allows users to access hosted Jupyter notebooks using computing power to deploy prototype models. Finally, the data that will be fed to our models consists of different datasets with monthly and weekly records.

4.2   Experiment 1: Comparison Between Models

This experiment compares the forecasting performance of the five DL models on the weekly and monthly avocado datasets. This experiment aims to seek a lower MAE value. In simple terms, the two models that get closer to real values will be used in the following two experiments.

4.3   Experiment 2: Best Models with Different Datasets

This experiment tests the best models using different datasets, such as the weekly and monthly red onion and cucumber datasets. This experiment aims to verify the generalization capabilities of the proposed models.

4.4   Experiment 3: Hyperparameter Tuning and Optimizer

This experiment evaluates the possibility of decreasing the metric error measurement and training time through some changes in different hyperparameters. We varied three hyperparameters: train-test ratio, look-back, and optimizer.

4.5   Experimental Setup

All the variations for the experiments are presented in Table 2. In summary, notice that in the three experiments that used SGDm, the LR varies between 10^{-7} and 10^{-5} thanks to the scheduler function. Besides, experiments one and two share several hyperparameters such as SGDm with momentum $= 0.9$, look-back, epochs, batch size, loss function, and train-test ratio. Lastly, Adam was used only for experiment three, and the hyperparameters were the following $LR = 10^{-3}$, $beta\_1 = 0.9$, $beta\_2 = 0.999$, $epsilon = 10^{-7}$, and amsgrad=False.

Table 2. Hyperparameter values for all experiments.

Hyperparameter	Value space	Observation
Batch size	32	Fixed value for all experiments
Epochs	200	Fixed value for all experiments
Loss function	MAE	Fixed metric for all experiments
Optimizer	SGDm, & Adam	SGDm is used in all experiments, Adam is used only for experiment three.
Learning rate	10^{-7}, 10^{-6}, 10^{-5}, & 10^{-3}	Scheduler callback function with SGDm, Adam has default setup
Train-test ratio	60:40, 70:30, & 80:20	70:30 ratio is used in all experiments, the others only for experiment three
Lookback	4, 8, & 16	4 value is used in all experiments. 8, &16 only for experiment three
Datasets	weekly, monthly: avocado, red onion, & cucumber	Avocado is used for experiment 1 & 3. The others only for experiment two

5 Results and Discussion

5.1 Comparison Between Models

Table 3 shows the general performance of the models in terms of training time, train MAE and test MAE for the weekly and monthly avocado dataset. Note that the lower values for each frequency are in bold. To start with training time, it is noticeable that for both temporalities, the RNN models outperform the others. In terms of train MAE, we obtained that the bidirectional LSTM model surprisingly got the lower value. Nonetheless, in the test part, it performs worse than all the models. Remember that we mostly care about the test MAE, so Bidirectional LSTM cannot be taken into consideration as the best model. Finally, the two best models for the test part are Conv-LSTM-MLPs and Conv-LSTM for weekly and monthly, respectively. Therefore, both models are going to be used for the next experiments. Figure 2 and Fig. 3 show a comparison between three models. We can see that weekly records allow the models to approach the real values, i.e., a lower error than monthly records.

Table 3. Results of experiment one using the avocado dataset.

Model	Train time(s)		Train MAE		Test MAE	
	Weekly	Monthly	Weekly	Monthly	Weekly	Monthly
MLPs	16.08	12.18	2.10	5.70	2.01	4.45
RNN	**14.17**	**11.27**	2.10	5.70	2.03	3.66
Bidirectional LSTM	18.48	13.45	**1.95**	**5.04**	2.23	3.60
Conv-LSTM	35.50	20.33	2.06	5.44	1.83	**3.02**
Conv-LSTM-MLPs	36.48	21.59	2.03	5.61	**1.80**	3.31

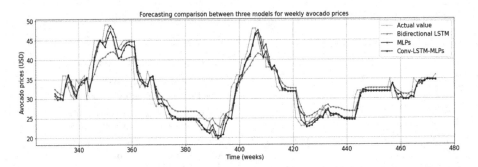

Fig. 2. Forecasting comparison between three models for weekly avocado prices on test dataset.

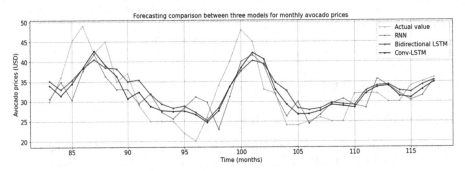

Fig. 3. Forecasting comparison between three models for monthly avocado prices on test dataset.

5.2   Best Model with Different Datasets

Table 4 and Table 5 show the experiments' outcomes for the red onion and the cucumber datasets, respectively. On the one hand, the Conv-LSTM model outperforms its version with MLPs at the end of the network. This performance is reflected in terms of training time, train MAE and test MAE for the weekly dataset. On the other hand, the cucumber dataset showed better results with Conv-LSTM-MLPs. It is worth mentioning that monthly frequency for both cases gave us the worst results, the same as the avocado dataset. Finally, Fig. 4 and Fig. 5 show the performance of both models with these datasets.

5.3   Hyperparameter Tuning and Optimizer

The results of all the experiments are summarized in Table 6. Firstly, the lookback value and train-test ratio influence a lot on the training time, i.e., if both grow, so does the training time. Secondly, SGDm optimizer takes less time for training in all the experiments in comparison with the Adam optimizer. Moreover, the train and test MAE results showed that SGDm works better with the look-back value set to 4 regardless of the train-test ratio. Likewise, Adam performs better with eight as the look-back value. The difference between iteration

Table 4. Results of experiment two using the red onion dataset.

Model	Train time(s)		Train MAE		Test MAE	
	Weekly	Monthly	Weekly	Monthly	Weekly	Monthly
Conv-LSTM	31.02	**16.00**	**3.01**	6.35	**2.80**	6.12
Conv-LSTM-MLPs	35	16.50	3.52	7.57	3.24	7.33

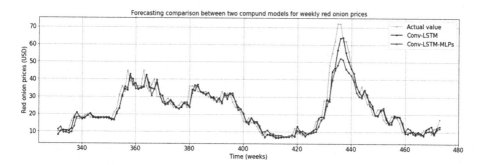

Fig. 4. Forecasting comparison between two compound models for weekly red onion prices on test dataset.

Table 5. Results of experiment two using the cucumber dataset.

Model	Train time(s)		Train MAE		Test MAE	
	Weekly	Monthly	Weekly	Monthly	Weekly	Monthly
Conv-LSTM	23.02	**16**	2.35	3.89	2.05	3.31
Conv-LSTM-MLPs	39.25	21	**1.80**	3.45	**1.50**	2.99

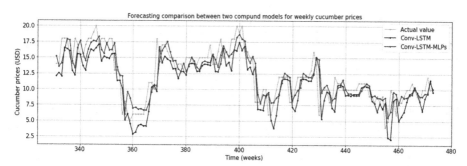

Fig. 5. Forecasting comparison between two compound models for weekly cucumber prices on test dataset.

13 and 16 for train MAE is 0.01 and for the test is 0.02. Besides, both experiments share the train and test ratio. Since their difference is small, Fig. 6 shows a part of the forecasting to see the differences between these iterations.

Table 6. Results of experiment three using the weekly avocado dataset.

Iteration	Model	Train-test ratio	Look-back value	Optimizer	Train time (s)	Train MAE	Test MAE
1	Conv-LSTM-MLPs	60:40	4	SGDm	**31.12**	1.73	1.65
2				Adam	35.23	1.85	1.71
3			8	SGDm	47.50	2.77	2.65
4				Adam	49.60	1.64	1.52
5			16	SGDm	58.20	2.01	1.97
6				Adam	61.36	1.96	1.76
7		70:30	4	SGDm	34.21	2.03	1.80
8				Adam	39.89	2.08	1.88
9			8	SGDm	51.32	2.06	1.90
10				Adam	55.01	1.69	1.61
11			16	SGDm	59.23	2.15	2.07
12				Adam	66.45	1.73	1.66
13		80:20	4	SGDm	37.25	**1.52**	**1.40**
14				Adam	40.63	1.63	1.47
15			8	SGDm	55.12	1.96	1.77
16				Adam	59.78	**1.53**	**1.38**
17			16	SGDm	64.87	1.86	1.67
18				Adam	68.95	1.77	1.67

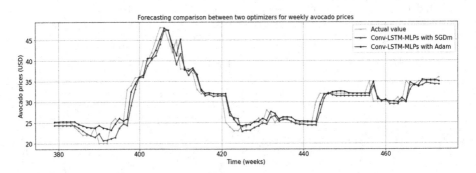

Fig. 6. Forecasting comparison between SGDm and Adam optimizers performance for weekly avocado prices using iteration 13 and 16 setup.

5.4 Discussion

There are many insights that can be driven from the experiments. It was clearly noticed that weekly forecasting results were better than monthly with the three datasets explored. One explanation is that weekly results data presents more observations. Notice that in the related work section, most of the authors work with monthly data. Thus, we can say that it does not depend on the time series frequency but on the amount of data we have. Related to the simple models tested, MLPs surprisingly perform well with both datasets. Thus, it can be considered a benchmark model. RNN is the most efficient model in terms of training time. However, its forecasting behavior was not the expected as the literature suggests, since MLPs were better with weekly data. Bidirectional LSTM showed the best results during the training stage. Nevertheless, the weekly test part showed worst results than all the other models. The performance of the last model is called over-fitting, which means to perform well on train data and worst in test data.

In the forecasting with compound models, combining the convolution layer with normal LSTM layers and/or MLPs layers guarantees better results in both train and test with red onion and cucumber datasets. Also, for weekly avocado and cucumber, the Conv-LSTM-MLPs outperform Conv-LTSM. However, for the weekly red onion, the opposite happened. Thus, we can conclude that more complexity does not mean necessary better results. Indeed, it seems to depend on the features of the dataset. For instance, the cucumber time series is chaotic compared to red onion records. Note also that compound models take double the time for training compared with simple models. This increase in training time is due to the convolution layer, which is an operation that uses more computational resources. Thus, under our experiments, these compound models are the perfect choice if we aim to sacrifice time and architecture complexity for gaining accuracy.

With respect to hyperparameter tuning, it was shown the importance of the right combination of train-test ratio, look-back value, and optimizer. Indeed, during all the experiments, it was clear that SGDm is still a good approach when the learning rate is properly tuned. However, in experiment three, the Adam optimizer has shown a slightly better result with basic settings. Thus, when working with DL models, the researcher should tune the most important hyperparameters to get promising results.

6   Conclusion

This work presents the acquisition, preparation, and forecasting of avocado, red onion, and cucumber prices from the Ibarra, Ecuador wholesale market. The results of our work show that the proposed methods are still suitable for time series forecasting; however, compound models outperform simple architectures in lower error. To continue, after the experimental phase, it was found that the algorithms performed better on weekly data in comparison with monthly data in terms of the MAE metric. Moreover, the importance of tuning the hyperparameters of DL models during training was demonstrated. For instance, the Conv-LSTM-MLPs obtain the most considerable error reduction. Nonetheless, compound models have some constraints, such as the complexity of the network. It means that since the model has two or three layers, it is necessary to have the right combination of each hyperparameter of each layer to perform the right task. That is, our model will work well with commodities prices; however, for other sequential tasks, this model may need another proper tuning.

We could obtain a prediction with better accuracy, but we must increase the model's complexity and thus also increase the training time. Further research should be expanded with the use of transformers algorithm along with multivariate time series to understand better all the variables that participate and affect the price of agricultural products.

References

1. Adämmer, P., Bohl, M.T.: Speculative bubbles in agricultural prices. Q. Rev. Econ. Finance **55**, 67–76 (2015)
2. Alameer, Z., Fathalla, A., Li, K., Ye, H., Jianhua, Z.: Multistep-ahead forecasting of coal prices using a hybrid deep learning model. Resour. Policy **65**, 101588 (2020)
3. Aliev, R., Fazlollahi, B., Aliev, R.R.: Soft computing and its applications in business and economics. In: Studies in Fuzziness and Soft Computing (2004)
4. Arsham, D.H.: Time Series Analysis for Business Forecasting, Aug 2020
5. Brownlee, J.: What is the difference between a batch and an epoch in a neural network? Machine Learning Mastery 20 (2018)
6. Chai, T., Draxler, R.R.: Root mean square error (rmse) or mean absolute error (mae). Geosci. Model Develop. Dis. **7**(1), 1525–1534 (2014)
7. Chee, J., Li, P.: Understanding and detecting convergence for stochastic gradient descent with momentum. In: 2020 IEEE International Conference on Big Data (Big Data), pp. 133–140. IEEE (2020)
8. Chen, G., Li, L., Zhang, Z., Li, S.: Short-term wind speed forecasting with principle-subordinate predictor based on conv-lstm and improved bpnn. IEEE Access **8**, 67955–67973 (2020)
9. Dolling, O.R., Varas, E.A.: Artificial neural networks for streamflow prediction. J. Hydraul. Res. **40**(5), 547–554 (2002)
10. Fang, H., Guo, G., Zhang, D., Shu, Y.: Deep learning-based sequential recommender systems: Concepts, algorithms, and evaluations. In: International Conference on Web Engineering, pp. 574–577. Springer (2019). https://doi.org/10.1145/3426723
11. Hochreiter, S., Schmidhuber, J.: Long short-term memory. Neural Comput. **9**, 1735–1780 (1997)
12. Kandel, I., Castelli, M.: The effect of batch size on the generalizability of the convolutional neural networks on a histopathology dataset. ICT Express **6**(4), 312–315 (2020)
13. Lucero, V., Noboa, S., Morocho-Cayamcela, M.E.: Plant disease classification and severity estimation: A comparative study of multitask convolutional neural networks and first order optimizers. In: Annual International Conference on Information Management and Big Data, pp. 313–328. Springer (2022). https://doi.org/10.1007/978-3-031-04447-2_21
14. Ly, R., Traoré, F., Dia, K.: Forecasting commodity prices using long-short-term memory neural networks. Soc. Sci. Educ. eJournal (2021)
15. Makridakis, S., Spiliotis, E., Assimakopoulos, V.: Statistical and machine learning forecasting methods: concerns and ways forward. PLoS ONE **13**, e0194889 (2018)
16. Manjunath, Y.S.K., Zhao, S., Zhang, X.P.: Time-distributed feature learning in network traffic classification for internet of things. arXiv preprint arXiv:2109.14696 (2021)

17. Mozaffari, L., Mozaffari, A., Azad, N.L.: Vehicle speed prediction via a sliding-window time series analysis and an evolutionary least learning machine: a case study on san francisco urban roads. Eng. Sci. Technol. Int. J. **18**(2), 150–162 (2015)
18. Nassar, L., Okwuchi, I., Saad, M., Karray, F., Ponnambalam, K.: Deep learning based approach for fresh produce market price prediction. In: 2020 International Joint Conference on Neural Networks (IJCNN), pp. 1–7 (2020)
19. Pantazi, X.E., Moshou, D., Alexandridis, T., Whetton, R.L., Mouazen, A.M.: Wheat yield prediction using machine learning and advanced sensing techniques. Comput. Electron. Agric. **121**, 57–65 (2016)
20. Pino, S., Aguilar, H., Apolo, A., Sisalema, L.: Contribution of the agricultural sector to the economy of ecuador. critical analysis of its evolution in the period of dollarization. years 2000–2016. Espacios **39**(32), 7 (2018)
21. Ramchoun, H., Idrissi, M.A.J., Ghanou, Y., Ettaouil, M.: Multilayer perceptron: architecture optimization and training. Int. J. Interact. Multim. Artif. Intell. **4**(1), 26–30 (2016)
22. Ribeiro, C.O., de Oliveira, S.M.: A hybrid commodity price-forecasting model applied to the sugar-alcohol sector. Agricult. Nat. Resour. Econ. eJournal **55**, 180–198 (2011)
23. Sabu, K.M., Kumar, T.M.: Predictive analytics in agriculture: forecasting prices of arecanuts in Kerala. Proc. Comput. Sci. **171**, 699–708 (2020)
24. Schuster, M., Paliwal, K.K.: Bidirectional recurrent neural networks. IEEE Trans. Signal Process. **45**(11), 2673–2681 (1997)
25. Sezer, O.B., Gudelek, M.U., Ozbayoglu, A.M.: Financial time series forecasting with deep learning: a systematic literature review: 2005–2019. Appl. Soft Comput. **90**, 106181 (2020)
26. Siami-Namini, S., Namin, A.: Forecasting economics and financial time series: Arima vs. lstm. ArXiv abs/1803.06386 (2018)
27. Solís, E., Noboa, S., Cuenca, E.: Financial time series forecasting applying deep learning algorithms. In: Conference on Information and Communication Technologies of Ecuador, pp. 46–60. Springer (2021) https://doi.org/10.1007/978-981-13-2035-4_3
28. Weng, Y., Wang, X., Hua, J., Wang, H., Kang, M., Wang, F.Y.: Forecasting horticultural products price using arima model and neural network based on a large-scale data set collected by web crawler. IEEE Trans. Comput. Soc. Syst. **6**, 547–553 (2019)
29. Yedida, R., Saha, S.: A novel adaptive learning rate scheduler for deep neural networks. arXiv preprint arXiv:1902.07399 (2019)
30. Yu, S., Ou, J.: Forecasting model of agricultural products prices in wholesale markets based on combined bp neural network -time series model. In: 2009 International Conference on Information Management, Innovation Management and Industrial Engineering, vol. 1, pp. 558–561 (2009)
31. Zaremba, W., Sutskever, I., Vinyals, O.: Recurrent neural network regularization. arXiv preprint arXiv:1409.2329 (2014)
32. Zhang, S.: China's artificial-intelligence boom. The Atlantic **20170216**, 20170924 (2017)

Assessing the COVID-19 Vaccination Process via Functional Data Analysis

Guido Tapia-Riera(✉) ⓘ, Lenin Riera-Segura ⓘ, Christian Calle-Cárdenas ⓘ, Isidro R. Amaro ⓘ, and Saba Infante ⓘ

School of Mathematical and Computational Sciences, Yachay Tech University, Urcuquí, Ecuador
{guido.tapia,lenin.riera,christian.calle,iamaro, sinfante}@yachaytech.edu.ec

Abstract. This manuscript aims to assess the evolution of the COVID-19 vaccination process in some American and European countries via Functional Data Analysis (FDA). Specifically, Functional Principal Components Analysis and Functional Clustering were implemented in a data set consisting of four COVID-19-related variables such as total cases per million, total deaths per million, total tests per thousand, and people fully vaccinated per hundred to explain heterogeneity in the vaccination process. We found that FDA methods are suitable to describe our study problem as, for example, the first two functional principal component corresponding to each variable explains above 96% of the variance. FDA techniques allow us to conclude that vaccines avoid people's deaths from COVID-19, but they do not stop the propagation of the virus.

Keywords: Functional Data Analysis · Functional Principal Components Analysis · Functional clustering · COVID-19

1 Introduction

At the end of 2019, the SARS-CoV-2 began an illness known as COVID-19 in the east of China. Because of its rapid spread at the beginning of March 2020, the World Health Organization (WHO) recognized this illness as a pandemic [1]. Although many actions have been taken to combat the effects caused by COVID-19, this disease continues to affect many countries worldwide, especially countries with poor vaccination campaigns or mitigation measures.

It is known that mathematical models have been thoroughly used to describe several aspects related to different epidemics and pandemics. For example, Daniel Bernoulli modeled several phenomena corresponding to the smallpox epidemic waves through a logistic model [2]. However, many of these models were developed in the previous century. The rapid advance in scientific research and the development of computational sciences have allowed the creation of new mathematical models that improve the results obtained by their predecessors. In this context, FDA has become a powerful technique to analyze data sets composed of observations picked in a time interval. Moreover, FDA has enormous advantages for better interpretation of data over time [2,3].

ⓒ The Author(s), under exclusive license to Springer Nature Switzerland AG 2022
J. Herrera-Tapia et al. (Eds.): TICEC 2022, CCIS 1648, pp. 152–170, 2022.
https://doi.org/10.1007/978-3-031-18272-3_11

1.1 Contribution and Related Work

In recent years, the number of researches and fields that use FDA's methodologies has been growing. For example, researchers have found FDA applications in economics, biology, medicine, meteorology, and others [2–4]. Even more, due to the COVID-19 pandemic, FDA has become a potent tool for modeling this phenomenon as it improves classical statistical approaches. For that reason, in this manuscript, we consider Functional Principal Component Analysis (FPCA) and Functional Clustering to understand the impact of the vaccination process. We do so by analyzing some COVID-19 variables related to the number of cases, deaths, tests, and people fully vaccinated during one year in some American and European countries. The contribution of this work is to provide a robust informative tool for assessing the COVID-19 vaccination process, mainly for policymakers of the aforementioned countries. Nevertheless, this tool is also helpful for policymakers of countries not considered in this work because they can know the keys to getting a successful vaccination campaign (such as Italy, France, or Ecuador) or what mitigation measures could be adapted to nations represented by them.

Now, let us summarize some related works about FDA's methodologies used to study the impact caused by the COVID-19 pandemic. It helps us to better contextualize our results and contributions.

Following the pandemic outbreak, researchers around the globe have proposed several models and techniques to study and forecast the pandemic's effects properly. In 2021, for example, Boschi et al. [5] investigated patterns of COVID-19 mortality across 20 Italian regions and their association with mobility, positivity, and socio-demographic, infrastructural and environmental covariates by means of FDA techniques. In France, Oshinubi et al. [2] used FDA methods to model daily hospitalized, deceased, intensive care unit cases and return home patient numbers along the COVID-19 outbreak, considered as functional data across different departments in France. Recently, Li et al. [6] exploited FDA methods to analyze the time series data of the case and death counts of COVID-19 that broke out in China during the Wuhan lockdown. Regarding the Latin American region, we can mention the work done by Martin-Barreiro et al. [7] and Chaglla et al. [8]. In [7], authors used functional and non-functional techniques to cluster South American countries based on the number of infected cases and deaths from COVID-19, whereas in [8], authors used FDA techniques to conduct an exploratory analysis on a dataset formed by the total cases per million, new cases, new tests, and stringency index of some Latin American countries. In Brazil, Collazos et al. [9] applied statistical methods for functional data to explain the heterogeneity in the deaths number evolution of COVID-19 over different regions of the country. In a broader region but outside of the FDA domain, Riera et al. [10] employed multivariate statistical techniques such as HJ-Biplot and Clustering to study the COVID-19 vaccination process of American and European countries. The present work can be understood as an improved extension of [10] in the sense that the data are no longer considered discrete but functional.

The present manuscript is organized as follows. Section 2 is dedicated to describe the data used, while Sect. 3 briefly introduces FDA's methodologies. A thorough discussion concerning the results is presented in Sect. 4. Conclusions and Further studies are exhibited in Sect. 5. Additional material to Sect. 4 is presented in Appendix A and B.

2 Materials

2.1 Data Description

The data contemplated in the present manuscript was collected from a GitHub public repository[1] which contains summary information from sites such as Our world in Data [11–13] and the Center for Systems Science and Engineering at Johns Hopkins University. In this work, we studied American and European countries, which are Mexico, Ecuador, Colombia, the United States (USA), and Guatemala from America; while, Italy, Germany, the United Kingdom (UK), Poland, and the Netherlands from Europe. To consider these nations, we selected the five that presented the highest population density value per km^2 together with a population greater than or equal to fifteen million, keeping with each continent.

In order to interpret the data from a functional perspective, we consider four variables which are: total cases per million (V1_TC), total deaths per million (V2_TD), total tests per thousand (V3_TT), and people fully vaccinated per hundred (V4_PFV). The values for selected data are accumulated and were taken from 01 April 2021 to 31 March 2022, producing 365 samples for each variable.

2.2 Handling the Missing Data

One of the most frequent problems in statistics is the missing data, which can be caused by numerous reasons, such as loss of follow-up, data collected retrospectively from medical records, etc. In obtaining the data, missing data were found in different observations of two variables (representing 2% of the total data), which are V3_TT and V4_PFV.

To counterbalance the missing data, there are several statistical packages in different programming languages to solve this problem. Most used and developed are AMELIA II [14], mice [15], linear and nonlinear regression, imputeTS, among others. In this work, we used the imputeTS algorithm, which specializes in univariate time series imputation [16] to handle the missing data since it delivers values that are very close to the expected values. This contrasts with the other methods that return as prediction data values lower and higher than the expected values, which no sense, since the considered data are accumulative. The imputeTS algorithm works because, being a univariate time series, it has to use temporal dependencies, whereas most imputation algorithms depend on correlations between attributes [16].

---

[1] https://github.com/owid/COVID-19-data/tree/master/public/data.

3   Methods: Functional Data Analysis

In this section, we briefly introduce some FDA topics. For a deeper understanding of these topics, we refer the reader to [17–20].

As we mentioned before, FDA is a fresh technique in statistics, the methodologies employed by this technique are quite related to Multivariate Statistical Analysis (MSA). Nevertheless, unlike MSA, the FDA's theory is supported mainly by Stochastic Processes, Probability Theory, and Mathematical Analysis. For this work, we use the functional space $L^2(\mathcal{T})$ which contains square integrable real-valued functions defined on the interval $\mathcal{T} \subseteq \mathbb{R}$, these functions can be considered as the realizations of a stochastic process. Formally, $L^2(\mathcal{T})$ is defined as follows

$$L^2(\mathcal{T}) = \left\{ f : \mathcal{T} \longrightarrow \mathbb{R} \ \middle| \ \int_{\mathcal{T}} |f(t)|^2 dt < +\infty \right\}. \tag{1}$$

As usual, the integral defined in (1) has to be computed in the Lebesgue sense. For $f, g \in L^2(\mathcal{T})$, the inner product is defined as follows

$$\langle f, g \rangle = \int_{\mathcal{T}} f(t)g(t)dt.$$

It is known that $L^2(\mathcal{T})$ is a Hilbert space. Now, we introduce formally the definition of Functional Datum.

Definition 1 (Functional Datum). *[17] If a random variable X is defined in a probability space $(\Omega, \mathcal{F}, \mathcal{P})$ and it takes values in a functional space, is known as a functional variable. Then an observation x of X is known a functional datum.*

Note that, for this work the functional space mentioned in the Definition 1 corresponds to $L^2(\mathcal{T})$. The functional variable $X = \{X(t) \ / \ t \in \mathcal{T}\}$ is commonly seen as second-order stochastic process, where $x_1(t), x_2(t), \ldots, x_n(t) \in L^2(\mathcal{T})$ are observations of X. Since in this work the data are taken daily, it follows that the data are equally spaced. FDA assumes that any observation can be expressed as a linear combination sufficiently large of known functions. More precisely, these known functions belong to a basis of functions $\{\phi_1(t), \ldots, \phi_n(t)\}$. It follows that

$$x_i(t) = \sum_{j=1}^{n} a_{ij}\phi_j(t), \quad i = 1, \ldots n,$$

where a_{ij} are called basis coefficients or weights. When the data are non-periodic is common to use a B-spline system as a basis of functions [20]. For further understanding of other bases such as Fourier, Wavelets, Power, and Exponential, the reader is referred to [18,20].

3.1   B-Spline Basis

These splines are piece-joined polynomial curves that are smooth and continuously differentiable. Among the most important characteristics we have that for an order $p \geq 0$: they consist of $p + 1$ pieces of polynomials of order p joined at p internal nodes, B-spline is positive in the domain spanned by $p + 2$ nodes and zero elsewhere, and $p + 1$ B-splines are nonzero for each point. De boor, C. [21] developed the most popular way of building B-spline; an advantage of this method is that several programming languages have implemented it, such as R and `MATLAB`. More precisely, it can be found as `create.bspline.basis()` in the R `fda` package. To determine the number n of functions in the B-spline basis system, we use the following criterion: **number of basis functions = order + number of interior knots** [20]. This relationship also works for any spline basis.

3.2   Smoothing Parameter

Smoothing techniques are helpful when the volume of data are relatively high, there is high variability, and the interpolation is rough. Let us denote the smoothing parameter as λ. The role of this parameter is basically to control the smoothness of a curve. The larger the λ, the closer the basis coefficients are to zero. So, if $\lambda \to +\infty$, we have a polynomial fit. Conversely, if $\lambda \to 0$, we use ordinary least squares, and the fit is linear. For this work, we use the generalized cross-validation (GCV) score [19,20]. To choose the optimal λ, we use the following formula

$$\text{GCV}(\lambda) = \left(\frac{\ell}{\ell - df(\lambda)} \right) \left(\frac{SSE}{\ell - df(\lambda)} \right), \tag{2}$$

where $df(\lambda)$ is the degrees of freedom of λ, SSE is the sum of squared errors (or residuals) between an observation and its estimator, and ℓ the number of sampling points. We are interested in the value of λ, which minimizes GCV.

3.3   Functional Principal Component Analysis (FPCA)

FPCA is an extension of the classical PCA, the latter being a well-known tool for dimension reduction used in MSA. The main difference between them is that through FPCA, unlike the classical PCA, we study the variability of an event according to its evolution over a period of time. Now, let us consider a square-integrable functional variable X, which is a second-order stochastic process, where the observations of X belong to $L^2(\mathcal{T})$. We define mean, covariance, and variance function, respectively. Then for all t, s in $\mathcal{T}$, we get

$$\mu(t) = \mathbb{E}[X(t)],$$
$$Cov_X(t, s) = \mathbb{E}[X(t)X(s)] - \mathbb{E}[X(t)]\mathbb{E}[X(s)],$$
$$Var_X(t) = \mathbb{E}[X(t)^2] - (\mathbb{E}[X(t)])^2.$$

We assume that X is centered, it follows that μ is equal to the zero function for all $t \in \mathcal{T}$. Otherwise, if X is not centered, the principal component analysis would be done through the centered process $X(t) - \mu(t)$. Now, let us define the covariance operator as $\Gamma : L^2(\mathcal{T}) \to L^2(\mathcal{T})$ given by

$$\Gamma[f(t)] = \int_{\mathcal{T}} Cov_X(t,s)f(s)ds, \quad \forall f \in L^2(\mathcal{T}).$$

It is easy to verify that the covariance operator is compact, self-adjoint, and positive. As a consequence of these properties and based on Mercer's Theorem, we have the following representation in $L^2(\mathcal{T})$ for the covariance function

$$Cov_X(t,s) = \sum_{i=1}^{+\infty} \alpha_i f_i(t) f_i(s), \quad \forall t, s \in \mathcal{T},$$

where α_i and f_i are eigenvalues and eigenfunctions of Cov_X, respectively. Even more, $\{\alpha_i\}_{i=1}^{+\infty} \subseteq \mathbb{R}_0^+$ is a decreasing sequence. On the other hand, given any i and j such that $i \neq j$, the eigenfunctions $\{f_i\}_{i=1}^{+\infty}$ satisfy

$$\int_{\mathcal{T}} f_i^2(t)dt = 1 \quad \text{and} \quad \int_{\mathcal{T}} f_i(t)f_j(t)dt = 0.$$

By the Karhunen-Loève Theorem, we have that any observation of X can be expressed as follows

$$x_i(t) = \mu(t) + \sum_{j=1}^{+\infty} \xi_{ij} f_i(t), \quad \forall i = 1, \dots, n, \tag{3}$$

where $\{f_i(t)\}_{i=1}^{+\infty}$ are the functional principal components (FPCs) and $\{\xi_{ij}\}_{j=1}^{+\infty}$ are FPC scores associated to each principal component. The first M FPCs can explain the variance that observations have. It follows that through the first M FPCs, we can approximate all the observations well [18, 19]. Then, without loss of generality, in practice, we commonly use a truncated version of (3), that is,

$$x_i(t) = \mu(t) + \sum_{j=1}^{M} \xi_{ij} f_i(t), \quad \forall i = 1, \dots, n.$$

In addition, it is of great interest to estimate the first M FPCs. Therefore, it is essential to choose an adequate number of FPCs, but this is subjective since it will depend on the type of research and researchers' criteria. However, the first M FPCs are usually chosen such that they can explain at least 85% of the total variance of all observations [19].

3.4 Functional Cluster Analysis

Cluster analysis has become an indispensable tool for researchers when the goal is to perform an exploratory analysis of a given data set. It consists of dividing a data set into subgroups so that their members are similar to each other but different from other subgroups according to a similarity measure. When it comes to functional data, cluster analysis operates similarly but with the additional difficulty that the data belongs to an infinite-dimensional space. As the functional data objects are curves, defining a meaningful distance between them is also a problem of concern. To address these problems, several methods have been proposed. These can be roughly classified into four groups: raw-data clustering, two-stage clustering, non-parametric clustering and model-based clustering [22]. This work uses a model-based clustering technique proposed by Bouveyron and Jacques [23] called functional high dimensional data clustering (funHDDC) because it yields the largest distance inter-cluster. This technique is based on a functional latent Gaussian mixture model and clusters functional data in group-specific subspaces of low dimensionality. As mentioned in [23] and [24], the appropriate number of clusters for a dataset is determined by the Bayesian information criterion (BIC) [25], and the model parameters and the group-specific functional subspaces are estimated by the EM algorithm [26]. Because this work studies four variables, we actually consider a novel general version of funHDDC, which deals with multivariate functional data and is described in [27].

4   Results and Discussion

4.1   Data Smoothing

In this section, we show the findings of applying FDA methodologies to COVID-19 data used in this work. To begin with, we use a B-spline system of order 4 as a functional basis because it minimizes the sum of squared errors (SSE) when we compare it with other basis systems such as Power system (see Appendix A). Therefore, the number of basis functions follows the criterion presented in Sect. 3.1, which means that 367 basis functions are employed for each variable. Also, we use a smoothing parameter $\lambda = 1$ because it minimizes the GCV. Then we plotted on Fig. 1 the data smoothing.

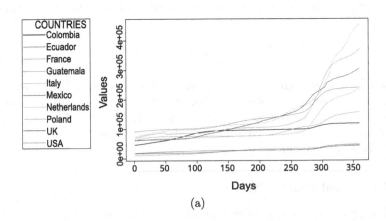

(a)

Fig. 1. Smoothed curves corresponding to (**a**) V1_TC, (**b**) V2_TD, (**c**) V3_TT, and (**d**) V4_PFV.

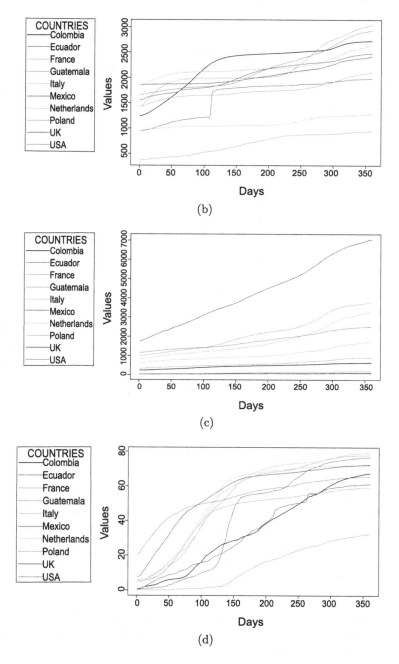

Fig. 1. (*continued*)

As expected, all the curves have an increasing behavior because data used are accumulative. However, France is the exception in Fig. 1(a), around 40 days (May 2021). It takes place due to France removed some false-positives cases from its database [28].

4.2   FPCA

As we mentioned in Sect. 3.3 we are interested in the first M FPCs. Then, we choose $M = 2$ because they explain at least 96% of the total variance. The variance percentage of the FPCs is shown in Table 1, while Fig. 2 presents graphically all the Functional Principal Components shown on Table 1. The first principal component (FPC1) is the most important because it explains the highest variance percentage.

Table 1. Variance explained by FPC1 and FPC2 for all variables.

Variable	FPC1	FPC2
V1_TC	93.6%	4.7%
V2_TD	93.7%	3.7%
V3_TT	99.5%	0.4%
V4_PFV	82%	14.2%

V1_TC. In Fig. 2(a), we note that after about 225 days (November 15, 2021), FPC 1 stops staying constant and starts to have a growing behavior till day 365 (March 31, 2022). Evidently, it might be caused mainly by events such as Halloween, Christmas, New Year's party, Carnival, and in a lesser way, other local celebrations. On the other hand, in the same time interval FPC2 begins to decrease rapidly.

V2_TD. In Fig. 2(b), we observe that FPC1 shows a slight increase during all the periods of time considered in this work. Due to early identification of the virus (through COVID-19 tests) for effective medical treatment and an effective vaccination campaign in each country, the increase in deaths has been slight rather than abrupt as at the pandemic's beginning. However, on the days where events mentioned for V1_TC have taken place, the growing behavior of FPC1 is more robust than on previous days of that events; the disrespect of people towards bio-security measures on that days could have caused this behavior. In contrast, FPC2 presents negative values between August 2021 to March 2022.

V3_TT. In Fig. 2(c), the growing behavior is maintained in FPC1. This behavior is a consequence of the increasing number of cases. On the other hand, FPC2 shows a continuous decrease.

V4_PFV. In Fig. 2(d), FPC1 peaked around day 125 (August 5, 2021), and then there was a decline in the following days considered in this work because people were receiving their recommended doses in the primary series. It is essential to mention that the rate at which FPC1 declined is less than the rate at which it grew before it peaked. Therefore, we deduce that the full vaccination rate was high about August, September, and October 2021, implying that for the events mentioned in V1_TC, many people had the necessary antibodies to fight COVID-19 and prevent their death.

Up to this point, we note the positive impact of the COVID-19 test and vaccination campaigns because it is evident that the increasing behavior of FPC1 of V1_TC is more pronounced than FPC1 of V2_TD. Also, we note that although people have received their recommended doses in the primary series, the number of COVID-19 tests has not diminished; on the contrary, it is growing. The previous two facts allow us to make one of our main deductions: vaccines do not stop the contagion of COVID-19, but they prevent the death caused by this disease, as the Pharmaceutical companies assure.

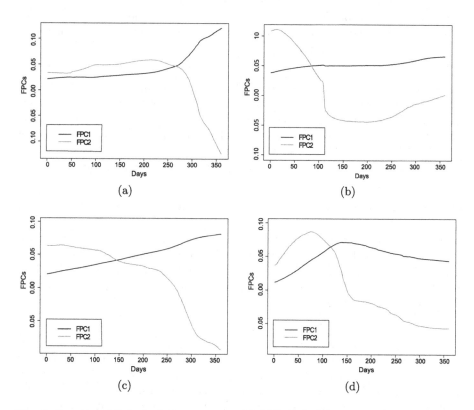

Fig. 2. Functional Principal Components of (a) V1_TC, (b) V2_TD, (c) V3_TT, and (d) V4_PFV.

4.3   FPC Scores

We now focus on describing countries' positions in the plane according to the FPC scores. For this section, we associate FPC scores with the behavior of each country for every one of the studied variables. We mean that if two (or more) countries have similar FPC scores for a specific variable, they have similar behavior regarding the phenomena that explain that variable. Analogous to the previous section, we analyze FPC1 and FPC2 while ignoring the rest of FPCs.

V1_TC. In Fig. 3(a), Ecuador, Mexico, and Guatemala almost have the same value, which is negative in FPC 1 and 2. In both FPCs, Italy, France, and the Netherlands have negative values, while UK and USA have positive values. Only Colombia and Poland have mixed values for the FPCs; specifically, negative for FPC1 and positive for FPC2. After this description, we deduce that Ecuador, Mexico, and Guatemala's behavior is similar. In the same sense, France and Netherlands' behavior is similar too.

V2_TD. In Fig. 3(b), France, the Netherlands, UK, Italy, and Poland have positive values; conversely, Ecuador and Guatemala have only negative values, both cases happen for FPC 1 and 2. The rest of the countries present positive values for FPC1 and negative for FPC2, with Colombia having the most negative value for FPC2. For this case, we identify two groups with similar behavior into its members, the first USA and Mexico and the second UK and Italy.

V3_TT. Analogous to the first case in Fig. 3(c), Ecuador, Mexico, and Guatemala almost have the same value, which is negative for both FPCs. Italia, Francia, UK, and USA have positive values for FPC1. However, the first two have negative values for FPC2, contrary for UK and USA. While Colombia, Poland, and the Netherlands have negative values for FPC1 and positive for FPC2. It is clear that Ecuador, Mexico, and Guatemala formed a group with similar behavior. Poland and Colombia form another group with similar behavior.

V4_PFV. Finally, in Fig. 3(d), UK and USA have positive values for both FPCs, while Mexico, Ecuador, and Colombia have negative values. Furthermore, Poland and Guatemala have positive values for FPC2 and negative for FPC1. On the contrary, France, Italy, and the Netherlands have positive values for FPC1 and negative for FPC2. Similar to all the previous cases, we recognize two groups with homogeneous behavior, which are Mexico and Colombia, while another group is France, Italy, and the Netherlands.

Neighboring countries do not necessarily have the same behavior regarding the COVID-19 pandemic. For instance, Ecuador and Colombia present different behaviors for all the variables. On the other hand, Mexico and Guatemala have similar behavior except in V2_TD and V4_PFV. Using this fact, we can deduce that when a government wants to know if some mitigation measures may work in its country, it should not be compared with the one that has successfully applied these measures. On the contrary, it should compare itself with a country statistically similar to its own.

Through Figs. 3(a)–3(d), we observe that FPC1 is the most important FPC. This is used to get the bulk of the statistical inferences. Also, we note the advantage of using FPCA over the classic PCA. In general, we can establish a relationship between FPC scores and smoothing data. For this case, the relationship is: if a country has a high positive for FPC score 1, then a high value is expected in the last days of the associated curve of that country in Fig. 1. While using the classical PCA, this relationship makes no sense because we do not know a country's behavior over a time interval. To illustrate it, see Appendix B.

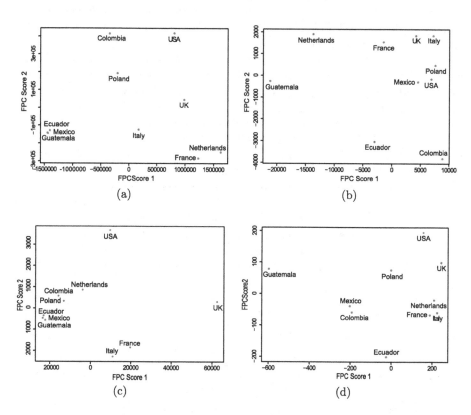

Fig. 3. FPCA scores for (a) V1_TC, (b) V2_TD, (c) V3_TT, and (d) V4_PFV.

4.4   Perturbations of the Mean Function

Figures 4, 5, 6, and 7 depict the principal component functions as perturbations of the mean function by adding and subtracting a multiple of each principal component, which is a typical representation in FDA [18,29]. The first FPC of V1_TC (Fig. 4(a)), which accounts for 93.6% of the variations, shows that variance increases significantly around day 265 (December 22, 2021) of the study period. This behavior may be unsurprisingly related to the holiday season. Looking at Fig. 4(b), we can note that the second FPC of V1_TC (accounting for 4.7% of the variations) follows a similar trend as the first one. However, there is an inversion at approximately January 26, 2022 (day 300), which may reflect the fact that some countries have a faster increase in the number of cases with respect to the mean while others have a slower decrease than the mean. Regarding the number of deaths (V2_TD), we can see that the first FPC, which accounts for 93.7% of the variations, shows a slow yet steady increase in variance.

In addition, there is an abrupt jump around day 111 (July 21, 2021) in the mean and both the perturbed means. This is due to the influence of the data from Ecuador (see Fig. 1(b)). Similar to the second FPC of V1_TC, there is also an inversion in this case. Coincidentally, it occurs around the same day we just mentioned. The amount of variance explained by this FPC (the second one of V2_TD) is 3.7%. With respect to V3_TT, we can see that its first FPC (see Fig. 6(a)), which explains 99.5% of the variations, increases steadily over the study period. This may be due to the significant difference between UK and the other countries. The second FPC of V3_TT behaves similarly to the previous ones and explains 0.4% of the variance. Finally, looking at Fig. 7, we can see that the first FPC of V4_PFV accounts for 82% of variability and reaches a breakpoint around day 160 (September 8, 2021). On this day, the increasing trend stops and becomes decreasing. The inversion of the second FPC (which accounts for 14.2% of variance) around the same day also reflects that change.

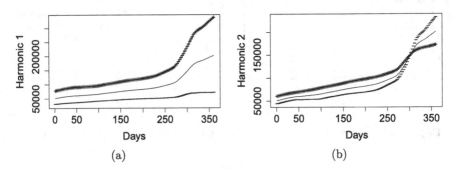

(a)   (b)

Fig. 4. Mean perturbation plot for **(a)** FPC 1 (Variability 93.6%) and **(b)** FPC 2 (Variability 4.7%) corresponding to V1_TC.

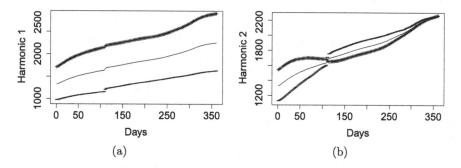

Fig. 5. Mean perturbation plot for (**a**) FPC 1 (Variability 93.7%) and (**b**) FPC 2 (Variability 3.7%) corresponding to V2_TD.

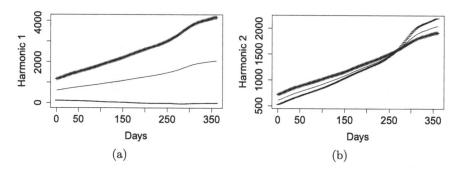

Fig. 6. Mean perturbation plot for (**a**) FPC 1 (Variability 99.5%) and (**b**) FPC 2 (Variability 0.4%) corresponding to V3_TT.

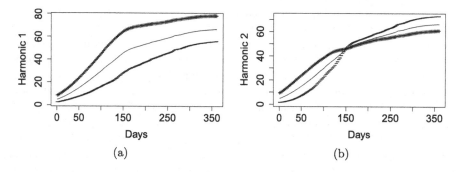

Fig. 7. Mean perturbation plot for (**a**) FPC 1 (Variability 82%) and (**b**) FPC 2 (Variability 14.2%) corresponding to V4_PFV.

4.5 Functional Clustering

Figure 8 exhibits the functional clustering results of applying the multivariate version of the `funHDDC` function [27] (which belongs to the homonymous R package). For a better interpretation, $k = 3$ groups were chosen. All the available models were tested (see [30]), and the selected one was `AKJBKQKDK` by means of the BIC [25] criterion. Additionally, `init="kmeans"` was set to initialize the E-M algorithm [26] (with `algo="EM"` by default) in the `funHDDC` method. The resulting clusters are homogeneous in number. Cluster 1 contains USA, UK, France, and the Netherlands. Mexico, Guatemala, and Ecuador belong to Cluster 2, while Colombia, Poland, and Italy are members of Cluster 3. Colombia's membership in Cluster 3 is surprising because one would expect it to belong to a cluster with Latin American neighbors.

Fig. 8. Clusters via multivariate functional clustering technique.

5 Conclusions and Further Studies

In this paper, we focus on summarizing temporal information regarding variations of variables associated with de pandemic of COVID-19, such as total cases per million (V1_TC), total deaths per million (V2_TD), total tests per thousand (V3_TT), and people fully vaccinated per hundred (V4_PFV). The values were taken from April 01, 2021 to March 31, 2022. FDA methodologies such as FPCA and FPCA scores demonstrated that the first functional principal component explains the total variance of data used in this manuscript well. This finding allows us to point out the importance of the first principal component when qualitatively describing and analyzing an observed phenomenon. The impact of vaccination campaigns is palpable because after events such as Halloween, Christmas, New Year's party, and Carnival. FPC1 of V2_TD does not grow as fast as FPC1 of PFC1 of V1_TC. It means that the vaccines avoid people's deaths from COVID-19, but they do not stop the propagation of the virus.

Unfortunately, except for FPC1, the rest of the FPCs have weak predictive power for variables used in this manuscript. Nevertheless, it does not mean we cannot get information from these FPCs. For example, as suggested in [2], with deeper research, we could predict the success of a vaccination campaign using FPC2. But, of course, we will need different tools and approaches than we used in this work to make it.

Lastly, for future works, our research group is interested in dividing data into two groups: before vaccination started and when vaccination has begun. To describe more phenomena associated with COVID-19 by applying FDA methodologies like the ones used in this work and others, such as canonical correlation analysis, functional regression methods, and functional time series.

Acknowledgements. This work was carried out under the project Functional Data Analysis: Methods and Applications, with registration REGINV-19-04054, Yachay Tech University.

Thanks to the anonymous referees for their helpful comments, which improved the quality of this work.

Appendix A − Sum of Squared Errors (SSE) of B-spline and Power system

SSE is a helpful tool for selecting a basis system. It is important to mention that other systems might produce a lower SSE value, but it does not imply that these systems represent graphically well data. For instance, using a Fourier system in this work makes no sense because selected data are accumulated, and with a Fourier system would seem that data were taken daily. While by using a Power system of order 4, we get similar graphical results to the B-spline system of the same order but with a higher SSE value. Let us see it in the following table (Table 2)

Table 2. SSE of B-spline and power system

System	V1_TC	V2_TD	V3_TT	V4_PFV
B-spline	163818459	57414.76	2473.42	13.02
Power	245511212315	8859360	5706165	30132.74

Appendix B − Classical PCA-Biplot

Figure 9 shows a PCA-Biplot representation of the data (all four variables) corresponding to the last day of this study. Such a condition is perhaps the main difference between functional and classical clustering, since the former considers the entire study period, while the latter considers just a representative day. In a sense, classical clustering is a snapshot of the data on a specific day (which takes into account the overall history until that day) whereas functional clustering provides a continuous representation of the data (like a movie, to be coherent with the analogy). To determine the clusters displayed in Fig. 9 (by color codes), we use the kmeans technique (Hartigan and Wong [31] algorithm) with parameter $k = 3$ beforehand. It produces the following clusters. Cluster 2 consists of USA, UK, and Italy. Cluster 2 contains all Latin American countries (Ecuador, Colombia, Mexico, and Guatemala) plus Poland, while Cluster 3 has France and the Netherlands as members.

Looking at Fig. 9, it can be noted that the first two principal components explain around 81.5% of the data variation. Compared to the functional approach, where the two principal components of all variables explain above 96%, the classical approach is inferior. Although the comparison is not appropriate, one can suspect that they differ because the classical approach deals with all four variables simultaneously. We can also observe that both approaches have some coincidences regarding clustering analysis. For example, USA and UK belong to the same cluster in both methods. Another group that is always together is Mexico, Ecuador, and Guatemala. This result is consistent with the groups reported in the FPC scores analysis in Subsect. 4.3, specifically when it comes to V1_TC and V3_TT. Both approaches also provide two other similar groups of countries. The first one consists of France and the Netherlands, and the second one of Colombia and Poland. Such groupings were already reported in Subsect. 4.3. The former was pointed out in the FPCA scores analysis of V1_TC and the latter in that of V3_TT.

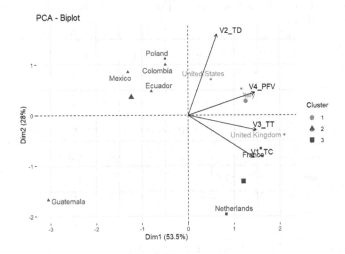

Fig. 9. PCA - Biplot (Clustering via kmeans technique)

References

1. World Health Organization: Report of the WHO-China joint mission on coronavirus disease 2019 (COVID-19) (2020). https://www.who.int/publications/i/item/report-of-the-who-china-joint-mission-on-coronavirus-disease-2019-(COVID-19)/. Accessed 3 May 2022

2. Oshinubi, K., Ibrahim, F., Rachdi, M., Demongeot, J.: Functional data analysis: application to daily observation of COVID-19 prevalence in France. AIMS Math. **7**(4), 5347–5385 (2022). https://doi.org/10.3934/math.2022298
3. Sánchez-Sánchez, M.L., et al.: Functional principal component analysis as a new methodology for the analysis of the impact of two rehabilitation protocols in functional recovery after stroke. J. NeuroEngineering Rehabi. **11**(34), 134 (2014). https://doi.org/10.1186/1743-0003-11-134
4. Padilla-Segarra, A., González-Villacorte, M., Amaro, I.R., Infante, S.: Brief review of functional data analysis: a case study on regional demographic and economic data. In: Rodriguez Morales, G., Fonseca C., E.R., Salgado, J.P., Pérez-Gosende, P., Orellana Cordero, M., Berrezueta, S. (eds.) TICEC 2020. CCIS, vol. 1307, pp. 163–176. Springer, Cham (2020). https://doi.org/10.1007/978-3-030-62833-8_14
5. Boschi, T., Di Iorio, J., Testa, L., Cremona, M.A., Chiaromonte, F.: Functional data analysis characterizes the shapes of the first COVID-19 epidemic wave in Italy. Sci. Rep. **11**(1), 1–15 (2021). https://doi.org/10.1038/s41598-021-95866-y
6. Li, X., Zhang, P., Feng, Q.: Exploring COVID-19 in mainland China during the lockdown of Wuhan via functional data analysis. Commun. Stat. Appl. Methods. **29**(1), 103–125 (2022). https://doi.org/10.29220/CSAM.2022.29.1.103
7. Martin-Barreiro, C., Ramirez-Figueroa, J., Cabezas, X., Leiva, V., Galindo-Villardón, M.: Disjoint and Functional principal component analysis for infected cases and deaths due to COVID-19 in South American Countries with sensor-related data. Sensors **21**(12), 4094 (2021). https://doi.org/10.3390/s21124094
8. Chaglla, D., Amaro, I.R., Infante, S.: An exploratory analysis of COVID-19 in Latin America using functional principal component analysis. In: Guarda, T., Portela, F., Santos, M.F. (eds.) ARTIIS 2021. CCIS, vol. 1485, pp. 221–233. Springer, Cham (2021). https://doi.org/10.1007/978-3-030-90241-4_18
9. Collazos, J.A., Dias, R., Medeiros, M.C.: Modeling the evolution of infectious diseases with functional data models: the case of COVID-19 in Brazil. arXiv preprint (2021). https://doi.org/10.48550/arXiv.2109.01952
10. Riera-Segura, L., Tapia-Riera, G., Amaro, I.R., Infante, S., Marin-Calispa, H.: HJ-biplot and clustering to analyze the COVID-19 vaccination process of American and European countries. In: Narváez, F.R., Proaño, J., Morillo, P., Vallejo, D., González Montoya, D., Díaz, G.M. (eds.) SmartTech-IC 2021. CCIS, vol. 1532, pp. 383–397. Springer, Cham (2022). https://doi.org/10.1007/978-3-030-99170-8_28
11. Mathieu, E., et al.: A global database of COVID-19 vaccinations. Nat. Human Behav. **5**(7), 947–953 (2021). https://doi.org/10.1038/s41562-021-01122-8
12. Ritchie, H., et al.: Coronavirus Pandemic (COVID-19). Our World in Data (2020). https://ourworldindata.org/coronavirus. Accessed 1 Apr 2022
13. Hasell, J., et al.: A cross-country database of COVID-19 testing. Sci. Data **7**(1), 345 (2020). https://doi.org/10.1038/s41597-020-00688-8
14. Honaker, J., King, G., Blackwell, M.: AmeliaII: a program for missing data. J. Stat. Softw. **45**(7), 1–47 (2011). https://doi.org/10.18637/jss.v045.i07
15. Buuren, S.V.: Flexible Imputation of Missing Data, 2nd edn. Chapman and Hall/CRC, Boca Raton (2018). https://doi.org/10.1201/9780429492259
16. Moritz, S., Bartz-Beielstein, T.: imputeTS: time series missing value imputation in R. R J. **9**(1), 207–218 (2017). https://doi.org/10.32614/RJ-2017-009
17. Ferraty, F., Vieu, P.: Nonparametric Functional Data Analysis. Springer, New York (2006). https://doi.org/10.1007/0-387-36620-2
18. Ramsay, J., Silverman, B.: Functional Data Analysis. Springer Series in Statistics. Springer, Heidelberg (2005). https://doi.org/10.1007/978-1-4757-7107-7

19. Sang, P.: New methods and models in functional data analysis (Doctoral dissertation, Science: Department of Statistics and Actuarial Science, Simon Fraser University, Burnaby, BC, Canada) (2018). https://summit.sfu.ca/item/18509
20. Ramsay, J.O., Hooker, G., Graves, S.: Functional Data Analysis with R and MATLAB, 1st edn. Springer, New York (2009). https://doi.org/10.1007/978-0-387-98185-7
21. De Boor, C.: On calculating with B-splines. J. Approx. Theory **6**(1), 50–62 (1972). https://doi.org/10.1016/0021-9045(72)90080-9
22. Jacques, J., Preda, C.: Functional data clustering: a survey. Adv. Data Anal. Classification **8**(3), 231–255 (2013). https://doi.org/10.1007/s11634-013-0158-y
23. Bouveyron, C., Jacques, J.: Model-based clustering of time series in group-specific functional subspaces. Adv. Data Anal. Classification **5**(4), 281–300 (2011). https://doi.org/10.1007/s11634-011-0095-6
24. Ruhao, W., Bo, W., Aiping, X.: Functional data clustering using principal curve methods. Commun. Stat. Theory Methods **51**, 7264–7283 (2021). https://doi.org/10.1080/03610926.2021.1872636
25. Schwarz, G.: Estimating the dimension of a model. Ann. Stat. **6**(2), 461–464 (1978). https://doi.org/10.1214/aos/1176344136
26. Dempster, A., Laird, N., Rubin, D.: Maximum likelihood from incomplete data via the EM algorithm. J. R. Stat. Soc. **39**(1), 1–38 (1977)
27. Schmutz, A., Jacques, J., Bouveyron, C., Chèze, L., Martin, P.: Clustering multivariate functional data in group-specific functional subspaces. Comput. Stat. **35**(3), 1101–1131 (2020). https://doi.org/10.1007/s00180-020-00958-4
28. Plateforme ouverte des données publiques françaises. https://www.data.gouv.fr/fr/datasets/donnees-relatives-aux-resultats-des-tests-virologiques-covid-19/. Accessed 3 May 2022
29. Wang, Z., Sun, Y., Li, P.: Functional principal components analysis of Shanghai stock exchange 50 index. Discrete Dyn. Nat. Soc. **2014**, 1–7 (2014). https://doi.org/10.1155/2014/365204
30. Schmutz, A., Jacques, J., Bouveyron, C.: funHDDC: Univariate and Multivariate Model-Based Clustering in Group-Specific Functional Subspaces (2021). R package version 2.3.1. Retrieved from https://CRAN.Rproject.org/package=funHDDC
31. Hartigan, J., Wong, M.: Algorithm AS 136: a K-means clustering algorithm. Appl. Stat. **28**(1), 100–108 (1979). https://doi.org/10.2307/2346830

A Methodology to Develop an Outdoor Activities Recommender Based on Air Pollution Variables

Pablo Arévalo[1] , Marcos Orellana[1](✉) , Priscila Cedillo[2] ,
Juan-Fernando Lima[1] , and Jorge Luis Zambrano-Martinez[1]

[1] Laboratorio de Investigación y Desarrollo en Informática - LIDI,
Universidad del Azuay, Cuenca, Ecuador
{pablo.loja,marore,flima,jorge.zambrano}@uazuay.edu.ec
[2] Universidad de Cuenca, Cuenca, Ecuador
priscila.cedillo@ucuenca.edu.ec

Abstract. Nowadays, the world faces a high level of environmental pollution. This phenomenon has become a constant challenge for our society due to its negative impact on health and the increased risk of disease. Considering this problem, applications, techniques and methodologies are generated that seek to relate atmospheric pollutants to each other to predict the state of the air. On the other hand, recommendation systems are present in numerous decision-making methods to find trends in various fields. Consequently, this work presents a methodology for a recommender system that provides people with the best hours to perform outdoor activities according to the pollutants found in the environment. The results obtained were verified through an evaluation and thus be able to contribute to the creation of new recommenders based on the previous topics.

Keywords: Recommender systems · Air quality · Data mining · Air pollutants · Meteorological variables

1 Introduction

Currently, the world faces high environmental air pollution [16], which this phenomenon directly affects health and increases the risk of diseases in people [3,32]. Furthermore, the short-term and long-term adverse effects of inhaling air pollutants on the respiratory and cardiovascular systems have been widely documented [16,28]. Hence, understanding the impact of pollutants and weather variables when doing outdoor activities is a constant challenge for our society [3,32]. Pollution is the result of combining multiple atmospheric variables. However, some of them are very disquieting because they have a more significant impact on human health, the predominant ones being: ozone (O_3), carbon monoxide (CO), nitrogen dioxide (NO_2), sulfur dioxide (SO_2), particulate matter ($PM_{2.5}$). These pollutants are part of the "Criteria Pollutants", a classification given by the Environmental Protection Agency (EPA) to all contaminants that are present in any place due to their nature and origin [2,36].

© The Author(s), under exclusive license to Springer Nature Switzerland AG 2022
J. Herrera-Tapia et al. (Eds.): TICEC 2022, CCIS 1648, pp. 171–185, 2022.
https://doi.org/10.1007/978-3-031-18272-3_12

At the same time, efforts to monitor and improve the air quality have been intensified, generating a wide field of research [27]. Monitoring the concentrations of atmospheric pollutants, calculating the pollution index and analysing the correlations and incidences between contaminants are the most relevant for an adequate air quality evaluation [27]. As a result of the monitoring, large volumes of data are available to develop tools, techniques, or methodologies that can relate the variables to each other [4,27,34]. It is essential to specify the best range of time in which an individual is exposed to less contamination. Doing activities in environments with high exposure to these pollutants affect health and performance, and this issue needs to be addressed as part of deep research.

Recommender systems are tools that provide suggestions about items that can be useful to the user. These recommendations are linked to a decision-making process focused on a particular issue [26]. Thus, this paper aims to develop a methodology for supporting the development of a recommender system based on atmospheric pollutants and meteorological variables through data mining techniques. In this case, the K-Means algorithm is considered as an unsupervised grouping method that allows objects to be grouped into k groups depending on whether they contain similarities. This technique does not require labeled attributes allowing the adaptation to new examples and its use of large data sets [9,12]. This document is structured as follows: Sect. 2 presents the related works, Sect. 3 describes each stage and result of the proposed methodology, Sect. 4 shows the evaluation of the proposed methodology, Sect. 5 discusses the threads of validity, and Sect. 6 presents the conclusions and future works.

2   Related Works

This section aims to guide among studies of artificial intelligence, data mining methodologies and techniques. Manohar et al. [17] apply the clustering analysis in Chennai, India to study awareness in the population to identify more predominant groups of questions and seek a reduction in air pollution. In other cases, the pollution forecast is performed using neural networks and the Dijkstra algorithm on the Hadoop MapReduce framework to search for a short route with less environmental pollution [30]. Likewise, Taneja et al. [35] present a study in Delhi, India, with techniques such as linear regression and multilayer perceptron, pollution trends to perform predictions through various emission sources such as vehicle emissions, industrial emissions, demolition, etc. [34].

Besides, other studies consider Relative Humidity (RH) and the air temperature as the concerting variables influencing the practice of multiple sports or physical activities. Thus, Chowdhury et al. [6] consider these two atmospheric variables to evaluate their influence on sports performance, such as the level of comfort for different sports disciplines. The results show that those parameters significantly impact sports performance for outdoor events.

A study developed in China reveal that pollutants such as $PM_{2.5}$, PM_{10}, SO_2, CO, and NO_2 are correlated with RH [39]. Similarly, another study focused on air quality shows that RH, air temperature, and wind speed are dominant factors influencing air quality due to their significant effects on the dispersion and transformation of pollutants [14]. In another study, Giri et al. [8] use meteorological conditions such as temperature, rain, humidity, atmospheric pressure, direction, wind speed, and concentrations of particulate matter and apply the Pearson's correlation coefficient to demonstrate the influence of PM_{10} and the RH, the wind speed and humidity. Thus, air temperature and RH are related to the heat index, indicating the relationship and impact on human health.

Recommendation systems are commonly found in most applications that detect trends in multiple sectors, such as: entertainment, news, and products' sales [15]. For example, recommendation systems are developed to extract educational data for predicting student learning outcomes [35]. Likewise, recommendation systems are created in the health field and well-being, for example, selecting the right person to practice a suitable sport based on parameters such as heart rate, speed, and height using k-means for grouping these data [1]. Public health care datasets are also considered to analyse the performance of different machine learning techniques to provide an intelligent health environment that evaluates health from multiple perspectives and recommends the most appropriate actions [31]. Collecting metrics of allergens and air quality from pollution stations, a recommender system is proposed to solve mobility problems of citizens by informing them which pedestrian routes minimize the time of exposure to allergens [7]. Finally, recommendation systems have different approaches, such as collaborative filtering, which seeks a method to emit recommendations considering user interactions in the past [37]. But the content-based approach learns to recommend items similar to what the user is interested in through a history [26, 37].

3   Methodology

Most recommender systems usually apply techniques and procedures from other areas such as Human-Computer Interaction (HCI) or Information Retrieval (IR) [26]. Also, they use an algorithm that can be interpreted as an instance of a data mining technique based on its three main steps, which are executed sequentially: i) previous data processing, ii) data analysis, and iii) interpretation of results. This methodology was focused on five main activities based on the three previous steps. The first activity was performed with the data collection for both atmospheric pollutants and meteorological variables. Then, the preprocessing of the collected data to avoid outliers to provide a clean dataset was performed as the second activity. Subsequently, in the third activity, grouping techniques were applied to generate groups of items with similar characteristics. In the fourth activity, it was essential to have evaluation metrics to qualify the results obtained and determine the optimal time with less pollution. Finally in the five activity the results was obtained, as shown in Fig. 1. It should be noted that these activities described above focus on the creation of a content recommender since, in each of the step, contaminants are considered as the basis for issuing recommendations, unlike demographic or collaborative filtering recommenders that place in the first place the opinions or characteristics of the users [26].

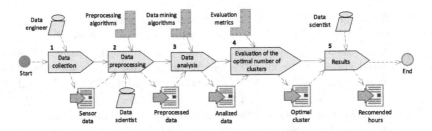

Fig. 1. Methodology for the outdoor activities recommender.

3.1 Data Collection

During 2018, a total of 52474 records were collected through the automatic monitoring station in Cuenca, Ecuador; the same one has a scope of four km, and stores these air pollution values by intervals of one minute, on the other hand, the meteorological variables are collected by intervals of 10 min [20], the Table 1 shows the descriptive values these variables.

Table 1. Collected pollutants and meteorological variable.

Description	Abbreviature	Measure
Pollutants		
Ozone	O_3	$\mu g/m^3$
Carbon monoxide	CO	mg/m^3
Nitrogen dioxide	NO_2	$\mu g/m^3$
Sulfur dioxide	SO_2	$\mu g/m^3$
Particulate matter	$PM_{2.5}$	$\mu g/m^3$
Meteorological variables		
Wind speed	$WINDSPEED\_AV$	m/s
Air temperature	$TEMPAIR\_AV$	$°C$
UV radiation (A)	UVA_AV	W/m^2
Global radiation	$RADGLOBAL\_AV$	W/m^2
Dew point	DP_AV	$°C$
Precipitation	$PREC\_SUM$	mm
Relative humidity	RH_AV	$\%$

3.2 Data Preprocessing

Data of the real world needs to be preprocessed, as the data is often unclean, missing or inconsistent [26]. In the first instance, the data must have a unified frequency since there is a time discrepancy between the records of atmospheric pollutants and meteorological variables. For this, the DateTime attribute was used to average the records of atmospheric pollutants in periods of ten minutes.

In this way, the meteorological variables and atmospheric pollutants are records that can be linked [19]. A data cleaning process was performed to identify possible errors in the records that can occur due to sensor failures, power outages, computer system failures, and contaminant levels below detection limits, among others [4]. To mitigate these possible drawbacks, three methods were implemented: i) fill missing values with zeros and filter all data with values greater than zero, ii) isolate each variable, and iii) apply the Local Outlier Factor (LOF) algorithm, which establishes a limit so that all values are below it [23]. In detail, two regularized methods of missing imputation, Lasso and Ridge regression were considered to determine the number of forwarding and backward points needed to estimate the value of a missing data point; that is, if a point is outside the threshold, it is considered an outlier [23].

3.3   Data Analysis

In this activity, the data mining methods were selected and applied. For this reason, as a first point, it was necessary to determine the attributes to consider in the following tasks. Those tasks are essential to recommend the best time to perform outdoor activities. All collected air pollutants were selected as they have a higher impact (criterion pollutants) on human well-being [2,36]. Regarding the meteorological variables and according to previously analysed studies, relative humidity relative and air temperature were considered relevant attributes due to their direct impact on pollutants and outdoor activities [14,17,24,39].

It was essential to have numeric type columns to avoid errors when applying the grouping algorithm. Subsequently, an attribute derivation of the date type attributes was performed to obtain only the hours, discarding the dates, minutes, and seconds. The optimum time range was set from 5:00 to 22:00 outside this range were discarded because they biased the results when searching for the best result. Although there was no high pollution in these discarded hours, they can be dangerous due to the absence of pedestrians and vehicles [10]. Afterwards, it was necessary to adjust the range of values when dealing with attributes of different units and scales. For this, the Z-transform was used, subtracting the mean of the data from all the values, and later the result obtained was divided by the standard deviation. The distribution obtained from the data had a mean of zero and a variance of one [12]. This normalisation technique is shared and used in various areas, and compared to other tools, it preserves the original distribution of the data and, unlike other normalisation methods, it is less influenced by outliers [12,18].

Finally, the K-Means algorithm was applied, which divides a data set of N elements into k separate subsets. Initially it is required to specify the number of subsets [22]; each one of them is defined by its members and by its centroid. The centroid of each group is the point at which the sum of the distances of all elements in that group is minimized. The algorithm works by randomly selecting the centroids [26]. Subsequently, all elements are assigned to the subset whose centroid is closest to them. The new cluster centroid must be updated to account for items that were added or removed from the cluster. This operation continues until there are no more elements that change their membership in a cluster [26]. Although a grouping method is less precise than a classification method, it can be implemented as a preliminary step to reduce the number of candidates or distribute them among different recommendations [26]. The application of the methods described above was done in Rapidminer, an open source tool that has a data/text mining engine for integration in its own products.

3.4 Evaluation of the Optimal Number of Clusters

Evaluation metrics were essential to validate the obtained results in our previous activities. Firstly, the elbow method is used to determine the optimal number of clusters [38]. The method executed the K-Means on the dataset for a range of k values after each k value, calculated the Sum of Squared Errors (SSE). The goal was to choose a small value of k that still has a low SSE, represented by the elbow [21]. The optimal number of clusters obtained was $k = 8$, as shown in Fig. 2.

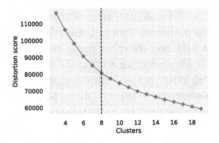

Fig. 2. The optimal number of clusters.

The method performed was graphical, facilitating the use of a large-scale dataset making it more desirable than other methods such as the silhouette index, which produces considerable computational overhead [38]. Subsequently, the best option of the result of the elbow method provided the most appropriate hours for outdoor activities as a recommendation. On the other hand, air pollutants were classified on six scales according to the health risk associated with air quality [14]. For this, it was necessary to use the air quality index, which indicates the possible impacts on health based on the actual concentrations of atmospheric pollutants in a range of 0 to 500 points [14]. Table 2 presents the quality standards for each of the input air pollutants used. These values were categorized according to the air quality index [14].

The meteorological variables were categorized using the heat and wind chill indices. The heat index is the temperature felt in the body when relative humidity is combined with temperature [11]. This index range was between 80 °F (26 °C) and 108 °F (42 °C), and it corresponding to RH_AV from 0% to 100%. Therefore, any value below that temperature range does not harm health since,

Table 2. Pollution index per pollutant.

Air quality	SO_2	NO_2	CO	O_3	$PM_{2.5}$
Excellent	0–50	0–40	0–2	0–100	0–35
Good	51–150	41–80	3–4	101–160	36–75
Light pollution	151–475	81–180	5–14	161–215	76–115
Moderate pollution	476–800	181–280	15–24	216–265	116–150
Strong contamination	801–1600	281–565	25–36	266–800	151–250
Severe contamination	>1601	>566	>37	–	>251

even if it has 100% humidity. The heat index does not indicate that it is dangerous, and their values correspond to shady places, so if they are exposed to direct sunlight, this index can increase by 15 °F, so it was considered to increase this range of 80 °F (26 °C) to 65 °F (18 °C) to cover this issue [11]. On the other hand, to determine the minimum temperature, the wind chill index was considered o refer to the loss of heat from the body to its environment during cold or windy days [13]. The available range is 5 °C to −50 °C [28]. Based on this, it was determined that the values that exceed 5 °C are suitable for outdoor activities since the risk due to low temperatures is minimised [13]. Table 3 summarise the ranges and health implication.

Table 3. Information about air temperature and RH.

TEMPAIR_AV	RH_AV	Health implication	Exerc.
Lees than 0	–	High risk of frostbite	No
0–5	0–100	Low risk of freezing	No
6–18	0–100	No harm to human health	Yes
19–26	0–100	No harm to human health/little probability	No
27–32	–	Fatigue is possible with prolonged exposure and/or physical activity	No
>32	–	High likelihood of heat cramps or heat exhaustion, and possible heat stroke	No

Data collected in Cuenca, Ecuador did not completely satisfy all the categories above. For this, the centroids in excellent air quality and allow outdoor activities were analyzed in each cluster.

3.5   Results

This subsection presents the results of the application of the proposed methodology. So, each cluster centroid was considered and the best option was chosen.

The centroids are a set of values that represent the behavior of the resulting clusters, in addition, depending on them, these groups can be categorized to issue recommendations [26]. As shown in Fig. 3, cluster number six presented an optimal result compared to the others after analysing each pollutant. This phenomenon can be observed in variables such as CO, SO_2, and $PM_{2.5}$. The centroids of this cluster were in the optimal range of air quality and allowed other clusters containing centroids with very high values to be quickly eliminated, as in the case of clusters number one, two, three, and seven.

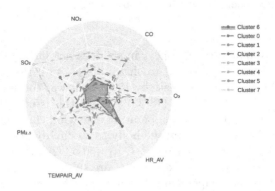

Fig. 3. The centroids of clusters.

Each centroid was denormalised to verify that these values allowed recommending the best hours for outdoor activities. This task was performed to observe their equivalence in the respective measurement units of each pollutant. Thus ratifying an excellent air quality and a temperature with humidity without risk to health. Although cluster six contained a high value in its centroid for RH_AV, this did not negatively influence having its centroid in $TEMPAIR\_AV$ in the optimal temperature range, and according to the heat index, there was no risk for activities outdoor. Likewise, this index allowed the elimination of clusters four and zero due to their high values at room temperature and possible complications in the open air such as fatigue.

Besides, considering O_3, cluster five was discarded. Once cluster 6 was determined as the best option, it is necessary to recommend the best time for outdoor activities. Kernel Density Estimation (KDE) smoothes observations with a Gaussian function, producing a continuous density estimate [22].

Figure 4 offers a comparison of the different hours for each cluster. In this case, the results determined that cluster six established that the best recommended hours to do outdoor activities cover a range from 5:00 to 8:00 and the night from 20:00 to 22:00. Table 4 shows the values of each centroid with the variables analysed. Concerning each atmospheric pollutant, SO, NO_2, CO, O_3, $PM_{2.5}$, the centroids, once denormalized, had values within excellent air quality. Therefore, there was a low level of air pollution, which is vital to avoid

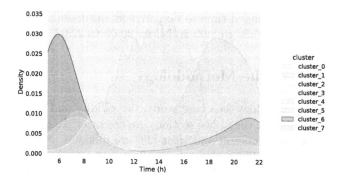

Fig. 4. KDE comparing each cluster to determine optimal time.

health damage. Otherwise, close to the noon-hour, atmospheric pollutants' values increased abruptly. This result was due to vehicular traffic, factories, and companies during working hours expelling pollutants and toxins into the environment in an uncontrolled manner, the same ones that, when found in the atmosphere, can combine, causing diseases of all kinds [33].

Table 4. Optimal clusters and related timestamps.

	Centroids	Denormalized centroids	Timestamp	Air quality
SO_2	−0.308	7.109	05:00–08:00 | 20:00–22:00	Excellent
NO_2	−0.223	15.328	05:00–08:00 | 20:00–22:00	Excellent
CO	−0.439	0.634	05:00–08:00 | 20:00–22:00	Excellent
O_3	−0.784	12.761	05:00–08:00 | 20:00–22:00	Excellent
$PM_{2.5}$	−0.44	7.093	05:00–08:00 | 20:00–22:00	Excellent
$TEMPAIR\_AV$	−1.127	12.167	05:00–08:00 | 20:00–22:00	Excellent
RH_AV	1.229	83.083	05:00–08:00 | 20:00–22:00	Excelent/Regular

Therefore, these hours were the worst time to perform activities outside and even worse if the person has respiratory or cardiac problems. Along with atmospheric pollutants, the centroid related to $TEMPAIR\_AV$ found a value of 12 °C, the optimal temperature to go outside. Therefore, concerning the thermal sensation index, there was no health risk due to low temperatures that can cause frostbite or diseases related to the respiratory system. On the other hand, considering the heat index, there was no risk of fatigue or sunstroke. As mentioned above, the RH_AV variable had a high relationship with the $TEMPAIR\_AV$. Although the value of the centroid is in an Excellent/Fair category, it has a $TEMPAIR\_AV$ that is outside the danger range of the heat index and does not have a negative effect. Based on these results analysed for each pollutant and atmospheric variable, it can be affirmed that the chosen cluster is the best option, and the recommended time to do activities outdoors that do not represent health risks is from 5:00 to 8:00 and from 20:00 to 22:00.

4   Evaluation of the Methodology

Evaluating this methodology as a case study, the validity and understanding of the methods presented in the above sections are essential. To perform this task, the steps proposed by Runeson and Höst [29] are followed for conducting and reporting this case study like a research in software engineering, were taken as a reference similar to any empirical study. The case studies, allow a more in-depth understanding of the phenomenon being studied in its current context.

4.1   Objectives and Research Questions

A case study investigates a flexible type in which planning is necessary for its development to be successful. From the Goal-Question Metric paradigm [5], the goal of this study is presented below:

- Evaluate the analysis phase of the proposed methodology based on atmospheric pollutants and meteorological variables.
- From the point of view of a Data scientist.
- Context: Research and development laboratory researchers.

The proposed methodology is based on the standard designed by Ricci [26] for recommenders in data mining, which focuses on any area. However, the presented methodology cannot be evaluated concerned another since no standard or similar examples of recommenders allow determining the best time for outdoor activities, considering atmospheric pollutants and meteorological variables as a basis [26]. The proposed research questions for the case study are:

- RQ1: Is the methodology presented to recommend outdoor activities based on pollutants and atmospheric variables perceived as useful and easy to use?.
- RQ2: Is there an intention to use this methodology in the future?.

4.2   Context and Survey Design

The context is represented by the proposed methodology of the outdoor activity recommender system that is evaluated. Researchers belonging to the Research and Development Laboratory were selected who have extensive knowledge in data mining techniques and work professionally in this same area. To answer the research questions, a survey based on the Technology Acceptance Model (TAM) has been included to provide evidence on the Perceived Ease Of Use (PEOU), Perceived Usefulness (PU), and Intention to Use (ITU) [25]. The Likert scale was considered, where one is regarded as a negative response, three as a neutral value and five as the highest value. These questions are shown in below list.

- PEOU1: The proposed methodology is simple and easy to follow.
- PEOU2: In general, the proposed methodology is easy to understand.
- PEOU3: The steps that must be followed to complete the methodology are clear and understandable.
- PEOU4: The proposed methodology is easy to learn.
- PEOU5: I think that the proposed methodology would be helpful as a basis for future projects.
- PU1: I consider that the proposed methodology would reduce the time and effort required to search for a recommender of outdoor activities.
- PU2: Generally, I consider the proposed methodology is useful.
- PU3: I consider the proposed methodology applicable when determining best time to perform outdoor activities.
- PU4: I think the methodology is detailed enough when guiding each of the steps focused on data science.
- PU5: This methodology provides an optimal method based on K-Means in the quest to determine the best time for outdoor activities.
- ITU1: If I were to provide training on air pollution and outdoor activities, I would consider this developed methodology.
- ITU2: If necessary, I would use this methodology in the future.
- ITU3: I would recommend the use of this methodology.

4.3 Results and Data Interpretation

For the case study to be successful, as a first task, an introduction was performed on the importance of the topic raised and the health benefit of being less exposed to atmospheric pollutants. Subsequently, the materials were delivered in digital format to the researchers, who performed the corresponding evaluation based on their reading and the model created in RapidMiner software. Once the data was obtained, the tabulations corresponding to each of the attributes were made: separate the questions according to the PEOU, the PU and the ITU. Table 5 shows the minimum and maximum values, and the means of the study variables, each of them consolidated (PEOU, PU, and ITU).

Table 5. Descriptive statistics for variables based on user perception.

Variable	Min	Max	Avg	Standard deviation	Error standard
PEOU	5.0	5.0	5.0	0.00	0.00
PU	4.0	5.0	4.6	0.40	0.28
ITU	4.0	5.0	4.67	0.33	0.23

The RQ raised can be answered based on the researchers who participated in the case study. The question seeks to perceive the usefulness of the methodology and ease of use. It can be concluded that it has been considered useful, based on the PU, where the mean has marked a value of 4.6 with a minimum of four and a maximum of five. Similarly, researchers found the methodology easy to use, with a 5/5 rating for PEOU. The second question focused on the ITU proposed methodology in the future. It averages of 4.67, implying that participants will consider the use of this methodology.

5   Threats to Validity

In this section we have analyzed the main threats that could interfere with the interpretation of the results. In relation to a validity of conclusion, there was a threat linked to the size and selection of the sample as well as the difficulty of finding data scientists. To mitigate this problem, expert researchers in this area belonging to the research laboratory were considered. In addition, due to the low significance of the sample size, experimental validation for a case study was eliminated. Similarly, they have proposed adding a more significant number of data scientists to corroborate the methodology with a larger sample in future work. Subsequently, considering an internal validity, a threat associated with the user's prior knowledge was presented, since they should have previously known the topics previously developed. To mitigate this threat, the selected researchers underwent initial training to state the research topic, its importance, and prior advances.

In the same way, there was a threat related to the validity of the survey presented. To mitigate this problem a Cronbach's alpha test of questions related to each subjective variable was performed to increase reliability. Being the minimum accepted threshold $\alpha = 0.70$, then, in PEOU $\alpha = 1$, in PU $\alpha = 0.937$, and ITU $\alpha = 0.75$. Validating the reality study applying TAM. Finally, to guarantee external validity, The participants were selected for convenience since they have a broad understanding of techniques, methods, and tools focused on data mining and know first-hand the analysed data of this study.

6   Conclusions

The use of the K-Means algorithm in developing our methodology resulted appropriate since it allows the use of large amounts of data on atmospheric pollutants and meteorological variables. However, these data must be normalised before their application to prevent larger-scale attributes from dominating the distances, affecting the results. For this purpose, it is required to have features that influence when doing outdoor activities depending on the location of the city. Atmospheric pollutants must be considered in their entirety since they mix within the environment, increasing their danger to health. The proposed methodology provides a solution to determine the best time for exercising outdoors. The selected time intervals are the best as there is no dangerous accumulation of these contaminants in the air, and the temperature and humidity do not represent a health hazard. Finally, based on the proposed case study, it is essential to indicate that a methodology is a valuable tool. Its ease of use allows its implementation without significant inconveniences. It can be used as a basis for future projects of contextualized recommenders, which consider the user's context, in this case the user's location with its respective air quality, humidity and temperature as the basis for the recommendations.

Acknowledgements. This work was partially supported by the Vice-Rector for Research of the University of Azuay for financial and academic support, as well as the entire staff of the Computer Science department and the Laboratory for Research and Development in Informatics - LIDI.

References

1. Abdulaziz, M., Al-motairy, B., Al-ghamdi, M., Al-qahtani, N.: Building a personalized fitness recommendation application based on sequential information. Int. J. Adv. Comput. Sci. Appl. **12**(1), 637–648 (2021). https://doi.org/10.14569/IJACSA.2021.0120173
2. Agency United States Environmental: Un resumen de la Ley de Aire Limpio (2007)
3. An, R., Zhang, S., Ji, M., Guan, C.: Impact of ambient air pollution on physical activity among adults: a systematic review and meta-analysis. Perspect. Public Health **138**(2), 111–121 (2018). https://doi.org/10.1177/1757913917726567
4. Arce, D., Lima, F., Orellana Cordero, M.P., Ortega, J., Sellers, C., Ortega, P.: Discovering behavioral patterns among air pollutants: a data mining approach. Enfoque UTE **9**(4), 168–179 (2018). https://doi.org/10.29019/enfoqueute.v9n4.411
5. Basili, V.R., Weiss, D.M.: A methodology for collecting valid software engineering data. IEEE Trans. Softw. Eng. **SE-10**(6), 728–738 (1984). https://doi.org/10.1109/TSE.1984.5010301
6. Chowdhury, A.S., Uddin, M.S., Tanjim, M.R., Noor, F., Rahman, R.M.: Application of data mining techniques on air pollution of Dhaka City. In: 2020 IEEE 10th International Conference on Intelligent Systems, IS 2020 - Proceedings, pp. 562–567 (2020). https://doi.org/10.1109/IS48319.2020.9200125
7. García-Díaz, J.A., Noguera-Arnaldos, J.Á., Hernández-Alcaraz, M.L., Robles-Marín, I.M., García-Sánchez, F., Valencia-García, R.: AllergyLESS. An intelligent recommender system to reduce exposition time to allergens in smart-cities. In: De La Prieta, F., Omatu, S., Fernández-Caballero, A. (eds.) DCAI 2018. AISC, vol. 800, pp. 61–68. Springer, Cham (2019). https://doi.org/10.1007/978-3-319-94649-8_8
8. Giri, D., Venkatappa, K., Adhikary, P.: The influence of meteorological conditions on PM10 concentrations in Kathmandu Valley. Int. J. Environ. Res. **2**(1), 49–60 (2008). (ISSN: 1735-6865)
9. Google: Machine Learning, June 2022. https://developers.google.com/machine-learning/clustering/algorithm/advantages-disadvantages
10. Guedes, I., Cardoso, C., Agra, C.: Emotional and insecurity reactions to different urban contexts—. GERN **2013**(1), 147 (2013)
11. Hass, A.L., Ellis, K.N., Mason, L.R., Hathaway, J.M., Howe, D.A.: Heat and humidity in the city: neighborhood heat index variability in a mid-sized city in the Southeastern United States. Int. J. Environ. Res. Public Health **13**(1), 117 (2016). https://doi.org/10.3390/ijerph13010117

12. Kotu, V., Deshpande, B.: Chapter 7 - clustering. In: Kotu, V., Deshpande, B. (eds.) Predictive Analytics and Data Mining, pp. 217–255. Morgan Kaufmann, Boston (2015). https://doi.org/10.1016/B978-0-12-801460-8.00007-0
13. Lankford, H.V., Fox, L.R.: The wind-chill index. Wilderness 'I&' Environ. Med. **32**(3), 392–399 (2021). https://doi.org/10.1016/j.wem.2021.04.005
14. Liu, Y., Wu, J., Yu, D., Hao, R.: Understanding the patterns and drivers of air pollution on multiple time scales: the case of Northern China. Environ. Manage. **61**(6), 1048–1061 (2018). https://doi.org/10.1007/s00267-018-1026-5
15. Lü, L., Medo, M., Yeung, C.H., Zhang, Y.C., Zhang, Z.K., Zhou, T.: Recommender systems. Phys. Rep. **519**(1), 1–49 (2012). https://doi.org/10.1016/j.physrep.2012.02.006
16. Mannucci, P.M., Franchini, M.: Health effects of ambient air pollution in developing countries. Int. J. Environ. Res. Public Health **14**(9), 1–8 (2017). https://doi.org/10.3390/ijerph14091048
17. Manohar, G., Devi, S., Rao, K.: A bi-level clustering analysis for studying about the sources of vehicular pollution in Chennai. Adv. Intell. Syst. Comput. **324**, 229–236 (2015). https://doi.org/10.1007/978-81-322-2126-5_26
18. Mohabeer, H., Soyjaudah, K.M., Pavaday, N.: Enhancing the performance of neural network classifiers using selected biometric features. In: SENSORCOMM 2011–5th International Conference on Sensor Technologies and Applications and WSNSCM 2011, 1st International Workshop on Sensor Networks for Supply Chain Management, pp. 140–144 (2011)
19. Orellana, M., Lima, J.F., Cedillo, P.: Discovering patterns of time association among air pollution and meteorological variables. In: Arai, K. (ed.) Advances in Information and Communication, pp. 205–215. Springer, Cham (2021). https://doi.org/10.1007/978-3-030-73103-8_13
20. Orellana, M., Salto, J., Cedillo, P.: Behavior analysis of atmospheric components and meteorological variables applying data mining association techniques. In: Arai, K. (ed.) Advances in Information and Communication, pp. 192–204. Springer, Cham (2021). https://doi.org/10.1007/978-3-030-73103-8_12
21. Pandey, A., Malviya, A.K.: Enhancing test case reduction by K-means algorithm and elbow method. Int. J. Comput. Sci. Eng. **6**(6), 299–303 (2018). https://doi.org/10.26438/ijcse/v6i6.299303
22. Pedregosa, F., et al.: Scikit-learn: machine learning in Python. J. Mach. Learn. Res. **12**, 2825–2830 (2011)
23. Peña, M., Ortega, P., Orellana, M.: A novel imputation method for missing values in air pollutant time series data. In: 2019 IEEE Latin American Conference on Computational Intelligence, LA-CCI 2019 (2019). https://doi.org/10.1109/LA-CCI47412.2019.9037053
24. Pezzoli, A., et al.: Effect of the environment on the sport performance: computer supported training - a case study for cycling sports. In: Cabri, J., Pezarat Correia, P., Barreiros, J. (eds.) Sports Science Research and Technology Support, pp. 1–16. Springer, Cham (2015). https://doi.org/10.1007/978-3-319-17548-5_1
25. Rahimi, B., Nadri, H., Afshar, H.L., Timpka, T.: A systematic review of the technology acceptance model in health informatics. Appl. Clin. Inform. **9**(3), 604–634 (2018). https://doi.org/10.1055/s-0038-1668091
26. Ricci, F., Rokach, L., Shapira, B., Kantor, P.B. (eds.): Recommender Systems Handbook. Springer, Boston (2011). https://doi.org/10.1007/978-0-387-85820-3
27. Rimensberger, N., Gross, M., Günther, T.: Visualization of clouds and atmospheric air flows. IEEE Comput. Graph. Appl. **39**(1), 12–25 (2019). https://doi.org/10.1109/MCG.2018.2880821

28. Rundell, K.W.: Effect of air pollution on athlete health and performance. Br. J. Sports Med. **46**(6), 407–412 (2012). https://doi.org/10.1136/bjsports-2011-090823
29. Runeson, P., Höst, M.: Guidelines for conducting and reporting case study research in software engineering. Empirical Softw. Eng. **14**(2), 131–164 (2009). https://doi.org/10.1007/s10664-008-9102-8
30. Sadiq, A., El Fazziki, A., Ouarzazi, J., Sadgal, M.: Towards an agent based traffic regulation and recommendation system for the on-road air quality control. SpringerPlus **5**(1), 1–19 (2016). https://doi.org/10.1186/s40064-016-3282-2
31. Sharma, R., Rani, S.: A novel approach for smart-healthcare recommender system. Adv. Intell. Syst. Comput. **1141**, 503–512 (2021). https://doi.org/10.1007/978-981-15-3383-9_46
32. Singla, S.: Air ality friendly route recommendation system. PhD Forum 2018 - Proceedings of the 2018 Workshop on MobiSys 2018 Ph.D. Forum, Part of MobiSys 2018, pp. 9–10 (2018). https://doi.org/10.1145/3212711.3212717
33. Swietlicki, E., Puri, S., Hansson, H.C., Edner, H.: Urban air pollution source apportionment using a combination of aerosol and gas monitoring techniques. Atmos. Environ. **30**(15), 2795–2809 (1996). https://doi.org/10.1016/1352-2310(95)00322-3
34. Taneja, S., Sharma, N., Oberoi, K., Navoria, Y.: Predicting trends in air pollution in Delhi using data mining. In: India International Conference on Information Processing, IICIP 2016 - Proceedings, pp. 1–6 (2017). https://doi.org/10.1109/IICIP.2016.7975379
35. Thai-Nghe, N., Drumond, L., Krohn-Grimberghe, A., Schmidt-Thieme, L.: Recommender system for predicting student performance. Procedia Comput. Sci. **1**(2), 2811–2819 (2010). https://doi.org/10.1016/j.procs.2010.08.006
36. Ubilla, C., Yohannessen, K.: Contaminación Atmosférica Efectos En La Salud Respiratoria En El Niño. Revista Médica Clínica Las Condes **28**(1), 111–118 (2017). https://doi.org/10.1016/j.rmclc.2016.12.003
37. Yu, L.: A35 - cloud storage-based personalized sports activity management in Internet plus O2O sports community. Concurr. Comput. **30**(24), 1–10 (2018). https://doi.org/10.1002/cpe.4932
38. Yuan, C., Yang, H.: Research on K-value selection method of K-means clustering algorithm. J. **2**(2), 226–235 (2019). https://doi.org/10.3390/j2020016
39. Zhou, H., et al.: Characteristics of air pollution and their relationship with meteorological parameters: Northern Versus Southern Cities of China. Atmosphere **11**(3), 253 (2020). https://doi.org/10.3390/atmos11030253

Improving with Metaheuristics the Item Selection in Parallel Coordinates Plot

David Cordero-Machuca [iD], Juan-Fernando Lima [iD], and Marcos Orellana[✉] [iD]

Universidad del Azuay, Cuenca 010204, Ecuador
{david.corderom,flima,marore}@uazuay.edu.ec

Abstract. Data visualization is one of the most powerful techniques to analyze and obtain reliable results based on the displayed outputs since it allows humans to improve decision-making by visually analyzing data behavior. Nevertheless, it could be disrupted by high data amounts in the visualization, as is the case with Parallel Coordinate Plot (PCP), where data behavior and associations of volumes of data are difficult to identify. This paper aims to reduce this issue with PCP and take advantage of metaheuristics for optimization problems through a Simulated Annealing (SA) algorithm. The proposed method was developed and tested using air pollution and meteorological variables. The obtained results presented a reduction in data volume, thus helping represent the most relevant data for the final user.

Keywords: Metaheuristic · Parallel coordinates plot · Filtering

1 Introduction

In recent years, the large volumes of daily generated data have opened the path for exploring and analyzing big data [13]. Big data allows using historical data to identify patterns useful for recent events, enabling a data analyst to make quick decisions based on big data analysis [1]. On the other hand, the constant growth of data has certain drawbacks, such as an increase in the algorithmic complexity required to process large amounts of data. This issue has pressured companies and academics to develop new systems and methodologies while generating innovative results [4].

Metaheuristic algorithms are processes that generate high-quality solutions by choosing a satisfactory solution through an iterative process with clear guidelines from a pool of possible solutions. They are implemented to avoid high algorithmic complexity. These algorithms include high-level and low-level procedures, such as a simple local search or a construction method [17] Metaheuristic algorithms are divided into two groups: the first group is single point-based methods, where each search space is gradually developed and includes some of the most known algorithms: Simulated Annealing (SA), trajectory/local search methods, tabu search, and simple evolutionary strategies [18]. The second group is population-based algorithms which include multiple trial points in the search

© The Author(s), under exclusive license to Springer Nature Switzerland AG 2022
J. Herrera-Tapia et al. (Eds.): TICEC 2022, CCIS 1648, pp. 186–200, 2022.
https://doi.org/10.1007/978-3-031-18272-3_13

space. Their results depend on their collective behavior, such as ant colony optimization, particle swarm optimization, and evolutionary strategies [18].

Data visualization is one of the most common techniques used to exploit big data and includes filtering irrelevant data, detecting multi-variable relationships, interacting with data representation, and observing data subsets in detail [9], making it easy to identify patterns, and is essential for information analysts [11]. Although previously, data visualization techniques were empirical and used to give a general idea of data representation, the difficulty of producing a quick analysis has required the generation of diverse data analysis techniques [5]. A lack of knowledge about new techniques, or the habit of using standard data visualization techniques, generates limitations for big data representation [22]. A clear example of the general lack of knowledge of visualization techniques is the Parallel Coordinates Plot (PCP), which is relatively unknown outside of the data visualization community [14,25]. This technique has some advantages, such as multi-variable relationships in a small space, data patterns between variables, and manipulation of data visualization by the user [10,12]. However, its main disadvantage is the difficulty of interpreting relationships between variables when handling big data [10,15]. Hence, to solve the data dispersion issue, Albazzaz and Wang [2] propose eliminating abnormal data and reducing the dimensions involved. Thus, we propose a metaheuristic algorithm that uses SA to show high levels of data concentration, based on various local results, to solve the disadvantage of PCP previously discussed.

The remaining paper is organized as follows: Sect. 2 presents the related work. Problem Formulation is in Sect. 3 which is divided into three stages: i) The data binning discretization, ii) The generation of alternative solutions, and iii) The optimal solution. Section 4 contains the results; and finally, Sect. 5 the conclusions and future works are presented.

2   Related Works

Data generally presents problems such as missing values, mixed formats, replicated entries, or lack of integrity rules [24]. It is important to apply preprocessing data techniques as the quality of results depends on cleaning the data of issues like those previously mentioned. In the field of data visualization, it is estimated that data scientists spend more than 50% of their time preparing data to be analyzed [24]. To deal with the PCP data dispersion problem, it is necessary to only reduce the data to the one relevant to the study. Meera and Sundar [19] propose a feature selection to reduce processing time and extract data from a database with big data, as it is a Hybrid method between Particle Swarm Optimization and Grammatical Evolution (PSO-GE).

Although PCP is a great advantage in representing multi-variables, its efficiency decreases when huge amounts of data are manipulated, thus presenting an overlapping issue. In order to reduce PCP representation complexity and make data easy to read, Berthold and Lawrence [6] apply fuzzy rules and even delimit the dimensions to be used to three, up to twenty. Also, variable selection reduces the amount of data processed. A good practice is establishing conditions and observations that are applied before analyzing and selecting variables [27].

Optimization problems can take advantage of metaheuristics. Abedinia et al. [21] propose a Shark Smell Optimization metaheuristic algorithm simulating shark behavior. The algorithm selects the best solution or "prey" by detecting higher odor concentration and forecasting the levels of solar energy by linking atmospheric components through a neural network.

Another research related to climate change, including metaheuristic algorithms and artificial intelligence tools, is the study by Dehghani et al. [8]. This study finds relationships between variables and data behavior and employs them to predict groundwater level behavior through a hybrid model on climatic variables. On the other hand, the analysis of climate variables does not exclusively use metaheuristics but also other artificial intelligence techniques. To find the best policy for drought regeneration systems, Mumtaz et al. [3] proposed the use of a Kernel Ridge Regression (KRR) model to split data and posed wet and dry scenarios, the Multivariate Empirical Mode Decomposition (MEMD) method to delimit multivariable climate indices, a Simulated Annealing (SA) model to define the most appropriate decomposed Intrinsic Mode Functions (IMFs) for the training period and feature selection strategy, and Random Forest (RF) to make decisions on a forecasting model. Another example of metaheuristics use is the one presented by Mohamed [20], where the algorithm seeks a relevant data subset by applying three different metaheuristic techniques: Particle Swarm Optimization (PSO), Cuckoo Search (CS), and Artificial Bee Colony (ABC).

Moreover, an example of the adaptability of metaheuristic algorithms to any optimization problem is the proposal by Bahadir and Serdar [16]. They employ SA to solve a p-median problem using a probabilistic metaheuristic and find the best threshold value for bi-level segmentation of gray-scale images, detecting optimal contour for edge-based images. In a different usage context, SA is used to find the optimal neighbor based on the power flow characteristics, within a real power system of nonlinear order and with a large combinatorial problem [26].

As observed, most of the studies implemented metaheuristics for global optimization. For this reason, our proposal contemplates using SA to define a rule for filtering relevant data in each selected variable. Thus, we use atmospheric variables, resulting in an understandable example of PCP optimization after filtering relevant data.

3   Problem Formulation

PCP is a visualization technique representing the relationships among related variables on the same graph. Usually, human intervention over the visualization graphs [7] results in data dispersion problems on PCP. These data dispersion issues highly increase the difficulty of interpreting a PCP, frequently becoming impractical to read. For this reason, this proposal aims to limit the amount of data presented by applying a SA metaheuristic algorithm. This section is divided into three parts: i) Visualization issue on PCP, ii) PCP visualization solution, and iii) Threats to validity.

3.1   Visualization Issue on PCP

To demonstrate the data dispersion issues, the analyzed dataset is managed by the municipality of Cuenca, Ecuador, which collects the atmospheric data measured in the city. A subset of this data, air pollution in the month of July 2018, has been chosen based on its completeness compared to other subsets. It includes five variables of air pollution: Carbon Monoxide (CO), Ozone (O_3), Nitrogen Dioxide (NO_2), Particulate Matter ($PM_{2.5}$), Sulfur Dioxide (SO_2), and a meteorological variable named air temperature ($°C$).

Then, preprocessing techniques were applied to the data. Table 1 presents the value range of variables, considering that the normality test failed for all of them. The PCP shown in Fig. 1 illustrates the selection of 3909 records belonging to the raw data for the month of July.

Table 1. Descriptive statistics of variables used for creating the visualization.

	Temperature ($°C$)	O_3 (ug/m^3)	CO (mg/m^3)	NO_2 (mg/m^3)	SO_2 (mg/m^3)	$PM_{2.5}$ (mg/m^3)
Min	5.30	4.74	0.25	0.0003	7.77	0.26
25%	12.20	11.40	0.55	5.19	9.95	5.29
Median	14.00	20.34	0.67	10.00	11.65	7.30
Mean	14.13	22.03	0.73	11.77	14.73	8.48
75%	16.00	30.44	0.83	16.23	15.87	9.82
Max	21.60	71.45	2.47	75.89	86.63	96.16

3.2   PCP Metaheuristic Solution

The proposed algorithm can filter records, thus reducing data presented to the most significant ones, to plot a clear image to show data behavior and relationships between variables. To aid human judgment, our proposed method aims to find the most relevant data in each variable based on user selection. Initially, each variable has the same amount of selected records. However, the data of

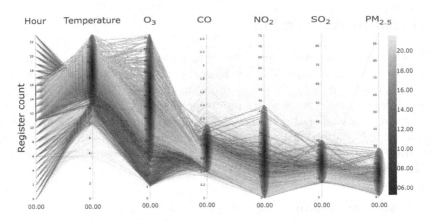

Fig. 1. PCP issue from July 2018.

a variable can be relevant in a different frequency and amplitude. The appropriate data selection method consists of three phases: i) The data distribution discretization phase receives prepossessed data as input, selects the ideal bin size, and detects the group of bars in the chosen variable. Then, ii) the alternative solutions phase calculates the minimum and maximum data from the selected dataset after the arithmetic means of each bin are calculated to decide if the current mean is unique; this value is added to the possible solutions array (threshold array). Finally, iii) the optimal solution phase chooses the better solution, the closest value to the frequency and amplitude conditions. The last two phases employ the SA algorithm, which has been divided into two algorithms for a better understanding: Algorithm 1 is responsible for finding alternative solutions, and Algorithm 2 is responsible for finding the optimal solution, obtaining between the two the SA algorithm and optimal threshold value.

To observe the data used in this study, Fig. 2 illustrates data for each variable in blue bars before it represents bins, and Fig. 3 depicts the dispersion of the raw data for the $PM_{2.5}$ variable.

Data Binning Discretization. Histograms are a type of graph that permit finding anomalies in data, such as dispersion, quantity counts of a bar (height or frequency) and the interval of a bar (width or amplitude). For this reason, histograms must be refined additionally for data preprocessing, as can be observed in Fig. 3.

Due to the dispersion presented was necessary to find a way to approach the histograms, one possibility being the division of the data into bins. There are different techniques to get a proper bin size, such as the equation of Sturge, normal of Scott, rule of Rice, and the Freedman-Diaconis equation [23]. To get a smoothness histogram, the Freedman-Diaconis equation was used in our dataset, as shown in Fig. 4 where the raw data of $PM_{2.5}$ are represented in Fig. 4a, and the division of that data into bins is represented in Fig. 4b.

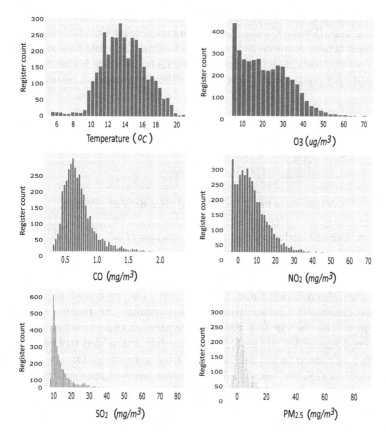

Fig. 2. Frequency and amplitude of selected variables. (Color figure online)

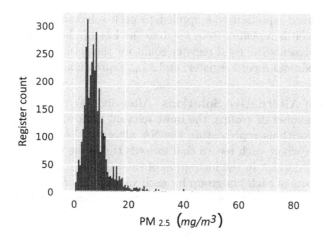

Fig. 3. $PM_{2.5}$ data dispersion.

Sahann et al. [23] show that the number of bins directly influences the distribution histogram. However, the same authors emphasize that the number of bins reaches a limit where no more bins can be added as the error rate stops decreasing. Based on the tests, the Freedman-Diaconis equation was chosen because it was balanced and sticks to the best bin size division for ideal results.

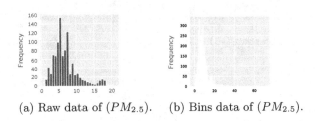

(a) Raw data of $(PM_{2.5})$.   (b) Bins data of $(PM_{2.5})$.

Fig. 4. Use of Freedman-Diaconis equation into $(PM_{2.5})$ variable data.

Once the data has been divided into bins, the bin groups (a sequence of bins) and their boundaries must be identified. The proposed algorithm went through the generated bins sequentially to determine the formed data groups. If the height of the current bar was more significant than or equal to the value of the Filtered Amount Criteria $()FAC)$, the bar was added to the current bin group (which is named in sequential order from zero to n). On the other hand, if the current bar register count (height) was not more significant than the value of Eq. 1, the bar was not added and the new bin group was defined. This process was repeated until all the bars in the histogram of each chosen variable were covered, producing an algorithmic complexity of $O(n^2)$.

$$FAC = \frac{\sum_{i=1}^{m} h_i}{(x_{max} - x_{min})} \qquad (1)$$

The mentioned equation was applied to each selected variable, where the height summation is repeated from $i = 1$ to the last bin height h_i of the actual variable. m represents the total register count for the actual variable, x_{max} represents the maximum record register, and x_{min} represents the minimum record.

Generation of Alternative Solutions. After dividing the data into bins and detecting the number of groups, the most relevant data was filtered by the two by the two algorithms representing the SA algorithm. Algorithm 1 defines a threshold value, where each record that exceeds this value is considered relevant data within the dataset in the histogram of each variable. Algorithm 1 explores the average values of each bin group for each variable. To reduce the complexity of the algorithm, initial control parameters are established, such as the possible solutions, which must be unique, and how many bin groups the algorithm can go through ("nNeighbours"). For our meteorological data, the value of "nNeighbours" was established as five neighbors since this value achieved the best test results.

In Algorithm 2, the input data refers to the list of variables to be analyzed $varList$, the current variable on analysis is $curVarible$, the complete data frame is $fulData$, the selected data frame is $selData$, the number of established neighbors is $nNeighbors$, and the number of bins from the actual variable is $nBinGroups$. As output data, the algorithm returns a vector of possible solutions $posibleSolutions$ and a vector of possible solutions expressed as a percentage $posibleSolutionsPct$.

Algorithm 1. Alternative solutions.

Require: $varList, curVarible, fulData, selData, nNeighbors, nBinGroups$
Ensure: $posibleSolutions, posibleSolutionsPct$
1: $minDataSel \leftarrow minseltData[]$
2: $maxDataSel \leftarrow maxseltData[]$
3: $minPerSel \leftarrow getPercenile(fulData[curVarible], minDataSel)$
4: $maxPerSel \leftarrow getPercenile(fulData[curVarible], maxDataSel)$
5: **for** seq in nNeighbor **do**
6:     $perMin \leftarrow 0$
7:     $perMax \leftarrow 100$
8:     **if** $minPerSel + seq \geq 0$ **then**
9:         $perMin \leftarrow minPerSel + seq$
10:    **end if**
11:    **if** $maxPerSel + seq \leq 100$ **then**
12:        $perMax \leftarrow maxPerSel + seq$
13:    **end if**
14:    $varMinPerSel \leftarrow getPercenile(fulData[curVarible], perMin)$
15:    $varMaxPerSel \leftarrow getPercenile(fulData[curVarible], perMax)$
16:    $tempData[] \leftarrow fulData[(fulData[curVarible] \geq varMinPerSel)$
17:    $and(fulData[curVarible] \leq varMaxPerSel)]$
18:    $n \leftarrow getHist(tempData[curVarible])$
19:    $tempSolution \leftarrow getAvg(n)$
20:    $tempPct[] \leftarrow getPct(curVarible, tempData[], nNeighbors)$
21:    **if** $tempSolution not in posibleSolutions$ **then**
22:        $posibleSolutions.add(tempSolution)$
23:        $posibleSolutionsPct.add(tempPct)$
24:    **end if**
25: **end for**

Optimal Solution. Algorithm 2 selects the optimal threshold value as the good enough solution. This threshold was found in the vector of bin groups chosen as possible solutions for each variable. This selection was produced through the application of predefined rules and fulfilled by the use of percentages such as the percentage of minimal width for acceptable data ($reqMinWidth$), the percentage of maximal width for acceptable data ($reqMaxWidth$), and the ideal amount of data ($reqHeight$) in each bin group chosen by each variable as a possible solution. Also, it is important to emphasize that the predefined rules were established according to the expertise of the data analyzer. Using the current dataset, and after testing possible best values for each rule, the best values were 5%, 42% and 10% for the variables *reqMinWidth*, reqMaxWidth, *reqHeight* respectively.

Therefore, those variables were taken as input data for the possible solutions *posibleSolutions*, the percentage of the possible solution *posibleSolutionsPct*, the minimum width required by the user for the selected data *reqMinWidth*, the maximum width required by the user for the selected data *reqMaxWidth*, and the height needed for the user for the selected data *reqHeight*.

Algorithm 2. Optimal solution.

Require: *posibleSolutions, posibleSolutionsPct*
Require: *reqMinWidth, reqMaxWidth, reqHeight*
Ensure: *optimalSolution*
1: **for** current in posibleSolutions **do**
2:     **if** *current* $\geq$ *reqMinWidth* **then**
3:         **if** *current* $\leq$ *reqMaxWidth* **then**
4:             **if** *current* $\geq$ *reqHeight* **then**
5:                 *optimalSolution* $\leftarrow$ *posibleSolutions[current]*
6:             **end if**
7:         **end if**
8:     **end if**
9: **end for**

Since the metaheuristic algorithm is executed on each analyzed variable, and each contains filtered data with different indexes, a final step is required for the selection of tuples to be displayed in the last PCP. For this reason, the union and the intersection of the filtered data indexes of each variable were tested, giving as best result in the merge of these indexes. The merge presented a loss of 6%, the minor data loss compared to the intersection loss of 11% of the indexes.

3.3 Threats to Validity

Although the study was performed and focused on multiple domains, some threats to its validity were identified, which are listed below to give an understanding and how to address them.

Threshold Value. The threshold values calculated as alternative solutions and the good enough solution for the SA proposed algorithm are based on their mean value, the most widely used metric. Notwithstanding, the threshold value can be calculated in other mathematical ways, such as the median, mode, or any other matter the data analyst considers. This study used the mean as the threshold value for each analyzed variable, meaning that whether different values could have produced better results or not is currently unknown.

Number of Bins. Due to the dispersion presented in the data used in our study, an approximation technique for histograms was sought to smooth the data. The method chosen was dividing the data into bins using the Freedman-Diaconis equation [23]. This equation provided the ideal size of bins to be applied to the data. However, it may not be the best in other data fields. For this reason, it is advisable to try other equations for obtaining the ideal bin size, such as the equation of Sturge, normal of Scott, normal of Rice, ruler of Rice, and Scot [23].

Control Variables. An expert in the problem domain must adjust the control variables in the SA algorithm according to whether or not they reduce data. The control variables must be adjusted to reduce the data to the most representative data, based on the judgment of a subject matter expert. However, this judgment may differ from the variable adjustment judgment of another subject matter expert. The variables; percentage of minimal width for acceptable data (*reqMinWidth*), percentage of maximal width for acceptable data (*reqMaxWidth*) and the ideal amount of data (*reqHeight*) set the initial rules for the algorithm by a percentage on each of them. The percentage per variable established in our proposal is based on the data analyzed; however, this data may be considered deficient depending on the expert analyst.

4 Results

The $PM_{2.5}$ air pollution variable was used to exemplify the first step of our proposal, where raw data was preprocessed, and then the data distribution discretization stage was applied. The steps presented in this section showed the results of all chosen variables for each step, not only the $PM_{2.5}$ variable.

Results in Data Distribution Discretization. While the $PM_{2.5}$ variable was used to follow the current process, the rest of the variables were not presented. Raw data of each missing variable was given against the data selected by the user and divided into the ideal number of bins. As shown in Fig. 5, the data represented on blue bars correspond to raw data, while green bars correspond to data selected by the user, which in our case includes the hour range from 11:00 to 16:00.

Results in Alternative Solutions. Once variables were preprocessed and their bins were defined, the possible solutions were established using Algorithm 1. As described in Sect. 3.2, each possible solution corresponds to an average value per bin, where it was added only if it was unique on the array of possible solutions for each variable. In Fig. 6, possible solutions are represented with a green color scale.

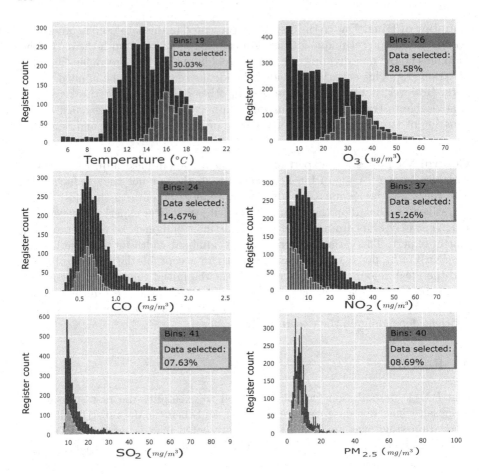

Fig. 5. Raw data versus selected data. (Color figure online)

Results in Optimal Solution. After applying the predefined rules, as mentioned in Sect. 3.2, the best possible solution was chosen. This optimal result reflects a threshold value used to filter the most relevant data from the users' initial selection. All data and bins that exceed the optimal solution value were considered necessary for marking a pattern of behavior within PCP. In contrast, the values below this mark were neglected for the analysis by the data expert. In Fig. 6, each optimal solution is presented with a red line per variable, where the left column shows the possible solutions (green color scale lines) and the optimal solution (red color line), while the right column shows the interaction of the possible solutions with the optimal solution of each variable.

In Fig. 7, the last PCP is shown, but only with the selection of the tuples obtained by the union of indexes of the analyzed variables, thus representing the data filtered by the metaheuristic algorithm.

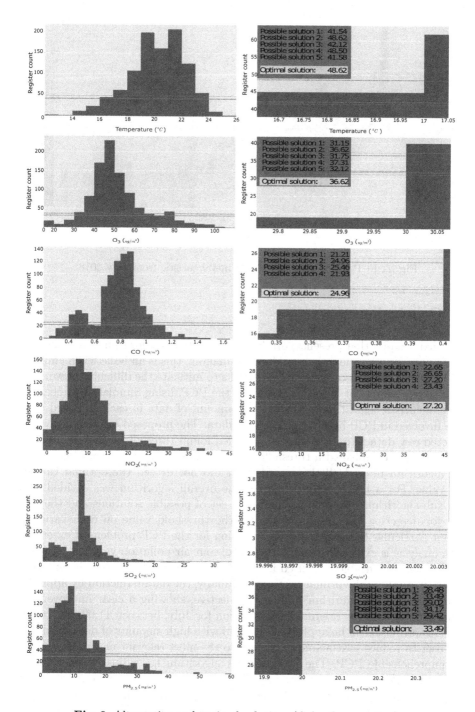

Fig. 6. Alternative and optimal solution. (Color figure online)

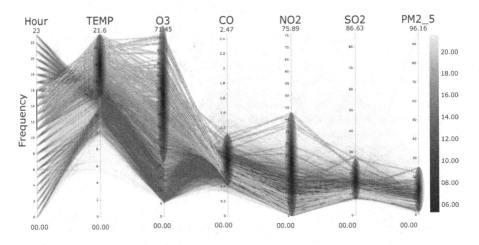

Fig. 7. PCP after being filtered by metaheuristic from July 2018.

5   Conclusions

Visualizing a plot that presents correlation and data behavior from large amounts of data can be a hurdle in human decision-making; this is an issue when employing PCP. For this reason, our proposal seeks to mitigate the difficulty of working with large amounts of data by optimizing the PCP, using Simulated Annealing, a metaheuristic algorithm, to reduce the amount of data in each analyzed variable involved in PCP by filtering relevant data. The proposed algorithm divided selected raw data into ideal bin groups, then found threshold values as possible solutions and established a threshold value as a good enough resolution. Thus, the algorithm filtered all the records that did not exceed the optimal threshold value. For a better understanding, the overall algorithm was divided into two sub-algorithms, the first for finding a set of possible solutions and the second for detecting the optimal value for the threshold value on each variable. In our particular case, the proposed solution for the PCP problem of extensive data analysis is explored through the use of four air pollution variables and one meteorological variable measured in the city of Cuenca, taking the air pollution $PM_{2.5}$ variable as the primary reference. Finally, the data reduction by applying the metaheuristic algorithm fulfills its objective, showing a clear improvement when interpreting the original data selection for July, between 11:00 and 16:00.

This proposal can be applied in any field with high amounts of data. It allows the user to reduce vast amounts of data to the most relevant and present it on a comprehensible PCP. The proposed SA algorithm has adjustment variables to find the best threshold value for each input variable. In future studies, the proposed algorithm will test with a larger dataset produced using a more significant number of sensor measurements in multiple locations of a country. Another adequate study for confirming the effectiveness of our proposal will be in the commerce field, as it generates enormous correlational data volume.

References

1. Agresi, A.: An Introduction to Categorical Data Analysis, 3rd Edn. Wiley (2018)
2. Albazzaz, H., Wang, X.Z.: Historical data analysis based on plots of independent and parallel coordinates and statistical control limits. J. Process Control **16**, 103–114 (2006). https://doi.org/10.1016/j.jprocont.2005.05.005
3. Ali, M., Deo, R.C., Maraseni, T., Downs, N.J.: Improving spi-derived drought forecasts incorporating synoptic-scale climate indices in multi-phase multivariate empirical mode decomposition model hybridized with simulated annealing and kernel ridge regression algorithms. J. Hydrol. **576**, 164–184 (2019). https://doi.org/10.1016/j.jhydrol.2019.06.032
4. Ansari, S., Mohanlal, R., Poncela, J., Ansari, A., Mohanlal, K.: Importance of big data. In: Handbook of Research on Trends and Future Directions in Big Data and Web Intelligence, pp. 1–19. IGI Global (2015)
5. Berinato, S.: Visualizations that really work. Harvard Bus. Rev. **94**(6), 93–100 (2016)
6. Berthold, M.R., Hall, L.O.: Visualizing fuzzy points in parallel coordinates. IEEE Trans. Fuzzy Syst. **11**, 369–374 (2003). https://doi.org/10.1109/TFUZZ.2003.812696
7. Dasgupta, A., Kosara, R.: The importance of tracing data through the visualization pipeline. In: Proceedings of the 2012 BELIV Workshop: Beyond Time and Errors-Novel Evaluation Methods for Visualization, pp. 1–5 (2012)
8. Dehghani, R., Poudeh, H.T., Izadi, Z.: The effect of climate change on groundwater level and its prediction using modern meta-heuristic model. Groundwater Sustain. Develop. **16**, 100702 (2022). https://doi.org/10.1016/j.gsd.2021.100702
9. Diehl, S.: Past, present, and future of and in software visualization. In: Past, Present, and Future of and in Software Visualization, pp. 3–11 (2015)
10. Fan, J., Li, R.: Statistical challenges with high dimensionality: feature selection in knowledge discovery. arXiv preprint arXiv:math/0602133 (2006)
11. Feng, M., et al.: Big data analytics and mining for effective visualization and trends forecasting of crime data. IEEE Access **7**, 106111–106123 (2019). https://doi.org/10.1109/ACCESS.2019.2930410
12. Groves, R.M., Fowler Jr, F.J., Couper, M.P., Lepkowski, J.M., Singer, E., Tourangeau, R.: Survey Methodology, vol. 561. Wiley (2011)
13. Gupta, A., Deokar, A., Iyer, L., Sharda, R., Schrader, D.: Big data & analytics for societal impact: recent research and trends. Inf. Syst. Front. **20**(2), 185–194 (2018)
14. Heinrich, J., Weiskopf, D.: State of the art of parallel coordinates. In: Eurographics (State of the Art Reports), pp. 95–116 (2013)
15. Johansson, J., Ljung, P., Jern, M., Cooper, M.: Revealing structure within clustered parallel coordinates displays. In: IEEE Symposium on Information Visualization, 2005. INFOVIS 2005, pp. 125–132. IEEE (2005)
16. Karasulu, B., Korukoglu, S.: A simulated annealing-based optimal threshold determining method in edge-based segmentation of grayscale images. Appl. Soft Comput. **11**, 2246–2259 (2011). https://doi.org/10.1016/J.ASOC.2010.08.005
17. Lev, B.: Meta-heuristics: advances and trends in local search paradigms for optimization. Interfaces **30**(4), 94 (2000)

18. Maier, H.R., et al.: Evolutionary algorithms and other metaheuristics in water resources: current status, research challenges and future directions. Environ. Model. Softw. **62**, 271–299 (2014). https://doi.org/10.1016/J.ENVSOFT.2014.09.013

19. Meera, S., Sundar, C.: A hybrid metaheuristic approach for efficient feature selection methods in big data. J. Ambient Intell. Humaniz. Comput. **12**(3), 3743–3751 (2020). https://doi.org/10.1007/S12652-019-01656-W

20. Mohamed, N.S., Zainudin, S., Othman, Z.A.: Metaheuristic approach for an enhanced MRMR filter method for classification using drug response microarray data. Exp. Syst. Appl. **90**, 224–231 (2017). https://doi.org/10.1016/J.ESWA.2017.08.026

21. Abedinia, O., Nima Amjady, N.G.: Solar energy forecasting based on hybrid neural network and improved metaheuristic algorithm. Comput. Intell. **34**, 241–260 (2018). https://doi.org/10.1111/COIN.12145

22. Perkhofer, L.M., Hofer, P., Walchshofer, C., Plank, T., Jetter, H.C.: Interactive visualization of big data in the field of accounting. J. Appl. Account. Res. **20**, 497–525 (2019). https://doi.org/10.1108/JAAR-10-2017-0114

23. Sahann, R., Müller, T., Schmidt, J.: Histogram binning revisited with a focus on human perception. In: 2021 IEEE Visualization Conference (VIS), pp. 66–70 (2021). https://doi.org/10.1109/VIS49827.2021.9623301

24. Sataloff, R.T., Johns, M.M., Kost, K.M.: Data Cleaning 2019. ACM Books Series (2019)

25. Siirtola, H., Räihä, K.J.: Interacting with parallel coordinates. Interact. Comput. **18**(6), 1278–1309 (2006)

26. Sousa, T., Soares, J., Vale, Z.A., Morais, H., Faria, P.: Simulated annealing metaheuristic to solve the optimal power flow. In: 2011 IEEE Power and Energy Society General Meeting, pp. 1–8 (2011). https://doi.org/10.1109/PES.2011.6039543

27. Weidele, D.K.I.: Conditional parallel coordinates. In: 2019 IEEE Visualization Conference (VIS), pp. 221–225 (2019). https://doi.org/10.1109/VISUAL.2019.8933632

Implementation of Clustering Techniques to Data Obtained from a Memory Match Game Oriented to the Cognitive Function of Attention

Marcos Orellana$^{(\boxtimes)}$, María-Inés Acosta-Urigüen ,
and Reinerio Rodríguez García

Universidad del Azuay, Cuenca, Ecuador
{marore,macosta}@uazuay.edu.ec, rrodriguez@es.uazuay.edu.ec

Abstract. Serious games are software applications with an explicit educational objective that have been thoroughly thought out and designed as a learning instrument or tool. They allow the user to experience situations similar to real life and learn from their mistakes through immediate feedback. These games have been developed in various fields, including business, industry, marketing, health, government, among others. For instance, some are used for cognitive training in human beings, where attention and memory are fundamental axes during the various stages of the human life cycle. In this context, the "memory match game" is a card game where many pairs of cards are laid face down, and its objective is to match pairs in the lowest time and with the minimum number of wrong clicks. This information is registered and stored along with the player's sociodemographic information. Thus, this article aims to analyze the dataset, applying clustering techniques in order to find behavioral patterns. The age variable was used to generate 4 age groups that served as the basis for applying the unsupervised machine learning algorithm, k-means. The results show the behavior of the data in relation to the age groups, it is evident that the more experience the players gain, times and scores improve, regardless of age.

Keywords: Serious games · K-means · Memory match game

1 Introduction

Cognitive functions directly influence educational and professional performance, socioeconomic achievement, health, and longevity. The study of the decrease in these capacities, although related to age, is also associated with deficiencies in the performance of daily activities when these fall outside normal ranges. In general, mild deficiencies in the aforementioned functions are considered normal in aging [1].

The cognitive functions include processing speed, attention, working memory, verbal and visual learning, and executive functions. Attention has components that measure vigilance, orientation, and detection. Detection is the component that quantifies the focus of attention on a stimulus for a time, even with the presence of distractions or

J. Herrera-Tapia et al. (Eds.): TICEC 2022, CCIS 1648, pp. 201–216, 2022.
https://doi.org/10.1007/978-3-031-18272-3_14

increased fatigue. For example, vigilance or sustained attention can be measured using sets of identical pairs, selective attention can be measured using the Stroop test [2, 3].

Serious Games (SG) are computer applications with purposes beyond the entertainment that can register and store data transparently during the gameplay [4, 5]. SG are mainly developed in the fields of military, health, science, and education. These games can include enhanced and interactive gameplay, levels and quests, and interaction with game objects [5, 6]. Some SG have been developed to support cognitive stimulation, training, and rehabilitation [6, 7], others try to modify the behavior or improve the health care [8].

Data science is an area of study focused on the prediction, exploration, and understanding of data [9]. The algorithms and techniques include supervised algorithms, unsupervised algorithms, and visualization techniques [10].

Unsupervised algorithms base the training process without previously defined labels or classes applied to the dataset. Clustering techniques and algorithms are considered unsupervised, and they measure the distance between two entities in a dataset, and, based on it, the clusters are formed [11]. K-means is an unsupervised algorithm which describes simple mathematical processes and has a fast convergence [12, 13].

The aim of this paper is to take, as an starting point, the results obtained by [14] and apply clustering techniques considering the level of the game in which the player is in order to evaluate the performance.

The paper is structured as follows: Sect. 2 presents the related works for the use of clustering algorithms in the field of serious games, Sect. 3 describes the methodology based on SPEM and its implementation, and finally, Sect. 4 presents the conclusions and future work.

2   Related Works

The implementation of data science techniques for the analysis of data from SG has been widely analyzed. For example, [15] presented a SG to predict math skill level of students with special capacities. The game consisted of a quiz with multiple choices (4 options) where each question had a predefined time limit. The quiz was applied to a sample of children with normal and special capacities, moreover, sociodemographic information was collected, along with the answers. To classify data, several ranges and percentages were calculated, and six data mining methods were used to analyze the data. The conclusions showed the correlation between sociodemographic variables when determining the level of math skills for the normal student, but this could not be found in the students with special needs group. The best accuracy was obtained using the JRIP algorithm.

The authors of [16] presented a SG to collect, analyze and visualize body movement information based on the data collected for the SG Hammer and Planks, whose objective is to rehabilitate patients with balance disorders. The user has to move the body in different directions in a 2D environment simulating the navigation on a ship. The hierarchical clustering algorithm was used to identify similar distribution of movements. However, the work does not mention scores related to the game performance, although it describes some visualization techniques to show the evolution of movements.

An adaptive rehabilitation bot based on the use of SG was proposed by [17]. RehaBot was developed for traditional therapy solutions. The application can adjust therapies to cover the whole body; includes a virtual assistant to address patients to perform the exercises correctly through 3D illustrations, and adjust the game's difficulty level in real-time according to the patients' abilities. The work presents the use of the mining techniques to predict improvement based on a schedule of exercises, but it does not describe the application of the techniques themselves.

A SG for science and technology presents a virtual world where players explore thematic islands to discover games, news, photos, and videos [18]. The players' information, performance, and interactions were stored and analyzed; the processes of detecting and removing outliers and extreme values were carried out; linear regression and clustering techniques were also applied. K-means technique was used, considering one dependent variable with two influential independent variables. The results demonstrate that the number of accesses to the game, the quests visited, and the advantages used are important factors that influence scores and time playing; the clustering allows to identify beginner, intermediate and advanced players according to their experience.

The authors of [14] presented a methodology to evaluate data from SG. The proposal included four stages, and the implemented data mining technique was clustering. Although several demographic variables were collected, only time, gender, and level were analyzed. The results showed a strong relationship between age and gender, and the proposed future work aims to compare models and techniques to obtain better results.

3   Application of the Methodology

The methodology is proposed in Fig. 1 through a diagram with the software process and the metamodel engineering systems 2.0 (SPEM 2.0). According to [19], the activities in the methodology describe the input and output of devices in the modeling process.

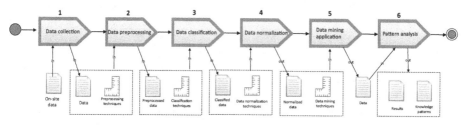

Fig. 1. Methodology to figure out knowledge patterns in serious games data.

The methodology is divided into data collection, processing, classification, normalization, mining techniques, and analysis. Data collection focuses on using in situ criteria for serious games data collection. The game of pairs consists of showing the tokens in a specific time and location for these to be covered for the subject to remember the initial position [20]. Sociodemographic variables and SG data execution variables are collected and stored in a single online data set for all players. The game is available in the website https://jserionew-8e818.web.app/#/.

The data processing stage describes a group of unprocessed data and its preliminary preparation by applying processing techniques such as the elimination of missing, faulty, extreme, among others, data values to obtain a clear data set. Within the collected data, there are several inconsistencies such as missing names, age, birth date or the time of a single game level. Lastly, the extreme values register time beyond half an hour to finish each level; these directly affect the participant's score. These registers are eliminated to obtain a clean data set and efficient results.

According to Hou, there is a data classification aimed to categorize the results because people's attention changes according to age [21]. Also, [22] applies a data classification based on the results of the participants' scores to group them in relation to their performance. For this study, four ranges have been considered: kids (up to 11 years), teenagers (from 12 to 20 years), adults (from 21 to 59 years), and elderly (from and beyond 60).

Data normalization applies the RapidMiner program to transform the scores and age in a standard scale for these two attributes using a value range from 0 to 1 [23].

This paper uses K-clustering and Neural Networks as data mining techniques to analyze and verify the most relevant technique to find efficient behaviors. This section uses K-clustering available in RapidMiner [24] to determine the K number of clusters to satisfy the criteria [25]; the K algorithm is a grouping method that allows to work in large data sets with significant values because it is capable to provide an efficient classification [21].

The data analysis stage uses the results from the data mining techniques. The data is statistically analyzed to determine the best distribution. In Fig. 2, it is possible to observe the quantity of score values obtained by the participants whose most frequent score is 1800 points; this is a significant value considering that the minimum score is 1000 and the maximum is 2000. The mean score of all participants is 1704.57, which is an acceptable value as the perfect score is 2000. The standard deviation is 208.62, so it is a relevant value to analyze and quantify in the data dispersion.

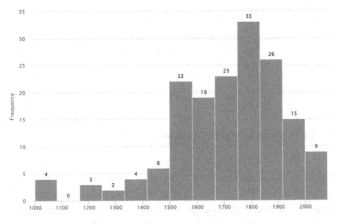

Fig. 2. Frequency of scores for all participants.

Table 1 presents the data distribution, where most data come from the adult category (21–58 years) with 67.66% (n = 112) of participants. For the other categories, teenagers (12–20 years) represent 19.16% (n = 32), kids represent 10.78% (n = 18), and elderly (beyond 60 years) represent 2.40% (n = 4).

Table 1. Data distribution of participants according to categories.

Category	Quantity	Percentage
Kids (up to 11 years)	18	10.78%
Teenagers (12–20 years)	32	19.16%
Adults (21–59 years)	112	67.66%
Elderly (from and beyond 60 years)	4	2.40%

Figure 3 presents a box plot of the categorized ages and scores to interpret the scores, laying out data quartiles and atypical values.

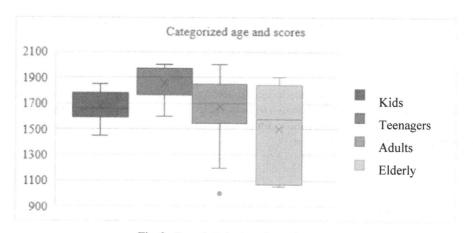

Fig. 3. Box plot of categories and scores.

The box plot portraying the Kids category is compact and not dispersed; the same pattern repeats for Teenagers and Adults. Conversely, in the Elderly category, there is more data dispersion due to the diversity in their scores, considering the lower quartile score and the minimum score compared to the other categories. This is due to the lower number of samples in the category, so a lower score affects all the results. Conversely, the Teenagers category has higher scores and less data dispersion; thus, this category's results show better attention in teenagers, representing a greater performance than the other categories.

Figure 4 presents the trials made by participants in the Kids category (0–11 years) in which five people made three trials, two people made four trials, and one person madefive5 trials in each of the 4 phases of the serious game. Every phase, according to the number of trials, shows an improvement in the time that take to finish each game's phase. As a result, they improve their attention. In the first phase of the game there is a slight increase in the time, but this increase is vastly irrelevant.

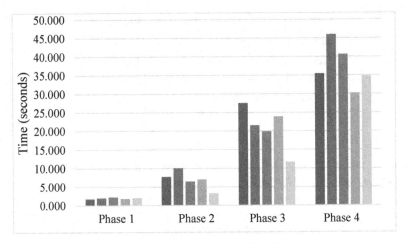

Fig. 4. Trials by the participants in the kids category.

Figure 5 depicts the trials made by the Teenagers category (12–20), in which 30 people made one trial and 2 made two trials of each of the 4 phases of the serious game. It can be appreciated that the time to finish each game's stages improves in each phase and according to the trial number.

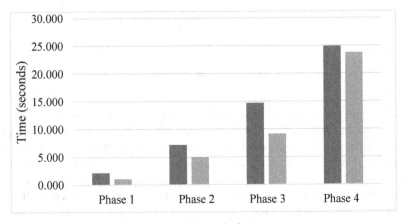

Fig. 5. Trials by the participants in the teenagers category.

In the Adults category, Fig. 6 portrays the trials performed by its participants in which 73 people made one trial, 15 people made two trials, seven people made three trials, and one person made 11 trials for each one of the phases of the serious game. In each phase, the time taken to finish the serious game improved in relation to the number of trials.

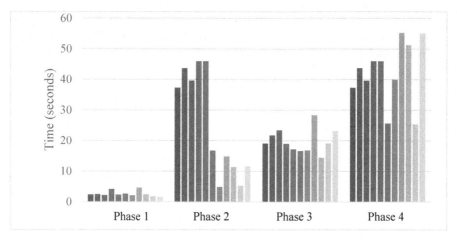

Fig. 6. Trials by the participants in the adults category.

In the category of Elderly (beyond 60 years), Fig. 7 shows the trials performed by its participants in which three people made one trial, and two made two trials in each of the SG phases. It is noticed that the time to finish the game improves as the number of trials increases.

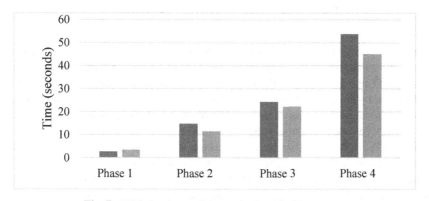

Fig. 7. Trials by the participants in the elderly category.

3.1   Cluster Application

For data classification, the Euclidean distance is used as a measurement of association. The formed groups contain similar individuals, so the distance between them is short.

Figure 8 shows that when the group of ages and participants' scores is classified, these can be divided into groups with similar values; cluster 5 is separated due to its two atypical values. A large amount of the values is concentrated within the range of less than 41 years and more than 1350 points. As a result, the vast majority of people younger than 40 years have higher scores, and after this age, other factors may affect the performance and efficiency to finish the game.

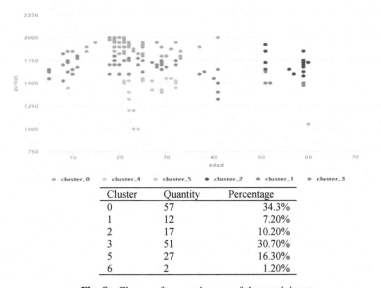

Cluster	Quantity	Percentage
0	57	34.3%
1	12	7.20%
2	17	10.20%
3	51	30.70%
5	27	16.30%
6	2	1.20%

Fig. 8. Cluster of age and score of the participants.

Figure 9 portrays the classification of data according to age and time of the first phase of the game, where the participants are divided into two groups defined by score similarity, defined according to their age and time into four groups. Also, cluster 2 is differentiated by an atypical value. A great quantity of the values concentrates in cluster zero with 126 data points, equivalent to 76% of the data set, meaning that people younger than 40 years end the first game's phase within 4 s.

Figure 10 displays the data set classification of age and time of the second phase of the game, which divides the participants into groups defined by the similarity of the values, thus, identifying four groups. Also, cluster 2 is differentiated due to an atypical value. A significant number of the values concentrate in cluster zero with 120 data points, equivalent to 72.3% of the data set, meaning that people younger than 37 years finish the second phase of the game in less than 14 s. Subsequently, there are dispersed values in cluster 1 for people between the ages of 20 and 26 years who exceed the 14 s.

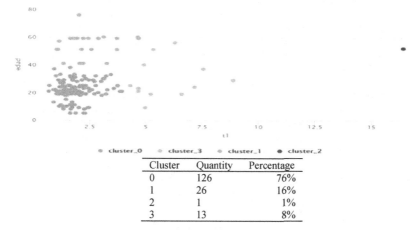

Cluster	Quantity	Percentage
0	126	76%
1	26	16%
2	1	1%
3	13	8%

Fig. 9. Data classification by age and time of the first phase.

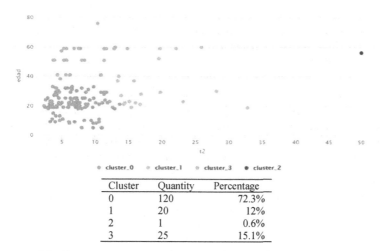

Cluster	Quantity	Percentage
0	120	72.3%
1	20	12%
2	1	0.6%
3	25	15.1%

Fig. 10. Data classification by age and time of the second phase.

Figure 11 depicts the data set classification of age and time of the third phase of the game, which divides the participants into groups defined by the similarity of the values; thus, identifying four cluster groups with dispersion. The largest concentration of data points is in cluster zero, with 59.6% of the data set, meaning that people older than 40 years finish the third phase of the game in 22 s or less. Then, cluster 1 is very close since it represents people older than 40 years with an estimated time between 12 and 38 s. Moreover, cluster 2 involves people between 5 and 38 years with a time between 20 and 35 s. Finally, cluster 3 has 8% of the data set depicting people between 5 and 40 years that take between 35 and 60 s to finish the game.

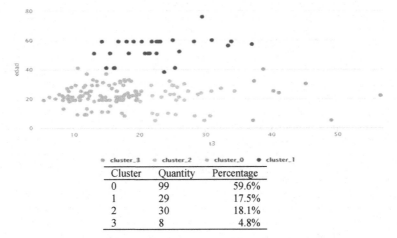

Fig. 11. Data classification by age and time of the third phase.

Cluster	Quantity	Percentage
0	99	59.6%
1	29	17.5%
2	30	18.1%
3	8	4.8%

Figure 12 depicts the data set classification of age and time of the third phase of the game, which divides the participants into groups defined by the similarity of the values; thus, identifying three cluster groups with dispersion. The largest concentration of data points is in cluster zero with 63.3% of the data set, meaning that people until 41 years finish the fourth phase of the game in less than 45 s. Then, cluster 1 represents 16.3% of the data set with people between 39 and 60 years with an estimated time between 25 and 45 s. Moreover, cluster 2 represents 1.8% of people between 55 and 68 years with a time between 60 and 85 s. Finally, cluster 3 has 18.7% of the data set depicting people between 5 and 39 years that take between 45 and 95 s to finish the game's phase.

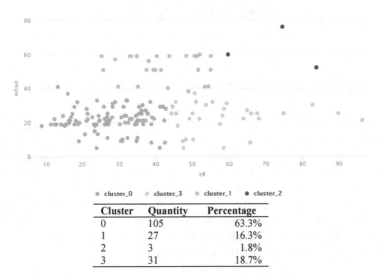

Fig. 12. Data classification by age and time of the fourth phase.

Cluster	Quantity	Percentage
0	105	63.3%
1	27	16.3%
2	3	1.8%
3	31	18.7%

To obtain data in the same scale, a normalization technique was applied to standardize the values in a common scale for the time variables for each game level (TPN1, TPN2, TPN3, TPN4), ages, scores, and sex. The objective is to analyze the data efficiently.

Once the data is normalized, a clustering technique is applied to classify it into four groups. Table 2 portrays the centroids of the four clusters and the different game variables.

Table 2. Normalized and classified data centroids.

	Cluster 1	Cluster 2	Cluster 3	Cluster 4
Trial	0.110	0.150	0.052	0.037
Age	0.311	0.516	0.203	0.289
Score	0.536	0.551	0.809	0.839
TPN1	0.201	0.243	0.193	0.132
TPN2	0.156	0.189	0.102	0.108
TPN3	0.424	0.493	0.198	0.162
TPN4	0.416	0.493	0.210	0.221
Sex	0	1	1	0

Figure 13 shows that the time variables in each level of the game, age, and sex are important in each cluster classification. This is why the analysis is more thorough in the trials of the participants in each level of the game. The aim is to verify the people in each category.

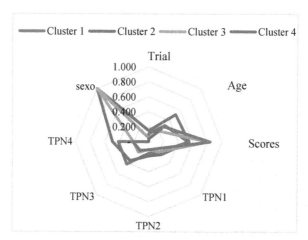

Fig. 13. Radial graph of the application of clustering with data from the centroids of the demographic variables.

Figures 14, 15, and 16 have centroids of the groups that include time variables in the different game levels (TPN1, TPN2, TPN3, TPN4) of each one of the trials. They show graphs that represent the classification of the data in each one of the trials of the game. From these, cluster 1 has a significant influence over the others, so it is thoroughly analyzed to identify the category of the people's ages in this classification. Tables 17, 19, and 21 reflect the different categories of age, quantity, and percentage of men and women found, the mean time of men (MTM) and the mean time of women (MTW) determine the time taken to finish the different levels of the game. Lastly, the mean scores of men (MSM) and mean scores of women (MSW) are portrayed too (Table 3).

Table 3. Results of the data for categories in Figure 15.

Category	Data quantity	Men quantity	Women quantity	MTM	MTW	MSM	MSW
Kids	5	2	3	16.4	19.2	1612.5	1725
Teenagers	30	22	8	12.0	12.9	1843.2	1890
Adults	73	35	38	17.8	15.6	1649.3	1718
Elderly	2	2	0	29.8		1062.6	
Total	110	61	49				
Mean				18.99	15.90	1541.9	1778

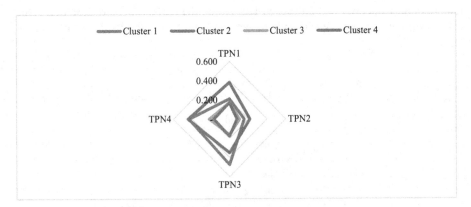

	Cluster 1	Cluster 2	Cluster 3	Cluster 4
TPN1	0.201	0.381	0.169	0.171
TPN2	0.156	0.217	0.107	0.080
TPN3	0.475	0.352	0.161	0.179
TPN4	0.435	0.445	0.218	0.168

Fig. 14. Graph of grouped centroids in trial 1.

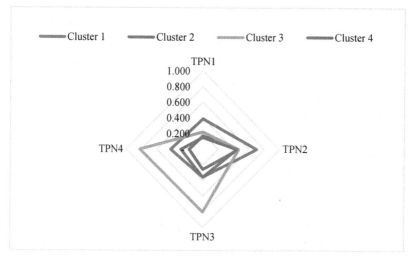

	Cluster 1	Cluster 2	Cluster 3	Cluster 4
TPN1	0.387	0.170	0.220	0.149
TPN2	0.701	0.466	0.467	0.443
TPN3	0.357	0.259	0.801	0.359
TPN4	0.418	0.178	0.821	0.285

Fig. 15. Graph of grouped centroids in trial 2.

Table 4. Results of the data for categories of trial 2 (Figure 15).

Category	Data quantity	Men quantity	Women quantity	MTM	MTW	MSM	MSW
Kids	5	3	2	19.77	20.062	1608.3	1650
Teenagers	2	2	1	9.59	9.862	1850	1950
Adults	16	10	6	19.94	16.928	1725	1579.2
Elderly	1	1	0	23.34		1725	
Total	24	15	9				
Mean				18.2	15.6	1727.08	1726.40

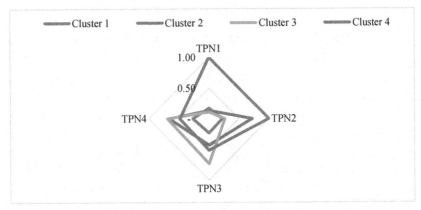

	Cluster 1	Cluster 2	Cluster 3	Cluster 4
TPN1	0.17	0.13	0.11	1.00
TPN2	0.22	0.72	0.27	1.00
TPN3	0.23	0.43	0.73	0.51
TPN4	0.27	0.65	0.69	0.48

Fig. 16. Graph of grouped centroids in trial 3

Table 5. Results of the data for categories of trial 2 (Figure 15).

Category	Data quantity	Men quantity	Women quantity	MTM	MTW	MSM	MSW
Kids	5	3	2	13.81	22.54	1783.3	1575
Adults	8	6	2	18.67	22.74	1716.6	1475
Total	13	9	4				
Mean				16.2	22.6	1750.5	1525

4   Conclusion

The data obtained from the serious game to assess attention was analyzed using data mining to understand the relevance within the variables of age, sex, score, and time to finish the game's levels. The clustering graphs draw two distinct patterns for men and women in relation to their mean time MTM and MTW and mean score MSM and MSW. While men finish the game faster than women, their score is lower than women. In Table 4, the data of the second trial, the mean´s difference in the sex category is irrelevant even if men take less time to finish than women but obtain a lower score. This data sample shows that adult men take, in average more time to finish than adult women. Also, Table 5 shows how men's time is lower and their scores higher in the Kids and Adults categories compared to women.

The data evaluation, through its grouping and normalization, determines that participants become more experienced as they play the game more, which improves the time and score. The age category is the most influential for the results because kids, teenagers, adults, and the elderly have a different attention span.

The future works aim to apply other techniques besides clustering, incorporating the analysis of other demographic variables such as level of education or health condition, and to increase the levels of difficulty that the SG has. Variables such as body mass index, exercise time per week and educational or work level will be analyzed to identify their importance in relation to the results obtained in serious play itself.

References

1. Lövdén, M., Fratiglioni, L., Glymour, M.M., Lindenberger, U., Tucker-Drob, E.M.: Education and cognitive functioning across the life span. Psychol. Sci. Public Interes. **21**(1), 6–41 (2020). https://doi.org/10.1177/1529100620920576
2. Burdick, K.E., Russo, M., Martin, J.: Neuropsychological assessment and psychological tests. Mt. Sinai Expert Guid., 24–27 (2016). https://doi.org/10.1002/9781118654231.ch5
3. Esterman, M., Rothlein, D.: Models of sustained attention. Curr. Opin. Psychol. **29**, 174–180 (2019). https://doi.org/10.1016/j.copsyc.2019.03.005
4. Alonso-Fernández, C., Martínez-Ortiz, I., Caballero, R., Freire, M., Fernández-Manjón, B.: Predicting students' knowledge after playing a serious game based on learning analytics data: a case study. J. Comput. Assist. Learn. **36**(3), 350–358 (2020). https://doi.org/10.1111/jcal.12405
5. Vidakis, N., Barianos, A.K., Trampas, A.M., Papadakis, S., Kalogiannakis, M., Vassilakis, K.: In-game raw data collection and visualization in the context of the "ThimelEdu" educational game. In: Lane, H.C., Zvacek, S., Uhomoibhi, J. (eds.) CSEDU 2019. CCIS, vol. 1220, pp. 629–646. Springer, Cham (2020). https://doi.org/10.1007/978-3-030-58459-7_30
6. Rego, P., Moreira, P.M., Reis, L.P.: Serious games for rehabilitation a survey and a classification towards a taxonomy (2002)
7. Palumbo, V., Paternò, F.: Serious games to cognitively stimulate older adults: a systematic literature review. In: Proceedings of the ACM International Conference on Proceeding Series, pp. 199–208 (2020). https://doi.org/10.1145/3389189.3393739
8. Yáñez-Gómez, R., Cascado-Caballero, D., Sevillano, J.-L.: Academic methods for usability evaluation of serious games: a systematic review. Multimedia Tools Appl. **76**(4), 5755–5784 (2016). https://doi.org/10.1007/s11042-016-3845-9
9. Blei, D.M., Smyth, P.: Science and data science. Proc. Natl. Acad. Sci. U. S. A. **114**(33), 8689–8692 (2017). https://doi.org/10.1073/pnas.1702076114
10. Alonso-Fernández, C., Calvo-Morata, A., Freire, M., Martínez-Ortiz, I., Fernández-Manjón, B.: Applications of data science to game learning analytics data: a systematic literature review. Comput. Educ. **141**, 103612 (2019). https://doi.org/10.1016/j.compedu.2019.103612
11. Kandasamy, I., Kandasamy, W.B.V., Obbineni, J.M., Smarandache, F.: Indeterminate likert scale: feedback based on neutrosophy, its distance measures and clustering algorithm. Soft. Comput. **24**(10), 7459–7468 (2019). https://doi.org/10.1007/s00500-019-04372-x
12. Yuan, C., Yang, H.: Research on K-value selection method of K-means clustering algorithm. J. **2**(2), 226–235 (2019). https://doi.org/10.3390/j2020016
13. Li, Y., Wu, H.: A clustering method based on K-means algorithm. Phys. Procedia **25**, 1104–1109 (2012). https://doi.org/10.1016/j.phpro.2012.03.206
14. Orellana, M., Lima, J.-F., Acosta Urigüen, M.-I., Patiño, A., Álvarez, N., Cordero, J.: Data mining applied to a serious game of memory and attention training. In: Narváez, F.R., Proaño, J., Morillo, P., Vallejo, D., González Montoya, D., Díaz, G.M. (eds.) SmartTech-IC 2021. CCIS, vol. 1532, pp. 58–68. Springer, Cham (2022). https://doi.org/10.1007/978-3-030-99170-8_5

15. Yuhana, U.L., Mangowal, R.G., Rochimah, S., Yuniarno, E.M., Purnomo, M.H.: Predicting Math performance of children with special needs based on serious game (2017). https://doi.org/10.1109/SeGAH.2017.7939276

16. Purwantiningsih, O., Sallaberry, A., Andary, S., Seilles, A., Azé, J.: Visual analysis of body movement in serious games for healthcare. In: Proceedings of the IEEE Pacific Visualization Symposium, pp. 229–233 (2016). https://doi.org/10.1109/PACIFICVIS.2016.7465276

17. Afyouni, I., Murad, A., Einea, A.: Adaptive rehabilitation bots in serious games. Sensors (Switzerland) 20(24), 1–30 (2020). https://doi.org/10.3390/s20247037

18. Benmakrelouf, S., Mezghani, N., Kara, N.: Towards the identification of players' profiles using game's data analysis based on regression model and clustering. In: Proceedings of the 2015 IEEE/ACM International Conference on Advances in Social Networks Analysis and Mining, ASONAM 2015, pp. 1403–1410 (2015). https://doi.org/10.1145/2808797.2809429

19. Standars Development Organization: Software & Systems Process Engineering Metamodel. https://www.omg.org/spec/SPEM/2.0/About-SPEM/

20. Khenissi, M.A., Essalmi, F., Jemni, M.: A learning version of memory match game. In: Proceedings of the IEEE 14th International Conference on Advanced Learning Technologies ICALT 2014, pp. 209–210 (2014). https://doi.org/10.1109/ICALT.2014.67

21. Hou, H.T.: Integrating cluster and sequential analysis to explore learners' flow and behavioral patterns in a simulation game with situated-learning context for science courses: a video-based process exploration. Comput. Human Behav. 48, 424–435 (2015). https://doi.org/10.1016/j.chb.2015.02.010

22. Slimani, A., Elouaai, F., Elaachak, L., Yedri, O.B., Bouhorma, M.: Learning analytics through serious games: data mining algorithms for performance measurement and improvement purposes. Int. J. Emerg. Technol. Learn. 13(1), 46–64 (2018). https://doi.org/10.3991/ijet.v13i01.7518

23. RapidMiner Named a Leader in The Forrester Wave™: Multimodal Predictive Analytics And Machine Learning, Q3 2020. RapidMiner (2020). https://rapidminer.com/news/rapidminer-named-leader-multimodal-predictive-analytics-machine-learning/

24. RapidMiner Inc.: RapidMiner _ Best Data Science & Machine Learning Platform, 2020 (2020)

25. Li, Y.G.: A clustering method based on K-means algorithm. Appl. Mech. Mater. 380–384, 1697–1700 (2013). https://doi.org/10.4028/www.scientific.net/AMM.380-384.1697

Q-Learning in a Multidimensional Maze Environment

Oscar Chang[1,2(✉)] ⬤, Stadyn Román Niemes[1] ⬤, Washington Pijal[1] ⬤,
Arianna Armijos[1,3] ⬤, and Luis Zhinin-Vera[1,2] ⬤

[1] School of Mathematical and Computational Sciences, Yachay Tech University,
100650 Urcuquí, Ecuador
{ochang,stadyn.roman,washington.pijal,arianna.armijos,
luis.zhinin}@yachaytech.edu.ec
[2] MIND Research Group - Model Intelligent Networks Development,
Urcuqui, Ecuador
[3] LoUISE Research Group, I3A, University of Castilla-La Mancha, Albacete, Spain

Abstract. Experiments with rodents in mazes demonstrate that, in
addition to visual cues, spatial localization and olfactory sense play a key
role in orientation, foraging and eventually survival. Simulation at some
level and understanding of this unique behavior is important for solving
optimal routing problems. This article proposes a Reinforcement Learning (RL) agent that learns optimal policies for discovering food sources
in a 2D maze using space location and olfactory sensors. The proposed
Q-learning solution uses a dispersion formula to generate a cheese smell
matrix S, tied in space time to the reward matrix R and the learning
matrix Q. RL is performed in a multidimensional maze environment,
in which location and odor sensors cooperate in making decisions and
learning optimal policies for foraging activities. The proposed method
is computationally evaluated using location and odor sensor in two different scenarios: random and Deep-Search First (DFS), showing positive
results in both cases.

Keywords: Q-learning · Agent · Multi-dimensional environment ·
Maze solving

1 Introduction

In the brain of a real-world rat trying to find a food source in a difficult maze,
a great deal of parallel data processing occurs. Even if the maze is brought
into total darkness, the animal will still go about its daily survival routines
of foraging, shifting its attention to senses other than sight such as the sense of
place [9] and the sense of smell [6]. It is evident that in total darkness the rat will
keep its learning ability intact and will be able to quickly learn a strategy that
defines its decision-making behavior and optimizes its path to the food source,
using only place and smell sense. Although some interesting theories have been
established over the years, no one knows exactly how the sense of place operates
in the rat brain [1,9,16].

© The Author(s), under exclusive license to Springer Nature Switzerland AG 2022
J. Herrera-Tapia et al. (Eds.): TICEC 2022, CCIS 1648, pp. 217–230, 2022.
https://doi.org/10.1007/978-3-031-18272-3_15

The rat's sense of smell is highly complex. It has been demonstrated that the utilization of stereo cues is critical for the detection of odor sources, as a rat can distinguish whether an odor is coming from the right or left in only 50 milliseconds with just one sniff. The rat's olfactory system appears to satisfy both the independent sampling and neural mechanisms criteria for stereo odor localization. According to the scientists, smelling in stereo has a number of evolutionary advantages, including the ability to swiftly detect the presence of a predator or prey with high precision [22,33]

On the other hand, in a totally dark environment, other senses come into play, such as the use of whiskers, since rats have a rather poor vision system. Whiskers change direction and allow the rat to move quickly in places it already knows or to explore new territories if the environment is new [2]. One type of neurons in the hippocampus are activated, the so-called *place cells* that respond maximally when the animal is in a specific location in an environment [17]. From these studies it is concluded that with little visual information, the rat activates the senses of localization and smell to the maximum.

In terms of computation, the rats quickly learn a decision-making policy that optimizes their way from anywhere in the maze to the food supply using only position (place) and odor detection information, even in complete darkness.

This paper proposes an extended 2D maze model in which a new dimension of odor is introduced to the environment in addition to the traditional location information (R coordinate matrix). The aim is to construct RL agents that emulate the learning behavior of rats operating in complete darkness while also incorporating the senses of "place" and "smell". A dispersion formula provides a cheese odor gradient in the maze space, which serves as the odor dimension. Additionally, the agent is equipped with odor sensors that are assembled into a gradient detection mechanism which complements an olfactory system.

For the implementation of this approach, the maze is one of the most important parts since using a modified Q-learning strategy generates an ideal scenario for the agent to learn to optimize routes and generate the expected results.

1.1   Q-learning

The Q-learning algorithm is a well known Reinforcement Learning technique first introduced in 1989 by J. Watkins for solving the Markov decision problems with incomplete information. It works with an agent in an environment that has to learn an action-value function that gives the expected utility for taking a given action in a given state [19]. It can also be thought of as an asynchronous dynamic method (DP). In other words, it enables agents to learn how to act optimally in Markovian domains by observing the effects of their actions instead of requiring them to build domain maps [32].

This agent-environment duo is widely used in data structures, educational algorithms, and research [3]. In this paper, an agent uses Q-learning to learn an efficient strategy by exploring and using place and odor sensors in a coordinated manner. As usual in this algorithm, exploration requires taking into account future events during the reward capture process.

Table 1. Overview of the main related works results that suggest solutions to solve the shortest path (STP) problem with Q-Learning, a RL algorithm.

Proposed method	Problem	Main results	Reference
Multi-Q-table Q-learning	Shortest path (STP) problem in a maze with considerable sub-tasks such as gathering treasures and evading traps	Manage the trouble of the lower average sum of compensations	[13]
ϵ-Q-learning	Slowly convergence speed during the location of the optimal paths in a given environment	The suggested ϵ-Q-Learning can find out more useful optimal paths with lower costs of searching, and the agent successfully evade all barriers or traps in an unfamiliar environment	[8]
ERTS-Q	The interaction between the environment and the agent for collecting real experiences is time-consuming and expensive	An adaptive tree structure integrating with experience replay for Q-Learning called ERTS-Q	[11]
Q-learning	Loss of resources to solve mobile robot maze	The robot can locate the briefest way to solve the maze	[12]
Multi-agent DQN system (N-DQN) model	Characteristics and conditions that are associated with the performance of reinforcement learning	N-DQN offers approximately 3.5 times more elevated learning performance compared to the Q-Learning algorithm in the reward-sparse environment in the performance evaluation	[14]
Improved Q-learning (IQL)	Even though numerous studies report the successful execution of Q-learning, its slow convergence related to the curse of dimensionality could restrict the performance in practice	The suggested techniques accelerate the learning speed of Improved Q-learning (IQL) compared to traditional Q-learning	[18]
A algorithm and Q-learning	Path planning for wheeled mobile robots on somewhat understood irregular landscapes is challenging since robot motions can be affected by landscapes with insufficient environmental information, such as impassable terrain areas and locally detected obstacles	The experimental results and simulation demonstrate that the developed path planning approach provides paths that bypass locally detected impassable areas and obstructions in a somewhat known irregular terrain	[34]
Bees Algorithm (BA) and Q-learning algorithm	Discover an optimal path in a two-dimensional environment for a mobile robot	The experimental results on various maps to validate the suggested method in the static and dynamic cases demonstrate the effectiveness and robustness of the presented method in discovering the optimal path	[4]

2   Related Work

Several ideas and methods have emerged from the study of biological agents' behavior and self-learning capacity in agent research, based on Q-learning and agent automatic learning in an unknown environment.

In [15] it is shown how a group of children learn from a totally unknown environment taking into account 2 conditions: Exploring freely into the maze and find a reward within the maze. Children were divided into 3 groups related to low, medium and high explorers. It was found that the later achieved a high percentage of exploration of the environment and a better performance when searching for rewards. An important conclusion is that children seem to have and innate behavior oriented toward DFS algorithm.

In the work of [23] the behavior of 20 different agents (mice) was analyzed. The mice were kept inside a cage next to a labyrinth. Half group have food and water at all times, while the rest were deprived from them. With this research it was appreciated how a biological agent is able to learn an efficient strategy from an unknown environment with the help of experience and exploration.

In previous work [5] a robotic structure that imitates an amino acid chain was proposed. Subsequently an agent uses reinforcement learning to explore new forms of folding that will lead toward rewards in terms of energy stability. Here the combination of two sensors, self bending and nearby molecules forces, is used by the agent to learn how to fold into proteins looking shapes. The agent was implemented with neural networks with a noise balance training algorithm.

In addition to these approaches, Table. 1 presents an overview of the most representative recent articles that use Q-Learning to solve maze and optimization problems. An initial search in Scopus using the keywords: "Maze, RL, Q learning" gave us 93 documents, of which 16 have been published in the last three years. This demonstrates the scientific interest in developing this type of work.

3   Methodology

The methodology to develop this approach requires an adequate generation of learning scenarios, the implementation of search algorithms and the RL approach for the agent to explore and learn.

3.1   Maze Design: Environment

A maze is a puzzling way that consists of a different branch of passages where the agent intends to reach his destination by finding the most efficient route in the shortest possible time. By definition, the agent can only move in 4 quadrants (up, down, left, and right), and walls cannot be passed through. The agent is evaluated to be the best in this procedure based on the least amount of time or steps required to reach the destination. There were various studies to automatically execute maze search even before reinforcement learning was discovered and explored. Figure 1 shows an illustration of a maze design.

Fig. 1. Graph of a 3D maze showing the proposed idea represented in this experiment, where as an illustration, the agent using RL is the rat and the target is represented by a cheese.

There are many peculiarities to consider when simulating this scenario. In real world, environments are multidimensional; for example, in a real-world cheese maze, a piece of cheese will react instantaneously with the surrounding air molecules, and a gradient of cheese odor will eventually penetrate the entire volume of the maze due to natural rules governing the environment [21]. On the other hand, odor information is hard to process because its high-dimensional data, and large amounts of computation are required to distinguish or separate odors. Odors are made up of a variety of odorant molecules (about 200–400 thousand). Most odor discrimination devices have been built for specific odors to decrease the dimensions of odor information. [20,27].

Rats, on the other hand, have an intrinsic ability to extract information from their environment using a highly developed set of sensors, including a strong sense of smell and olfactory gradients, which complicates the experiment. These rodents utilize it to improve their abilities to locate food sources fast in a maze [7]. It's important to note that if the food source is steady, the rat will utilize its sense of smell to develop a policy that optimizes its path to the largest reward in the shortest time possible [31]. This is the type of scenario addressed in this work, in which odor plays an important part in the agent's self-learning process.

To simulate the environment, we create a matrix R that depicts the maze's space as well as the distribution of rewards. Then, using an exponential decay algorithm, a new dimension is provided by simulating the dispersion of the cheese (reward) odor throughout the maze. This dispersion formula can be as complicated as needed, and it can even incorporate a time variation.

Odor information is stored in a matrix S that has the same dimension as and is bounded in space-time by the matrix R. The greatest value of odor in S is in the same row-column location as the cheese in this arrangement. When agent is so far away from the cheese, the intensity of the odor reduces exponentially. Figure 2 shows a graphical representation of the environment with colors representing the odor intensity.

Fig. 2. In the context of the analyzed environment, this 2D graphical representation shows the odor gradient, the cheese (yellow) and the agent (red). (Color figure online)

For the purpose of this work a 28×28 cell maze is used, where the agent has to learn efficient policies using an expanded version of Q-learning where the sense of location (place) and the sense of smell cooperate to learn efficient food location policies. The agent's learning capabilities are tested with Random Search and Deep-Search First (DSF) modalities [24,30]. Finally, both implementations' performance and outcomes are analyzed and compared.

3.2   Depth-First Search (DFS)

Reachability in a directed graph is frequently determined using depth-first search in sequential algorithms. A depth-first spanning tree is built by recursively exploring all successors from a given vertex. Each vertex is marked before visiting its successors to avoid looping, and a marked vertex is not searched again [28].

DFS is a technique for traversing a graph that uses a last-in, first-out (LIFO) scheme and a stack as the underlying data structure [26]. Following the LIFO concept, insertion (push) and removal (pop) are performed at the top or front [10].

DFS on a graph with n vertices and m edges takes $O(m + n)$ runtime. DFS traversal starts at one vertex and branches out to corresponding vertices until it reaches the final or destination point. DFS traversal of a graph performs the following [26]:

– Visits all vertices and edges of G
– Determine whether G is connected

- Computes the connected components
- Computes the spanning forest of G

This algorithmic approach together with a random search are used in this work to compare the effectiveness of our approach in combination with the new dimension we incorporated: odor.

3.3 How the Agent Explores and Learns

Efficient maze solving plays a key role in some branches of Artificial Intelligence [25]. The Q-learning algorithm, in particular, is an effective way for enabling agents to capture rewards and learn an optimal policy in maze path solutions. The agent main goal is to interact with the environment (maze) by trial and error, and use evaluative feedback systems (rewards and penalties) to achieve decision-making optimization [29].

The learning process begins after the multidimensional environment has been prepared. The first step is for the agent to begin exploring and determining the optimal policies by itself. This is accomplished by a modified version of the conventional Q-learning method, in which the agent takes input from both the R and S matrices to make a choice. The outcome of these choices is stored in a Q matrix, which finally becomes the optimal policy.

In order to fill the knowledge matrix Q, the Bellman equation is used, which is defined as:

$$Q(s,a) = R(s,a) + \gamma \cdot \max_{a'} Q(s',a') \tag{1}$$

The concept is that when the agent finds the cheese, Q gets filled depending on the immediate reward in R as well as the highest possible reward from Q based on future states. The *gamma* parameter, often defined as the discount rate, determines the contribution of future steps.

In our model, the smell matrix S is the one that supplies the data that will be used, thereby transforming it into a reward matrix that considers odor gradient. As a result, the Bellman equation is as follows:

$$Q(s,a) = S(s,a) + \gamma \cdot \max_{a'} Q(s',a') \tag{2}$$

Using both Random Search and Depth-First Search algorithms, the impacts of having a new odor dimension in the maze environment and an improved agent with odor sensing skills are evaluated. When odor capacities are activated, the agent now considers data from R or S in its decision-making, and the learning process becomes more efficient and closer to biological processes.

The Random Search algorithm is an adaptation of the original method with minor changes. Normally, Random Search would be unconcerned by odor, but in this case, with a gradient to take, the agent's behavior is more greedy and odor-oriented. To prevent gradient traps, the agent's decision-making is also Markovian. When the odor gradient is insufficient to cover the entire maze, the agent reverts to random decision-making. In this way, the agent's search strategy

---

Algorithm 1: Odor Random Search Pseudocode

---

do
> **if** *there is no odor around* **then**
> > | Move to a random neighbor.
>
> **else**
> > | Search the best neighbor according to S.
> > | Move to that neighbor.
>
> **end**
> | Update Q according to (2).

while *reward* **not** *captured*;

---

devolves into a random search aided by odor. Algorithm 1. shows the algorithm that controls the behavior of this type of agent.

In the case of the DFS approach, the algorithm performs as expected, that is, it creates the DFS path and visited lists. The main loop then utilizes DFS and the odor to determine where to move, then executes the move and stores the information. This is shown in Algorithm 2.

Algorithm 2: Odor DFS Main Pseudocode

Initialize the path list P.
Initialize the visited list V.
Put the agent in a random starting position.
do
> | Use Odor DFS to get the next move.
> | Make the move.
> | Search the best neighbor (according to Q).
> | Update Q according to (2).

while *reward* **not** *captured*;

The environment, the path and visited sets, the knowledge matrix, and the agent's initial position are used by the Odor DFS method. The ideal route for solving the maze determined by the algorithm is P, whereas V represents all the cells visited by the agent during the procedure. This method functions similarly to a standard DFS, with the exception that it makes decisions using the S matrix and chooses the agent's next step in a markovian way rather than traversing the entire maze at once. Algorithm 3 illustrates this approach.

3.4 Implementation Details

The algorithm was implemented using C++ and the Borland C++ graphic libraries. The code was run in an Intel Core i5 processor of 10th generation @ 1.00 GHz. The programs used for the project are hosted in this GitHub repository: https://github.com/StadynR/q-learning-multidim-maze.

Algorithm 3: Odor DFS Pseudocode
Save the current position in both P and V.
Initialize the unvisited list U.
Get the unvisited neighbors from the current position and save them in U.
if U *is empty* **then**
| Remove the current position from P.
| Backtrack to get the next move.
else
| Search the best unvisited neighbor according to S.
| Get the next move from the previous step.
end
return the next move.

4 Results

The simulation was performed with and without the odor gradient to determine the efficiency of the additional dimension. This means that the following four scenarios were explored: Random Search, Odor Random Search, DFS, and Odor DFS. In the non-odor cases, equation (1) was used to fill Q, while in the opposite cases, Equation (2) is used. For every case, the simulation was run in a total of 10 instances. An instance is the period of time that the agent takes to learn, i.e., the time in which the Q matrix is stabilized (does not change between iterations). Total execution time and total steps were used to determine the duration of the instances.

Table 2. Results of the runs of the algorithms: Random Search, Odor Random Search, DFS, and Odor DFS.

	Random Search		Odor R. Search		DFS		Odor DFS	
Instance	Time (s)	Steps	Time (s)	Steps	Time (s)	Steps	Time (s)	Steps
1	4023.777	135869	1540.11	44341	**134.283**	**3710**	208.202	5667
2	3427.708	115328	1648.718	45788	311.473	9730	262.389	7656
3	**1566.016**	**59395**	3257.644	56041	235.346	6673	208.767	5594
4	5010.259	192674	1508.734	42475	270.83	7807	228.717	6431
5	3932.311	126950	1755.688	47486	147	4211	273.018	7746
6	6673.376	184338	1665.358	46345	285.029	8948	129.092	3656
7	6403.862	215333	932.847	**25821**	220.893	6569	205.488	5859
8	4941.812	150560	**860.624**	28770	274.576	7783	**78.892**	**2267**
9	2683.155	94152	1420.08	39247	259.253	7747	259.264	7392
10	4120.635	137179	1869.393	53112	240.848	6848	289.283	8236

Table 2 shows the results when the agent uses Random Search to fill the Q matrix. It takes an average of 141178 steps and 4278.291 s to reach a stable

Q matrix. The values obtained are very high due to the fact that the agent uses a totally Random Search. In the same table, the improvement in learning efficiency when the agent uses Random Search supported by the Odor gradient (Odor Random Search), which information is taken from the S matrix. It takes and average of 42942 steps and 1645.92 s to reach a stable Q matrix. In this search, the results improve greatly due to the odor gradient that guides the agent.

When the agent uses DFS to fill the Q matrix, the utilized stop criteria is the same as the rest. It takes an average of 7002 steps and 237.953 s to stabilize the matrix Q. With this type of search, the agent has a great advantage over all the previous techniques. It is one of the most stable compared to the others.

In addition, the improvement in learning efficiency when the agent uses DFS assisted by the odor gradient is shown in the same table (Odor DFS). This technique presents the lowest average in both number of steps and seconds to achieve stabilization of the Q matrix, with 6050 steps and 214.311 s. This last type of search turns out to be the best of all, giving very low search averages, therefore being the fastest method for learning.

Finally, Fig. 3 shows the comparison between the four types of search, taking as parameters the instances and the steps needed to stabilize the Q matrix in each of them. It is clearly noticeable that the most unstable results are obtained when the agent explores its environment in a random manner. At the same time there is a great difference between pure random search with the other three methods, with Odor DFS being the most stable and appropriate technique for the agent studied.

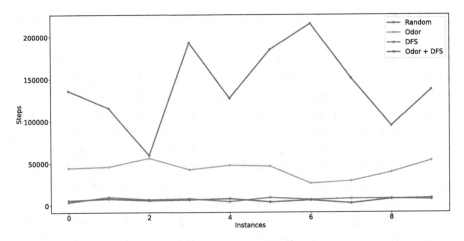

Fig. 3. Comparison of the evolution of instances vs steps of the different results of the executed algorithms.

5   Discussion

As can be observed from the results, introducing an odor matrix aids the agent's decision-making while also complicating it. In particular, if we compare each pair, we can clearly see the improvement. The difference between random search and odor random search is significant, with odor random search learning 3 times faster (using average steps as a measure) than its non-odor counterpart. Odor random search appears to be a viable option for more complex maze traversal strategies.

When we look at the DFS-odor pair, the improvement is a small but significant 1.16 ratio. It's astonishing that odor matrix information can increase the performance of a top contender, given that DFS is one of the most efficient search algorithms known, used by biological entities with millions of years of evolution.

Random search (both odor and non-odor) frequently stabilizes Q in less episodes than DFS, which is worth noting. This is because DFS is highly direct and prioritizes speed above maze coverage, whereas random search usually ends up traversing the majority, if not all, of the maze cells. This suggests that random search fills Q with more information in a single episode than DFS. Even so, on a wide scale, this fact is immaterial since, while DFS requires more episodes, the steps and time spent in each episode are significantly lower than in random search, making DFS solutions a clear winner.

In general, it is evident that adding odor as a new dimension not only allows for more realistic maze models to be created, but it also improves the agent's behavior and learning speed. In fact, by including more matrices into the model, additional dimensions can be added to the simulation.

6   Conclusions

This paper added a new point of view to the classical *rat in a maze* scenario, in which an agent must learn a policy that optimizes reward capturing paths during exploitation. The additional dimension reflects a cheese odor gradient that occurs naturally in real-life scenarios; it is represented by the matrix S and constructed using an exponential decay dispersion algorithm. Along from its sense of location, the used agent has a rodent-like sense of smell, which allows it to identify odor gradients that aid in decision-making and efficient learning.

In a random search situation, a computer simulation shows that coordinating the senses of place and smell greatly improves the Q-learning process, which becomes up to three times more efficient. The DFS ambient also shows an increase in learning efficiency, which is a notable feat inside a high-performance method. The proposed technique enables the addition of extra dimensions and the creation of more realistic maze models.

7   Future Work

In principle, other dimensions could be incorporated to obtain more realistic maze models. For example, our research team has performed initial tests with an additional matrix U of self-generated odor, typical in the rodent world and created by urination, special glands, among others. Another proposal would be to implement this type of approach to solve more complex optimization problems such as finding optimal routes in situations that require moderate use of computational power. Another additional approach would be to compare our algorithm with metaheuristic algorithms focused on solving the rat in a maze problem, to know how better or worse our algorithm performs in comparison. Ultimately, this research can be used as a way to improve on the methods exposed, and create simulations closer and closer to the real world.

References

1. Abbott, A.: Brains of norway. Nature **514**(7521), 154–157 (2014)
2. Arkley, K., Grant, R., Mitchinson, B., Prescott, T.: Strategy change in vibrissal active sensing during rat locomotion. Curr. Biol. **24**(13), 1507–1512 (2014). https://doi.org/10.1016/j.cub.2014.05.036
3. Bakale, V.A., Kumar VS, Y., Roodagi, V.C., Kulkarni, Y.N., Patil, M.S., Chickerur, S.: Indoor navigation with deep reinforcement learning. In: 2020 International Conference on Inventive Computation Technologies (ICICT), pp. 660–665. IEEE (2020)
4. Bonny, T., Kashkash, M.: Highly optimized q-learning-based bees approach for mobile robot path planning in static and dynamic environments. J. Field Robot. **39**(4), 317–334 (2022)
5. Chang, O., Gonzales-Zubiate, F.A., Zhinin-Vera, L., Valencia-Ramos, R., Pineda, I., Diaz-Barrios, A.: A protein folding robot driven by a self-taught agent. Biosystems **201**, 104315 (2021)
6. Deschenes, M., Moore, J.D., Kleinfeld, D.: Sniffing and whisking in rodents. Curr. Opin. Neurobiol. **22**, 243–250 (2012)
7. Findley, T., et al.: Sniff-synchronized, gradient-guided olfactory search by freely-moving mice. eLife 10 (05 2021). https://doi.org/10.7554/eLife.58523
8. Gu, S., Mao, G.: An improved Q-learning algorithm for path planning in maze environments. In: Arai, K., Kapoor, S., Bhatia, R. (eds.) IntelliSys 2020. AISC, vol. 1251, pp. 547–557. Springer, Cham (2021). https://doi.org/10.1007/978-3-030-55187-2_40
9. Hafting, T., Fyhn, M., Molden, S., Moser, M.B., Moser, E.: Microstructure of a spatial map in the entorhinal cortex. Nature 436, 801–6 (09 2005). https://doi.org/10.1038/nature03721
10. Hsu, L.H., Lin, C.K.: Graph theory and interconnection networks (2008)
11. Jiang, W.C., Hwang, K.S., Lin, J.L.: An experience replay method based on tree structure for reinforcement learning. IEEE Trans. Emerg. Topics Comput. **9**(2), 972–982 (2019)

12. Jin, C., Lu, Y., Liu, R., Sun, J.: Robot path planning using q-learning algorithm. In: 2021 3rd International Symposium on Robotics & Intelligent Manufacturing Technology (ISRIMT), pp. 202–206. IEEE (2021)
13. Kantasewi, N., Marukatat, S., Thainimit, S., Manabu, O.: Multi q-table q-learning. In: 2019 10th International Conference of Information and Communication Technology for Embedded Systems (IC-ICTES), pp. 1–7. IEEE (2019)
14. Kim, K.: Multi-agent deep Q network to enhance the reinforcement learning for delayed reward system. Appl. Sci. **12**(7), 3520 (2022)
15. Kosoy, E., et al.: Exploring exploration: Comparing children with RL agents in unified environments. arXiv preprint arXiv:2005.02880 (2020)
16. Krupic, J., Bauza, M., Burton, S., Barry, C., O'Keefe, J.: Grid cell symmetry is shaped by environmental geometry. Nature 518, 232–5 (2015). https://doi.org/10.1038/nature14153
17. Kulvicius, T., Tamosiunaite, M., Ainge, J., Dudchenko, P., Wörgötter, F.: Odor supported place cell model and goal navigation in rodents. J. Comput. Neurosci. **25**(3), 481–500 (2008)
18. Low, E.S., Ong, P., Low, C.Y., Omar, R.: Modified q-learning with distance metric and virtual target on path planning of mobile robot. Expert Syst. Appl. **199**, 117191 (2022)
19. Namalomba, E., Feihu, H., Shi, H.: Agent based simulation of centralized electricity transaction market using bi-level and Q-learning algorithm approach. Int. J. Electr. Power Energy Syst. **134**, 107415 (2022)
20. Okuhara, K., Nakamura, T.: Explore algorithms in olfactory system of mice. Softw. Biol. **3**, 20–25 (2005)
21. Radvansky, B.A., Dombeck, D.A.: An olfactory virtual reality system for mice. Nature Commun. **9**(1), 1–14 (2018)
22. Rajan, R., Clement, J.P., Bhalla, U.S.: Rats smell in stereo. Science 311(5761), 666–670 (2006). https://doi.org/10.1126/science.1122096
23. Rosenberg, M., Zhang, T., Perona, P., Meister, M.: Mice in a labyrinth: Rapid learning, sudden insight, and efficient exploration (2021). https://doi.org/10.1101/2021.01.14.426746
24. Russell, S., Norvig, P.: Artificial intelligence: a modern approach (2002)
25. Sadik, A.M., Dhali, M.A., Farid, H.M., Rashid, T.U., Syeed, A.: A comprehensive and comparative study of maze-solving techniques by implementing graph theory. In: 2010 International Conference on Artificial Intelligence and Computational Intelligence, vol. 1, pp. 52–56. IEEE (2010)
26. Sagming, M., Heymann, R., Hurwitz, E.: Visualising and solving a maze using an artificial intelligence technique. In: 2019 IEEE AFRICON, pp. 1–7 (2019). https://doi.org/10.1109/AFRICON46755.2019.9134044
27. Soh, Z., Suzuki, M., Tsuji, T., Takiguchi, N., Ohtake, H.: A neural network model of the olfactory system of mice: computer simulation of the attention behavior of mice for some components in an odor. Artif. Life Robot. **12**(1–2), 75–80 (2008)
28. Steier, D.M., Anderson, A.P.: Depth-First Search, pp. 47–62. Springer, US, New York, NY (1989). https://doi.org/10.1007/978-1-4613-8877-7_5
29. Sutton, R.S., Barto, A.G.: Reinforcement learning: An introduction. MIT press (2018)
30. Tarjan, R.: Depth-first search and linear graph algorithms. SIAM J. Comput. **1**(2), 146–160 (1972)
31. Wallace, D.G., Gorny, B., Whishaw, I.Q.: Rats can track odors, other rats, and themselves: implications for the study of spatial behavior. Behav. Brain Res. **131**(1), 185–192 (2002). https://doi.org/10.1016/S0166-4328(01)00384-9

32. Watkins, C., Dayan, P.: Technical note: Q-learning. Machine Learning 8, 279–292 (1992). https://doi.org/10.1007/BF00992698
33. Wolfe, J., Mende, C., Brecht, M.: Social facial touch in rats. Behav. Neurosci. **125**(6), 900 (2011)
34. Zhang, B., Li, G., Zheng, Q., Bai, X., Ding, Y., Khan, A.: Path planning for wheeled mobile robot in partially known uneven terrain. Sensors **22**(14), 5217 (2022)

Cyberbullying Through the Lens of Data Science

Alexandra Bermeo[(✉)] ⓘ, María-Inés Acosta-Urigüen ⓘ, Marcos Orellana ⓘ,
and Sebastián I. Valdivieso Albán ⓘ

Universidad del Azuay, Cuenca, Ecuador
{alexbermeo,macosta,marore}@uazuay.edu.ec,
sebasva@es.uazuay.edu.ec

Abstract. The objective of this systematic literature review is to find the scientific contributions that involve the topics of cyberbullying, data science techniques and microlearning. The proposed research question is how data science engages with data treatment for microlearning about fighting bullying and cyberbullying. To answer it, four important digital libraries were selected, and the search was performed using an established search string. Two hundred eighty-three studies were preliminary found; after an initial review, 69 were chosen to be part of the process. This literature review follows the guidelines established by Kitchenham and Charters. After applying the review protocol, which guarantees the rigour and replicability of the study, it was found that not many studies involve the initial terms; therefore, this scientific article is an initial step toward an in-depth analysis of this area of study.

Keywords: Data science · Cyberbullying · Microlearning

1 Introduction

Nowadays, the study of cyberbullying has become a key topic in the scientific community (Castillo et al. 2019), due to the ever-growing phenomenon of cyberbullying among children and teens, through the use of technology (Reyes Ortega and Gonzalez-Bañales 2014). This issue is mainly reflected in the harassment, intimidation or personal attacks on a specific person, causing psychological and physical injuries to the bullied person (Gimenez Gualdo et al. 2013).

Moreover, data science is a growing field, with an important range of applications on any topic or area. In the cyberbullying domain, it is of extreme importance to create knowledge from the data, which could be reached with the application of data science techniques (Castillo et al. 2019). T.k. et al. (2021) presented a study where they used machine learning algorithms to analyze how to approach social media content. Then, Yang et al. (2020) created a framework for the detection of depression from information gathered on social networks. Lastly, Khairy et al. (2021) presented a survey to automatically detect cyberbullying and abusive language in social networks.

Although, all these contributions use data science techniques to attend issues related to cyberbullying or harassment, they all are isolated solutions, but do not answer a more important question related to cyberbullying and data science, and do not even

© The Author(s), under exclusive license to Springer Nature Switzerland AG 2022
J. Herrera-Tapia et al. (Eds.): TICEC 2022, CCIS 1648, pp. 231–249, 2022.
https://doi.org/10.1007/978-3-031-18272-3_16

name any type of educational involvement. Therefore, this systematic literature review (SLR) proposes to answer the research question of how data science engages with data treatment for microlearning about fighting bullying and cyberbullying. For this, four important digital libraries were selected, using an established search string, based on the research method of Kitchenham and Charters (2007). Here, 283 studies were preliminary found, and, after an initial review, 69 were chosen to be part of the complete study.

This paper's structure presents, on Sect. 2, the related work. Then, on Sect. 3 the research method for the SLR and Sect. 4 has the conclusions and future work.

2   Related Work

There are few systematic literature reviews (SLR) that engage with data science and cyberbullying at the same time.

One of them is the contribution presented by Rosa et al. (2019), which analyzed 22 studies that used Machine Learning (ML) and Natural Language Processing (NLP) techniques to detect cyberbullying. The authors highlight several challenges regarding cyberbullying detection, mainly the difficulty in the definition and classification of this phenomenon, and production of datasets. Also, they regard the repetitive nature of cyberbullying as a key aspect, meaning that datasets that label single messages or posts as cyberbullying undermine the quality of the research, which most of the datasets analyzed. Leaving behind key aspects of cyberbullying may result in flawed characterizations. For this reason, the authors argue that studies on automatic cyberbullying detection produce isolated online aggression classifications, instead of cyberbullying classifications. The paper concludes that research on cyberbullying detection fails to properly address key aspects of cyberbullying; thus, it remains an unsolved task.

Furthermore, Al-Garadi et al. (2019) analyzed prediction models produced by ML algorithms to detect and predict cyberbullying on social media (SM). The authors identified multiple issues in the formulation of cyberbullying prediction models, which range from defining cyberbullying, collecting data (building datasets), and features: engineering, the cultural context, language dynamics, and human bias. Similarly, to the previously named paper, the authors of this one present concerns regarding a mischaracterization of cyberbullying due to the subjectivity of its definition; this paper asserts that human interactions are constantly evolving and exist in a cultural and social context. Al-Garadi et al. (2019), discuss that language and social dynamics, such as the friendly use of swear words among friends or the appearance of new slang in communities, increase the difficulty of detecting harassment. These subjectivities involving cyberbullying are present while building datasets, which are then used to train ML models.

Finally, a systematic literature review on cyberbullying detection algorithms by Kim et al. (2021) showed similar issues as those raised by the previous papers. That is the lack of a consistent definition of cyberbullying. The analysis found that, while aggressiveness or hostility through electronic mediums was almost universally associated with cyberbullying, less than half of the papers reviewed included repetitiveness as a key attribute, and almost a fourth of the papers did not include the power imbalance between victims and perpetrator. Additionally, Kim et al. (2021), highlight the importance of using contextual and temporally varying data in cyberbullying detection to aid the classifiers, as the content of posts is not enough by itself. The authors also included information on the classifiers used in the studies analyzed, Support Vector Machines making up almost half of them, followed by Naïve Bayes Classifiers, then Random Forest, Regression techniques, Tree-based models, and Adaboos.

Therefore, as far as it is known to the date, there are not secondary studies that address the topics of cyberbullying, data science and microlearning together, thus, the need for the present work.

3 Systematic Literature Review

A systematic literature review's objective is to identify, collect and synthesize the scientific evidence available which meet certain criteria to determine the answer to a research question (Piper 2013). To reach this objective, it is required to follow a scientific methodology, so the review is rigorous and reproducible. The methodology proposed by Kitchenham and Charters (2007) is used for this study. It has three defined phases: planning, conducting and reporting the review (Kitchenham and Charters 2007), which are presented on the following sections.

3.1 Planning the Review

This phase mainly consists of the definition of the research questions, search strategy and quality assessment of the papers that will be reviewed, therefore, defining the review protocol. This protocol is the roadmap that will be followed through the complete development of the SRL and was prepared and approved by the authors. This planning stage has the following steps, according to the guidelines proposed by Kitchenham and Charters (2007): i) identification of the need for a review, ii) *commissioning a review*, iii) establishing the research question and sub-questions; iv) developing a review protocol, and v) *evaluating the review protocol*. Also, taking into consideration the authors' notes, the step (ii) is not mandatory, and therefore not applied on this contribution, because this SLR is not done in a commercial basis. For the last step, the protocol was evaluated by the team whom are developing the systematic review.

Identification of the need of a review. To determine this first step, an initial search was performed on the main digital libraries, looking for SLR on the topics of cyberbullying, data science and education. However, there were not satisfactory results from this search, motivating to define the protocol and the development of this systematic review.

Research question and sub-questions. For starters, the research question in which the review will focus is "*How does data science engage with data treatment for microlearning about fighting bullying and cyberbullying?*". Moreover, to answer the research question in an orderly and rigorous manner, three sub-questions are proposed: **RQ1**. What data science techniques and methodologies are used for gathering information on bullying and cyberbullying? **RQ2**. What are the activities, interfaces and requirements used in the development of microlearning content? and **RQ3**. What is the state of the research in the area of data science related to microlearning about bullying and cyberbullying?

Review protocol. This will specify the exact steps to take when performing the SLR, to reduce the possibility of researcher bias when selecting the studies and synthesizing the information. The main aspects which are included within the protocol are defined below.

Search strategy. To perform the search, the most representative digital libraries and journals are selected, either on cyberbullying, data science or education. Firstly, for the automatic search, it will be performed on Scopus, Scielo, Redalyc, Springer Link and Science Direct; and the search string used is (Tech* OR Meth*) AND (Cyberbullying) AND ("data science" OR "data mining") AND (Education or Microlearning).

The aforementioned search will be conducted by applying the search string to the same metadata, in this case title and abstract, on all the selected libraries. The string needed to be adapted for each of the libraries, according to each of its own requirements. Moreover, for the manual search, the same keywords will be used. Here, any paper related to the main topics, and which was not retrieved from the automatic search, will be added to the total count, using the most relevant journals and conferences on the area.

Study selection criteria and procedures. Once the primary studies are obtained from the automatic and manual searches, each one of them will be evaluated by the authors, to decide whether the paper is or not included on the final selection. This selection is done based on the review of the title, abstract and keywords of the paper. In case of discrepancies in the selection, the authors will pursue the whole paper to reach a decision. The criteria applied to the SLR state that, any study that meets at least one of the following inclusion criteria, will be included: i) Studies presenting information about the use of technology to prevent cyberbullying, ii) Studies presenting information about education methods or techniques to prevent cyberbullying and iii) Studies presenting information about data science and data mining related to cyberbullying.

Moreover, any study that meets at least one of the following exclusion criteria will be excluded: i) Introductory papers for special issues, books, and workshops, ii) Works such as indexes, books, chapters, among others that are not articles, iii) Duplicate reports of the same study in different sources, iv) Short papers with less than five pages and v) Studies that have not been written in English or Spanish.

Data extraction strategy. To answer each of the research sub-questions, the data extraction strategy applied is to define a set of possible answers for each of them. Therefore, the data extraction applied to the final papers is the same and the results are replicable on future investigations. Table 1 presents the extraction criteria applied on this SLR.

Quality assessment. On top of applying the inclusion and exclusion criteria previously defined, it is necessary to assess the quality of the primary studies, based on the content of the papers and the relevance on the academic community. For this, a three-point Likert scale will be used into a questionnaire which contains two subjective closed-questions and two objective closed-questions. The subjective questions are: i) The study presents issues about information of cyberbullying related to education and ii) The study presents issues about data science that reference to cyberbullying. Moreover, the objective questions are: i) The study has been published in a relevant journal or conference, and ii) The study has been cited by other authors.

Table 1. Extraction criteria

RQ1: What data science techniques and methodologies are used for gathering information on bullying and cyberbullying?

EC1	Techniques	Decision trees, Naïve Bayes classifiers, Support vector machines, K-nearest neighbour, Neural networks, Regression, Clustering, Other, None
EC2	Used for gathering information on bullying	Yes, No
EC3	Used for gathering information on cyberbullying	Yes, No

RQ2: What are the activities, interfaces and requirements used in the development of microlearning and educational content?

EC4	Type of content	Educational, Microlearning
EC5	Interfaces	App, Website, Social networks, Other
EC6	Techniques (Educational)	Changes to school culture, Awareness activities, Anti-bullying programs, Other
EC7	Activities (Microlearning)	Video, Interactive elements, Visual aids, Self-assessments, Other
EC8	Requirements (Microlearning)	Short time demand, Brief units, Accessibility, Other

RQ3: What is the state of the research in the area of data science related to microlearning about bullying and cyberbullying?

EC9	Phase(s) in which the studies are based	Analysis, Design, Implementation, Testing
EC10	Type of validation	Proof of concepts, Survey, Experiment, Quasi-experiment, Prototype, Case study, Other
EC11	Approach scope	Industry, Academy
EC12	Methodology	New, Extension
EC13	Country	
EC14	Year	

3.2 Conducting the Review

Once the review protocol has been approved by the authors involved in the development of this SLR, it is executed. This section presents the obtained results. With the application of the search string on the mentioned digital libraries, and the filter of dates from 2009 to 2021, the initial results add up to 283 scientific papers. After the application of the inclusion and exclusion criteria, the chosen papers to be reviewed for the RSL are 69. Figure 1 presents the initial number of papers found for each library and the definitive ones, where it is shown that most of the studies are obtained from Redalyc.

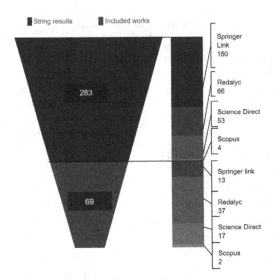

Fig. 1. Preliminary and definitive results from string search

Methods of analysis and synthesis. This stage presents the results and findings of the RSL. For this study, the results will be presented firstly, through statistical tables that show the number of studies that answer to each extraction criterion, and bubble graphs, which will aid to answer the research questions previously stated and will be further discussed.

The chosen research works come from twenty-two countries, most of them from North America and Latin America, as presented on Fig. 2. Yet, Spain has the largest number of published papers on the study topic, 28,99% of the total analyzed. Mexico follows with 14,49% and the United States with 11,59%. The remaining 44,93% of papers come from other nineteen countries. Since 43,48% of the papers come from Spanish-speaking countries, it was relevant to add Spanish as a language in the primary selection criteria, which also is in line with the library from which most of the papers were retrieved. Regardless of cyberbullying being a global issue, North America and Latin America are pioneers in this field's research. Given the relevance of the studied issue, it is necessary to promote research in Europe, Africa, Asia, and Oceania while continuing to nurture the growing research community in Latin America.

Starting in 2009, taking as a keystone the data of the National Center for Education Statistics of the United States (2021), the number of contributions related to cyberbullying, education, and data science shows a growing trend that reaches a plateau between 2017 and 2018, as presented on Fig. 3. The number of publications decreases again between 2019 and 2020 which could be related to the importance given to health-related papers during the pandemic's year zero. The trend stabilizes in 2021 as the effects of the pandemic on mental health and education become relevant in the research community. It is clear how research on this issue has become more important as technological development and interconnectedness through social media platforms intensify. Though, considering the overall small number of research papers obtained for this review, it

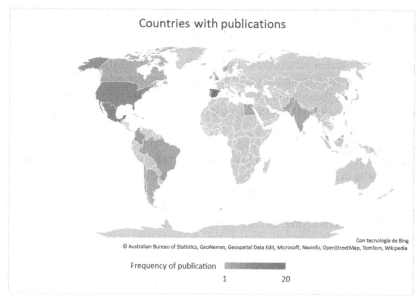

Fig. 2. Countries with publications on the topic.

is necessary to foster further research about digital educational techniques to prevent cyberbullying.

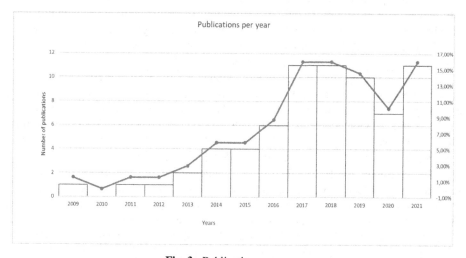

Fig. 3. Publications per year

Out of the 69 analyzed studies, only 23% (n = 16) of them presented the use of data science techniques, and 13 of those were about or mentioned, cyberbullying. For a better understanding of the selected papers, an additional bibliography has been created, it is shown at the end of this document, as Appendix 1. Some of the techniques used are Machine Learning algorithms (Decision Trees (DT), Support Vector Machines

(SVM), k-Nearest Neighbors (kNN), Bayesian Optimization, Naïve Bayes Classifiers (NBC), Linear Regression, Logistic Regression, Classification and Regression Trees (CART), Random Forest, AdaBoost, Neural Networks (NN)) as well as Natural Language Processing techniques (Opinion Mining/Sentiment Analysis). The majority of studies use data science techniques to detect, and/or predict cyberbullying and/or acts of cyber aggression, these being [S1] [S2] [S40] [S41] [S44] [S51] [S61] [S62] [S66] [S67]. Three studies, [S31] [S39] [S68], used data science techniques to analyze surveys about bullying and cyberbullying.

Regarding the first group, it is important to distinguish between cyber aggression or cyber harassment (these terms can be used interchangeably) and cyberbullying. It is important to note that while acts of cyber aggression are an intrinsic element of cyberbullying, it is often defined as a pattern of repetitive attacks on someone vulnerable, similar to traditional bullying. The work [S62] is an example of a study that conflates cyber aggression with cyberbullying, as it analyzes an Intrusion Detection System designed to detect early Denial of Service (DoS) and Distributed Denial of Service (DDoS) attacks. Authors categorize it as cyberbullying; the study does not offer any context or explanation regarding why DoS and DDoS attacks are considered cyberbullying instead of cyber aggression. Then, the authors of [S1] present a model for analyzing web mined data and detecting cyberbullying vocabulary, which means that the model detects the presence of cyber aggression rather than detecting cyberbullying itself. Other authors have noticed this issue; such is the case of [S40], a survey on cyberbullying detection in Arabic content from social networks. The authors highlight the definition of cyberbullying as a repetitive act, and they observed that all the datasets present in the survey labelled single posts as cyberbullying, which may be misleading. Authors of [S66] classify sentences or statements as bullying, while the authors of [S44] detect singular acts of cyber aggression on Twitter to detect cyberbullying (although there is an emphasis on detecting bullying-related posts). Finally, [S67] analyzes and labels individual tweets, although this study targets hate speech rather than cyberbullying.

However, detecting and recognizing individual acts of cyber aggression is a key to build a cyberbullying profile with which the phenomenon can be detected, predicted, and analyzed, but it is not the only identifiable factor. Many of the studies mine metadata for their cyberbullying detection model, such as [S2] [S39] [S40] [S42] [S44] [S67], the last of which uses purely metadata for their model, to add context to the content being analyzed and classified. The contribution of [S39] links students' socioeconomic status with the geographic location of their schools, either urban or rural, and their susceptibility to being bullied. Moreover, authors of [S31] find a correlation between a young person's gender and sexuality, and their likelihood to commit or receive, cyberbullying. [S42] mention that, from previous studies, users may be more vulnerable if they display risky social networking behaviour. Therefore, this study considers the user's personality, language, and social influence. Furthermore, [S67] relies exclusively on metadata for detecting cyberbullying; more specifically, it compares the use of spatiotemporal crime patterns in the physical world to using digital microenvironment metadata for identifying hate speech patterns in the online world.

However, while metadata is beneficial for cyberbullying detection models, its unavailability is a concern in several studies. The authors of [S2] correlate the presence of cyberbullying with the age and education of users, yet are unable to obtain this information due to most social networks keeping users' demographic information inaccessible; instead, the authors opt for using textual and users features to infer their demographic information. Similarly, [S40] recognizes that most social networks keep personal information private, rendering it unavailable to be mined. The authors of [S67] delve further into this issue, as their hate speech detection method relies solely on metadata; they note that while their contribution could be valuable across different social media platforms, currently social networks tend to restrict access to metadata. Both [S40] and [S67] acknowledge that Twitter is often used for data mining purposes, due to the platform's open access to a wide range of data.

Despite the metadata and context data, most of the studies that present models for classifying cyber aggression and/or cyberbullying reported high accuracy rates and F1 score, which is the harmonic mean of precision and recall. [S1] is a study that aims to detect cyberbullying vocabulary, and their AdaBoost algorithm obtained the highest accuracy at 97%, followed by their NN algorithm with an accuracy of 92.5%. Authors of [S41] present a survey on ML algorithms for analyzing social media that considers two studies on detecting cyberbullying. The first uses Bow, SVM, Linear Discriminant Analysis, and a Semantic-Enhanced Marginalized Denoising Auto-Encoder. When using a Twitter-generated dataset, it obtained an accuracy of 84.9% and an F1 score of 71.9%, and, when using a Myspace-generated dataset, its accuracy was 89.7%, and its F1 score was 77.6%; the second study uses SVM and Artificial NN to detect cyberbullying with 70.5% accuracy using a Twitter dataset. Moreover, [S51] uses a tuned SVM (by way of using a radial basis function to adjust the hyperparameters of the model) as part of a scheme for analyzing social network behaviour to prevent cyber hazards; this tuned SVM obtained results of 91% accuracy, 89% recall, and an F1 score of 89%. [S61] uses two transformer deep learning models to detect cyber aggression: Bidirectional Encoder Representations from Transformers (BERT) with 85% accuracy and Efficiency Learning an Encoder that Classifies Token Replacements Accurately (ELECTRA) with 84.92% accuracy. [S66] uses many ML algorithms: NBC, Naïve Bayes Kernel, DT, Gradient Boosted Trees, ID3, Rule Induction, and a multi-layer feed-forward ANN; all of them obtained, at minimum, an accuracy of 86.2% and an F1 score of 91.91%. Lastly, [S68] uses CART, and their final model obtained an overall accuracy of 59.8% at classifying adolescents in the 'bullied' category.

Finally, [S40] is a survey of cyberbullying and abusive language in Arabic on social networks detection models and as such there are analyses of a plethora of studies. Among them, two studies used NBC with an accuracy of 95.9% and 90%, respectively. Two different studies used SVM, one producing an F1 score of 79.7%, and the other, which made use of word-level features and n-gram features and included multiple pre-processing techniques, obtained an accuracy of 90.05%. Other studies in [S40] include an n-grams character-based deep learning classifier that could classify tweets with a 90% F1 score; a Sentiment Analysis algorithm with some metadata that maintained accuracy of 73% at a minimum; a term frequency-inverse document frequency (tf-idf) extraction method that when applied to a dataset could achieve an accuracy of 99.90% when applying the ridge regression algorithm; one study that uses Recurrent Neural Networks (RNN) only obtained an accuracy of 98.7%, while one that uses RNN in conjunction with Convolutional NN and Arabic pre-trained word embedding on a balanced dataset achieved an 84% F1 score. Finally, a model that used RNN, a Gated Recurrent Unit, and Long-Short Term memory, along with tf-idf features, produced a best macro-F1 score of 83%, and a model of Convolutional NN with bidirectional GRU obtained an F1 score of 85.9% for offensive language detection and an F1 score of 75% for detecting hate speech. It must be noted that the authors of [S40] stress the fact that all the studies they analyzed classified single instances of cyber aggression as cyberbullying. Then, the authors of [S67] use Random Forests and attain a precision of 98% at minimum, along with a recall of 60% or more, and an F1 score of 78% or higher; however, it solely analyzes tweets produced after the 2017 London Bridge attack.

Given that bullying, and cyberbullying by extension, is a phenomenon that manifests predominantly in educational environments, guidelines or suggestions for dealing with bullying is found in some of the studies so far discussed. Authors of [S1] mention that the results of their cyberbullying detection models establish the main variables involved in cyberbullying, which can be used to develop a plan to implement security measures; this plan would include identifying acts and actors of aggression and implementing procedures for students to help promoting defense and prevention strategies, for families to be involved in protecting and helping victims. [S44] analyzes risk factors related to cyberbullying vocabulary in South Korean websites; its obtained results point towards power dynamics playing an important factor in cyberbullying and suggest educational programs as a way for people involved to understand how these dynamics work. [S66] is a study on cyberbullying in Virtual Learning Communities (VLC) that develops a framework for combining VLC and Physical Learning Communities (PLC) while reducing aggression through the application of sociocultural learning theories. [S68], a study on environmental factors related to being bullied, concludes that individual, family, peer, and school factors play a key role in preventing peer victimization, so bullying prevention must include modifications to parental support, friendship quality, academic pressure, and school performance. Age-modified interventions were also highlighted as necessary to deal with vulnerability factors that are different for adolescents according to their age ranges. To round up this section, [S2] and [S39] are studies that analyzed surveys filled by students to detect the relationship between cyberbullying and gender, and between bullying and reading performance, respectively. [S2] notes in their conclusions that to tackle cyberbullying based on gender and sexuality, programs that educate adolescents on romantic relationships are important. [S39] stresses the importance of public policy that aims to reduce bullying, bringing up as an example a Colombian law that created guidelines for educational institutions to foster the recognition of diversity and peaceful relations.

As a further analysis, Fig. 4 portrays the majority of the papers in the analysis stage of research that either applies or do not use data science techniques in their research. While Clustering is the only technique that no research work applies, indistinctively of its phase, after the alternative methods, the figure shows, in order of importance, Regression and Neural Networks, Support Vector Machines and Naïve Bayes Classifiers, and Decision Trees and K-nearest Neighbor. [S65] is one of the works whose research goes along all four investigation phases while using one of the classic data science techniques. Yet, its main research focus is obesity prevention, which uses cyberbullying prevention in social media as a means to achieve it. Accordingly, the research works in the figure use data science approaches undergoing the analysis phase with a decreasing trend along with the other three phases. Even though the analysis phase stands out with the use of the data science techniques, more papers use alternative data science techniques in all the investigation phases than within the pre-established techniques in the criteria. For example, [S66] uses an alternative data science method in all the research phases to evaluate the influence of Virtual Learning Communities or VLCs on the ehaviour of bullying perpetrators; it shows that VLCs can promote collaborative work and positive interaction among all group members when taken to these platforms meanwhile AI linguistic surveillance can detect any bullying incident between equals. Conversely, [S60] uses one of the classic research approaches, Neural Networks, along with the alternative method of ontological analysis of text from an open database to understand the importance and influence of social media policies and regulations to prevent and stop cyberbullying in secondary education. This could suggest that current research focuses more on the analysis of educational methods to prevent cyberbullying, but the nature of the research requires different data science approaches.

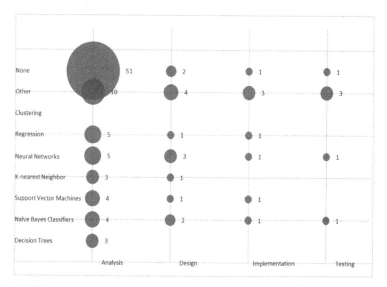

Fig. 4. EC1: Data science techniques vs. EC9: Phase(s) in which the studies are based

Moreover, according to Fig. 5, the vast majority of research papers, that either gather or do not information about cyberbullying, are in the analysis stage of research. This trend decreases along the next stages: design, implementation, and testing. Yet, more papers gather information about cyberbullying within the analysis stage of research. There is a single work that overlaps the criteria EC3: Used for gathering information on cyberbullying and the EC4: Type of Content, with Microlearning content. The authors of [S23] suggest that there is a limited number of programs designed to prevent and fight cyber-bullying developed with current technological tools and whose efficacy has not been properly tested. Nevertheless, the majority of works focus on educational content that excludes micro learning. From these, only [S53] undergoes the four research study phases in the EC9 criteria: analysis, design, implementation, and testing. Authors of [s53] explain, through a Game Learning Analytics (GLA) and Learning Analytics Model (LAM) analysis, how Serious Games, for awareness and prevention of cyberbullying, should apply evidence-based assessment following LAM to extract the collected data and evaluate the game's performance; games that apply this principle improves the design and implementation for educational frameworks.

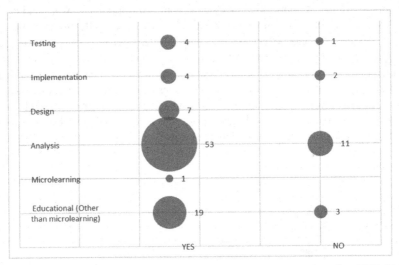

Fig. 5. EC4: Type of Content vs. EC9: Phase(s) in which the studies are based vs. EC3: Used for gathering information on cyberbullying

4 Conclusions

Once the proposed systematic literature review has been executed, it is important to note that, there are not many studies that relate the three main topics: data science, cyberbullying and microlearning, therefore, it is a need to perform extensive research in these topics. It has been found that most of the studies use basic descriptive statistics as their analysis, while more deep data science techniques are often not used, just named. This opens a breach for the application of said techniques in a more widespread manner, allowing for the acquisition and better management of data in this specific topic, therefore, contributing to the developing of better tools and solutions for cyberbullying situations, and to have a better understanding of this issue. In general, research does not use data science techniques to study cyberbullying per se, moreover, it tends to focus more on teenager's issues linked to cyberbullying, such as obesity. Also, papers tend to use alternative data science techniques when studying cyberbullying or mixes data science techniques with qualitative research methods or statistics to study the issue.

As future works, it is important to study the relation among microlearning, cyberbullying and data science, because the importance of the latter in the data analysis and the acquisition and definition of learning patterns.

Acknowledgements. The authors would like to thank to Corporación Ecuatoriana para el Desarrollo de la Investigación y Academia - CEDIA for the financial support given to the present research, development, and innovation work through its program, especially for the IMPLEMENTACIÓN Y DESPLIEGUE DE CÁPSULAS DE APRENDIZAJE PARA COMBATIR EL BULLYING Y EL CIBERBULLYING EN NIÑOS, NIÑAS Y ADOLESCENTES fund.

Appendix 1

List of selected papers used in this systematic literature review, it is shown the code used for identification in the RLS, authors and title of each paper.

Code	Authors	Title
S1	Castillo I., Munoz J., Lopez J.I., Rodriguez L., Romero L.D., Gonzalez M., Ponce J.C	Helping Students Detecting Cyberbullying Vocabulary in Internet with Web Mining Techniques
S2	Lee P.-J., Hu Y.-H., Chen K., Michael Tarn J., Chen L.-E	Cyberbullying detection on social network services
S3	Rodríguez, C; Trujillo, JM; Moreno, AJ; Alonso, S	Educación en seguridad digital: estudio bibliométrico sobre el cyberbullying en web of science
S4	Ramos-Jiménez, A, Esparza del Villar, O, Castro-Valles, A, Hernández-Torres, R, Murguía-Romero, M, Villalobos-Molina, R	Systematic Validation of a Self-Administered Questionnaire to Assess Bullying: From Elementary School to High School and by Sex
S5	Saez, V	Confirmatory factor analysis, school violence, internal reliability, emotional health
S6	Caetano, A.; Freire, I	Violence, dating, university students, young people, systematic review: Multiple voices to the development of a critical and responsible citizenship
S7	Malganova, I; Dokhkilgova, D; Saralinova, D	The transformation of the education system during and post covid-19
S8	Gimenez Gualdo, A.; Sanchez, P; Maquilon Sanchez, J	Causas, medios y estrategias de afrontamiento en la agresión online en escolares de Murcia)
S9	Bosch, N; Gil-Juarez, A	Un acercamiento situado a las violencias machistas online y a las formas de contrarrestarla

(continued)

(continued)

Code	Authors	Title
S10	Torres-Acuña, G; Rivera Hernández, C; Navarro Rangel, Y	Validación de una escala para medir afrontamiento ante ciberagresiones entre universitarios Revista electrónica de investigación educativa
S11	Osorio Tamayo, D, Millán Otero, K	Adolescentes en internet: la mediación entre riesgos y oportunidades
S12	Mendieta Toledo, L, Arteaga Ureta, F, Chamba Zambrano, J	El acoso escolar en la educación general básica, institución Santo Domingo de los Tsáchilas
S13	Domínguez-Alonso, J, Vázquez-Varela, E, Nuñez-Lois, S	Cyberbullying escolar: incidencia del teléfono móvil e internet en adolescentes
S14	Redondo, J; Luzardo-Briceño, M; García-Lizarazo, K; Inglés, C	Impacto psicológico del ciberbullying en estudiantes universitarios: un estudio exploratorio
S15	Etxeberria, F, Intxausti, N, Azpillaga, V	School Climate in Highly Effective Schools in the Autonomous Region of the Basque Country (Spain)
S16	Albert Gómez, M, Ortega Sánchez, I, García Pérez, M	Educación en derechos humanos: formación ética-cívica de los educadores sociales como medio para prevenir el ciberbullying
S17	Ortega Reyes, J, González Bañales, D	El ciberacoso y su relación con el rendimiento académico
S18	Cerezo Ramírez, F, Rubio Hernández, F	Medidas relativas al acoso escolar y ciberacoso en la normativa autonómica española. Un estudio comparativo
S19	Valdés Cuervo, A; Carlos Martínez, E; Torres Acuña, G	Propiedades psicométricas de una escala para medir cibervictimización en universitarios
S20	Rivadulla López, J; Rodríguez Correa, M	Ciberacoso escolar: experiencias y propuestas de jóvenes universitarios
S21	Herrera-López, M; Romera, E; Ortega-Ruiz, R	Bullying y Cyberbullying en Latinoamérica. Un estudio bibliométrico
S22	Pérez Rubio, J	¿Cómo se relacionan las características de los profesores con el bullying escolar?
S23	Colmenero Martínez, S	¿Son eficaces los programas de prevención anti-bullying que utilizan herramientas audiovisuales? Una revisión sistemática

(continued)

(continued)

Code	Authors	Title
S24	Sánchez Romero, C; Álvarez González, E	Actitudes nocivas y riesgos para los menores a través de los dispositivos móviles
S25	Zapata-Rivera, I; Guerrero-Zapata, Y	Por la ruta trazada: manifestaciones del bullying en bachillerato y superior en la unidad regional centro-norte de la uas
S26	Rodríguez Correa, M; Rivadulla López, J	Percepción y experiencias sobre el ciberbullying en estudiantes universitarios
S27	Sabater Fernández, C; López-Hernáez, L	Factores de Riesgo en Ciberbullying. Frecuencia y Exposición de los Datos Personales en Internet
S28	Gutiérrez Martín, A; Torrego González, A	Educación Mediática y Didáctica. Propuesta para la Formación del Profesorado en TIC y Medios
S29	Medina Cascales, J; Reverte Prieto, M	Violencia escolar, rasgos de prevalencia en la victimización individual y grupal en la Educación Obligatoria en España
S30	Bartrina Andrés, M	Conductas de ciberacoso en niños y adolescentes. Hay una salida con la educación y la conciencia social
S31	Donoso-Vázquez, T; Rubio Hurtado, M; Vilà Baños, R	Las ciberagresiones en función del género
S32	Gamito, R; Aristizabal, P; Olasolo, M	La necesidad de trabajar los riesgos de internet en el aula
S33	Hamodi Galán, C; Jiménez Robles, L	Modelos de prevención del bullying: ¿qué se puede hacer en educación infantil?
S34	Astorga-Aguilar, C; Schmidt-Fonseca, I	Peligros de las redes sociales: Cómo educar a nuestros hijos e hijas en ciberseguridad
S35	Gabard, S; Orellana Alonso, N; Pérez Carbonell, A	La comunicación adolescente en el mundo virtual: Una experiencia de investigación educativa
S36	Serrano Sobrino, M; Pérez Carbonell, M	FORMACIÓN DEL PROFESORADO DE EDUCACIÓN SECUNDARIA OBLIGATORIA SOBRE EL BULLYING
S37	Prieto Quezada, M; Carrillo Navarro, J; Lucio López, L	Violencia virtual y acoso escolar entre estudiantes universitarios: el lado oscuro de las redes sociales

(continued)

(continued)

Code	Authors	Title
S38	Pérez-Carbonell, A; Ramos-Santana, G; Serrano Sobrino, M	Formación del profesorado de educación secundaria obligatoria para la prevención e intervención en acoso escolar. Algunos indicadores
S39	Botello Peñaloza, H	Efecto del acoso escolar en el desempeño lector en Colombia
S40	Khairy, M, Mahmoud, T, Abd-El-Hafeez, T	Automatic Detection of Cyberbullying and Abusive Language in Arabic Content on Social Networks: A Survey,
S41	Balaji T, Rao Annavarapu, C, Bablani, A	Machine learning algorithms for social media analysis: A survey,
S42	Yang, X, McEwen, R, Robee Ong, L, Zihayat, M	A big data analytics framework for detecting user-level depression from social networks,
S43	Altarturi, H, Saadoon, M, Anuar, N	Cyber parental control: A bibliometric study,
S44	Tae-Min Song, Juyoung Song	Prediction of risk factors of cyberbullying-related words in Korea: Application of data mining using social big data,
S45	Valdivia, A, Luzón, M, Cambria, E, Herrera, F	Consensus vote models for detecting and filtering neutrality in sentiment analysis,
S46	Biernesser, C, Sewall, C, Brent, D, Bear, T, Mair, C, Trauth, J	Social media use and deliberate self-harm among youth: A systematized narrative review,
S47	Tahaei, H.; Afifi, F.; Asemi, A.; Zaki, F.; Anuar, N	The rise of traffic classification in IoT networks: A survey,
S48	Alakrot,A.; Murray, L.; Nikolov, N	Dataset Construction for the Detection of Anti-Social Behaviour in Online Communication
S49	Moustaka, V.; Theodosiou, Z.; Vakali, A.; Kounoudes, A.; Anthopoulos, L	Enhancing social networking in smart cities: Privacy and security borderlines,
S50	Rahman, M.; Zaman, N.; Asyhari, A.; Nazmus Sadat, N.; Pillai, P.; Abdullah Arshah, R	SPY-BOT: Machine learning-enabled post filtering for Social Network-Integrated Industrial Internet of Things,
S51	Bryce, J, Klang, M	Young people, disclosure of personal information and online privacy: Control, choice and consequences

(continued)

(*continued*)

Code	Authors	Title
S52	Alonso-Fernandez, C.; Cano, A.; Calvo-Morata, A.; Freire, M.; Martinez-Ortiz, I.; Fernandez-Manjan, B	Lessons learned applying learning analytics to assess serious games,
S53	Ferreira, P.; Veiga Simão, A.; Paiva, A.; Martinho, C.; Prada, R.; Ferreira, A.; Santos, F.:	Exploring empathy in cyberbullying with serious games,
S54	Alonso-Fernandez, C.; Freire, M.; Martinez-Ortiz, I.; Fernandez-Manjan, B	Improving evidence-based assessment of players using serious games,
S55	Rathore, S.; Kumar Sharma, P.; Loia, V.; Jeong, Y.; Hyuk Park, J	Social network security: Issues, challenges, threats, and solutions,
S56	Quayyum, F.; Cruzes, D.; Jaccheri, L	Cybersecurity awareness for children: A systematic literature review,
S57	Kumar, A.; Sachdeva, N	Cyberbullying detection on social multimedia using soft computing techniques: a meta-analysis
S58	Thomas, K.; McGee, C	The Only Thing We Have to Fear is…
S59	Pasquini, L.; Evangelopoulos, N	Sociotechnical stewardship in higher education: a field study of social media policy documents
S60	Taharat, T.; Rifat Sadik, A.; Ahmed, S	Abusive Bangla comments detection on Facebook using transformer-based deep learning models
S61	Hassan, M.; Faisal, Z.; Kashif, B.; Qureshi, N.; Kausar, S.; Rizwan, M.; Jeon, G	Deep learning based cyber bullying early detection using distributed denial of service flow
S62	Farahmand, F.; Yadav A.; Spafford, E	Risks and uncertainties in virtual worlds: an educators' perspective
S63	Binti, M.; Abdelsalam, M.; Busalim. H.; Abuhassna, H.; Hasnaa, N.; Mahmood, N	Understanding students' behavior in online social networks: a systematic literature review
S64	Wen-ying; Chou, S.; Prestin, A.; Kunath, S	Obesity in social media: a mixed methods analysis
S65	Nikiforos, S.; Tzanavaris, S.; Kermanidis, K	Virtual learning communities (VLCs) rethinking: influence on behavior modification bullying detection through machine learning and natural language processing
S66	Miró-Llinares, F.; Moneva, A.; Esteve, M	Hate is in the air! But where? Introducing an algorithm to detect hate speech in digital microenvironments

(*continued*)

(*continued*)

Code	Authors	Title
S67	Seek, S.; Heeyoung, M.; Kristen, K.; Eusebius, S.; Youn, S.; Kim, K	Ecological Factors of Being Bullied Among Adolescents: a Classification and Regression Tree Approach
S68	Thomas, S.; Weinstein, E.; Selman, R	Did I Cross the Line?: Gender Differences in Adolescents' Anonymous Digital Self-Reports of Wrongdoing in an Online Anonymous Context
S69	Lee, B	Explaining Cyber Deviance among School-Aged Youth

References

Al-Garadi, M.A., et al.: Predicting cyberbullying on social media in the big data era using machine learning algorithms: review of literature and open challenges. IEEE Access **7**, 70701–70718 (2019). https://doi.org/10.1109/ACCESS.2019.2918354

Castillo, I., et al.: Helping students detecting cyberbullying vocabulary in internet with web mining techniques. In: Proceedings - 2019 International Conference on Inclusive Technologies and Education, CONTIE 2019, pp. 21–27 (2019). https://doi.org/10.1109/CONTIE49246.2019.00014

Gimenez Gualdo, A.M., et al.: Causas, medios y estrategias de afrontamiento en la agresión online en escolares de Murcia (España). Texto Livre: Linguagem e Tecnologia, **6**(2), 2–18 (2013). https://doi.org/10.17851/1983-3652.6.2.2-18

Khairy, M., Mahmoud, T.M., Abd-El-Hafeez, T.: Automatic detection of cyberbullying and abusive language in Arabic content on social networks: a survey. Procedia CIRP **189**, 156–166 (2021). https://doi.org/10.1016/j.procs.2021.05.080

Kim, S., et al.: A human-centered systematic literature review of cyberbullying detection algorithms. Proc. ACM Hum.-Comput. Interact. **5**(CSCW2) (2021). https://doi.org/10.1145/3476066

Kitchenham, B., Charters, S.: Guidelines for performing Systematic Literature Reviews in Software Engineering (Issue EBSE 2007–001) (2007)

National Center for Statistics Education of the USA. Fast Facts: Access to the internet (46). NCES Access to the Internet (2021). https://nces.ed.gov/fastfacts/dis-play.asp?id=46&_ga=2.45730599.2083730396.1643241977-479983204.1642562341

Piper, A.R.J.: How to write a systematic literature review: a guide for medical students. Natl. AMR, Fostering Med. Res. **1**, 1–8 (2013)

Reyes Ortega, J.I., Gonzalez-Bañales, D.L.: Análisis del impacto del cyber-bullying en el rendimiento académico de estudiantes de nivel medio superior. In: Departamento De La Gestión De La Calidad Del Colegio Científico Y Tecnológico Del Estado De Durango, Vol. 40, Issue 2 (2014). https://doi.org/10.13140/RG.2.1.4213.6489

Rosa, H., et al.: Automatic cyberbullying detection: a systematic review. Comput. Hum. Behav. **93**, 333–345 (2019). https://doi.org/10.1016/j.chb.2018.12.021

T.k., B., Annavarapu, C. S. R., & Bablani, A.: Machine learning algorithms for social media analysis: a survey. Comput. Sci. Rev. **40**, 100395 (2021). https://doi.org/10.1016/j.cosrev.2021.100395

Yang, X., McEwen, R., Ong, L.R., Zihayat, M.: A big data analytics framework for detecting user-level depression from social networks. Int. J. Inf. Manage. **54**(October 2019), 102141 (2020). https://doi.org/10.1016/j.ijinfomgt.2020.102141

Software Development

Comparative Study of Image Degradation and Restoration Techniques

Washington Pijal[1,2(✉)] [ID], Israel Pineda[1,2,3] [ID],
and Manuel Eugenio Morocho-Cayamcela[1,2,3] [ID]

[1] School of Mathematical and Computational Sciences, Yachay Tech University,
Hda. San José s/n y Proyecto Yachay, San Miguel de Urcuquí, Ecuador
[2] Yachay Scientific Computing Group (SCG), Urcuqui, Ecuador
washington.pijal@yachaytech.edu.ec
[3] Deep Learning for Autonomous Driving, Robotics, and Computer Vision
(DeepARC Research), Urcuqui, Ecuador
http://www.yachaytech.edu.ec, http://www.yachay-scg.com,
http://www.deeparcresearch.com

Abstract. This paper implements airy disk smoothing, Poisson noise, Gaussian smoothing, Hanser's phase term, and Zernike polynomial phase term as degradation techniques on images from the DIV2K dataset. These actions allows the generation of gray-scale degraded images to study the performance of the inverse filter, Wiener filter, and the Richardson-Lucy algorithm as image restoration techniques. Our experiments are conducted on two representative tasks: (i) intense image degradation, and (ii) image restoration from the degraded images. To measure the image degradation and the image approximation to the original image, this paper uses four similarity metrics: global dimensionless relative error of synthesis (ERGAS), mean squared error (MSE), spectral angle mapper (SAM), and visual information fidelity (VIFP). These similarity metrics determine which restoration technique can estimate the original image in more precisely, and enable the analysis of the required conditions for the estimation.

Keywords: Inverse filter · Wiener filter · Image restoration · Image processing · Computer vision

1 Introduction

Digital images make it possible to record and display helpful information; however, they are vulnerable to defects or degradation during image acquisition [1]. One of the most common defects is *blurring* (a form of bandwidth compression of the original digital image) owing to the defective image formation process [2]. Blurring can be caused by movement between the original scene and the camera, weather disturbances, irregularities in the optical system, or simply the camera system being out of focus [3]. In addition to blurring effects, noise continually degrades any recorded image [4]; this noise is introduced by random scattering or absorption effects when the digital image is generated.

© The Author(s), under exclusive license to Springer Nature Switzerland AG 2022
J. Herrera-Tapia et al. (Eds.): TICEC 2022, CCIS 1648, pp. 253–265, 2022.
https://doi.org/10.1007/978-3-031-18272-3_17

Image restoration and reconstruction techniques try to solve these defects during image acquisition and recover or estimate the original digital image [5]. These techniques are oriented toward modeling the degradation and applying the inverse process to recover the original image [6]. They are extensively applied in many fields [7], such as astronomical imaging, remote sensing, medical imaging, microscopy, and imaging.

For the previously shown, this paper tries to measure and analyze restoration techniques' performance, and determine the optimal option to estimate an original image and under which kind of degraded image works. For measuring and analyzing the degradation techniques, as well as the performance of restoration techniques, this paper uses image similarity metrics between the original images from the DIV2K dataset and degraded-recovered images.

2   Degradation Restoration Modeling

The overall degradation/restoration process can be modeled as in Fig. 1, where the function $f(m, n)$ represents the original image, and m and n are coordinates of a point on the original image, H is the degradation function that degrades the original image [8], $\eta(m, n)$ is an additive noise term, $g(m, n)$ is the observed image after the degradation and noise addition, and $\hat{f}(m, n)$ represents the restored image.

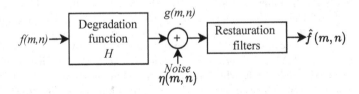

Fig. 1. An overview of the degradation-restoration pipeline followed by our reconstruction methodology.

This relation is expressed in Eq. (1), where the operator ($\star$) constitutes convolution, and the representation in the frequency domain is given by Eq. (2), where $G(u, v)$, $H(u, v)$ and $F(u, v)$, are the Fourier transforms of $g(m, n)$, $h(m, n)$ and $f(m, n)$, respectively.

$$g(m, n) = (h \star f)(m, n) + \eta(m, n) \tag{1}$$

$$G(u, v) = H(u, v)F(u, v) + N(u, v) \tag{2}$$

The digital image restoration process can be observed as the process of estimating the original image as close as possible [5] (i.e., the approximation of $f(m, n)$, given the values of $g(m, n)$ and $\eta(m, n)$).

2.1 Degradation Functions

Gaussian Smoothing. Gaussian blur is a type of *image-blurring* filter that uses a Gaussian function for determining the transformation to apply to each pixel in the digital image [9]. In 2-dimensions, the filter is expressed as the product of two Gaussian functions (one in each dimension), where x is the distance from the source in the horizontal axis, y is the distance from the source in the vertical axis, and σ is the standard deviation of the Gaussian distribution [10] (as shown in Eq. (3)). This formula produces a surface whose contours are concentric circles with a Gaussian distribution from the center point.

$$G(x,y) = \frac{1}{2\pi\sigma^2}e^{-\frac{x^2+y^2}{2\sigma^2}} \tag{3}$$

Airy Disk Smoothing. The airy disk smoothing filter is a representation of the diffraction model resulting from a consistent illumination, where the circular aperture has a bright central region [11]. The output of the airy disk smoothing filter ($I(\theta)$) can be denoted by Eq. (4), where I_0 is the highest intensity of the model at the airy disk center, J_1 is the Bessel function of the first order, a is the radius of the hole, $k = 2\pi/\lambda$ is the wave-number, and θ represents the angle between the axis of the circular aperture, and the line between the aperture center and the observation point.

$$I(\theta) = I_0\left[\frac{2J_1(k\,a\sin\theta)}{k\,a\sin\theta}\right]^2 = I_0\left[\frac{2J_1(x)}{x}\right]^2 \tag{4}$$

Poisson Noise. The Poisson noise is a signal-dependent additive noise that can be seen on images and is also known as *quantum noise* [12]. Due to its signal dependency, the Poisson noise is more challenging to filter than Gaussian noise and other signal-independent noises [13]. The degradation model due to Poisson noise is represented in Eq. (5), where $f(i,j)$ is the original image, λ is the intensity, and $g(i,j)$ is the degraded image. In the Poisson($\cdot$) function, the input is the mean of the Poisson distribution [14], and the output value is a Poisson random generation function that produces Poisson random numbers.

$$g(i,j) = \frac{1}{\lambda}Poisson(\lambda f(i,j)) \tag{5}$$

Hanser's Phase Term. This degradation function is based on Hanser's theorem, where appropriate deconvolution yields a point spread function (PSF) that contains aberrations [15]. Furthermore, phase recovery techniques can be implemented to generate a compact and flexible description of a microscope system, including measurements [15]. These pupil functions can generate a smoothing image that models the microscope error acquisition.

Zernike Polynomial Phase Term. In this work, we consider the Fourier analysis to represent the structure of measured deformations and aberrations for this degradation function. For the effect, we have employed Zernike functions to form a complete, orthogonal basis, over the unit circle [16]. This degradation function attempts to estimate structural deformations in circular optical components, such as ocular and mirrors optical fibers [17], modelling the aberrations of the optical wavefronts caused by these deformations.

2.2   Restoration Filters

Unfortunately, it is challenging to select a specific degradation model. In this work, the inverse degradation process is derived from the degradation model [18], and it can be applied to restore the degraded image $g(m, n)$. After the inverse degradation process, we can obtain $\hat{f}(m, n)$, which represents an estimate of the original image $f(m, n)$. Based on the five degradation functions described in this paper, we implement and analyze the inverse filter, Wiener filter, and the Richardson-Lucy algorithm to restore degraded images.

Inverse Filter. This filter is the simplest approach to restoration [19], where we compute an estimate $\hat{f}$ of the transformed image [5]. This filter is defined in Eq. (6), where $\hat{F}$ and $N(u, v)$ represents the inverse Fourier transform of the estimated image and the noise respectively, and tells that even if we identify the degradation function, we cannot obtain the exactly inverse Fourier transform of $F(u, v)$ because $N(u, v)$ is not known [19]. Furthermore, in Eq. (6) there is a probability of reaching a division by zero in the known, derived, or estimated degradation function $H(u, v)$, and cause a computing problem. Moreover, $H(u, v)$ might become very small, resulting in very large values of N. One technique to trade with this obstacle is to use the restoration cutoff-frequency to avoid small values of $H(u, v)$ [6]; in other words, we can limit the restoration to a specific radius about the origin on the spectrum plane.

$$\hat{F} = F(u, v) + \frac{N(u, v)}{H(u, v)} \tag{6}$$

Wiener Filter. To consider the noise effect, we have exploited the minimum mean square error (Wiener filter) [6]. This filter excludes the addition of noise, and inputs the blurring simultaneously, performing an optimal trade-off among filtering and noise smoothing [5]. Therefore, the restored image in the spatial domain is given by the inverse Fourier transform of the frequency-domain estimate $\hat{f}(\cdot)$. The Wiener filter is defined by Eq. where $S_f(u, v)$ represents the power spectrum of the signal process, obtained by taking the Fourier transform of the signal autocorrelation, and $S_\eta(u, v)$ represents the power spectrum of the noise process, obtained by taking the Fourier transform of the noise autocorrelation. In the latter equation, the magnitude of the complex quantity squared, is equal to the product of a complex quantity with its conjugate [5]. Note that in

Eq. (7), the Wiener filter might have problems when the degradation function drops to values close to zero (e.g., if the entire denominator is zero for the same value(s) of u and v, and the noise is zero; then the noise power spectrum vanishes and the Wiener filter reduces to the inverse filter).

$$\hat{F}(u, v) = \left[\frac{H^*(u, v)S_f(u, v)}{S_f(u, v)|H(u, v)|^2 + S_\eta(u, v)} \right] G(u, v) \qquad (7)$$

Richardson-Lucy Algorithm. The Richardson-Lucy algorithm is an iterative method for recovering an underlying image that has been smoothed by a known point spread function [20]. We have started with an initial estimate $f_{(0)}$, and iteratively updated the estimated value to obtain a de-smoothing $f_{(k)}$ filter at the kth iteration [20]. The Richardson-Lucy update can be expressed by Eq. (8), where k represents the iteration index, $f_{(k)}$ is the current deblur estimate ($f_{(0)}$ is usually selected as the smoothing input image), H is the known point spread function, H^T represents the transposed matrix of H, and g represents the input.

$$f_{(k+1)} = f_{(k)}.H^T \star \frac{g}{H \star f_k} \qquad (8)$$

3   Results of Modeling

This section describes the similarity metrics used to compare the original image with the degraded image and the approximation images, then it presents the evaluation results of the inverse filter, wiener filter, and Richardson-Lucy algorithm. The performance metrics shown in Table 1, 2, 3, 4 correspond to the mean of the test of 100 random images from the DIV2K dataset.

3.1   Dataset

The original images are taken from DIV2K, a popular single-image super-resolution dataset [21]. The DIV2K dataset offers high-quality instances for image restoration tasks (with a 2k pixel resolution). The DIV2K dataset consists of 100 test images, 800 training images, and 100 validation images [22].

3.2   Measuring Similarity

It is straightforward for the human eyes to describe how identical the two provided images are. For instance, in Fig. 2 it is easy to compare the differences between the original image and the degraded images. However, to quantify this difference, we have used the following mathematical expressions:

- **MSE** represents the cumulative squared error between the image approximation and the original image [23].

- **ERGAS** is a global quality index that indicates the shifting and dynamic range modification between the image approximation and the original image [24].
- **SAM** is an automatic method for directly comparing image approximation spectra to an original image spectrum. This method is insensitive to illumination [25].
- **VIFP** is an image quality assessment index based on natural scene statistics and image knowledge extracted by the human visual system [26].

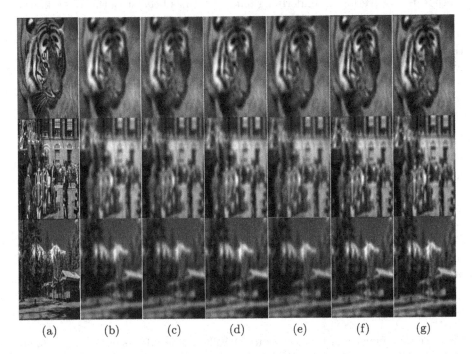

(a)   (b)   (c)   (d)   (e)   (f)   (g)

Fig. 2. Comparison of (a) the original image, and degradation functions: (b) airy disk smoothing, (c) airy disk smoothing-Poisson noise, (d) Gaussian smoothing, (e) Gaussian smoothing-Poisson noise, (f) Hanser's smoothing, (g) Zernike polynomial smoothing.

3.3   Image Degradation Results

In this subsection, we analyze the results of the degradation functions and the similarity of the degraded image with the original image. Table 1 shows us the degradation mean obtained by applying the different degradation functions to 100 random images from the DIV2K dataset. The process followed to obtain this data is represented in Fig. 3. Notice that the image similarity metrics in Table 1 show that the Airy smoothing with noise generates values farthest from the original values' column than other degradation functions; that means, It is the strongest degradation function. On the other hand, Zernike smoothing generates weaker degradation because their similarity metrics values are near the original values' column.

Table 1. Image degradation score after implementing similarity metrics, the *original* column displays the score after comparing the original image with itself to set the perfect score. The remaining columns indicate the score after degrading the image using different methods. Note that we can determine how strong a degradation is by observing how far this value is for the perfect score. The farthest metric values from the original image are highlighted.

Similarity metrics	Original	Airy smoothing	Airy smoothing with noise	Gauss smoothing	Gauss smoothing with noise	Image Hanser defocus	Image Zernike defocus
MSE	0	0.01086	**0.01122**	0.01007	0.01042	0.00926	0.00906
ERGAS	0	7459.59625	**7800.09669**	7148.55913	7554.26969	6822.14768	6740.09872
SAM	0	0.28383	**0.2889**	0.27424	0.27941	0.26307	0.26
VIFP	1	**5.29286**	2.54479	4.21729	2.28176	2.29291	2.23269

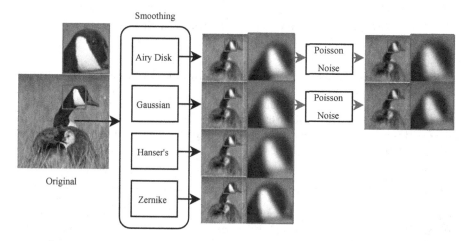

Fig. 3. The degradation process followed by this paper including the four smoothing stages and the additive noise blocks.

3.4   Image Restoration Results

We test three different restoration filters to find the restoration filter that can best manage the different degradation function types and recover or estimate the original image, the process followed is represented in Fig. 4.

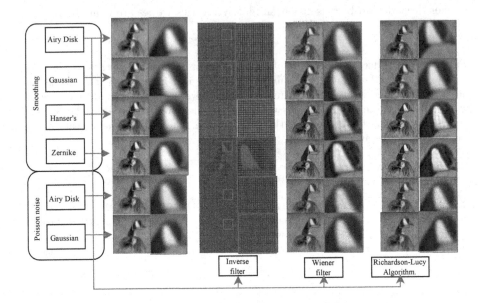

Fig. 4. The restoration process followed by this paper.

Table 2. Image estimation score after implementing similarity metrics, the *original* column displays the score after comparing the original image with itself to set the perfect score. The remaining columns indicate the score after estimating the image using the *inverse filter*. Note that we can determine how good estimation is by observing how near this value is for the perfect score. The nearest values from the original metric are highlighted.

Similarity metrics	Original	Airy smoothing	Airy smoothing with noise	Gauss smoothing	Gauss smoothing with noise	Image Hanser defocus	Image Zernike defocus
MSE	0	406778.2087	212332913.1	423447.8209	189002159.2	10095.80554	**24.11695**
ERGAS	0	3561138.536	6192614.019	3603621.897	3246913.968	3361802.141	**1279206.371**
SAM	0	1.56641	1.5709	1.56729	1.57111	1.56156	**1.37682**
VIFP	1	0.000005	0.0000008	0.000005	0.0000009	0.00002	**0.00052**

Table 3. Image estimation score after implementing similarity metrics to the estimated images by *Wiener filter*.

Similarity metrics	Original	Airy smoothing	Airy smoothing with noise	Gauss smoothing	Gauss smoothing with noise	Image Hanser defocus	Image Zernike defocus
MSE	0	0.01345	0.01437	0.01286	0.01378	0.00550	**0.00543**
ERGAS	0	14550.44147	31216.37728	18700.80513	15158.59544	8191.83503	**6757.34522**
SAM	0	0.30702	0.31847	0.29931	0.31079	0.19763	**0.19622**
VIFP	1	1.75518	**0.8686**	1.53956	0.85413	1.41639	1.63231

Table 4. Image estimation score after implementing similarity metrics to the estimated images with the *Richardson-Lucy algorithm.*

Similarity metrics	Original	Airy smoothing	Airy smoothing with noise	Gauss smoothing	Gauss smoothing with noise	Image Hanser defocus	Image Zernike defocus
MSE	0	0.01258	0.01408	0.01176	0.01326	0.00518	**0.00495**
ERGAS	0	7997.599	9003.374	7733.38	8865.484	8835.901	**7645.249**
SAM	0	0.30415	0.32246	0.29411	0.31262	0.19031	**0.18571**
VIFP	1	1.49307	0.60581	1.35376	0.62817	1.14394	**1.33563**

The mean results of inverse filter, Wiener filter, and Richardson-Lucy algorithm are described in Table 2, 3, 4, respectively. Notice that the three restoration filters have accomplish satisfactory metrics in the estimation from degraded images generated by the Zernike smoothing degradation function.

This result is explained since the degraded images generated by Zernike smoothing degradation function have similar metrics to the original images than other degraded images by others degradation functions. On the contrary, if we analyze the Table 2, 3, 4, we note that the Richardson-Lucy Algorithm metrics on Table 4 have the best performance to recover or estimate the original image from the different degradation functions implemented in this paper. These results are illustrated in Fig. 5, 6, 7. The inverse filter results are not considered in these figures due to their inferior results during image estimation.

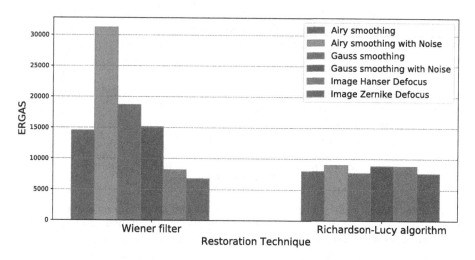

Fig. 5. Shifting and dynamic range modification between the image approximation and the original image. Note that the restoration technique with better image approximation in various degradation is the Richardson-Lucy algorithm, where the optimal value is 0.

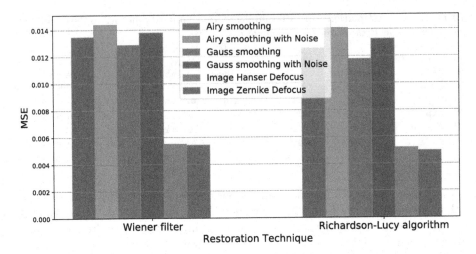

Fig. 6. The cumulative squared error between the image approximation and the original image. Note that the restoration technique with better image approximation in various degradation is the Richardson-Lucy algorithm, where the optimal value is 0.

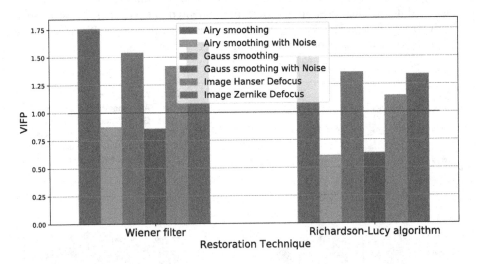

Fig. 7. Image quality assessment index between original image and image approximation. Note that the restoration technique with better image approximation in various degradation is the Richardson-Lucy algorithm, where the optimal value is 1.

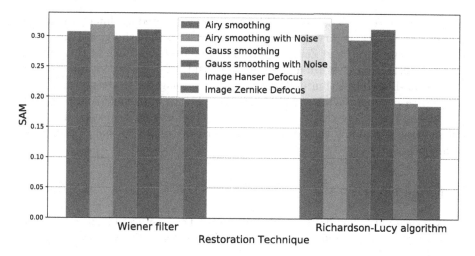

Fig. 8. Difference between an image approximation spectrum with the original image spectrum. This method is insensitive to illumination. Note that the restoration technique with better image approximation in various degradation is the Richardson-Lucy algorithm, where the optimal value is 0.

3.5   Evaluation Results

If we visually analyze the degradation process described in Fig. 3, all the degraded images by the different degradation functions appear like they do not have a noticeable difference. However, the implemented similarity metrics demonstrate the difference between all degradation functions. Furthermore, Table 1 shows that the Airy smoothing degradation function with Noise can generate stronger distortion on the original images than all the different degradation functions described and implemented in this paper. On the other hand, the comparison of the results between Table 2, 3, 4 shows that the Richardson-Lucy Algorithm is the restoration filter that can best estimate the original images from all different degraded images. This algorithm is a viable alternative for image pre-processing to improve the dataset quality instead of artificial intelligence-based techniques. Thus, we consider the Richardson-Lucy Algorithm to be implemented in many tasks such as image captioning [27], hyperspectral imaging [28], or modeling [29], improving the results obtained in the experiments in these research fields.

4   Conclusions

This paper determines that the Richardson-Lucy algorithm is the more suitable image restoration filter to recover or estimate degraded images. The estimated images generated by this restoration filter have proved to have similar spectrum metrics to the original image than other estimated images generated by inverse

filter or Wiener filter. The degraded images were generated by different degradation functions such as airy disk smoothing, Gaussian smoothing, Poisson noise,
Hanser's phase term, and Zernike polynomial phase term. Each of these degradation functions have shown a different magnitude of degradation; however, the
Richardson-Lucy algorithm demonstrates better image estimations when compared with other restoration techniques. We plan to implement and study the
Richardson-Lucy algorithm on RGB, near-infrared, and multispectral images as
future work, expanding the current possibilities of traditional image processing
techniques.

References

1. Neelamani, R., Choi, H., Baraniuk, R.: Forward: Fourier-wavelet regularized deconvolution for ill-conditioned systems. IEEE Trans. Signal Process. **52**(2), 418–433
   (2004)
2. Aizenberg, I., Bregin, T., Butakoff, C., Karnaukhov, V., Merzlyakov, N., Milukova,
   O.: Type of blur and blur parameters identification using neural network and its
   application to image restoration. In: Dorronsoro, J.R. (ed.) ICANN 2002. LNCS,
   vol. 2415, pp. 1231–1236. Springer, Heidelberg (2002). https://doi.org/10.1007/3-
   540-46084-5_199
3. Aoki, H., Watanabe, E., Nagata, A., Kosugi, Y.: Rotation-invariant image association for endoscopic positional identification using complex-valued associative
   memories. In: Mira, J., Prieto, A. (eds.) IWANN 2001. LNCS, vol. 2085, pp. 369–
   376. Springer, Heidelberg (2001). https://doi.org/10.1007/3-540-45723-2_44
4. Andrews, H.C., Hunt, B.R.: Digital image restoration (1977)
5. Wods, R.E., Gonzalez, R.C.: Digital Image Processing. Pearson, 4th global edition
   (2017)
6. Wen, C.-Y., Lee, C.-H., et al.: Point spread functions and their applications to
   forensic image restoration. Forensic Sci. J. **1**(1), 15–26 (2002)
7. Khare, C., Nagwanshi, K.K.: Implementation and analysis of image restoration
   techniques. In: International Journal of Computer Trends and Technology-May to
   June (2011)
8. Sur, K., Chauhan, P.: Dynamic trend of land degradation/restoration along Indira
   Gandhi canal command area in Jaisalmer district, Rajasthan, India: a case study.
   Environ. Earth Sci. **78**(15), 1–11 (2019)
9. Wink, A.W., Roerdink, J.B.T.M.: Denoising functional MR images: a comparison
   of wavelet denoising and gaussian smoothing. IEEE Trans. Med. Imag. **23**(3), 374–
   387 (2004)
10. Hsiao, P.Y., Chou, S.-S., Huang, F.-C.: Generic 2-D gaussian smoothing filter for
    noisy image processing. In TENCON 2007–2007 IEEE Region 10 Conference, pp.
    1–4. IEEE (2007)
11. Peng, R., Ye, Y., Tang, Z., Zhao, C., Wen, S., Fan, D.: Smoothing effect in the
    broadband laser through a dispersive wedge. Optics Commun. **265**(1), 106–110
    (2006)
12. Le, T., Chartrand, R., Asaki, T.J.: A variational approach to reconstructing images
    corrupted by poisson noise. J. Math. Imag. Vision. **27**(3), 257–263 (2007)
13. Salmon, J., Harmany, Z., Deledalle, C.-A., Willett, R.: Poisson noise reduction
    with non-local PCA. J. Math. Imag. Vision **48**(2), 279–294 (2014)

14. Zhang, B., Fadili, J.M., Starck, J.-L.: Wavelets, ridgelets, and curvelets for poisson noise removal. IEEE Trans. Image Process. **17**(7), 1093–1108 (2008)
15. Hanser, B.M., Gustafsson, M.G.L., Agard, D.A., Sedat, J.W.: Phase-retrieved pupil functions in wide-field fluorescence microscopy. J. Microscopy **216**(1), 32–48 (2004)
16. Tian, C., Yang, Y., Wei, T., Ling, T., Zhuo, Y.: Demodulation of a single-image interferogram using a zernike-polynomial-based phase-fitting technique with a differential evolution algorithm. Opt. Lett. **36**(12), 2318–2320 (2011)
17. Milanetti, E., Miotto, M., Di Rienzo, L., Monti, M., Gosti, G., Ruocco, G.: 2D zernike polynomial expansion: finding the protein-protein binding regions. Comput. Struct. Biotechnol. J. **19**, 29–36 (2021)
18. Lagendijk, R.L., Biemond, J.: Basic methods for image restoration and identification. In: The Essential Guide to Image Processing, pp. 323–348. Elsevier (2009)
19. Mohapatra, B.R., Mishra, A., Rout, S.K.: A comprehensive review on image restoration techniques. Int. J. Res. Advent Technol. **2**(3), 101–105 (2014)
20. Laasmaa, M., Vendelin, M., Peterson, P.: Application of regularized Richardson-Lucy algorithm for deconvolution of confocal microscopy images. J. Microsc. **243**(2), 124–140 (2011)
21. Kim, S., Jun, D., Kim, B.-G., Lee, H., Rhee, E.: Single image super-resolution method using CNN-based lightweight neural networks. Appl. Sci. **11**(3), 1092 (2021)
22. Ayazoglu, M.: Extremely lightweight quantization robust real-time single-image super resolution for mobile devices. In Proceedings of the IEEE/CVF Conference on Computer Vision and Pattern Recognition, pp. 2472–2479 (2021)
23. Pu, Y., Wang, W., Xu, Q.: Image change detection based on the minimum mean square error. In: 2012 Fifth International Joint Conference on Computational Sciences and Optimization, pp. 367–371. IEEE (2012)
24. Renza, D., Martinez, E., Arquero, A.: A new approach to change detection in multispectral images by means of ERGAS index. IEEE Geosci. Remote Sens. Lett. **10**(1), 76–80 (2012)
25. Yang, C., Everitt, J.H., Bradford, J.M.: Yield estimation from hyperspectral imagery using spectral angle mapper (sam). Trans. ASABE, **51**(2), 729–737 (2008)
26. Thakur, N., Devi, S.: A new method for color image quality assessment. Int. J. Comput. Appl. **15**(2), 10–17 (2011)
27. Castro, R., Pineda, I., Lim, W., Morocho-Cayamcela, M.E.: Deep Learning Approaches Based on Transformer Architectures for Image Captioning Tasks. IEEE Access (2022)
28. Pineda, I., Alam MD, N., Gwun, O.: Calyx and stem discrimination for apple quality control using hyperspectral imaging. In: Botto-Tobar, M., Pizarro, G., Zúñiga-Prieto, M., D'Armas, M., Zúñiga Sánchez, M. (eds.) CITT 2018. CCIS, vol. 895, pp. 274–287. Springer, Cham (2019). https://doi.org/10.1007/978-3-030-05532-5_20
29. Pineda, I., Gwun, O.: Leaf modeling and growth process simulation using the level set method. IEEE Access **5**, 15948–15959 (2017)

IOWA Rough-Fuzzy Support Vector Data Description

Ramiro Saltos[1,2](✉) [iD] and Richard Weber[3] [iD]

[1] Facultad de Innovación y Tecnología, Universidad Del Pacífico,
Km. 7.5 Vía a la Costa, Guayaquil, Ecuador
ramiro.saltos@upacifico.edu.ec, rjsaltos1989@gmail.com
[2] Escuela de Negocios y Economía, Facultad de Ciencias Económicas
y Administrativas, Pontificia Universidad Católica de Valparaíso,
Amunátegui 1838, Viña del Mar, Chile
[3] Department of Industrial Engineering, FCFM, Universidad de Chile,
Av. Beaucheff 851, Santiago de Chile, Chile
richard.weber@uchile.cl

Abstract. Rough-Fuzzy Support Vector Data Description is a novel soft computing derivative of the classical Support Vector Data Description algorithm used in many real-world applications successfully. However, its current version treats all data points equally when constructing the classifier. If the data set contains outliers, they will substantially affect the decision boundary. To overcome this issue, we present a novel approach based on the induced ordered weighted average operator and linguistic quantifier functions to weigh data points depending on their closeness to the lower approximation of the target class. In this way, we determine the weights for the data points without using any external procedure. Our computational experiments emphasize the strength of the proposed approach underlining its potential for outlier detection.

Keywords: Support Vector Data Description · OWA Operators · Outlier detection · Soft-computing

1 Introduction

An outlier is a data point that is significantly different from the rest of the data. They are also called abnormalities, discordants, deviants, or anomalies [1]. Eventually, these outliers have useful information about abnormal characteristics of the systems that impact the data generation process. The detection of such unusual characteristics provides useful insights in many application domains [2,24,26]. Since outlier detection is relevant in any data science task, many techniques have been proposed in the literature [5,25,29]. Among them, the support vector data description (SVDD) [27,28] has been widely used given its flexibility and applicability to real-world problems [3,6,11,30]. However, SVDD does not consider the data distribution, and consequently, all observations contribute equally to the hypersphere and thus to the decision boundary [12].

J. Herrera-Tapia et al. (Eds.): TICEC 2022, CCIS 1648, pp. 266–280, 2022.
https://doi.org/10.1007/978-3-031-18272-3_18

As stated by Tax and Duin [27, 28] and Ben Hur et al. [4], the support vectors define the contour of dense data regions. Therefore they should contribute more to the decision boundary than other data points. In consequence, many research works have been proposed in the literature to deal with the equally-treated data when building the SVDD classifier [7, 9, 10, 12, 13, 15, 36, 37]. All these works introduced a weight, usually called membership degree[1], into the mathematical formulation of the SVDD model. In this way, each data point receives a different membership degree reflecting its importance to the decision boundary. On the other hand, they differ in the mechanisms used to compute the membership degrees for each observation. These mechanisms usually rely on external methods like k-nearest neighbor approaches, clustering algorithms, and density-based methods, among others.

In this paper, we present the Induced Ordered Weighted Average Rough-Fuzzy Support Vector Data Description (IOWA-RFSVDD). This novel approach combines the concepts defined in fuzzy logic and rough set theory to compute the observations' degrees of membership of being outliers. At the same time, it assigns a weight to these data points, reducing their influence on the decision boundary. The main contributions of our work are:

- The IOWA-RFSVDD uses two values to assess the importance of a data point to construct the classifier: (1) a membership degree that measures its belongingness to the target class, and (2) a weight that controls its contribution to the decision boundary. As we show in Sect. 2.3, state-of-the-art approaches only use the weights to reduce the effect of noise data on the decision boundary.
- The weight generation mechanism of the IOWA-RFSVDD relies on linguistic quantifier functions which are not data-dependent. In this way, our approach avoids using local and global data centers, which are usually computationally expensive to calculate.
- The target class is a rough-fuzzy set instead of a fuzzy set like in state-of-the-art approaches. This way, data points are classified either in the lower approximation or the fuzzy boundary. We compute the membership degrees for these elements using the information available in the kernel matrix. This property is inherited from the base method, the rough-fuzzy support vector data description (RFSVDD) introduced in [21].
- The IOWA-RFSVDD does not rely on any external algorithm to obtain the data points located in sparse regions, which are possible outliers.

The rest of the paper is arranged as follows: Sect. 2 provides the basics of the RFSVDD algorithm, the OWA and IOWA operators, and an overview of the relevant literature. In Sect. 3 the proposed methodology for IOWA-RFSVDD is presented. Its potential is shown in Sect. 4 in several computational experiments. Section 5 concludes our work and hint at possible future developments.

---

[1] This term is not to be confused with the well-known concept of membership as defined in fuzzy logic.

2   Literature Review

2.1   Rough-Fuzzy Support Vector Data Description

In 2015, Saltos and Weber [21] presented a soft-computing version of the classical Support Vector Data Description (SVDD) Algorithm [27,28] called Rough-Fuzzy Support Vector Data Description (RFSVDD), which is the basic method of the approach introduced in this paper. The contribution made by RFSVDD is constructing a rough-fuzzy description of the dataset where outliers can be clearly identified and separated from the main classes.

The RFSVDD algorithm has two phases that will be explained below in more detail. First, there is a *training phase*, in which the classic SVDD is used to obtain a hypersphere (in a higher-dimensional, projected feature space) that encloses most of the data points. All observations that fall outside this sphere are usually considered outliers. Then, a *fuzzification phase* is performed over those objects that were classified as outliers in the first stage. The novelty of RFSVDD lies in this step, in which each outlier gets a membership degree of being or not an outlier. A formal description of the phases follows.

Training Phase. Let $X = \{\mathbf{x}_i \in \mathcal{R}^d / i = 1, \ldots, N\}$ be the set of N data points of dimension d. The first step projects the data to a reproducing kernel Hilbert space (RKHS), in which we construct a hypersphere with minimal radius that encloses most of the training samples. The following quadratic optimization problem is solved:

$$\min_{R,a,\xi} \; z = R^2 + C \sum_{i=1}^{N} \xi_i \tag{1}$$

s.t.

$$\| \phi(\mathbf{x}_i) - \mathbf{a} \|^2 \leq R^2 + \xi_i \qquad\qquad \forall i = 1, \ldots, N \tag{2}$$

$$\xi_i \geq 0 \qquad\qquad \forall i = 1, \ldots, N, \tag{3}$$

where R is the radius of the sphere and $\mathbf{a}$ its center; ϕ is a non-linear mapping; ξ is a vector of slack variables used to allow some observations falling outside the hypersphere; $\| \cdot \|$ is the Euclidean norm; and $C \in [0,1]$ is a constant regularization parameter that controls the trade-off between the volume of the sphere and the number of data points it includes. The dual formulation of the model (1)–(3) is as follows:

$$\max_{\beta} \; z_D = \sum_{i=1}^{N} \beta_i K(\mathbf{x}_i, \mathbf{x}_i) - \sum_{i=1}^{N}\sum_{j=1}^{N} \beta_i \beta_j K(\mathbf{x}_i, \mathbf{x}_j) \tag{4}$$

s.t.

$$\sum_{i=1}^{N} \beta_i = 1 \tag{5}$$

$$0 \leq \beta_i \leq C \qquad\qquad \forall i = 1, \ldots, N, \tag{6}$$

where β are Lagrange multipliers and $K(\mathbf{x}_i, \mathbf{x}_j) = \phi(\mathbf{x}_i) \cdot \phi(\mathbf{x}_j)$ is the kernel function. A widely used kernel is the Gaussian kernel, which is given by:

$$K(\mathbf{x}_i, \mathbf{x}_j) = e^{-q\|\mathbf{x}_i - \mathbf{x}_j\|^2} \tag{7}$$

where $q > 0$ is a parameter that controls the kernel's width [23]. From the optimal solution of the model (4)–(6) we get:

- Data points with $\beta_i = 0$ are called *inside data points* (ID) since they lie inside the hypersphere.
- Data points with $0 < \beta_i < C$ are called *support vectors* (SV) and define the decision boundary.
- Data points with $\beta_i = C$ are called *bounded support vectors* (BSV) since they lie outside the hypersphere. For this reason they are also called outliers.

Data points are assigned in any of two classes: the target class and the rejection class. The target contains the data points whose images lie inside the enclosing hypersphere, while the rejection class/outlier class contains the bounded support vectors. These classes together with the decision boundary define the description of the data set [27, 28].

Fuzzification Phase. Saltos and Weber [21] proposed a fuzzification phase to calculate the membership degrees of bounded support vectors to the target class. The procedure is:

1. Cast the hard data description structure of the training phase into a rough-fuzzy one with two components: a lower approximation and a fuzzy boundary.
2. Assign the support vectors and inside data points to the lower approximation of the target class.
3. Assign the bounded support vectors to the fuzzy boundary.
4. Calculate the membership degree μ_i of bounded support vector i to the target class with the following equation:

$$\begin{aligned} \mu_i = \mu(BSV_i, SV_i) &= K(BSV_i, SV_i) \\ &= e^{-q\|BSV_i - SV_i\|^2} \end{aligned} \tag{8}$$

where SV_i is the closest support vector to the bounded support vector i.

A simple example of the RFSVDD method using a two-dimensional toy data set is available in [22].

2.2 Ordered Weighted Average

Yager [32] presented the ordered weighted average (OWA) operator to aggregate numbers coming from different information sources. Formally, an OWA operator of dimension n is a mapping from $\mathcal{R}^n$ to $\mathcal{R}$ that has associated a weighting vector $\mathbf{w} \in \mathcal{R}^n$ such that $\sum_{j=1}^{n} w_j = 1$ and $w_j \in [0,1]$. The OWA function is given by:

$$\text{OWA}(a_1, \ldots, a_n, \mathbf{w}) = \sum_{j=1}^{n} w_j b_j \tag{9}$$

where b_j is the j-th largest a_j. A wide range of possible aggregation operators can be obtained when varying the weighting vector. The next ones are worth noting among others [8,19]:

- If $w_1 = 1$ and $w_j = 0$ for all $j \neq 1$, the OWA operator becomes the maximum.
- If $w_n = 1$ and $w_j = 0$ for all $j \neq n$, the OWA operator becomes the minimum.
- If $w_j = \frac{1}{n}$ for all $j = 1, 2, \ldots, n$, we get the arithmetic mean.

A critical step when using the OWA operator is how to set the weight vector $\mathbf{w}$. Fortunately, there are many approaches in the literature for setting these weights [8,14,19]. A common approach relies on using linguistic quantifiers [16]. The weights are generated by a regular increasing monotone (RIM) function $Q \colon \mathcal{R} \to \mathcal{R}$ as follows:

$$w_j = Q\left(\frac{j}{n}\right) - Q\left(\frac{j-1}{n}\right) \qquad \forall j = 1, 2, \ldots, n \tag{10}$$

Some common RIM quantifiers available in the literature are [16,17]:

- The basic linguistic quantifier:

$$Q(r) = r^\alpha \tag{11}$$

- The quadractic linguistic quantifier:

$$Q(r) = \frac{1}{1 - \alpha \cdot r^{0.5}} \tag{12}$$

- The exponential linguistic quantifier:

$$Q(r) = e^{-\alpha \cdot r} \tag{13}$$

- The trigonometric linguistic quantifier:

$$Q(r) = \arcsin(\alpha \cdot r) \tag{14}$$

where $\alpha > 0$. The OWA operator is monotonic, commutative, bounded, and idempotent [32].

Another relevant aggregation operator is the Induced Ordered Weighted Average (IOWA) introduced by Yager and Filev in 1999 [34]. It is an extension of the OWA function. The main difference is in the ordering step. The IOWA operator uses a second variable to induce the order of the argument variables. The IOWA operator fits well in applications where the argument variables are not comparable. For example, in this paper, the argument variables are $d-$dimensional data vectors which are clearly not comparable. Formally, the IOWA operator is a function given by:

$$\text{IOWA}\left(\langle a_1, u_1 \rangle, \ldots, \langle a_n, u_n \rangle, \mathbf{w}\right) = \sum_{j=1}^{n} w_j b_j \qquad (15)$$

where the vector $\mathbf{b}$ is the vector $\mathbf{a}$ sorted in decreasing order based on the values of the variable $\mathbf{u}$. The variable $\mathbf{u}$ is the order-inducing variable, and $\mathbf{a}$ is the argument variable. The IOWA operator is also monotonic, bounded, idempotent, and commutative [34]. Other properties and special cases of the IOWA operator are discussed in [33,34]. The OWA and the IOWA operator have been applied successfully in many areas such as engineering, medicine, and finance, among others [8,18,31,35].

2.3   Recent Advances on SVDD

The RFSVDD without the fuzzification phase leads to the classical SVDD algorithm proposed by Tax and Duin [27,28] in 1999. From the derivation of the dual form of the model (1)–(3) we get that:

$$a = \sum_{i=1}^{n} \beta_i \phi(\mathbf{x}_i) \qquad (16)$$

where a is the center of the hypersphere in the projected feature space. From the Eq. (16) we note that only support vectors ($\beta_i \in (0, C)$) and bounded support vectors ($\beta_i = C$) affect this center, and therefore, the decision boundary. Since $\beta_{SV} < \beta_{BSV}$ and the number of SVs is usually lower than the number of BSVs, it is clear that the BSV data influences more on the sphere's center than non-BSV data. This issue originates from the fact that all data points have the same importance when building the classifier. Several works have been proposed in the literature to reduce or solve this issue. In what follows, we explain some of the most relevant and recent approaches.

The first approaches looking at reducing the importance of the training samples when constructing a support vector classifier were proposed by Liu and Huang [15] and Lin and Wang [13] in the context of binary classification using support vector machines (SVM). In their works, the authors cast the crisp nature of the training set to a fuzzy one in which every data point receives a membership degree to the new fuzzy training set. Their approaches differ in how they compute the membership degrees for the data points. Liu and Huang [15] used an outlier detection combination of techniques for separating the extreme data points from the main target class. Then, the membership degrees are computed based on the distance of the data points to the center of the main body (target class). On the other hand, Lin and Wang [13] proposed a function of the time of arrival of the data point to the training set to get the membership degrees. In this way, recent observations are more important than older ones.

The first approach that explicitly incorporates the notion of the relative importance of the training samples into the SVDD model is due to Zheng et al. [37] within the context of Support Vector Clustering (SVC) [4]. Given that the SVC algorithm uses the SVDD model in the training phase, the authors proposed the approach for both the SVDD and the SVC algorithms simultaneously by introducing the following optimization problem:

$$\min_{R,a,\xi} \; z = R^2 + C\sum_{i=1}^{N} w_i \xi_i \tag{17}$$

s.t.

$$\| \phi(\mathbf{x}_i) - \boldsymbol{a} \|^2 \le R^2 + \xi_i \qquad \forall i = 1,\ldots,N \tag{18}$$

$$\xi_i \ge 0 \qquad \forall i = 1,\ldots,N, \tag{19}$$

where $w_i \in [0,1]$ is the membership degree assigned to data point $\mathbf{x}_i$ and represents the relative importance it has in the training set. The Wolfe dual of the model (17)–(19) is:

$$\max_{\beta} \; z_D = \sum_{i=1}^{N} \beta_i K(\mathbf{x}_i,\mathbf{x}_i) - \sum_{i=1}^{N}\sum_{j=1}^{N} \beta_i \beta_j K(\mathbf{x}_i,\mathbf{x}_j) \tag{20}$$

s.t.

$$\sum_{i=1}^{N} \beta_i = 1 \tag{21}$$

$$0 \le \beta_i \le w_i C \qquad \forall i = 1,\ldots,N, \tag{22}$$

The only difference between the model (4)–(6) and the model (20)–(22) is the upper bound of the Lagrange multipliers. Zheng et al. used a k-nearest neighbor (K-NN) approach to set up the membership degrees for each data point. Since Zheng's work, other approaches have been proposed in the literature [7,9,10,12,36]. All use the same mathematical formulation but differ on how they set the membership degrees.

Fan et al. [9] proposed the Grid-based Fuzzy Support Vector Data Description (G-FSVDD). The membership degrees are computed based on grids. The key idea relies on grouping the data points based on the dense regions surrounded by sparse regions. The authors divided the data space into grids at different scales several times. After obtaining enough grids, the apriori algorithm finds the grids with high density. After that, the membership values are set for each observation. On the other hand, Zhang et al. [36] used the improved possibilistic c-means to compute the membership degree of each data point to the cluster found in the kernel reproducing Hilbert space. Then, these membership degrees are used as weights in the model (20)–(22).

Hu et al. [10] used a completely different approach for setting up the membership degrees for the fuzzy support vector data description (F-SVDD). Based on the Rough Set theory [20], they divide the training set into three regions.

Then, a neighborhood model of the samples is used to discriminate the data points in each region. Finally, the weight value is computed based on the region of the data point. Consequently, different weight values are assigned based on the locations of the observations.

Similarly to Zheng's work, Cha et al. [7] introduced a density approach for the SVDD. In this case, the weights reflect the density distribution of a dataset in real space using the k-nearest neighbor algorithm. Then, each data point receives its weight according to the data density distribution. By applying this idea in the training process, the data description prioritizes observations in high-density regions. Eventually the optimal description shifts toward these dense regions. Finally, Li et al. [12] presented a method called Boundary-based Fuzzy-SVDD (BF-SVDD). BF-SVDD uses a local-global center distance to search for the data points near the decision boundary. Then, it enhances the membership degrees of that data using a k nearest neighbor approach and the global center of the data.

Based on the literature reviewed, we can conclude that almost all of the related work focuses on how to compute the weights for each training sample to give them different importance when building the classifier. Most rely on external techniques like k-nearest neighbor, clustering algorithms, or outlier detection methods in a pre-processing step of the SVDD task. To the best of our knowledge, aggregation operators were not used to compute weights to affect the contribution of the training samples when constructing the SVDD classifier. In this paper, we propose a methodology using the IOWA operator and the rough-fuzzy version of SVDD that naturally obtain the membership degrees with the information of the kernel matrix.

3   Proposed Methodology for IOWA-RFSVDD

As stated in Sect. 2, the RFSVDD algorithm builds a rough-fuzzy description of the data set by computing the membership degrees of data samples depending on whether they belong to the lower approximation or the fuzzy boundary. In this section, we use the classical RFSVDD together with the IOWA aggregation function to weigh the contribution of each data point to the decision boundary. Instead of assigning a weight to each data point for constructing the classifier, we propose using two values: (1) a membership degree that measures the belongingness of a data point to the target class, and (2) a weight that controls the contribution of the data point to the decision boundary.

In the training phase of the RFSVDD, we replace the model (1)–(3) by the model (17)–(19). Next, by setting up $w_i = 1$ for all $i = 1, 2, \ldots, N$, we solve the optimization model to get the support vectors, bounded support vectors, and inside data points. Then, we run the fuzzification phase to obtain membership degrees μ_i of each data sample. After that, using a linguistic quantifier, we recalculate the weights w_i only for those data points that are bounded support vectors and assign the weights based on the order-induced variable μ_i. In this way, BSVs closer to the decision boundary will have higher weights than BSVs that are far away (outliers). Finally, we update the constant penalty parameter

C and repeat the above steps until convergence or the maximum number of BSV data is achieved. We call this novel approach Induced Ordered Weighted Average Rough-Fuzzy Support Vector Data Description (IOWA-RFSVDD). Algorithm 1 presents its details.

Algorithm 1: IOWA Rough-Fuzzy Support Vector Data Description

---

Input: Data set X, parameters $q > 0$, $v \in (\frac{1}{N}, 1)$, and $\lambda > 0$.
Output: Rough-fuzzy data description with $[0, 1]$-membership matrix for data points.

1 Initialize $w_i = 1$ for all $i = 1, 2, \ldots, N$.
2 Compute the kernel matrix $K = k(\mathbf{x}_i, \mathbf{x}_j)$ for $\mathbf{x}_i, \mathbf{x}_j \in X$.
3 Set $v' = v$.
4 **while** *stopping criteria is not achieved* **do**
5   Run the training phase of the SVDD algorithm using model (17)–(19) with parameters q and v'.
6   Obtain the set of support vectors (SV), bounded support vectors (BSV), and inside data points (ID).
7   Assign support vectors and inside data points to the lower approximation of the target class.
8   Assign bounded support vectors to the fuzzy boundary of the target class.
9   **for** *each $x_i \in SV \cup ID$* **do**
10   Set $\mu_i = 1$.
11   Set $w_i = 1$.
12   **for** *each $x_i \in BSV$* **do**
13   Compute the membership degree μ_i using equation (8).
14   Compute the weights w_i using any linguistic quantifier function where n is the number of BSVs. See equations (11)–(14).
15   Sort descending the BSV data based on their membership degrees.
16   Assign the weights w_i to the sorted BSVs using equation (15) .
17   Set $v' = \frac{vN - |BSV|}{N}$.

In the first iteration of Algorithm 1, the steps 5–13 are the traditional RFSVDD method since the weights w_i are the same for all data points. The steps 14–16 which correspond to weight generation, BSV data ordering, and weight assignment, are the IOWA phase of the proposed approach. Finally, step 17 updates the value of the constant penalty parameter C to control the number of BSV data in each iteration and to guarantee convergence. We present the following example to illustrate the proposed method.

The Motivation Data Set [22] is an artificially generated data set with 316 instances, 16 of which are outside the main classes (Fig. 1(a)). The parameters of the SVDD algorithm $q = 12$ and $v = 0.074$ were fixed based on the values reported in [22]. After the training phase, support vectors, bounded support vectors, and inside data points are identified as is shown in Fig. 1(b), where red points are SV, orange points are BSV, and the remaining ones are inside data.

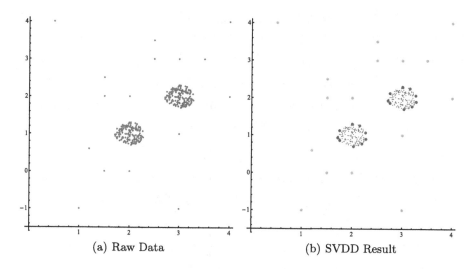

(a) Raw Data   (b) SVDD Result

Fig. 1. Motivation Data Set

Table 1. Results for bounded support vectors

BSV	x	y	β_i	β_i^*	$\downarrow$ (%)	μ_i
301	4.00	4.00	0.0428	0.0048	88.80	0.0000
302	2.50	3.00	0.0428	0.0062	85.54	0.0001
303	3.50	3.00	0.0428	0.0066	84.46	0.0003
304	3.00	3.00	0.0428	0.0140	67.21	0.0028
305	2.50	3.50	0.0428	0.0052	87.78	0.0000
306	4.00	2.00	0.0428	0.0072	83.10	0.0017
307	1.20	0.60	0.0428	0.0339	20.83	0.0111
308	1.50	2.00	0.0428	0.0058	86.42	0.0001
309	2.00	2.00	0.0428	0.0108	74.84	0.0028
310	1.50	2.50	0.0428	0.0050	88.32	0.0000
311	3.00	1.00	0.0428	0.0091	78.79	0.0027
312	1.50	0.00	0.0428	0.0055	87.15	0.0001
313	2.00	0.00	0.0428	0.0080	81.31	0.0027
314	3.00	−1.00	0.0428	0.0046	89.22	0.0000
315	1.00	−1.00	0.0428	0.0044	89.60	0.0000
316	0.50	4.00	0.0428	0.0043	89.94	0.0000

Table 2. Results support vectors

SV	x	y	β_i	β_i^*	↑ (%)	μ_i
15	1.75	0.87	0.0173	0.0457	264.62	1
19	2.27	1.07	0.0110	0.0302	274.24	1
28	2.15	1.26	0.0177	0.0477	268.82	1
38	1.75	1.13	0.0234	0.0625	266.61	1
49	2.00	1.30	0.0217	0.0605	278.72	1
70	2.19	0.77	0.0007	0.0009	132.40	1
93	2.03	0.70	0.0313	0.0863	275.71	1
117	1.71	0.93	0.0093	0.0285	306.88	1
148	2.28	0.90	0.0253	0.0700	276.05	1
165	2.75	1.87	0.0177	0.0457	258.61	1
169	3.27	2.07	0.0112	0.0303	271.31	1
178	3.15	2.26	0.0176	0.0476	270.97	1
188	2.75	2.13	0.0230	0.0621	269.43	1
199	3.00	2.30	0.0219	0.0606	276.91	1
220	3.19	1.77	0.0009	0.0010	112.46	1
243	3.03	1.70	0.0311	0.0862	277.42	1
267	2.71	1.93	0.0096	0.0291	304.29	1
298	3.28	1.90	0.0251	0.0699	277.87	1

Table 1 presents the results for bounded support vectors after running both RFSVDD and IOWA-RFSVDD algorithms. The columns β_i and β_i^* show the optimal values of the Lagrange multipliers when all data points are weighted equally and differently, respectively. Due to the newly proposed weighting mechanism, the contribution of BSV data has been reduced by an average of 80% approximately. At the same time, the membership degrees of these data points are close to zero, indicating them as outliers.

Similarly, Table 2 presents the results for support vectors. As can be seen, the contribution of the support vectors to the decision boundary has been increased by more than 100%. At the same time, the membership degrees prevent SV data from being treated incorrectly as BSV data which is a common issue in state-of-the-art approaches cited in Sect. 2. For example, Li et al. [12] argue most weighting mechanisms are based on the k-nearest neighbor method, and some support vectors will be located in sparse areas with relatively fewer neighbors than others, producing their misclassification as BSVs.

As can be seen, the IOWA-RFSVDD reduces the influence of possible outliers in the construction of the SVDD classifier. The proposed approach uses the RIM quantifier function to generate the weights and the membership degrees as an order-induced variable for the assignation. In this way, our method does not require external procedures like the k-nearest neighbors or clustering algorithms, among others. Finally, using the membership degrees, as proposed in this paper, avoids the misclassification of SV data as BSVs due to their location in sparse areas.

4   Computational Experiments

To assess the effectiveness of the proposed approach, we performed computational experiments on nine data sets where eight are from the UCI Machine Learning Repository. Additionally, we introduced outliers randomly to the data sets to show how IOWA-RFSVDD reduces their effect on the decision boundary (sphere radius). We set the parameters for RFSVDD and IOWA-RFSVDD according to [22]. Table 3 shows the parameters fixed for each data set tested. Note since both methods use the same parameters, we report them once.

Table 3. Algorithms' Parameters

Instance	q	v
Motivation	12	0.074
BankNote	0.25	0.1
Cancer	0.0001	0.20
Glass	0.1	0.1
Quake	1	0.2
Abalone	5	0.05
WineOut	0.0001	0.1
IrisOut	0.5	0.14
ConcreteOut	0.00005	0.05

Based on the optimal solution of model (17)–(19), the distance of any data point $\mathbf{x}$ to the center of the hypersphere is given by:

$$d(\mathbf{x}, a) = \sqrt{K(\mathbf{x}, \mathbf{x}) - 2\sum_{i=1}^{N} \beta_i K(\mathbf{x}, \mathbf{x}_i) + \sum_{i=1}^{N}\sum_{j=1}^{N} \beta_i \beta_j K(\mathbf{x}_i, \mathbf{x}_j)} \qquad (23)$$

Then, the radius of the hypersphere is $R = d(\mathbf{x}, a)$ where $\mathbf{x}$ is a support vector. Using (23), we computed the radius of the sphere for both RFSVDD and IOWA-RFSVDD. Table 4 shows these results for all data sets tested.

From Table 4, we can see that IOWA-RFSVDD reduces the sphere radius in almost all data sets tested. Hence, the decision boundary is tighter than in the RFSVDD approach since BSV data does not significantly influence the sphere center. Therefore, the proposed method is less prone to misclassifying outliers in an unsupervised setting. These results show the potential that IOWA-RFSVDD has to outperform the SVDD and RFSVDD algorithms for outlier detection tasks.

Table 4. Sphere Radius

Instance	RFSVDD	IOWA-RFSVDD
Motivation	0.973962	0.922660
BankNote	0.992739	0.992604
Cancer	0.983732	0.976560
Glass	0.914629	0.888286
Quake	0.984919	0.980202
Abalone	0.900619	0.919713
WineOut	0.953004	0.941470
IrisOut	0.932424	0.902718
ConcreteOut	0.981190	0.979499

5   Conclusions and Future Work

In this paper, we proposed the IOWA Rough Fuzzy Support Vector Data Description. IOWA-RFSVDD is a novel approach to treat available data points differently for SVDD classifier construction according to their position in the feature space. The main advantages of the method are:

1. It uses two values to assess the importance of a data point for the construction of the classifier: (1) a membership degree that measures the belongingness of a data point to the target class, and (2) a weight that controls the contribution of the data point to the decision boundary.
2. The weight generation mechanism of the IOWA-RFSVDD relies on linguistic quantifier functions which are not data-dependent. These functions only need the number of BSVs.
3. It does not rely on external algorithms to obtain the data points of sparse regions.

We performed several computational experiments on diverse data sets to evaluate the effectiveness of our approach. The results showed that IOWA-RFSVDD tightens the decision boundary reducing the possibility of misclassifying outlier data. Finally, the proposed method can be extended to other support vector-based algorithms like support vector machines for classification, regression, or clustering.

Acknowledgements. Both authors acknowledge financial support from FONDECYT Chile (1181036 and 1221562). The second author received financial support from ANID PIA/BASAL AFB180003.

References

1. Aggarwal, C.C.: Outlier Analysis. 2 edn. Springer, Cham (2017). https://doi.org/10.1007/978-3-319-47578-3

2. Bansal, R., Gaur, N., Singh, S.N.: Outlier detection: applications and techniques in data mining. In: 6th International Conference Cloud System and Big Data Engineering, pp. 373–377. IEEE (2016)

3. Bellinger, C., Sharma, S., Japkowicz, N.: One-class classification-From theory to practice: a case-study in radioactive threat detection. Expert Syst. Appl. **108**, 223–232 (2018)

4. Ben-Hur, A., Horn, D., Siegelmann, H.T., Vapnik, V.: Support vector clustering. J. Mach. Learn. Res. **2**, 125–137 (2001)

5. Boukerche, A., Zheng, L., Alfandi, O.: Outlier detection: methods, models, and classification. ACM Comput. Surv. (CSUR) **53**(3), 1–37 (2020)

6. Bu, H.G., Wang, J., Huang, X.B.: Fabric defect detection based on multiple fractal features and support vector data description. Eng. Appl. Artif. Intell. **22**(2), 224–235 (2009)

7. Cha, M., Kim, J.S., Baek, J.G.: Density weighted support vector data description. Expert Syst. Appl. **41**(7), 3343–3350 (2014)

8. Csiszar, O.: Ordered weighted averaging operators: a short review. IEEE Syst. Man Cybern. Mag. **7**(2), 4–12 (2021)

9. Fan, Y., Li, P., Song, Z.: Grid-based fuzzy support vector data description. In: Wang, J., Yi, Z., Zurada, J.M., Lu, B.-L., Yin, H. (eds.) ISNN 2006. LNCS, vol. 3971, pp. 1273–1279. Springer, Heidelberg (2006). https://doi.org/10.1007/11759966_189

10. Hu, Y., Liu, J.N., Wang, Y., Lai, L.: A weighted support vector data description based on rough neighborhood approximation. In: IEEE 12th International Conference on Data Mining Workshops, pp. 635–642. IEEE (2012)

11. Lee, S.W., Park, J., Lee, S.W.: Low resolution face recognition based on support vector data description. Pattern Recogn. **39**(9), 1809–1812 (2006)

12. Li, D., Xu, X., Wang, Z., Cao, C., Wang, M.: Boundary-based Fuzzy-SVDD for one-class classification. Int. J. Intell. Syst. **37**(3), 2266–2292 (2022)

13. Lin, C.F., Wang, S.D.: Fuzzy support vector machines. IEEE Trans. Neural Netw. **13**(2), 464–471 (2002)

14. Lin, M., Xu, W., Lin, Z., Chen, R.: Determine OWA operator weights using kernel density estimation. Econ. Research-Ekonomska istraživanja **33**(1), 1441–1464 (2020)

15. Liu, Y., Huang, H.: Fuzzy support vector machines for pattern recognition and data mining. Int. J. Fuzzy Syst. **4**(3), 826–835 (2002)

16. Luukka, P., Kurama, O.: Similarity classifier with ordered weighted averaging operators. Expert Syst. Appl. **40**(4), 995–1002 (2013)

17. Maldonado, S., Merigó, J., Miranda, J.: Redefining support vector machines with the ordered weighted average. Knowl. Based Syst. **148**, 41–46 (2018)

18. Maldonado, S., Merigó, J., Miranda, J.: IOWA-SVM: a density-based weighting strategy for SVM classification via OWA operators. IEEE Trans. Fuzzy Syst. **28**(9), 2143–2150 (2019)

19. Merigó, J.M., Gil-Lafuente, A.M.: The induced generalized OWA operator. Inf. Sci. **179**(6), 729–741 (2009)

20. Pawlak, Z.: Rough Sets: Theoretical Aspects of Reasoning about Data, vol. 9. Springer Science & Business Media (1991). https://doi.org/10.1007/978-94-011-3534-4

21. Saltos, R., Weber, R.: Rough-fuzzy support vector domain description for outlier detection. In: 2015 IEEE International Conference on Fuzzy Systems (FUZZ-IEEE), pp. 1–6. IEEE (2015)

22. Saltos, R., Weber, R.: A rough-fuzzy approach for support vector clustering. Inf. Sci. **339**, 353–368 (2016)
23. Schölkopf, B.: Learning with Kernels. MIT Press (2002). https://doi.org/10.1198/jasa.2003.s269
24. Singh, K., Upadhyaya, S.: Outlier detection: applications and techniques. Int. J. Comput. Sci. Issues (IJCSI) **9**(1), 307 (2012)
25. Smiti, A.: A critical overview of outlier detection methods. Comput. Sci. Rev. **38**, 100306 (2020)
26. Ranga Suri, N.N.R., Murty M, N., Athithan, G.: Outlier Detection: Techniques and Applications. ISRL, vol. 155. Springer, Cham (2019). https://doi.org/10.1007/978-3-030-05127-3
27. Tax, D.M., Duin, R.P.: Support vector domain description. Pattern Recogn. Lett. **20**(11–13), 1191–1199 (1999)
28. Tax, D.M., Duin, R.P.: Support vector data description. Mach. Learn. **54**(1), 45–66 (2004)
29. Wang, H., Bah, M.J., Hammad, M.: Progress in outlier detection techniques: a survey. IEEE Access **7**, 107964–108000 (2019)
30. Wang, S., Yu, J., Lapira, E., Lee, J.: A modified support vector data description based novelty detection approach for machinery components. Appl. Soft Comput. **13**(2), 1193–1205 (2013)
31. Xu, Z., Da, Q.L.: An overview of operators for aggregating information. Int. J. Intell. Syst. **18**(9), 953–969 (2003)
32. Yager, R.R.: On ordered weighted averaging aggregation operators in multicriteria decision making. IEEE Trans. Syst. Man Cybern. **18**(1), 183–190 (1988)
33. Yager, R.R.: Induced aggregation operators. Fuzzy Sets Spystems **137**(1), 59–69 (2003)
34. Yager, R.R., Filev, D.P.: Induced ordered weighted averaging operators. IEEE Trans. Syst. Man Cybern. Part B (Cybernetics) **29**(2), 141–150 (1999)
35. Yager, R.R., Kacprzyk, J., Beliakov, G.: Recent developments in the ordered weighted averaging operators: theory and practice, vol. 265. Springer (2011). https://doi.org/10.1007/978-3-642-17910-5
36. Zhang, Y., Chi, Z.X., Li, K.Q.: Fuzzy multi-class classifier based on support vector data description and improved PCM. Expert Syst. Appl. **36**(5), 8714–8718 (2009)
37. Zheng, E.-H., Yang, M., Li, P., Song, Z.-H.: Fuzzy support vector clustering. In: Wang, J., Yi, Z., Zurada, J.M., Lu, B.-L., Yin, H. (eds.) ISNN 2006. LNCS, vol. 3971, pp. 1050–1056. Springer, Heidelberg (2006). https://doi.org/10.1007/11759966_154

Preparation of a Social Engineering Attack, from Scratch to Compromise: A USB Dropper and Impersonation Approach

Jorge Sánchez Freire[✉] and Benjamín Garcés

CrySeg Information Security Consultants, Ambato, Ecuador
info@cryseg.com

Abstract. Although there are different kind of tools to fight against cyber attackers, there is one vulnerability that is exploited daily due to the nature that it represents and the damage which might cause, the human being. Studies claim people are the weakest link in a security chain, so intrusions might occur taking advantage of this, leading cybercriminals to enter into organizations and provoking several damages. For a successful attack, it is important a well thought out plan, a good analysis of the target and a great performance. In this research two Social Engineering Techniques will be presented, USB dropper and impersonation using hardware and software to collect data from a target's PC, demonstrating how attacks are born and how are they implemented on the field.

Keywords: Impersonation · USB dropper · Social engineering · Bad USB

1 Introduction

1.1 Motivation

As new security strategies for computer systems are developed, attackers also improve their methodologies to attack them. These cyber-attacks are increasing year by year and are more common nowadays.

There are many tools attackers use to achieve their goals like WannaCry. This ransomware dealt several damages to thousands of computers around the world, taking advantage of a Windows misconfiguration in the Server Message Block, allowing intruders to execute remote code. This vulnerability is publicly known as Eternalblue (MS17–010) [1, 2]. This kind of attack raises questions about the need of complex preparation and robust coding of tools, taking several hours in front of the computers to search for vulnerabilities in the applications or operative systems to take control of an entity. Still, there is a vulnerability that is present in almost any IT structure and cannot be patched, the human being [3].

People represent the weakest link in a cybersecurity chain. Globally and historically, many organizations have used this security failure to compromise entire countries [4].

A popular tool used to exploit such flaw is Dragonfly, which uses a Social Engineering technique called spear-phishing that is more effective than traditional phishing

J. Herrera-Tapia et al. (Eds.): TICEC 2022, CCIS 1648, pp. 281–293, 2022.
https://doi.org/10.1007/978-3-031-18272-3_19

because it's focused on a certain population making use of custom PDFs sent via compromised legitimate accounts. This way, the virus could be used to infiltrate and spy power infrastructures in United States and Europe [5].

Like the spear-phishing technique, there are many other ways to vulnerate computer users. These tools or methodologies are called Social Engineering Techniques which utilize a science whose purpose is to manipulate people and make them do determined actions. This can be either employed for better or worse and it's aimed mainly to gather information, but it can be used as a backdoor in a secure system [6].

1.2 Goals

This research focuses on the preparation of a Social Engineering attack, using two techniques which include impersonation and USB dropper approaches. The preparation of the attack is one of the main activities that must be done to achieve success and it's important to consider which steps are needed to create an attack from scratch. Furthermore, the use of different tools is important, so this research proposes the necessary tools to ease the attacker's job for each technique.

The knowledge of planning, strengths and risk areas which might be under the scope of attackers is to be used as a basis to detect and avoid such attempts.

2 Background

2.1 Social Engineering

Defining Social Engineering requires exploring a lot of different meanings depending on the author. For instance, according to Mitnick [6] Social Engineering uses persuasion to convince people that they are not being attacked, so the intruder can take advantage and gather information of the target (owner of the desired information). This agrees with Conteh and Schmick who claim that Social Engineering is the "art of tricking" [7].

With this preamble, Social Engineering can be defined as the art of manipulation, trying to convince the target for giving information without raising any alarm. It is also remarkable that some authors like Engebretson [8] define Social Engineering as one of the simplest methods to obtain data. To sum it up, it is important that Social Engineering does not always require advanced tools and can be performed by anyone with the proper knowledge [9].

2.2 Common Attacks

According to Krombholz et al. [10], there are physical, social, technical and sociotechnical techniques used on Social Engineering attacks and approaches. Each of them aiming to obtain something from the target, each one differs on how the attacker proceeds. Social engineering attacks adapt to the target and the information that wants to be obtained, for instance, the most common technique used is called phishing which consists in using a fake login access that looks like the real one. This tricks the target into writing their information and giving their data to the attacker [11]. This can be complemented with spear-phishing which uses data gathering in order to be specific about the kind of attack that has to be performed (taking into consideration the fields of study, work, connections and applications used by the potential target) [12].

Another way to perform a Social Engineering attack is vishing, which has the same goal as phishing, but it uses a phone call instead of a web page. Creating a fake application that resembles an app commonly used by the target is an effective way to create an access point to achieve his goal [13]. The scope of this research is centered on the use of a physical and socio-technical approach. In the first approach the attacker is present to lead the course of action using applications and technical knowledge to develop the adequate program that will gather information automatically [14].

2.3 Human Weakness Exploitation

But why is Social Engineering a successful technique? Humans are vulnerable because of their feelings and thoughts. It is important to remember that as Junger [15] and Hasan [16] claim in their research "Humans tend to trust each other", so attackers make use of this failure in the nature of the human being to benefit from it [17], gather information, gain privileged access and even convincing others to attack for him/her through the use or persuasion which means someone influence on the behaviour or decisions of another person [18].

Persuasion has six principles which can be used to succeed: authority, liking, conformity, scarcity, commitment and reciprocity [19]. The attacker has to evaluate the situation and use these principles according to the relationship with the target.

2.4 Tailgating

Tailgating is a common technique to get access into restricted facilities, where the attacker follows a person who has access and uses some pretext to convince the target to hold the door open, the most common pretext is carrying something heavy and hoping the target is usually enough [20].

2.5 Empathy

A good way to have privileged access with the help of the target is by creating empathy. Eisenberg and Strayer [21] interpreted this as the capacity to experience another's ideas and feelings. In other words, establishing a bond may help the attacker ease his work.

Empathy used as a tool requires some abilities from the researcher, it's important to create a good bonding with the target. This can be achieved by studying human behavior. Humor is also a good way to improve the atmosphere. Detecting hidden emotions might help the attacker to bond with people [22].

2.6 Attack Structure

In every attack there must be some steps to follow in order to achieve the final goal which in this research is to gather information. As Antokoletz explained in his work [23], Social Engineering attacks possess an anatomy. They need to accomplish certain steps to escalate its access, in this work the steps contemplated are: target's acknowledgement, roles definition, credibility accomplishment, attention deviation, gaining trust and empathy and exploiting. All these steps can be compressed as Luo et al. presented in their research [24], reducing it to: Information Gathering, Developing Relationship, Exploitation and Execution.

There are different tools that can be used for information gathering such as publicly available data, technical tools to automatic exfiltration like the ones used in this research, looking for valuable information in trash, shoulder surfing and many others [25].

2.7 USB Dropper

This is a kind of Social Engineering attack which uses USB drives to gain the attention of the potential targets and relies on baiting. The target finds this USB drive and connects it to his computer [26]. Once connected to the system, the behavior of the information inside may be different, it might have malicious code, the user clicks on one file and it executes code inside the target's machine; the USB drive might lead the attacked person to a phishing website to steal credentials [27].

There are several investigations about this kind of attack, Tischer et al. Found that this kind of attack has a high success rate, from the 98% of USB drives found, 45% were plugged in [28]. The targets usually claim they usually connect the USB drive to find the owner [29].

2.8 Bad USB Drive

A Bad USB is a special appliance which acts like a Human Interface Device, this means it can be detected and accepted as a keyboard, then it can perform actions programmed on it like writing arbitrary code automatically [30].

There are many kinds of these devices, mainly they use an ATMEGA32U4 micro-controller which allows them to interact with the Arduino framework and be programmed [31]. These USB drives can be easily bought in online stores (such as Aliexpress). Some of them come in blank and must be programmed from scratch, while others have already some software/firmware that facilitates their use. The differences between each one of them are the way they are programmed and how they interact with the computer.

The first type of Bad USB drive considered in this work uses an external micro-SD card. In this case, using the Arduino framework, the micro-controller is programmed to act as a keyboard and to receive input from an external device (i.e., the SD card). Through the usage of an SD card, there is a.txt file with a special scripting language used to program the device keyboard instructions (which it will do after being plugged in) called Ducky Script. It has commands that can bring up strings, keyboard keys and waiting times to perform an attack after gaining access to the target's computer [32].

The next device does not use an external card to store instructions but it is programmed directly in the micro-controller to act as a keyboard and to perform steps that the attacker needs to achieve his goal. To program this type of Bad USB drive, the Arduino framework is used.

There is a variant of this USB device called Evil Crow Cable which has similar characteristics to the previous bad USB variant but this one is disguised as a wire which can be used with other approaches using Social Engineering Techniques [33]. It is also programmed directly without the use of an external SD.

The most common commercialized device is sold by the Hack5 group which uses a technology as the first one described with an SD card to store the commands that will be performed at the time the USB drive is attached. The behavior remains undetected because it is recognized as a keyboard so it can bypass antivirus [34].

2.9 Impersonation

Redmon affirms that impersonation is "the most valuable tool of a social engineer" [35]. With this characteristic, an attacker takes the role of someone else. Inside a company, the attacker might be someone from the personnel to obtain privileged access or act as a police officer to gather information from the target. There are several options of the roles that can be assumed to achieve a goal. The objective needs to be studied to determine the best course of action This means to define the role that is going to be played and practice it. One good example of this is Stanley Mark Rifkin who faked being a computer worker of an institution to perform one of the biggest bank robberies in history. He managed to access a restricted area where he found a secret code used for bank transfers, he memorized it and returned it. After a while he called the bank pretending to be from the bank's international division and asked for a money transfer, he had the secret code, so he did not raise any alert [36].

2.10 Pretext

Pretext always goes by the hand with impersonation because the attacker needs to create a false story and make it credible [37]. To achieve this technique, the attacker must be aware of the unexpected events and questions that might surge in the conversation with the target. A script is often used to ease the learning of the fake story, but also a structure is necessary to know how to act if something does not go as planned, the ability to adapt to the circumstances is crucial.

When performing a penetration testing by using Social Engineering techniques, it is appropriate to allow the target to suspect something is going on, so it is recommended not to be too perfect when using pretext and be careful about how the target reacts [38].

2.11 Persuasion

One of the best tools that an impersonation approach needs is persuasion, this needs all the abilities of an attacker because he must study the target while he is speaking, it's important to notice micro expressions, gesticulation, voice tone, and have some good conversational subjects in order to gain empathy and ask for access or convince the target that the attacker is the new IT guy [39].

2.12 Social Engineering in the Enterprise

Using the human vulnerability, organizations and enterprises suffer constant attempts to access their information [40]. The main targets are the ones who work with large customer databases, sensitive data and critical infrastructures [41]. Also, attackers aim at non-technical people who aren't commonly aware of these dangers. That is why security policies are important and must train all employees about cybersecurity threats, to increase their knowledge and increase detection of possible attacks, reducing the probability of leaks and infiltrations [42].

2.13 Awareness

To mitigate possible threats that might damage the entity, awareness is necessary for all the employees. Aldawood affirms that the lack of Social Engineering knowledge is one of the main cybersecurity risks [43]. That is why educational programs are important for reducing and preventing attacks [44]. For this reason, companies must provide training to all the personnel involved in the company to create concern about information security problems and their possible implications if they succeed [45].

3   Methodology

To perform any kind of attack, proper preparation is needed. Study the target in order to know exactly what kind of information is going to be collected from it. This research was focused on the preparation of two studied techniques, USB Dropper and impersonation, so the tools which are used are harmless for the target. They are prepared to collect only system information and private IP data.

There are a different set of tools and ways to get closer to the targets for these two main approaches. The tools must be prepared to be quick and effective, so they are programmed to ease the attacker's job by performing their instructions automatically and collecting data as fast as possible.

3.1   The Preparation

Before going deep inside the attack, it is important to know everything possible about the targets and the environment they're involved in. For instance, who are the targets, where do they work, what are their habits, likes, and anything that can be used to get into their minds and be reliable while performing the attacks.

It is important to determine the kind of targets and how they might react, it is not the same to attack the CEO of the company or a secretary, or even a guard. They have different roles in the entity, and different mindsets so it is important to know how to approach each one of them.

After determining the possible targets is important to know the facilities that are going to be the target of the attack. Learn where is the server room, the guard's desk, the waiting room, and other important places inside the entity.

Self-confidence is important for the attacker performing the job. Avoid being nervous to avoid raising alerts and also be kind and easygoing with everyone surrounding. It is important to generate empathy and gain the trust of the possible targets, which is crucial in the impersonation attack.

USB Dropper. For the USB Dropper attack, knowing the public places of the target entity is vital, whether it has a cafeteria, library, recreational spaces, and bathrooms. Places where most people pass by and may "accidentally" drop a prepared USB drive there, waiting for someone to pick it up and connect it to a PC.

Due to the restrictions of today's operative systems and the impossibility to use the autorun feature, the USB drive must contain information that might lead the target to click on one malicious file. Here, filenames are very important, so it is necessary to create a few and also leave some clean files. For instance, a name which gains attention inside an entity is a "to be fired.doc" file, where most people might have the curiosity to click on it and know who is going to be fired or if their names are on the list leading the target's PC to be compromised.

Impersonation. This technique requires a higher level of knowledge and performance due to the risk it represents for the attacker because it's needed to be present at that moment by using a special tool designed to simplify the attack. Usually, attackers impersonate workers from the same company, for example, pretending to be part of the IT team. The attacker tries to get the trust of the target, a prepared script is highly recommended, but it is important to notice every possible change that might occur during the attack.

The attacker must be an easygoing person, who can lead people to trust him easily by using a proper speech, knowing the target, and trying to inspire empathy. Furthermore, it is necessary to know the facilities to not get lost while performing the attack and be sure where to go afterward. The main goal of this attack is to gain access to the target's computer and plug in the special tool which is described in Sect. 3.2.

3.2 Tools

A social engineering attack depends on how well it is planned and implemented by the attacker itself. That's why it is important to have some tools prepared.

Since the aim of the research is for educational purposes only, the presented tools only collect non sensitive data like system and network information.

The USB Dropper Attack technique must use a malicious file inside of a fake file like the ones seen on Fig. 1 which are dubbed *"Fotografías chicas playa"*, *"Base de datos exámenes periodo 2020- 2021"*, a word file called *"Respuestas exámenes"*.

When the target finds the USB drive and connects it to a computer, the files are seen. After a malicious file is clicked, a small Visual Basic code is executed; this code only calls another one in PowerShell. This is done to avoid showing something on the target's screen so everything is executed backgrounds. Then, the information collected by the PowerShell script (*systeminfo* and *ipconfig*) is sent to a prepared website where the information is processed, converted into a.txt file and presented by date to the person behind the attack in order to process it. Furthermore, this script is also programmed to open a prepared website. In this example the website is designed to create awareness of the target by telling them the importance of being cautious when connecting a strange USB found outside (see Fig. 2).

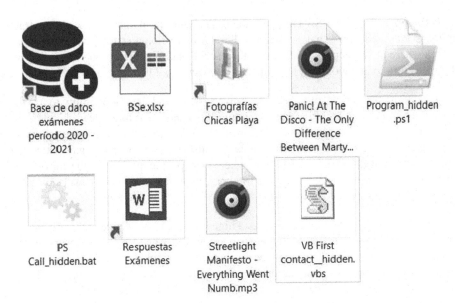

Fig. 1. Example of files stored and hidden inside the dropped USB.

Uh oh!

Tal parece que te has encontrado ésta usb.

Si estás viendo ésto pudiste ser víctima de un virus informático, te informo que esta usb está diseñada para enviarte a este sitio cuando des click sobre alguno de los archivos que encuentres allí, pero no te preocupes, esta vez no es un virus sino solo una advertencia para que tengas mucho cuidado cuando encuentres este tipo de dispositivos por la calle ya que representa una posible vulnerabilidad para tu PC. Mantén tu información a salvo y ten prácticas adecuadas de ciberseguridad. Y si encuentras una USB perdida, entrégala al departamento de TI

Recuerda que, si tienes dudas acerca del manejo de la Seguridad de la Información en la institución y cómo puedes protegerte, puedes acercarte a los responsables del área, el Director de Seguridad de la Información (CISO) o el Delegado de Protección de Datos (DPO).

Fig. 2. Warning deployed after the target clicks an infected file.

For the impersonation approach, a more elaborated tool is prepared and designed. Due to the risk it represents for the attacker, the need of automatization and the lack of time are essential factors to analyze. The attacker must use all of the knowledge at hand to fake being part of the entity and gain access to the facilities and target's computers. The tool that is presented is called a BAD USB. In this research there are two examples of these devices to be used, one of the uses an external SD card to receive instructions (see the left device Fig. 3.) and the other one that relies in instructions programmed directly into it (see the right de- vice Fig. 3).

For both BAD USB drives, the script opens a CMD and calls to PowerShell where no harmful information is collected due to the educational purposes of this research (*systeminfo* and *ipconfig*). As the USB dropper technique, the collected information is sent to a prepared website where it is transformed and analyzed.

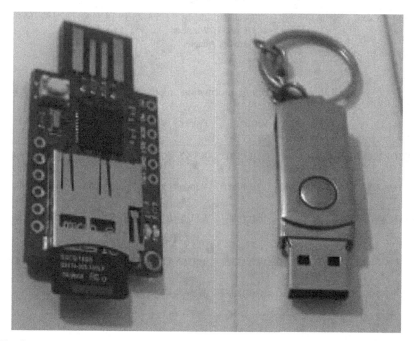

Fig. 3. BAD USB sticks (Left: Using a micro-SD card, Right: Without an external card).

4 Results and Discussion

As the main goal remains on the preparation of the attack, the results are based on which information is gathered by the different tools prepared for both techniques, the USB Dropper, and the impersonation approaches.

5 controlled tests were held by the researcher using the different approaches presented. Subsequently, the targeted information gathered is ordered and filtered in the tables below.

Table 1. *Ipconfig* information ordered and filtered.

Hostname	Adapter type	Description	Physical address	Ip address
DESKTOP-LXXXXX	Wi-Fi	Intel(R) Wireless-AC 9560 160MHz	18–56–80-F6–66-3E	192.168.47.77
DESKTOP-AXXXX	Wi-Fi	Intel(R) PRO/100 MT Desktop Adapter	08–00–27–59-59-3A	10.0.2.15
JSXXXXXX	Ethernet	Qualcom Atheros AR9287 Wireless Network Adapter	18-D6-C7-B9–11-52	172.16.18.39
PXXXXXXZ	Wi-Fi	Intel(R) Dual Band Wireless-AC 8265	1C-4D-70-9B-FA-78	192.168.1.4
LAPTOP-XXXXC	Wi-Fi	Qualcom Atheros QCA9377 Wireless Network Adapter	F8–28-19-DC-49-B7	192.168.0.136

Table 2. *Systeminfo* information ordered and filtered.

Hostname	Operative system	Version	Property of	System manufacturer	Model
DESKTOP-LXXXXX	Windows 10 Home	10.0.18362	XXXXXXX	Acer	Predator PH315–51
DESKTOP-AXXXXX	Windows 10 Pro	10.0.10586	Windows User	Toshiba	Satellite pro r40-d-111
JSXXXX	Windows 10 Pro	10.0.16299	USUARIO	System manufacturer	System Product Name
PXXXZ	Windows 10 Home	10.0.18362	19179XXXXXXX	ASUStek Computer Inc	GL503VD
LAPTOP-XXXXXC	Windows 10 Home	10.0.18362	Windows User	LENOVO	80YY

The metrics to determine the success level of the attack are presented by the number of entries and the number of tries the attacker performs, which are reported on Tables 1 and 2. As it can be seen, the complete information requested by this design was gathered on each of the 5 tries, which indicates an efficient build and performance of the tests mentioned above. As it can be seen, only the system and network information are gathered, avoiding the collection of sensitive data.

Preparation determines the success ratio of a Social Engineering attack. Other approaches like phishing techniques and whaling (a form of a spear phishing attack consisting in targeting the CEO of a company through fake email campaigns) need a broader, time-consuming preparation in order to achieve a specific goal, studying the likes, and dislikes of the target are crucial, knowing in deep about the feelings about certain topics is also recommended to prepare an email campaign which might lead to successful access to the target's information [46]. In contrast, an impersonation app-roach demands mostly a company's public information and general knowledge of social behavior, which are more easily gathered [47].

With the use of crafted tools, like the ones presented in this research, the costs of obtaining commercial tools which are sold nowadays are considerably reduced (saving about 50 to 60 USD) making them easier to get and having the same result. The difference between the commercial rubber ducky and the self-crafted ones consists in the need of programming these devices. These tools need to be configured to act as a keyboard in Arduino and also upload the necessary payload depending on the type (if it's with or without microSD card) while the commercial ones are prepared just to receive the payloads through a microSD card but having the same results because both devices are programmed to detect and execute ducky scripting. With these tools the time needed to complete the information gathering is minimized, this is caused by the lack of manual intervention during the attack, letting the attacker distract the target while the tool does its work. To perform this attack manually, it has to be considered that the attacker must introduce the commands by hand, save them in a specific file and send it to a repository to analyze later, which takes an average of 3 − 4 min that are reduced to seconds with a prepared attack and tool. The use of the tools presented in this research help the attacker automatize the procedure.

Social Engineering is a wide area of study and it has a variety of attacks, techniques, and tools, which make it so difficult to stop because it aims to the one system that can't be patched, the human being.

References

1. Mohurle, S., Patil, M.: A brief study of wannacry threat: ransomware attack 2017. Int. J. Adv. Res. Comput. Sci. **8**(5) (2017)
2. C. V. E. Details, Vulnerability Details: CVE-2017–0144 (2017). https://www.cvedetails.com/cve/CVE-2017-0144/. Accessed March 2021
3. Heartfield, R., Loukas, G.: Detecting semantic social engineering attacks with the weakest link: implementation and empirical evaluation of a human-as-a-securitysensor framework. Comput. Secur. **76**, 101–127 (2018)
4. Ghafir, I., et al.: Security threats to critical infrastructure: the human factor. J. Supercomput. **74**(10), 4986–5002 (2018)
5. Cert, U.: Russian government cyber activity targeting energy and other critical infra- structure sectors", Us Cert, pp. 1–19 (2018)
6. Mitnick, K.D., Simon, W.L.: The Art of Deception: Controlling the Human Element of Security. John Wiley & Sons (2003)
7. Conteh, N.Y., Schmick, P.J.: Cybersecurity: risks, vulnerabilities and countermeasures to prevent social engineering attacks. Int. J. Adv. Comput. Res. **6**(23), 31 (2016)
8. Engebretson, P.: The basics of hacking and penetration testing: ethical hacking and penetration testing made easy. Elsevier (2013)
9. Beckers, K., Pape, S.: A serious game for eliciting social engineering security requirements. In: 2016 IEEE 24th International Requirements Engineering Conference (RE). IEEE, pp. 16–25 (2016)

10. Krombholz, K., Hobel, H., Huber, M., Weippl, E.: Social engineering attacks on the knowledge worker. In: Proceedings of the 6th International Conference on Security of In- formation and Networks, pp. 28–35 (2013)
11. Jagatic, T.N., Johnson, N.A., Jakobsson, M., Menczer, F.: Social phishing. Commun. ACM **50**(10), 94–100 (2007)
12. Binks, A.: The art of phishing: past, present and future. Comput. Fraud Secur. **2019**(4), 9–11 (2019)
13. Yasin, A., Fatima, R., Liu, L., Yasin, A., Wang, J.: Contemplating social engineering studies and attack scenarios: a review study. Secur. Privacy **2**(4), e73 (2019)
14. Stasiukonis, S.: Social engineering, the USB way, Dark Reading, vol. 7 (2006)
15. Junger, M., Montoya, L., Overink, F.-J.: Priming and warnings are not effective to prevent social engineering attacks. Comput. Hum. Behav. **66**, 75–87 (2017)
16. Hasan, M.I., Prajapati, N.B.: An attack vector for deception through persuasion used by hackers and crackers. In: 2009 First International Conference on Networks & Communications. IEEE, pp. 254–258 (2009)
17. Bullée, J.-W.H., Montoya, L., Pieters, W., Junger, M., Hartel, P.H.: The persuasion and security awareness experiment: reducing the success of social engineering attacks. J. Exp. Criminol. **11**(1), 97–115 (2015)
18. Gass, R.H., Seiter, J.S.: Persuasion: Social Influence and Compliance Gaining. Routledge (2015)
19. Ferreira, A., Coventry, L., Lenzini, G.: Principles of persuasion in social engineering and their use in phishing. In: International Conference on Human Aspects of Information Security, Privacy, and Trust, Springer, pp. 36–47 (2015)
20. Akati, J., Conrad, M.: Anti-tailgating solution using biometric authentication, motion sensors and image recognition. In: 2021 IEEE Intl Conf on Dependable, Autonomic and Secure Computing, Intl Conf on Pervasive Intelligence and Computing, Intl Conf on Cloud and Big Data Computing, Intl Conf on Cyber Science and Technology Congress (DASC/PiCom/CBDCom/CyberSciTech), pp. 825–830. IEEE, October 2021
21. Eisenberg, N., Strayer, J.: Empathy and its development. CUP Archive (1990)
22. Piscitelli, E.: El Arte de Engañar al Usuario - Parte 2: Técnicas y herramientas (2017). https://blog.smartfense.com/2017/05/e1-arte-de-enganar-alusuario-parte-2.htmls. Accessed March 2021
23. Antokoletz, D., Antokoletz Huerta, D.: Ingeniería social, vol. 1, pp. 17–23, August 2018
24. Luo, X., Brody, R., Seazzu, A., Burd, S.: Social engineering: the neglected human factor for information security management. Inf. Resour. Manage. J. (IRMJ) **24**(3), 1–8 (2011)
25. Beckers, K., Schosser, D., Pape, S., Schaab, P.: A structured comparison of social engineering intelligence gathering tools. In: International Conference on Trust and Privacy in Digital Business, Springer, pp. 232–246 (2017)
26. Barseghyan, A.: Cyber criminal mechanisms employed in social engineering and technical tricks (2010)
27. Talamantes, J.: USB Drop Attacks: The Danger of "Lost And Found" Thumb Drives (2017). https: / / www . redteamsecure . com / blog / usb - drop - attacks - the - danger-of-lost-and-found-thumb-drives/. Accessed March 2021
28. Tischer, M., et al.: Users really do plug in USB drives they find. In: 2016 IEEE Symposium on Security and Privacy (SP). IEEE, pp. 306–319 (2016)
29. Tischer, M.A.: Testing the malicious USB anecdote, PhD thesis (2015)
30. Nohl, K., Lell, J.: Badusb-on accessories that turn evil, Black Hat USA, vol. 1, no. 9 (2014)
31. Arduino, Arduino Framework, https://www.arduino.cc/en/Main/Software. Accessed March 2021
32. Cannoles, B., Ghafarian, A.: Hacking experiment by using USB rubber ducky scripting. J. Systemics **15**, 66–71 (2017)

33. Santana, J., Sanchez, E.:bEvil Crow Cable Github (2017). https://github.com/joelsernamor eno/BadUSB-Cable. Accessed March 2021
34. Team, H.: Rubber Ducky presentation (2010). https://www.hak5.org/episodes/episode-709. Accessed March 2021
35. Redmon, K.C.: Mitigation of Social Engineering Attacks in Corporate America. East Carolina University, Greenville (2005)
36. Becker, J.: Rifkin, a documentary history. Computer/LJ **2**, 471 (1980)
37. Ivaturi, K., Janczewski, L.: A taxonomy for social engineering attacks. In: International Conference on Information Resources Management, Centre for Information Technology, Organizations, and People, pp. 1–12 (2011)
38. Hadnagy, C.: Social Engineering: The Art of Human Hacking. John Wiley & Sons (2010)
39. Siddiqi, M.A., Pak, W., Siddiqi, M.A.: A study on the psychology of social engineering-based cyberattacks and existing countermeasures. Appl. Sci. **12**(12), 6042 (2022)
40. Wilcox, H., Bhattacharya, M.: A human dimension of hacking: Social engineering through social media. In: IOP Conference Series: Materials Science and Engineering, IOP Publishing Ltd., vol. 790, p. 012–040 (2020)
41. Švehla, Z.L., Sedinĺc, I., Pauk, L.: Going white hat: security check by hacking employees using social engineering techniques. In: 2016 39th International Convention on Information and Communication Technology, Electronics and Microelectronics (MIPRO). IEEE, pp. 1419–1422 (2016)
42. Hagen, J.M., Albrechtsen, E., Hovden, J.: Implementation and effectiveness of organizational information security measures. Inf. Manage. Comput. Secur. (2008)
43. Aldawood, H., Skinner, G.: Reviewing cyber security social engineering training and awareness programs—pitfalls and ongoing issues. Future Internet **11**(3), 73 (2019)
44. Aldawood, H.: Educating and raising awareness on cyber security social engineering: a literature review. In: 2018 IEEE International Conference on Teaching, Assessment, and Learning for Engineering (TALE). IEEE, pp. 62–68 (2018)
45. Ma, Q., Schmidt, M.B., Pearson, J.M.: An integrated framework for information security management. Rev. Bus. 30(1) (2009)
46. Kalaharsha, P., Mehtre, B.M.: Detecting Phishing Sites--An Overview. arXiv preprint arXiv:2103.12739 (2021)
47. Hwang, Y.W., Lee, I.Y., Kim, H., Lee, H., Kim, D.: Current status and security trend of OSINT. Wireless Commun. Mobile Comput. (2022)

Information Security at Higher Education Institutions: A Systematic Literature Review

Daisy Imbaquingo-Esparza[1,2,3](✉), Javier Díaz[2], Mario Ron Egas[1,2], Walter Fuertes[2], and David Molina[1,2]

[1] Universidad Nacional de La Plata, 08544 La Plata, NJ, Argentina
daisy.imbaquingoe@info.unlp.edu.ar
[2] Universidad de Las Fuerzas Armadas ESPE, Sangolquí, Ecuador
[3] Universidad Técnica del Norte UTN, Ibarra, Ecuador

Abstract. Information is considered an essential asset in Higher Education Institutions (IES) either public or private, specifically since the pandemic there has been a rise in academic and administrative security risks at such institutions, hence an increase in cloud services. As expected, IES have proposed new risk- prevention methods instead of the traditional ones seen as obsolete, considering security programs modifications made in digital transformation demands. This study identifies issues generated by IES information security tools and security measures implemented for information protection security processes. As per the systematic literature review, 47 English written scientific articles were analyzed from the following bibliographical bases: *IEEE Xplore, ScienceDirect, SpringerLink, ResearchGate, PeerJ*, belonging to quartiles Q1, Q2 y Q3. In the articles, responses to research questions were found. Results obtained allowed for the recognition of security issues affecting IES institutions security measures and tools containing security threats. To conclude, the seriousness of applying security policies, technical measures, and constant critical security assessments regarding information security in IES is outlined.

Keywords: Information security · Data protection · Security techniques · Security measures · Higher Education Institutions

1 Introduction

The complex development of information technologies, particularly the excessive use of the Internet, business transactions and information processing have become more vulnerable to security threats therefore, user and organizations concerns are eminent [1]. Some of the most common threats are on the Internet which is an open space for professional cyber attackers or even cyber beginners who put information security at risk.

Information security attacks make organizations reflect on the importance of solving these issues therefore, reference frameworks have been proposed to evaluate comprehensive security maturity, establish security levels, pinpoint system weaknesses and

J. Herrera-Tapia et al. (Eds.): TICEC 2022, CCIS 1648, pp. 294–309, 2022.
https://doi.org/10.1007/978-3-031-18272-3_20

mitigation plans to be implemented. Organizations implementing such frameworks evaluate security levels in their information systems, run deficiencies analyses and create treatment plans so that information systems have adequate risk control measures.

Information systems are immersed in the integral management from any organization. Los sistemas de información se encuentran inmersos dentro de la gestión integral de cualquier organización. Information is an imperative resource considered a sensitive asset for institutions where technology plays a protagonist role, thus information systems are generally the norm in any environment at present. Higher Education Institutions—IES are no exemption (IES).

IES invest a great deal of money to control security threats and IT environment protection with the use of combined tools from antivirus software/ antispyware, firewalls, detection systems, intrusion prevention and filtering content software [4]. Public IES require a vision, mission and objectives that measure results to evaluate management in terms of efficiency and finance. (Zambrano, María; Armada, 2018) That is why IES institutions challenge the government to become a role model in the implementation of IT systems, since security threats are capable to cause serious issues to an institution's information resources (Imbaquingo Esparza & Pusdá Chulde 2015).

This research work performs a Literature Systematic Review (SRL) to obtain data from previous research in regards to security issues at IES in Ecuador. Methodology applied to this study for the production of SLR detailed as follows:

2   Methodology and Tools

Review process presented in Fig. 1 comprised by 4 phases: (i) Research questions (ii) Document search, (iii) Article selection (iv) Relevant data mining.

Phases explained:

2.1   Research Questions

For the development of this study, three research questions were implemented (PI) Table 1 which are considered guidelines in the reviews process of the study topic addressing security information issues at IES. Research was addressed by a 5-member research team from Ecuador who analysed 5 scientific data bases: *IEEE Xplore, ScienceDirect, SpringerLink, ResearchGate y PeerJ*.

Table 1. Research questions (PI)

Code	Research questions	Goal
PI1	What are the main information security issues faced by IES?	Identify information security issues faced by IES
PI2	Impact caused to society by the lack of information security	Identify the impact caused information security failures at IES
PI3	What security measures IES implement for information protection?	Identify information protection techniques and methods implemented for the prevention mitigation incidents at IES

2.2 Document Search

Table 2, illustrates search chains used in bibliographical data bases. The main chain: "information AND security AND in AND higher AND education AND institutions". Also, more variables were used in search chains for optimum results. 50 scientific articles were found from which 4 belong to *IEEE Xplore*, 2 to *SpringerLink, 41 to ScienceDirect, 2 to ResearchGate and 1 to PeerJ.*

Research questions (3)

Document research (50)

Article selection (47)

Relevant data mining

Fig. 1. Protocol diagram used in SLR

Table 2. Research chains used in scientific databases

Criteria	Science direct	SpringerLink	IEEE Xplore	ResearchGate	PeerJ
Search chain	"Information AND security AND in AND higher AND education AND institutions"	"Information AND security AND problems AND in AND higher AND education AND institutions A ND in AND developed AND countries"	"Information AND security AND management AND for AND higher AND education AND institutions"	"Information A ND security AN D issues AND i n AND institutions AND of AN D higher AND education AND today"	"Information n AND sec urity AND strategy A ND in AN D higher A ND education AND institutions"
Total	41	2	4	2	1

2.3 Article Selection

Article selection included three phases: In the first phase inclusion and exclusion criteria were applied as all computer science, engineering, research and education discipline-related work published in the last 17 years in English were analyzed (2004–2021). In the second phase, chain search criteria were applied and documents within categories Q1, Q2, Q3 were included, considering quality and relevance. Lastly, in the third phase selected article content was reviewed so answers to proposed research questions were

Table 3. Article selection for SLR

Data base	Phase I	Phase II	Phase III
ScienceDirect	40	40	39
SpringerLink	2	2	2
IEEE Xplore	4	4	4
ResearchGate	2	2	1
PeerJ	1	1	1
Total	**49**	**49**	**47**

analyzed aiming to verify relevance. The total number of documents recovered after running the phases is shown in Table 3.

Detail of the 47 scientific articles selected is illustrated in Table 4.

Table 4. Selected articles for SLR

Code	Title	Bibliographical data base	Year	Country
A1	"Organizational culture on information security: case study"	Springer	2016	USA
A2	"Information security policy compliance model in organizations"	ScienceDirect	2016	United Kingdom
A3	"Self-efficacy information security: Its influence on end users' information security practice behavior"	ScienceDirect	2009	USA
A4	"Securing higher education against cyberthreats: from an institutional risk to a national policy challenge"	ResearchGate	2021	USA
A5	"Information Security Management for Higher Education Institutions"	Springer	2014	Chinese
A6	"Information Security Management in academic institutes of Pakistan"	IEEE	2013	Pakistan
A7	"Cybersecurity maturity assessment framework for higher education institutions in Saudi Arabia"	PeerJ	2021	Saudi Arabia

(*continued*)

Table 4. (*continued*)

Code	Title	Bibliographical data base	Year	Country
A8	"A study on integrating penetration testing into the information security framework for Malaysian higher education institutions"	IEEE	2015	Malaysia
A9	"Performance evaluation of the recommendation mechanism of information security risk identification"	ScienceDirect	2017	Netherlands
A10	"Information security investments: An exploratory multiple case study on decision-making, evaluation, and learning"	ScienceDirect	2018	United Kingdom
A11	"A safety/security risk analysis approach of Industrial Control Systems: A cyber bowtie – combining new version of attack tree with bowtie analysis"	ScienceDirect	2017	United Kingdom
A12	"An economic modelling approach to information security risk management"	ScienceDirect	2008	United Kingdom
A13	"A new BRB model for security-state assessment of cloud computing based on the impact of external and internal environment"	ScienceDirect	2018	United Kingdom
A14	"Cyber ranges and security testbeds: Scenarios, functions, tools and architecture"	ScienceDirect	2020	United Kingdom
A15	"The impact of information security threat awareness on privacy-protective behavior"	ScienceDirect	2018	United Kingdom
A16	"Issues of information security analyses in Indian context"	ScienceDirect	2014	United Kingdom
A17	"Information security assessment in public administration"	ScienceDirect	2020	United Kingdom

(*continued*)

Table 4. (*continued*)

Code	Title	Bibliographical data base	Year	Country
A18	"Information security risks management framework - A step towards mitigating security risks in university network"	ScienceDirect	2017	India
A19	"On the Information Security Issue in the Information Construction Process of Colleges and and Universities"	IEEE	2016	Chinese
A20	"An exploratory prioritization of factors affecting current state of information security in Pakistani university libraries"	ScienceDirect	2021	Pakistan
A21	"Information Security Awareness at the Knowledge-Based Institution: Background and Measures"	ScienceDirect	2015	USA
A22	"Information security awareness in higher education: An exploratory study"	ScienceDirect	2008	United Kingdom
A23	"Cyber security education is as essential as "The three R's"	ScienceDirect	2019	USA
A24	"Riskio: A Serious Game for Cyber Security Awareness and Education"	ScienceDirect	2020	United Kingdom
A25	"Teaching for Conceptual Change in Security Awareness: A Case Study in Higher Education"	IEEE	2009	Egypt
A26	"The least secure places in the universe? A systematic literature review on information security management in higher education"	ScienceDirect	2018	United Kingdom
A27	"An empirical analysis on information security culture—key factors framework"	ScienceDirect	2021	United Kingdom
A28	"Incorporating global information security and assurance in I.S. education"	ScienceDirect	2013	USA

(*continued*)

Table 4. (*continued*)

Code	Title	Bibliographical data base	Year	Country
A29	"Information security policy compliance model in organizations"	ScienceDirect	2016	USA
A30	"Information security management needs more holistic approach: A literature review"	ScienceDirect	2016	USA
A31	"One secure data integrity verification scheme for cloud storage"	ScienceDirect	2019	USA
A32	"Towards automatic fingerprinting of IOT devices in the cyberspace"	ScienceDirect	2019	USA
A33	"Distributed password cracking with BOINC and hash cat"	ScienceDirect	2019	USA
A34	"Android User Enabled Security"	ScienceDirect	2018	USA
A35	"Assessing information security risks in the cloud: A case study of Australian local government authorities"	ScienceDirect	2020	USA
A36	"Towards a reliable firewall for software - defined networks"	ScienceDirect	2019	USA
A37	"Institutional governance and protection motivation: Theoretical insights into shaping employees' security compliance behavior in higher education institutions in the developing world"	ResearchGate	2018	USA
A38	"Evaluating the explanatory power of theoretical frameworks on intention to comply with information security policies in higher education"	ScienceDirect	2019	Saudi Arabia

(*continued*)

Table 4. (*continued*)

Code	Title	Bibliographical data base	Year	Country
A39	"Enhancing employees information security awareness in private and public organizations: A systematic literature review"	ScienceDirect	2019	Indonesia
A40	"Assessment of Information System Risk Management with Octave Allegro at Education Institution"	ScienceDirect	2021	Pakistan
A41	"Information security breaches and IT security investments: Impact on competitors"	ScienceDirect	2018	United Kingdom
A42	"Shall we follow? Impact of reputation concern on information security managers' investment decisions"	ScienceDirect	2019	Malaysia
A43	"Information security policy compliance eliciting requirements for a computerized software to support value-based compliance analysis"	ScienceDirect	2020	USA
A44	"Information security policy unpacked: A critical study of university policies content"	ScienceDirect	2022	Sweden
A45	"IS professionals' information security behavior in Chinese IT organizations for information security protection"	ScienceDirect	2009	Indonesia
A46	"A systematic literature review on information security management in higher education"	ScienceDirect	2022	USA

2.4 Relevant Data Mining

The 47 selected articles were reviewed by our team members for validity and relevancy verification. In case the articles were related to more than one research question, they were classified in one group for better interpretation and result discussion.

Information extracted from the articles was obtained based on research questions. First, main information security issues faced by IES were determined then, information security protection measures were analyzed. Next, the impact that possible failures on information security may have in society was studied. Finally, a 150-word summary containing the most critical information from each article was written.

3 Results

Obtained results from each research question asked in this study as follows in Table 1:

PI 1 What are the main information security issues faced IES?

Difficulties/Misinformation when implementing security measures at IES.

Due to authority's misinformation regarding techniques as infiltration tests or ethical hacking, authorities have not been able to protect their own information against computer hackers [11] nor the need to implement an information security management system (SGSI) to design policies facing security threats [12]. Furthermore, the IT Administration Centralized Security Information Department has inappropriately taken little action since there is a lack of budget forecast for the implementation of preventive security measures despite an expansion of digital systems boosting residual risks [13].

Risks' identification may be biased by misinformation or lack of updated information resulting in subsequent errors [14].

Most security testing Banks and cyber ranks focus on qualitative evaluation [14].

On the other hand, confidentiality, integrity and availability are essential to protect privileged information and the continuity of business during natural or man-made disasters. Such characteristics may be achieved by designing survival skills and resilience in the critical information structure of an organization [47], leading to an increase of information security levels in public administration which have significantly limited identifiable irregularities [17].

Financial Situation

This is one of the primary issues IES go through, as a result they are no table to effectively act before a security incident, causing an irreparable impact on student information security [15].

Some IES do not have appropriately trained personnel for the protection of information, consequently lacking of necessary information backup or information is unseemly stored [16].

Furthermore, there is no defined approach to evaluate an investment required in the field of information security technology from a financial perspective that includes security resources evaluating in relation to security threats and information systems vulnerability [12].

Environmental Situation

Information security investments from organizations are driven, for the most part by external factors related to the environment [49].

Table 5 illustrates the leading information security issues faced by IES.

Table 5. What are the leading information security issues faced by IES?

Leading issues	Selected articles	N.-Articles
Difficulties/misinformation to implement security measures at IES	A5, A6, A40, A46, A9, A14,	2
Financial situation	A39, A38	2
Environmental situation	A10	1
Total		4

PI2 What kind of impact the lack of information security may have?

Financial Loss. – as identity theft occurs, personal information is openly exposed to criminals using such information to their benefit [4] by the free publication of personal and confidential data or altering information [18]. Second, there may be a financial loss of about two to three percent from a company profits [1].

Destruction of Information. - Occurs as non- authorized individuals have access to programs or data as in the case of hackers [17]. Additionally, computer equipment loss or deterioration likely to happen due to malicious operation [19].

Table 6 enlists the number of articles containing answers to the following security question.

Table 6. Impact caused to society by information security systems failure

Impact to society	Selected articles	No. of articles
Financial Loss	A1, A4, A40, A43, A45, A46	6
Destruction of information	A33, A36, A31	3
Total		9

PI3 What information protection security measures are implemented by IES?

Vulnerability Evaluation
Higher education institutions in Saudi Arabia have implemented SCMAF—a comprehensive maturity evaluation framework in line with local and international security standards. This is a self-evaluation method that determines security levels and highlights system weaknesses and defines mitigation plans to be implemented [2].

Attack Tree Analysis
This approach combines the bow tie analysis commonly used in a normal security analysis with a new expanded version of the Attack Tree introduced for the security analysis pertaining to industrial control security systems [11].

Security Policies
Policies guaranteeing adequate protection security levels and liability for files containing information regardless of the environment in which they are stored must be established [20]. The exchange of security knowledge information, collaboration, intervention and expertise have a significant impact on employee's attitude towards the compliance of an organization information security policies [3].

Attitude has a compelling impact on information security—related behavior. Cyber-security measures that governments may adopt to enhance resilience in the Higher Education sector against cyber threats are analyzed with the purpose of prevent and correct security vulnerability inherent to an increase in digitalization processes [21].

Access Control—Restricted Data
One of the paramount security measures is to limit information access. The smaller number of individuals having access to information, the lesser the risk for compromised information, therefore, the need for the implementation of a system that hinders unnecessary access to data is vital [22].

Security Back-Up Systems
[23] Having a periodical security back-up system that guarantees IES to recover data before catastrophic events, prevents data loss in addition to recovering the system in minutes.

Highly Undecipherable Passwords
Access to platforms used by IES (e-mail, security back-up server and the like) must be performed by entering highly secure passwords preventing effortless deciphering by hackers since the implementation of secure passwords functions as far-reaching information security measures at IES [24]. Participants in the study reacted swiftly to the security violation and privacy news by the use of highly undecipherable passwords and selective personal information dissemination [50].

Email Protection
Most communication that takes place at IES is through email therefore, another security measure is the use of antispam filters and messages encryption systems to ensure protection and privacy of the information contained [24].

BRB Based Model
May be efficiently used to determine unknown parameters whose initial values are generally provided by an expert, likely to yield inaccurate results. Additionally, there is an optimum algorithm based on maximum likelihood for the training of assessment model parameters [51].

Table 7 summarized security measures implemented by IES for information protection.

Table 7. What security measures are implemented by IES for information protection?

Security measures	Selected articles	No. of articles
Vulnerability assessment	A2, A40, A47, A11	4
Security policies	A3, A7, A8	3
Restricted information access control	A35	1
Perform security back-up	A32	1
Using highly undecipherable passwords	A37, A15	2
Email protection	A37	1
Total		**12**

4   Discussion

Analyzed articles in this literature review reveal information security issues and pre-ventive measures to prevent and face computer attacks at Higher Education Institutions. Implementation of security measures is a challenge to undertake since total commitment is required from the interested parties.

Figure 2 illustrates a diagram regarding information security level of difficulty faced by Higher Education Institutions.

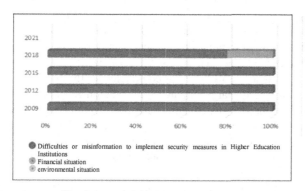

Fig. 2. Issues faced by IES regarding IS.

A large number of reviewed articles focus on individuals as vital to address informa-tion security at IES. Attitude has an indicative impact on behavioral intention in regard to complying with information security [20].

Consequently, establishing security polices together with personnel training as secu-rity measure has demonstrated favorable results. There are measures that governments may adapt to enhance information security in the Higher Education sector.

Reviewed articles assess security issues policy compliance and security management. Information security commitment is a widely talked-about topic thus not addressing attention to this issue may be catastrophic not only for IESs but also for organizations and the public in general as shown in Fig. 3.

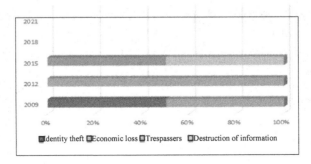

Fig. 3. Possible impact for the lack of security information.

5 Conclusions

Analyzed articles detail the ultimate issues that Higher Education Institutions face in terms of information security, since in some institutions teres is little or no commitment for this type of security. The impact had on IESs organizations by the increase of information and communication data processing technology has made organizations more vulnerable to information asset [21].

Higher Education Institutions have started policies for the protecting of administrative procedures. However, the large amount of information generated at IES requires the implementation of regulations guaranteeing data, confidentiality, integrity and availability. Prince Sultan University in Saudi Arabia has started the implementation of the use of information maturity evaluation mechanisms through SCMAF a framework used as self-evaluating to establish security levels, outline system's weaknesses and mitigation plans to be implemented [2].

The role played by individuals in the security field is crucial, for this reason, some researchers mentioned that the exchange of knowledge regarding information security has an exceptional impact on people's attitude towards information security policy compliance in the organization.

Analyzed security measures included in this document provide a clearer idea of the emphasis on the application of processes such as security policies, technical and permanent evaluation techniques implementation to critical information security areas at Higher Education Institutions, being misinformation the most concerning limitation by the management.

References

1. Tang, M., Li, M., Zhang, T.: The impacts of organizational culture on information security culture: a case study. Inf. Technol. Manage. **17**(2), 179–186 (2015). https://doi.org/10.1007/s10799-015-0252-2
2. Sohrabi Safa, N., Von Solms, R., Furnell, S.: Information security policy compliance model in organizations. Comput. Secur. **56**, 70–82 (2016). https://doi.org/10.1016/j.cose.2015.10.006
3. Rhee, H.S., Kim, C., Ryu, Y.U.: Self-efficacy in information security: its influence on end users' information security practice behavior. Comput. Secur. **28**(8), 816–826 (2009). https://doi.org/10.1016/j.cose.2009.05.008
4. Pan, J.-S., Snasel, V., Corchado, E.S., Abraham, A., Wang, S.-L. (eds.): Intelligent data analysis and its applications, volume I. AISC, vol. 297. Springer, Cham (2014). https://doi.org/10.1007/978-3-319-07776-5
5. Pan, J.-S., Snasel, V., Corchado, E.S., Abraham, A., Wang, S.-L. (eds.): Intelligent data analysis and its applications, volume II. AISC, vol. 298. Springer, Cham (2014). https://doi.org/10.1007/978-3-319-07773-4
6. Rehman, H., Masood, A., Cheema, A.R.: Information security management in academic institutes of Pakistan. In: Conf. Proc. - 2013 2nd Natl. Conf. Inf. Assur. NCIA 2013, pp. 47–51 (2013). https://doi.org/10.1109/NCIA.2013.6725323
7. Almomani, I., Ahmed, M., Maglaras, L.: Cybersecurity maturity assessment framework for higher education institutions in Saudi Arabia. PeerJ Comput. Sci. **7**, e703 (2021). https://doi.org/10.7717/peerj-cs.703
8. Kang, C.M., Josephng, P.S., Issa, K.: A study on integrating penetration testing into the information security framework for Malaysian higher education institutions. In: 2015 Int. Symp. Math. Sci. Comput. Res. iSMSC 2015 - Proc., pp. 156–161 (2016). https://doi.org/10.1109/ISMSC.2015.7594045
9. Wei, Y.C., Wu, W.C., Chu, Y.C.: Performance evaluation of the recommendation mechanism of information security risk identification. Neurocomputing **279**, 48–53 (2018). https://doi.org/10.1016/j.neu-com.2017.05.106
10. Weishäupl, E., Yasasin, E., Schryen, G.: Information security investments: an exploratory multiple case study on decision-making, evaluation and learning. Comput. Secur. **77**, 807–823 (2018). https://doi.org/10.1016/J.COSE.2018.02.001
11. Abdo, H., Kaouk, M., Flaus, J.M., Masse, F.: A safety/security risk analysis approach of Industrial Control Systems: a cyber bowtie – combining new version of attack tree with bowtie analysis. Comput. Secur. **72**, 175–195 (2018). https://doi.org/10.1016/j.cose.2017.09.004
12. Bojanc, R., Jerman-Blažič, B.: An economic modelling approach to information security risk management. Int. J. Inf. Manage. **28**(5), 413–422 (2008). https://doi.org/10.1016/J.IJINFOMGT.2008.02.002
13. Wei, H., Hu, G.Y., Zhou, Z.J., Qiao, P.L., Zhou, Z.G., Zhang, Y.M.: A new BRB model for security-state assessment of cloud computing based on the impact of external and internal environments. Comput. Secur. **73**, 207–218 (2018). https://doi.org/10.1016/j.cose.2017.11.003
14. Yamin, M.M., Katt, B., Gkioulos, V.: Cyber ranges and security testbeds: scenarios, functions, tools and architecture. Comput. Secur. **88**, 101636 (2020). https://doi.org/10.1016/j.cose.2019.101636
15. Mamonov, S., Benbunan-Fich, R.: The impact of information security threat awareness on privacy-protective behaviors. Comput. Human Behav. **83**, 32–44 (2018). https://doi.org/10.1016/j.chb.2018.01.028
16. Chaturvedi, M., Singh, A.N., Gupta, M.P., Bhattacharya, J.: Analyses of issues of information security in Indian context. Transform. Gov. People, Process Policy, **8**(3), 374–397 (2014). https://doi.org/10.1108/TG-07-2013-0019

17. Szczepaniuk, E.K., Szczepaniuk, H., Rokicki, T., Klepacki, B.: Information security assessment in public administration. Comput. Secur. **90** (2020). https://doi.org/10.1016/j.cose.2019. 101709
18. Joshi, C., Singh, U.K.: Information security risks management frame-work – a step towards mitigating security risks in university network. J. Inf. Secur. Appl. **35**, 128–137 (2017). https://doi.org/10.1016/j.jisa.2017.06.006
19. Nie, J., Dai, X.L.: On the Information Security Issue in the Information Construction process of colleges and universities. In: Proc. - 12th Int. Conf. Comput. Intell. Secur. CIS 2016, pp. 582–585 (2017). https://doi.org/10.1109/CIS.2016.140
20. Khan, A., Ibrahim, M., Hussain, A.: An exploratory prioritization of factors affecting current state of information security in Pakistani university libraries. Int. J. Inf. Manag. Data Insights **1**(2), 100015 (2021). https://doi.org/10.1016/j.jjimei.2021.100015
21. Ahlan, A.R., Lubis, M., Lubis, A.R.: Information security awareness at the knowledge-based institution: its antecedents and measures. Pro-cedia Comput. Sci. **72**, 361–373 (2015). https://doi.org/10.1016/j.procs.2015.12.151
22. Rezgui, Y., Marks, A.: Information security awareness in higher education: an exploratory study. Comput. Secur. **27**(7–8), 241–253 (2008). https://doi.org/10.1016/j.cose.2008.07.008
23. Venter, I.M., Blignaut, R.J., Renaud, K., Venter, M.A.: Cyber security education is as essential as 'the three R's. Heliyon, **5**(12), 1–7 (2019). https://doi.org/10.1016/j.heliyon.2019.e02855
24. Hart, S., Margheri, A., Paci, F., Sassone, V.: Riskio: a serious game for cyber security awareness and education. Comput. Secur. **95** (2020). https://doi.org/10.1016/j.cose.2020. 101827
25. Chan, Y.Y., Wei, V.K.: Teaching for conceptual change in security awareness: a case study in higher education. IEEE Secur. Priv. **7**(1), 68–71 (2009). https://doi.org/10.1109/MSP.200 9.22
26. Bongiovanni, I.: The least secure places in the universe? a systematic literature review on information security management in higher education. Comput. Secur. **86**, 350–357 (2019). https://doi.org/10.1016/j.cose.2019.07.003
27. Tolah, A., Furnell, S.M., Papadaki, M.: An empirical analysis of the information security culture key factors framework. Comput. Secur. **108**, 102354 (2021). https://doi.org/10.1016/j.cose.2021.102354
28. White, G.L., Hewitt, B., Kruck, S.E.: Incorporating global information security and assurance in I.S. education. J. Inf. Syst. Educ. **24**(1), 11–16 (2013)
29. Rubén, A.: INTELIGENCIA. ¿QUÉ SABEMOS Y QUÉ NOS FALTA POR INVESTIGAR?, January 2011. http://www.scielo.org.co/sci-elo.php?script=sci_arttext&pid=S0370-39082011000100009. Accessed 28 June 2021
30. Soomro, Z.A., Shah, M.H., Ahmed, J.: Information security management needs more holistic approach: a literature review. Int. J. Inf. Manage. **36**(2), 215–225 (2016). https://doi.org/10.1016/j.ijinfo-mgt.2015.11.009
31. Fan, Y., Lin, X., Tan, G., Zhang, Y., Dong, W., Lei, J.: One secure data integrity verification scheme for cloud storage. Futur. Gener. Comput. Syst. **96**, 376–385 (2019). https://doi.org/10.1016/j.future.2019.01.054
32. Yang, K., Li, Q., Sun, L.: Towards automatic fingerprinting of IoT devices in the cyberspace. Comput. Netw. 148, 318–327 (2019). https://doi.org/10.1016/j.com-net.2018.11.013
33. Hranický, R., Zobal, L., Ryšavý, O., Kolář, D.: Distributed password cracking with BOINC and hashcat. Digit. Investig. **30**, 161–172 (2019). https://doi.org/10.1016/j.diin.2019.08.001
34. Hoog, A.: Android device, data, and app security (2011)
35. Ali, O., Shrestha, A., Chatfield, A., Murray, P.: Assessing information security risks in the cloud: a case study of Australian local government authorities. Gov. Inf. Q. **37**(1), 101419 (2020). https://doi.org/10.1016/j.giq.2019.101419

36. Hu, H., et al.: Towards a reliable firewall for software-defined networks. Comput. Secur. **87**, 101597 (2019). https://doi.org/10.1016/j.cose.2019.101597
37. Khan, I., Saeed, K., Khan, I.: Nanoparticles: properties, applications and toxicities. Arab. J. Chem. **12**(7), 908–931 (2019). https://doi.org/10.1016/J.ARABJC.2017.05.011
38. Hina, S., Panneer Selvam, D.D.D., Lowry, P.B.: Institutional governance and protection motivation: theoretical insights into shaping employees' security compliance behavior in higher education institutions in the developing world. Comput. Secur. **87**, 101594 (2019). https://doi.org/10.1016/j.cose.2019.101594
39. Rajab, M., Eydgahi, A.: Evaluating the explanatory power of theoretical frameworks on intention to comply with information security policies in higher education. Comput. Secur. **80**, 211–223 (2019). https://doi.org/10.1016/j.cose.2018.09.016
40. Khando, K., Gao, S., Islam, S.M., Salman, A.: Enhancing employees information security awareness in private and public organisations: a systematic literature review. Comput. Secur. **106**, 102267 (2021). https://doi.org/10.1016/j.cose.2021.102267
41. Suroso, J.S., Fakhrozi, M.A.: Assessment of information system risk management with octave allegro at education institution. Procedia Comput. Sci. **135**, 202–213 (2018). https://doi.org/10.1016/j.procs.2018.08.167
42. Jeong, C.Y., Lee, S.-Y.T., Lim, J.-H.: Information security breaches and IT security investments: impacts on competitors. Inf. Manag. **56**(5), 681–695 (2019). https://doi.org/10.1016/j.im.2018.11.003
43. Shao, X., Siponen, M., Liu, F.: Shall we follow? Impact of reputation concern on information security managers' investment decisions. Comput. Secur. **97**, 101961 (2020). https://doi.org/10.1016/j.cose.2020.101961
44. Szczepaniuk, E.K., Szczepaniuk, H., Rokicki, T., Klepacki, B.: Information security assessment in public administration. Comput. Secur. **90**, 101709 (2020). https://doi.org/10.1016/J.COSE.2019.101709
45. Baham, C.: Improving business product owner commitment in student scrum projects. J. Inf. Technol. Educ. Res. **19**, 243–258 (2020). https://doi.org/10.28945/4549
46. Younas, M., Jawawi, D.N.A., Ghani, I., Fries, T., Kazmi, R.: Agile development in the cloud computing environment: a systematic review. Inf. Softw. Technol. **103**, 142–158 (2018). https://doi.org/10.1016/J.INFSOF.2018.06.014
47. Srivastava, A., Bhardwaj, S., Saraswat, S.: SCRUM model for agile methodology. In: Proceeding - IEEE Int. Conf. Comput. Commun. Autom. ICCCA 2017, vol. 2017, pp. 864–869, December 2017. https://doi.org/10.1109/CCAA.2017.8229928

Author Index

Acosta-Urigüen, María-Inés   201, 231
Aguiar-Salazar, Evelyn   32
Alario-Hoyos, Carlos   117
Almeida-Galárraga, Diego   32
Amaro, Isidro R.   152
Arcentales-Carrion, Rodrigo   85
Arévalo, Pablo   171
Armijos, Arianna   217

Bermeo, Alexandra   231

Calle-Cárdenas, Christian   152
Carrera Villacrés, David Vinicio   73
Cedillo, Priscila   171
Cerezo Ramirez, Johanna Carolina   3
Cerón-Andrade, Bryan   32
Chang, Oscar   217
Cordero-Machuca, David   186
Cortez-Orellana, Santiago Angel   101
Cruz Felipe, Marely del Rosario   59
Cuenca Macas, Leduin José   18
Cuenca, Erick   137
Cuzme-Rodríguez, Fabián   46

De La Cruz-Ramirez, Nadezhda Tarcila   101
De La Cruz-Ramirez, Yuliana Mercedes   101
Delgado Kloos, Carlos   117
Díaz, Javier   294
Domínguez-Limaico, Mauricio   46
Duran, Ricardo   73

Farinango-Endara, Henry   46
Fiallos-Ayala, Xiomira   32
Flores-Siguenza, Pablo   85
Freire, Jorge Sánchez   281
Fuertes, Walter   294

Garcés, Benjamín   281
Garcés, Rodney Alberto   73
García, Reinerio Rodríguez   201

Imbaquingo-Esparza, Daisy   294
Infante, Saba   152

Lima, Juan-Fernando   171, 186
Loor Zamora, Darwin Patricio   59
Luque-Nieto, Miguel-Ángel   46

Maldonado-Mahauad, Jorge   117
Molina, David   294
Morocho-Cayamcela, Manuel Eugenio   253
Murillo López, José Luis   3

Negrete-Bolagay, Daniela   32
Niemes, Stadyn Román   217
Noboa, Sherald   137

Olaza-Maguiña, Augusto Felix   101
Orellana, Marcos   171, 186, 201, 231
Otero, Pablo   46

Perez-Sanagustin, Mar   117
Pijal, Washington   217, 253
Pineda, Israel   18, 253

Raura, Geovanny   73
Riera-Segura, Lenin   152
Ron Egas, Mario   294

Saltos, Ramiro   266
Siguenza-Guzman, Lorena   85
Solís, Erik   137
Sucozhañay, Dolores   85
Suntaxi-Dominguez, Diego   32

Tapia-Riera, Guido   152
Tierra Criollo, Alfonso Rodrigo   73
Tirado-Espín, Andrés   32

Valdivieso Albán, Sebastián I.   231
Valenzuela-Guerra, Andrea   32
Vásquez-Salinas, Bernarda   85
Villalba-Meneses, Fernando   32
Vinces Mendieta, Manuel Eduardo   59

Weber, Richard   266

Yoo, Sang Guun   3

Zambrano-Martinez, Jorge Luis   171
Zhinin-Vera, Luis   217

Printed in the United States
by Baker & Taylor Publisher Services